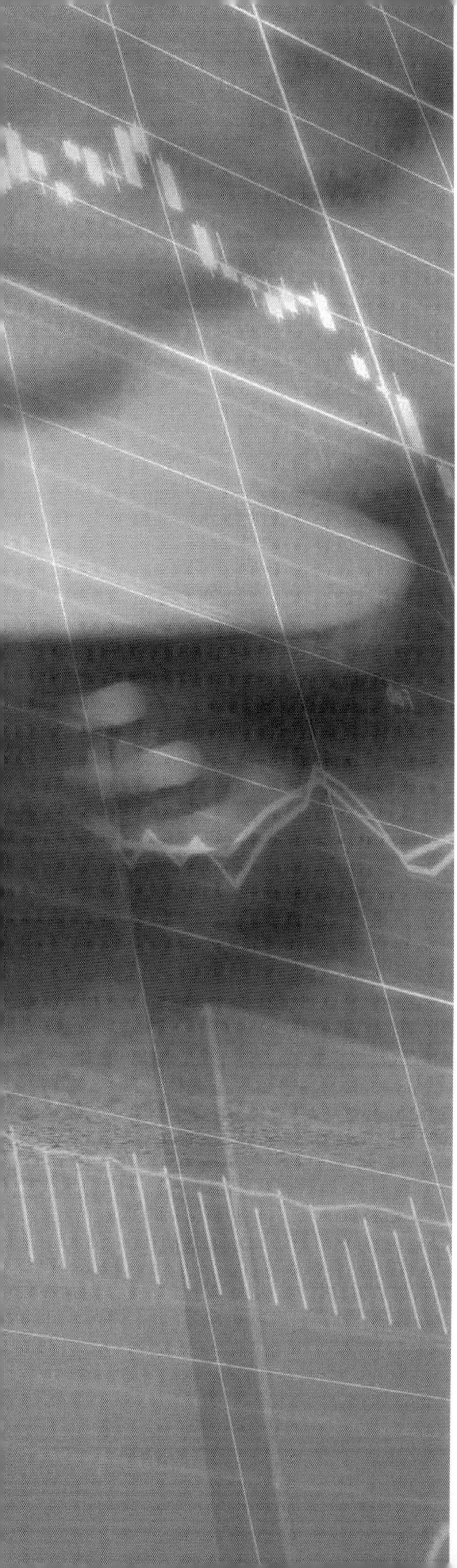

CISI
INSTITUTE FOR
& INVESTMENT

Capital Markets Programme

Derivatives

Edition 13, July 2017

This learning manual relates to syllabus version 17.0 and will cover examinations from **11 October 2017 to 10 October 2018**

CHARTERED INSTITUTE FOR SECURITIES & INVESTMENT

APPROVED WORKBOOK

CISI
CHARTERED INSTITUTE FOR SECURITIES & INVESTMENT

Welcome to the Chartered Institute for Securities & Investment's Derivatives study material.

This workbook has been written to prepare you for the Chartered Institute for Securities & Investment's Derivatives examination.

Published by:
Chartered Institute for Securities & Investment

20 Fenchurch Street
London
EC3M 3BY
Tel: +44 20 7645 0600
Fax: +44 20 7645 0601

Email: customersupport@cisi.org
www.cisi.org/qualifications

Author:
Bob Morrissey

Reviewers:
Alan Green
Alan Burr

A learning map, which contains the full syllabus, appears at the end of this workbook. The syllabus can also be viewed on cisi.org and is also available by contacting the Customer Support Centre on +44 20 7645 0777. Please note that the examination is based upon the syllabus. Candidates are reminded to check the Candidate Update area details (cisi.org/candidateupdate) on a regular basis for updates as a result of industry change(s) that could affect their examination.

The questions contained in this workbook are designed as an aid to revision of different areas of the syllabus and to help you consolidate your learning chapter by chapter.

Learning workbook version: 13.2 (December 2017)

Learning and Professional Development with the CISI

The Chartered Institute for Securities & Investment is the leading professional body for those who work in, or aspire to work in, the investment sector, and we are passionately committed to enhancing knowledge, skills and integrity – the three pillars of professionalism at the heart of our Chartered body.

CISI examinations are used extensively by firms to meet the requirements of government regulators. Besides the regulators in the UK, where the CISI head office is based, CISI examinations are recognised by a wide range of governments and their regulators, from Singapore to Dubai and the US. Around 50,000 examinations are taken each year, and it is compulsory for candidates to use CISI workbooks to prepare for CISI examinations so that they have the best chance of success. Our workbooks are normally revised every year by experts who themselves work in the industry and also by our Accredited Training Partners, who offer training and elearning to help prepare candidates for the examinations. Information for candidates is also posted on a special area of our website: cisi.org/candidateupdate.

This workbook not only provides a thorough preparation for the examination it refers to, it is also a valuable desktop reference for practitioners, and studying from it counts towards your Continuing Professional Development (CPD). Mock examination papers, for most of our titles, will be made available on our website, as an additional revision tool.

CISI examination candidates are automatically registered, without additional charge, as student members for one year (should they not be members of the CISI already), and this enables you to use a vast range of online resources, including CISI TV, free of any additional charge. The CISI has more than 40,000 members, and nearly half of them have already completed relevant qualifications and transferred to a core membership grade. You will find more information about the next steps for this at the end of this workbook.

CISI
CHARTERED INSTITUTE FOR SECURITIES & INVESTMENT

1 2 3 4 5 6 7 8 9

It is estimated that this manual will require approximately 100 hours of study time.

What next?

See the back of this book for details of CISI membership.

Need more support to pass your exam?

See our section on Accredited Training Partners at the back of this book.

Want to leave feedback?

Please email your comments to learningresources@cisi.org

CHARTERED INSTITUTE FOR SECURITIES & INVESTMENT

Chapter One

Introduction to Derivatives

This syllabus area will provide approximately 7 of the 100 examination questions

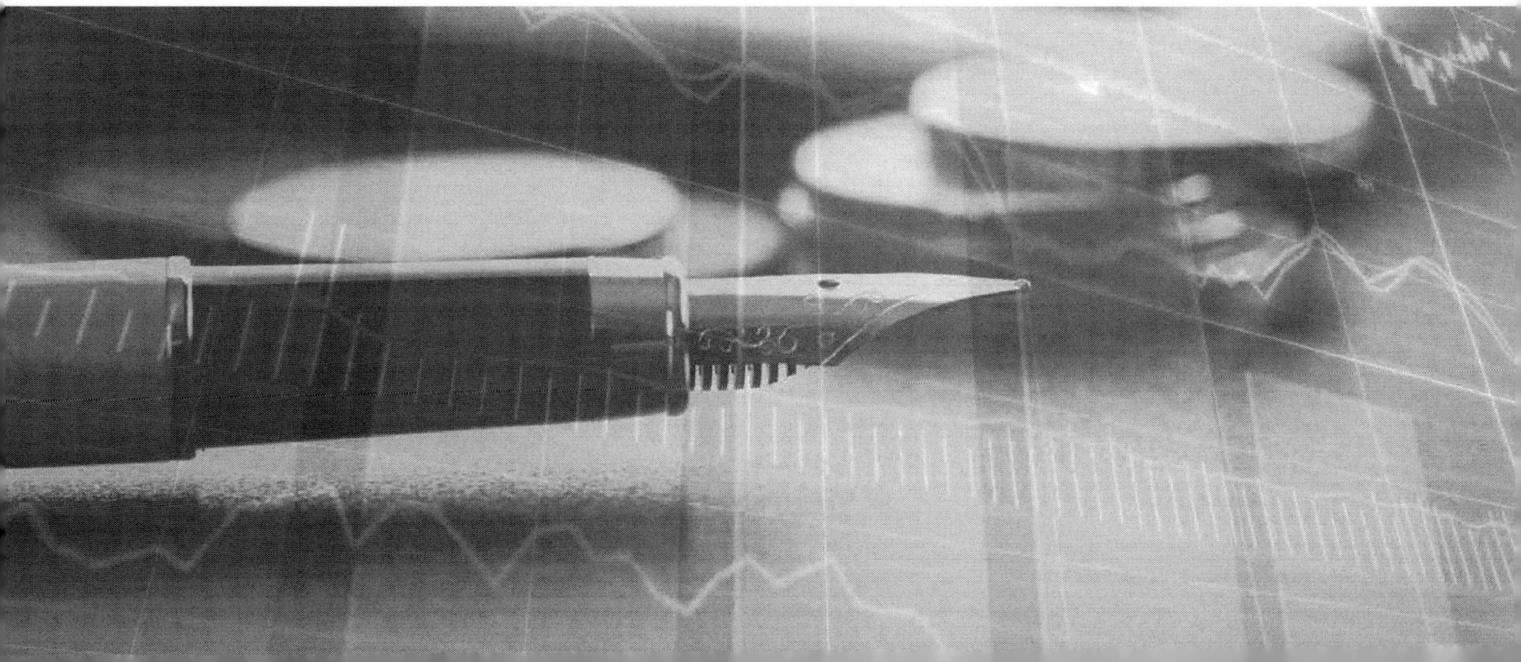

1. General Introduction

Mention **derivatives** and people tend to think of high-risk instruments that are impenetrably complex. Derivatives *can* be high-risk; after all, it was mainly trading in derivatives that brought about the collapse of Lehman Brothers and massive monetary losses at many other organisations during the recent credit crunch. However, it is not necessarily true that these instruments are inherently dangerous – they are chiefly designed to be used to reduce the risk faced by organisations and individuals (technically referred to as hedging).

In fact, many of these derivatives are not particularly complex, either. To illustrate the underlying simplicity, imagine that you want to purchase a new sofa from a furniture showroom.

You make your choice of sofa and see that it will cost £1,000. On enquiry, you discover from the sales assistant that the sofa is currently out of stock in the warehouse. However, you can sign a contract to accept delivery of the sofa in two months' time (when the stock will be replenished) and at that stage the store will charge the £1,000 to your credit card. If you sign, you have agreed to defer delivery for two months – and you have entered into a derivative (it is derived from something else – here, a sofa). This is very similar to a **futures** contract. You have contracted to buy an underlying asset (the sofa) and pay a pre-agreed sum of money (£1,000) in two months' time (the future date). The furniture store has contracted to sell the underlying (the sofa) in exchange for £1,000 in two months' time.

So, this is an example of a futures-type contract that we could refer to as a sofa future. In the jargon of the derivatives markets, you are **long** a sofa future because you have agreed to buy at a future date. The furniture store is short a sofa future because it has agreed to sell at a future date.

Futures are not the only type of derivative – there are also **options**. To illustrate how options differ from futures, we can use the same example of a sofa in a furniture store. This time, the sales assistant tells you the sofa you want is not in stock at present, but there is a small batch of ten sofas due for delivery in two months' time. Of these ten sofas, nine have been pre-sold. You cannot make up your mind whether to go ahead and commit to buy the tenth sofa or to try a few other stores to see if anything else catches your eye. Noticing this, the sales assistant makes you an offer. If you pay £30 now, he will give you the right to reserve the tenth sofa. It will become yours on the payment of £1,000 in two months' time and, in the intervening period, the sales assistant cannot sell it to anyone else.

Again, this is a derivative transaction (derived from something else – the sofa). If you agree to it, you will be paying a non-returnable sum of money (£30) that gives you the right to buy the sofa for £1,000 in two months' time. This is a sofa option and, using derivatives jargon, you are long the option because you have the right to do something (here, the right to buy the sofa for £1,000). You are not obliged to buy the sofa, but, if you decide not to buy, you will lose the £30 you paid at the outset. As far as the furniture store is concerned, they are short the option because they have granted the right to do something (by giving you the right to buy the sofa for £1,000) in return for the receipt of an agreed sum (here £30).

2. Futures

Learning Objective

1.1.1 Understand the basic concepts and fundamental characteristics of: forward and futures contracts; contracts for differences

2.1 What is a Future?

A future is a legal agreement between two parties to make or take delivery of a specific quantity and quality of a specified asset on a fixed future date at a price agreed today.

Unlike our example of a sofa future above, futures are often described as futures contracts because they are traded on organised exchanges, such as **Euronext** Derivatives, the CME Group in the US, the Singapore Exchange (SGX) and the Dubai Mercantile Exchange (DME) in the United Arab Emirates (UAE).

The terms of each contract are standardised in a legal document called the contract specification. This is because it would not be financially viable for an exchange to precisely satisfy every single trader's requirements regarding particular underlying assets. The aim of the contract specifications is to allow participants to take positions on general price movements in any given market. Contract specification also promotes transparency across all users of the exchange.

Futures originated in the agricultural market, where they were based on commodities, such as grain. The Chicago Board of Trade (CBOT), now part of the CME Group, trades wheat futures, where the full-sized contract is based on a set of specific grades of wheat and the specific quantity is 5,000 bushels, ie, each individual contract represents 5,000 bushels of wheat. The specified asset is obviously wheat, but of what quality? The contract specification goes to great lengths to detail precisely what is acceptable under the terms of each contract. For example, the CBOT's wheat future specifies that the grain must be a specific deliverable grade, a list of which is set out by the exchange. It also specifies what form of delivery is acceptable by listing the names of storage/warehouses to which delivery must be made.

The price is agreed between the buyer and the seller. In fact, it is the sole element of the futures contract that is open to negotiation. However, the exchange does specify the minimum permitted movement in price and the method of quotation. For a wheat future contract, the quote is on a per bushel basis and the minimum movement is 0.25 of a cent ($0.0025) per bushel (known as the full **tick** size) and, because each contract represents 5,000 bushels, the value of the minimum price movement per contract (the full tick value) is $12.50 per contract.

The fixed future date is also laid down by the exchange. Although it is a set day within the month, the fixed future date is often referred to as the contract month. In respect of wheat futures traded on the CBOT, the delivery months are March, May, July, September and December.

Alongside these commodity futures there are also financial futures, which are based on interest rates, **bonds**, currency exchange rates and stock market indices.

For all futures contracts, the contract specification standardises the futures product and, as long as the contracts have a common underlying asset and a common delivery date, the contract is said to be fungible, ie, identical to, and substitutable with, others traded on the same exchange.

For example, all March long gilt futures on ICE Futures Europe, London are fungible. A March long gilt future on ICE Futures, London is not fungible with a June long gilt future on the same exchange, because the delivery dates are different.

The consequences of standardisation and fungibility are:

- traders know what they are trading
- traders know what their delivery obligations are (buyers know the cost of the asset they have bought, and sellers know the amount they will receive and the quality of the asset they have sold)
- contracts are easy to trade as they have set terms
- it is possible to trade large volumes (multiple contracts), and
- the concentration of activity provides liquidity and, therefore, efficiency to the market.

The fungible nature of contracts also means that a trader can remove any delivery obligations by taking an equal and opposite position. For example, a trader who has bought a future and is required to buy a specified quantity of the underlying asset can simply sell a fungible future. The result is that they have agreed to both buy and sell the same item at the same future date. The trader is described as having closed out his position.

2.1.1 How Do Futures Work?

Futures positions are opened by going long (buying) or short (selling).

By opening either a long or short futures position, the trader becomes exposed to changes in the futures price and the position will incur profits or losses as a result of the movement in price.

Holding the contract to expiry will oblige the trader to meet the delivery obligations. If the price of the asset rises, the futures buyer will make a profit. The trader will take delivery at the lower price and be able to sell the asset in the cash market at the higher price.

Conversely, if the price is lower than the agreed price, the trader's counterparty (the futures seller) will make a profit.

2.2 Forwards

Forwards are very similar to futures contracts, as they are similarly legally binding agreements to make or take delivery of a specified quantity of a specific asset at a certain time in the future for a price that is agreed today. They may not be marked to market daily or, if they are, the resulting profits are not paid out until maturity and any losses must be paid to the exchange clearing house if they are traded on-exchange. Forwards are, therefore, settled only on the delivery date.

They are usually traded off-exchange, commonly known as **over-the-counter (OTC)**, but they can also be traded on-exchange. For example, the London Metal Exchange (LME) lists a number of forward contracts.

In the physical markets (where **physical delivery** is common), an airline might, for example, use forward prices on jet fuel to lock in one of their major costs. They would agree a price today for delivery in a future month.

The LME trades and clears both futures and OTC contracts for certain non-ferrous metals, steel and minor metals, such as cobalt. An OTC-like steel forward allows a construction company to lock in today the price of steel, which is a major input cost, when submitting a bid for a building project. In this case, a steel forward is similar to any other forward, in that it allows the contract's buyer to lock in today the price of steel that will be delivered at a future date.

Forwards are derivatives – the future price agreed for a forward is based on the **spot price** of the underlying asset (usually known as just 'the underlying'); in the case of a currency it will be adjusted for the interest rates in the relevant currencies.

Most forwards are OTC contracts, usually with banks or investment firms. Outright forwards are a common product traded in the **foreign exchange (FX)** market. Companies, institutional investors and banks themselves use forwards to manage their FX transaction risks. If an organisation is importing or exporting goods (or investing) in another currency, they can use forwards to protect against adverse currency movements. Forward contracts are also used to lock in the price of physical commodities, such as energy, metals (see the example above) and foodstuffs.

The main advantages of forwards compared with futures (which are always, by definition, exchange-traded) are:

- flexibility (size, date)
- wide range of underlyings
- are available from most commercial banks.

Their main disadvantages are potential counterparty risk, cost and in some cases, liquidity. With exchange-traded futures, counterparty risk is reduced considerably by **novation** through the central clearing house (see Chapter 6, Section 1.1).

Forwards can also be used for the same purposes as futures.

2.3 Contracts for Differences (CFDs)

Some futures contracts are based on tangible goods such as grain and oil. If the contract is carried through to expiry there will be an exchange of the underlying for the pre-agreed cash sum. These contracts are described as being physically deliverable.

However, many people trade in futures contracts where the underlying is intangible – a stock market index, for example. At the end of the contract, physical delivery of the underlying is either impossible or impractical. These contracts, where the underlying is intangible, are known as contracts for differences (CFDs) and are cash-settled.

Example 1

An investor buys a **FTSE 100** future at an agreed 'price' of 6900 points and at expiry the index stands at 7050 points. The investor has made a profit, not by buying or selling a tangible asset such as shares, grain or a bond, but by receiving a set amount of cash for each point gained. The amount of money for each point is specified in the futures contract.

In the case of ICE Futures Europe FTSE 100 futures, that amount is £10, so the seller of the future simply pays the buyer 150 points multiplied by £10, ie, £1,500.

Exercise 1

An investor has the view that economic growth will slow down in the next 12 months. This slower growth will cause metals' prices to fall, due to a drop in demand. Based on this view, he sells 20 contracts of the LME's June (one-year maturity) **LMEX** futures at 3400.

The LMEX is a cash-settled index-based futures contract that is based on the weighted average of the price of the LME's six primary metals.

One month before its maturity the June LMEX future is trading at 3190. The contract's specification is $10 per index point. What is the investor's profit or loss?

The answer can be found in the appendix at the end of this chapter.

2.4 Spread Betting

An alternative way of entering into a CFD is to place a bet with a spread-betting firm. One of the most popular of these types of trades involves a **short-term interest rate** (STIR) contract, such as the three-month short sterling future.

Example 2

If an investor thinks a particular market will continue to rise over the short term, they could place an **up bet**. Say they believe the FTSE 100 Index of leading UK shares is going to rise after their recent sell-off. If the FTSE 100 is currently 7200 index points, a spread-betting firm may be quoting 7250/7275 for three months into the future.

Let's say the investor places an up bet at £10 a point at the quote of 7275 (the choice of pounds per point is up to the investor), and a month later the index has risen to 7350. The quote from the spread-betting firm is now 7375/7400 and the investor decides to cash in their close-out (profitable position). This is achieved by placing a **down bet** of £10 per point at 7375. The difference between the buy and sell prices is 100 index points (7375 – 7275), which, multiplied by £10, gives a gain of £1,000.

This gain is not subject to capital gains tax.

Obviously, if an investor thinks it likely that the FTSE 100 (the London Stock Exchange's (LSE's) main share index of 100 largest listed companies) will fall, they could speculate by placing a down bet via a spread-betting firm.

2.5 Uses of Futures

There are three ways futures can be used:

2.5.1 Speculation

Speculators take a view on the market's direction and seek to make a profit from price movements by buying or selling futures contracts. Speculative investments may involve a high degree of risk and usually have short holding periods. If an investor feels the price of the underlying is going to go up, they can speculate by buying the underlying itself or, alternatively, by buying futures contracts on that underlying.

Futures are often seen to be more attractive than the underlying because they can be highly geared. Put simply, this means that a small expenditure/initial investment gives the holder a big exposure to a market, ie, the potential for large profits or losses. However, a speculator has to allow for **margin** requirements and must have sufficient liquidity to manage the open position.

2.5.2 Hedging

People who want to guard themselves against adverse price movements **hedge** using futures. A hedger seeks to protect a position, or anticipated position, in the spot market by taking an opposite position in the futures market. A perfect hedge is a risk-free position. For example, a fund manager can remove or reduce their exposure to a stock market fall that will affect the portfolio of shares they manage. They do this by taking a temporary short position in futures in an equity index. It will deliver profits to offset the impact a fall in the stock market would have (the extent to which the risk is offset will depend on how closely their portfolio is correlated to the index). Fund managers often use these hedging strategies as temporary 'shields' against market movements.

2.5.3 Arbitrage

Arbitrageurs exploit price anomalies in two markets. They observe that the same underlying asset or financial instrument is selling at two different prices in two different markets. They undertake a transaction whereby they buy the asset or instrument at the lower price in one market and sell it at the higher price in the other market. **Arbitrage** gives them a risk-free profit that will be realised when the prices in the two markets come back into line and the arbitrageur closes out the position.

2.6 Futures Profit and Loss Profiles

Learning Objective

1.1.3 Understand the risks and rewards associated with derivatives: market risk

2.6.1 Long Futures

The outcome for a buyer or seller of a future when it reaches its expiry date is driven by the price of the underlying asset at that time. Because the market price can vary, this is known as the market risk.

A futures buyer commits to buy at a pre-agreed price (eg, £115) and will make a profit as long as the underlying asset is trading above this price at expiry. This can be represented graphically as follows:

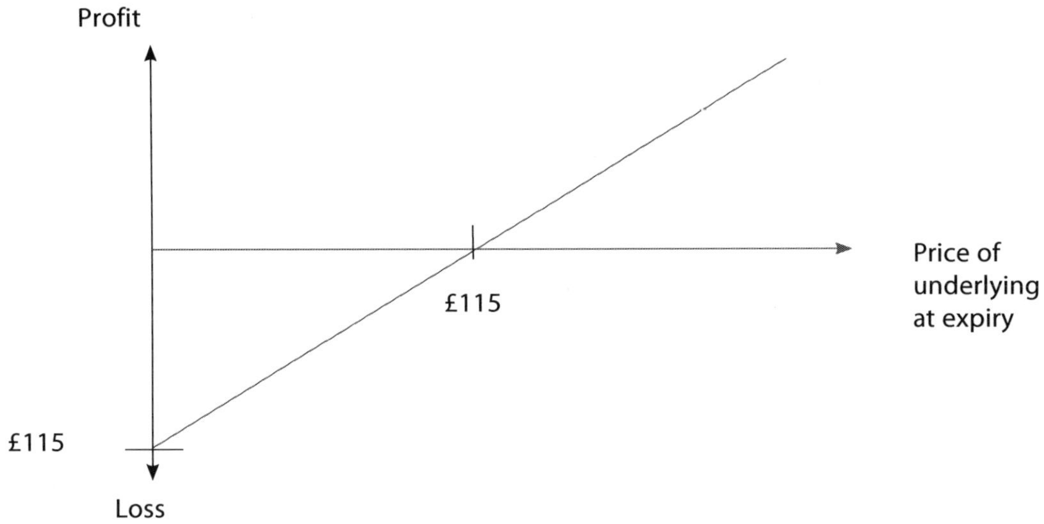

As shown, the risk to the buyer of a futures contract is maximised when the value of the underlying at expiry falls to zero. In that case, the buyer will pay the pre-agreed sum (£115) for an asset worth nothing, losing the £115. The reward to the buyer is, theoretically, unlimited – the higher the price of the underlying at expiry, the higher the profit made by the futures buyer.

2.6.2 Short Futures

Because the seller of a future is the other side of the transaction from the buyer of the future, the outcome is a mirror image of the outcome for the buyer. It is driven by the price of the underlying asset at expiry and a profit is made if the underlying asset's price falls below the pre-agreed level. A loss will be made if the underlying asset at expiry is priced above the pre-agreed futures price. This can be represented graphically as follows:

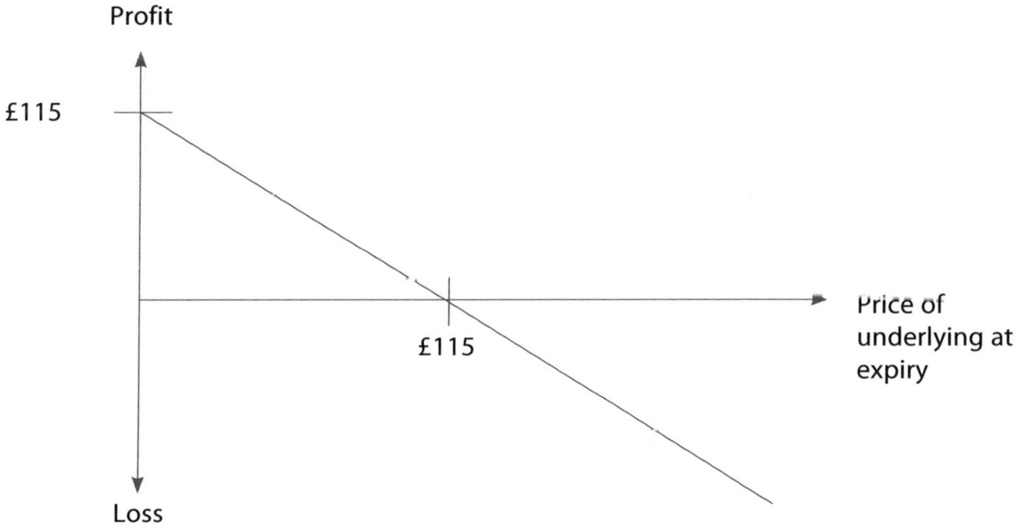

The risk to the seller of a futures contract is, theoretically, unlimited. As the price of the underlying asset rises above the pre-agreed level at expiry, the futures seller suffers a loss since they must pay the higher market price and sell at the lower pre-agreed price to the futures buyer. The futures seller's reward increases as the price of the underlying asset falls below the pre-agreed level and is limited to the futures price, whereas the seller can deliver the underlying asset that has cost nothing in exchange for the pre-agreed futures price.

2.7 Other Risks

Learning Objective

1.1.3 Understand the risks and rewards associated with derivatives: counterparty risk, liquidity risk

In addition to the market risk, there are two other risks that arise on futures contracts.

Whenever a buyer or seller enters into a futures contract, there is a risk that the other side (the counterparty) of the contract does not or cannot honour its obligations. This is known as counterparty risk. It should be noted that in the case of futures, counterparty risk is extremely low, when compared to most OTC derivatives. This is due to the fact that futures are exchange-traded contracts; therefore, once a trade takes place, the exchange becomes the counterparty to both the buyer and the seller. This will be explained in Chapter 3.

Counterparty risk exists between:

- the broker and their client, and
- the broker and the clearing house.

The second risk is liquidity risk. Liquidity risk arises from situations in which a party interested in trading a specific contract or asset cannot do so because no-one in the market is willing to quote a price for that contract or asset at which the party is prepared to trade. Liquidity risk becomes particularly important when a market participant wishes to buy or sell a contract/asset that they currently hold, since it affects their ability to close out an open position. See Section 5 of this chapter for a full explanation of liquidity.

The third type of risk is operational risk, which is defined as a risk incurred by a failure in an organisation's internal activities – in this case, the risk associated with a loss from a derivative trade that was caused by a problem/fault in a firm's processing of the transaction. Operational risk is broadly defined as focusing on the risks arising from the people, systems and processes through which a company operates. It can also include other classes of risk, such as fraud, legal, physical and environmental.

A widely used definition of operational risk is in the Basel II regulations. This states that operational risk is:

> *'the risk of loss resulting from inadequate or failed internal processes, people and systems, or from external events.'*

Operational risk management differs from other types of risk because it is not used to generate profit. It occurs only due to a failure within a firm's/market participant's internal structure/systems.

Basically, operational risk is the prospect of any loss resulting from inadequate or failed procedures, systems or policies due to:

- employee errors
- systems failures
- fraud or other criminal activity
- any event that disrupts business processes.

3. Options

Learning Objective

1.1.2 Understand the basic concepts and fundamental characteristics of options contracts, including: basic puts and calls; options on cash and futures; American, European, Asian; common path-dependent and average pricing options

3.1 What is an Option?

An option is a contract that gives the buyer the right, but not the obligation, to sell or buy a particular asset at a particular price, on or before a specified date. The seller of the option, conversely, assumes an obligation in respect of the underlying asset upon which the option has been traded. As illustrated by the sofa option in the introduction to this chapter, an option is a contract that allows an investor to buy (or sell) a product for a fixed price, on or before a future date.

Options are available on a variety of underlying assets – physical assets, like oil and sugar, and financial assets, such as cash shares and FX forwards. The option may be based on a futures contract, where the underlying asset is a future; these are known as options on futures.

As with futures, investors attempting to place directional bets in options are known as speculators, but options can also be used to hedge existing positions. Options are trading and risk management tools which offer an extremely wide set of choices for investors and fund managers with differing attitudes to market direction and **volatility** and with differing appetites for risk.

3.2 Options Terminology

A **call option** is an option to buy an asset (the underlying) for a specified price (the **strike or exercise price**), on or before a specified date. Remember this by thinking that the buyer can call away the asset from the seller.

A **put** option is an option to sell an asset for a specified price on or before a specified date. Remember this by thinking that the buyer can put the asset on to someone else (the seller of the option), demanding the pre-agreed sum in exchange.

The buyer of an options contract is said to be long, or the holder or owner of the contract. The seller of an options contract is said to be short, or the writer of the contract.

An option's **premium** is the cost of the option to the buyer. Premiums are non-returnable and are paid by the option holder to the option writer.

The exercise style of an option describes how it may be exercised. A **European-style option** is an option that can be exercised on its expiry day only (remember 'E' for 'European' and 'Expiry day'). An **American-style option** is an option that the holder can exercise on any day during its life (remember 'A' for 'American' and 'Any day').

There are also a number of exotic path-dependent types of options (ie, those whose pay-offs are based on how the underlying's asset price moves over the whole or part of the option's life). Here is a brief list of the most common types that are currently traded:

- A **lookback option** is path-dependent and is where the option owner has the right to buy (or sell) the underlying instrument at its lowest (or highest) price over some preceding period.
- An **Asian option** is an option where the pay-off is not determined by the underlying price at maturity, but by the average underlying price over the entire length or a specified part of the contract. For example, a three-month **Asian call option** might pay the difference between the underlying asset's average price over the call's three-month life and its price at expiration. Remember, if the asset's reference price is less than the three-month average, the option will expire unexercised and no payment will be made. In the same circumstances, an **Asian put option** would purchase the buyer the difference between the three-month average price and the underlying asset's price at expiration, since this option's strike price is higher than the asset's current price.
- A **barrier option** is a type of option whose existence and pay-off depends on whether or not the underlying asset has reached a predetermined price. There are two types of barrier options: a knock-in and a knock-out. A knock-in option is one that is activated or starts to exist once the underlying asset has reached the predetermined price, while a knock-out option is the opposite: when it is purchased, it exists, but it ceases to exist if the underlying asset reaches the predetermined price.
- A **binary option** (also known as a **digital option**) pays a fixed amount, or nothing at all, depending on the price of the underlying instrument at maturity.
- A **Bermudan option** is an option (call or put) where early exercise is restricted to certain dates during its life. It derives its name from the fact that its exercise characteristics are somewhere between those of the American (exercisable at any time during the life of the option) and the European (exercisable only at the expiration of the option) styles of option. Bermudan options offer the buyer several exercise dates over the life of the option. This can be a series of dates over the contract's life that are usually spaced in regular intervals. Since Bermudan options are more flexible than European options, but less flexible regarding exercise than American-style options, their premiums are more expensive than the former but cheaper than the latter, if all other factors are the same.

3.3 Options – Risks, Rewards and Profit and Loss Profiles

Learning Objective

1.1.8 Understand how to interpret basic options diagrams (long call, long put, short call, short put)

The following examples are based on American-style options on the shares of two fictional companies – ABC plc and XYZ plc.

3.3.1 Buying a Call

eg, March ABC plc 700 Call @ 30

The buyer of the option pays the premium (30p), which is the amount due per share, quoted in pence to the seller. The buyer is the holder of the option (and said to be long a call). The holder now has the right, but not the obligation, to buy one share in ABC for 700p.

They can do this at any point on any business day during the published trading times until the defined time on the expiry day in March. The option premium is paid upfront and is non-returnable.

The premium is paid by the buyer via their broker and then passed on to the clearing house for the account of the counterparty's broker.

What Happens at Expiry?

It will depend on the price of ABC shares on the expiry day:

- If the share price prevailing in the market is below 700p, the option expires worthless and the holder will **abandon** the option. Would you pay 700p for the share if you could buy it for less in the market?
- If the prevailing share price is above 700p, the holder has the right to buy the shares for 700p, a lower price than in the cash market. They will, therefore, exercise the option, paying 700p for the share, and then may sell it in the market for the higher price. Even if the market price is 701p the option is worth exercising as the holder will make a profit of 1p, which can be used to offset the upfront cost of the premium.
- The break-even price of the call is its strike plus its premium; in this case the break-even is 730p.

The potential for gain or loss can be represented diagrammatically, with profit or loss shown on the Y axis and the price of the underlying at expiry on the X axis:

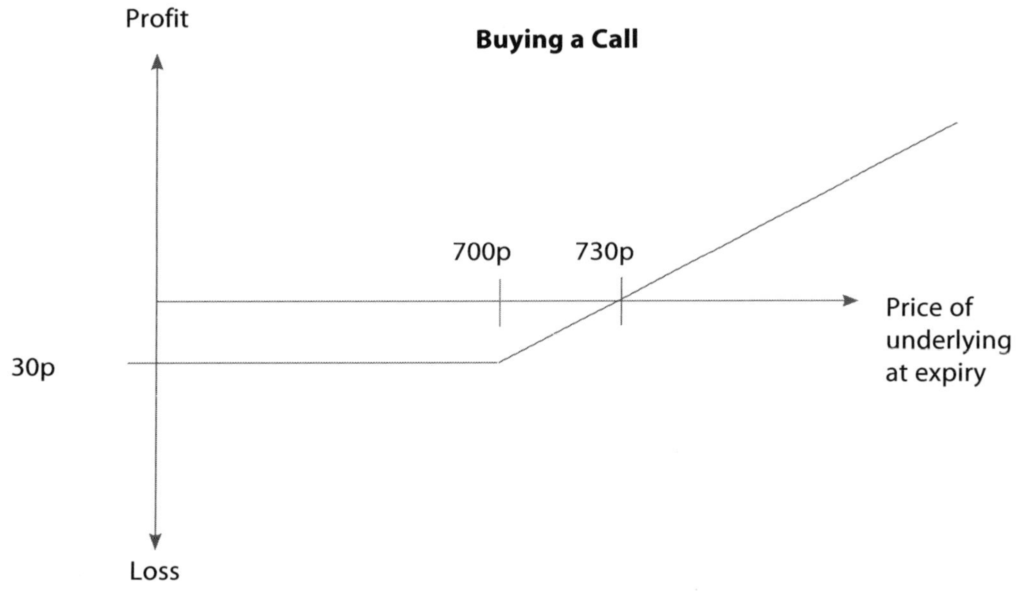

In Summary

- The maximum cost to the buyer is limited to the premium paid, which is paid regardless of the outcome at expiry.
- A net profit will be made by the buyer if the profit on exercise exceeds the premium paid.
- The break-even point is the strike price plus the premium.
- The maximum potential profit is unlimited as the long call option will become increasingly valuable to the buyer as the share price rises above the exercise price.

3.3.2 Selling a Call

eg, March ABC plc 700 Call @ 30

The seller of the option immediately receives the premium (30p) from the buyer, which is the amount due per share. The seller is now under an obligation to deliver the share should the holder of the option decide to exercise at any time up to and including expiry (as it is an American-style exercise).

What Happens at Expiry?

- If the share price prevailing in the market is below 700p, as indicated in the first example, the holder will abandon the option and the seller/writer will no longer hold any obligation. The premium has already been received and provides the seller's profit.
- If the prevailing share price is above 700p, the holder will exercise the option against the writer. The writer is obliged to deliver the share for 700p. They may not already own the share and have to acquire it in the market at a higher price and take the loss. As long as the loss is lower than the premium received, the writer will still make an overall profit.

Diagrammatically:

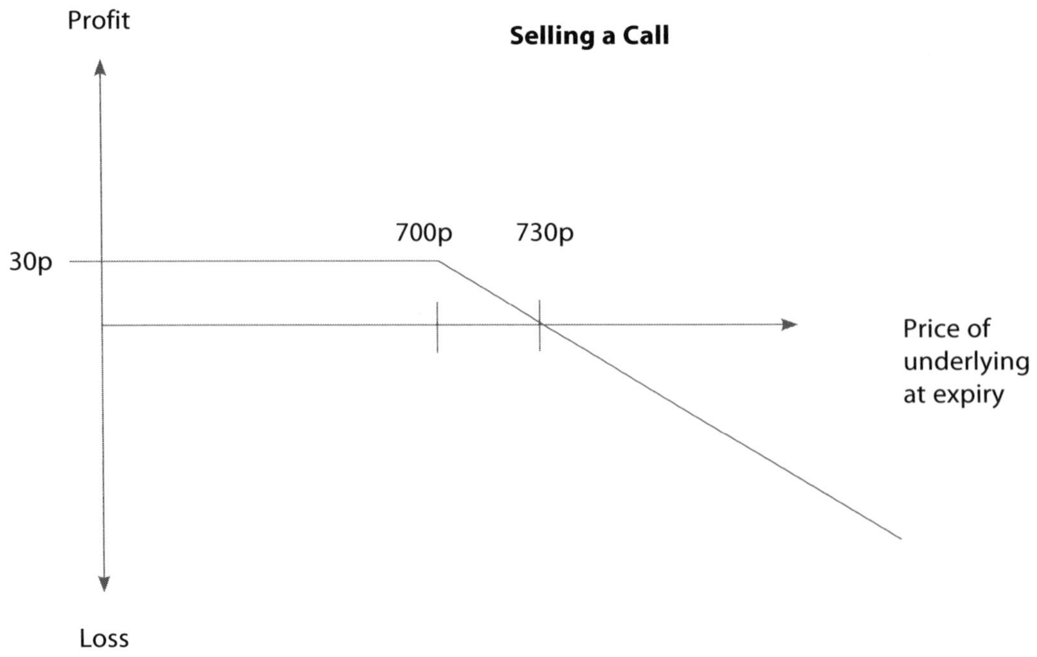

In Summary

- The maximum loss for the seller is potentially unlimited.
- A net loss will be made by the seller if the loss on exercise exceeds the premium already received.
- The seller's break-even point is the strike price plus the premium.
- The seller's maximum potential profit is limited to the premium received.

3.3.3 Buying a Put

eg, March XYZ plc 450 Put @ 17

Similarly to the earlier examples, the buyer of the option pays the premium (this time, say, 17p) to the seller and becomes the holder of the put option (they are now long a put). The holder now has the right to sell one share in XYZ for 450p, again under American-style terms.

What Happens at Expiry?

It will depend on the price of XYZ shares on the expiry day:

- If the share price is above 450p, the holder will abandon the option. The option is worthless. Would you sell the share for 450p if you could sell it for more in the market?
- If the share price is below 450p, the holder can buy the share in the cash market at the lower price, then exercise the option at the 450p strike price, thus selling the share at the higher price (450p) to make a profit. Even if the market price is 449p, the option is worth exercising as the holder will make a profit of 1p, which can be used to offset the cost of the original premium.

Diagrammatically:

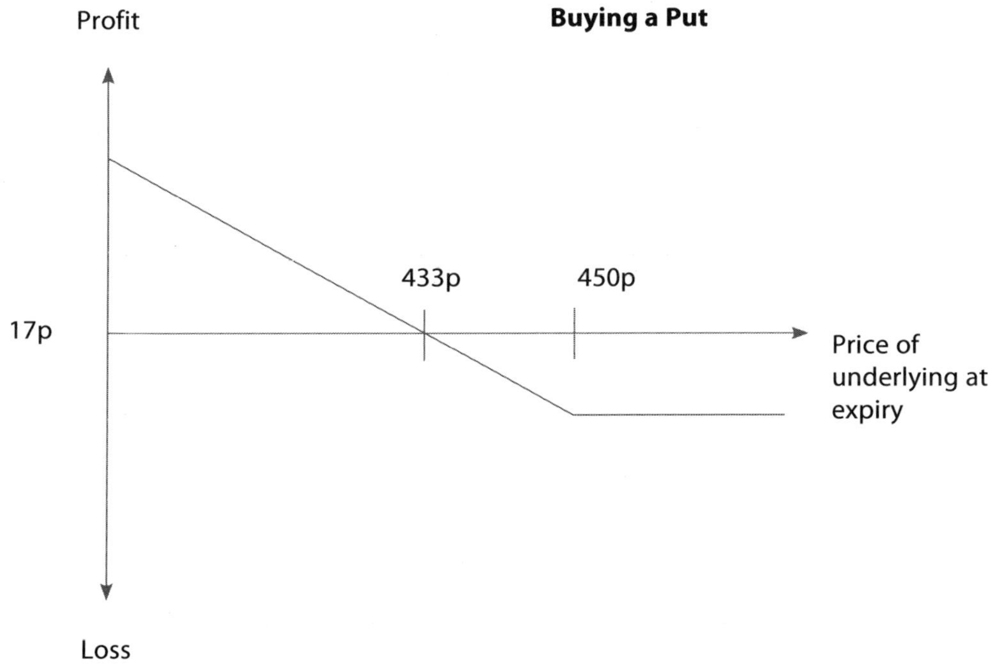

In Summary

- The maximum loss to the buyer is limited to the premium paid.
- A net profit will be made by the buyer if the profit on exercise exceeds the premium paid.
- The break-even point is the strike price less the premium.
- Maximum potential profit will arise if the share price falls to zero, and is the strike price less the premium.

3.3.4 Selling a Put

eg, March XYZ plc 450 Put @ 17

The seller of the option receives the premium (17p) from the option buyer and is the writer of the option. The writer is now under an obligation to buy XYZ shares for 450p each if the holder decides to exercise.

What Happens at Expiry?

As you might expect by now, it will depend on the price of XYZ shares on expiry day:

- If the share price is above 450p, the holder will abandon the option (as they can receive a higher price in the market for the share, as explained earlier). The seller keeps the premium received.
- If the share price is below 450p, the holder will exercise the option (as the holder can achieve a higher price by exercising than is possible in the market). The option writer will be obliged to buy the share for 450p and sell it on in the market at the lower price and take the loss. As long as the loss is lower than the premium received, the writer will still make an overall profit.

Diagrammatically:

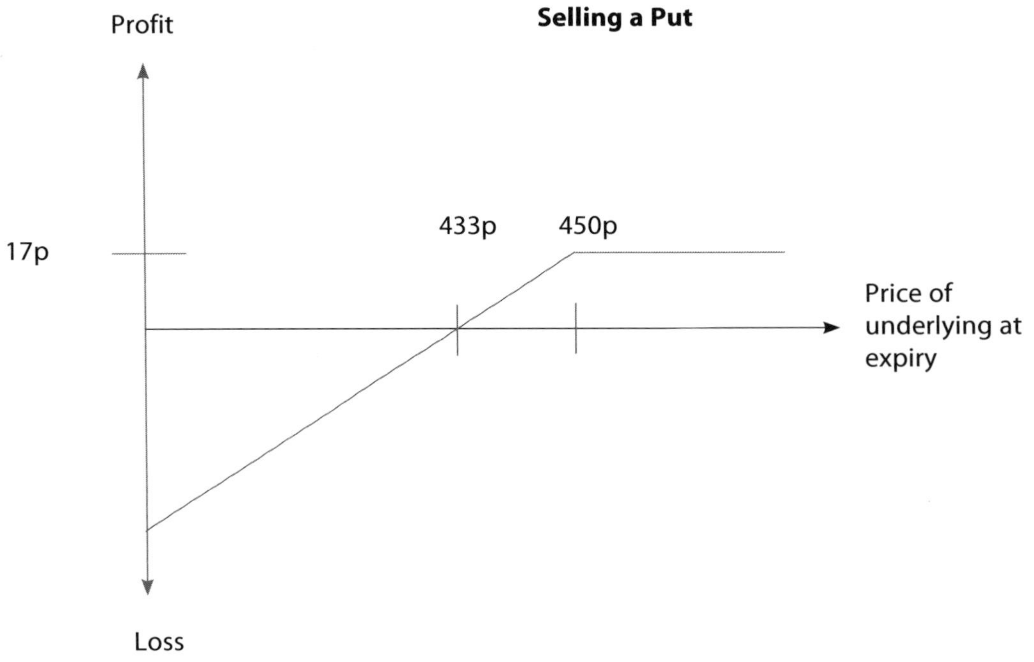

In Summary

- The seller's maximum profit is limited to the premium received.
- A net loss will be made by the seller if the loss on exercise exceeds the premium received.
- The seller's break-even point is the strike price less the premium.
- Maximum potential loss will arise if the share price falls to zero, and is the strike price less the premium.

3.4 Risk and Reward Summary

Learning Objective

1.1.3 Understand the risks and rewards associated with derivatives: counterparty risk; market risk; liquidity risk; risks to the buyer of options; risks to the writers of options

The following table summarises the potential risks and rewards in each of the four option positions:

Position	Risk	Reward
Long call	Limited to premium	Unlimited
Short call	Unlimited	Limited to premium
Long put	Limited to premium	Strike price less premium (asset price would have to fall to zero)
Short put	Strike price less premium (asset price would have to fall to zero)	Limited to premium

The counterparty risk associated with options reflects the fact that, when an option is **out-of-the-money (OTM)**, there is no risk that it will be exercised. Therefore, for an option seller, under normal circumstances, they do not have any counterparty risk once they have received the premium, since after that the buyer has no obligation to the seller.

In the case of an option buyer, they do have counterparty risk relative to the seller, but only when the option has **intrinsic value (IV)** – that is, when it is **at-the-money (ATM)** or **in-the-money (ITM)**. This is based on the fact that the seller will have to either buy the underlying asset, in the case of a put, or sell the underlying asset, in the case of a call, at a loss, based on its current market price.

3.5 Profit and Loss Calculator

The following table provides the formulae for calculating the profit or loss made on each of the four positions at expiry:

	Expiry price < strike	Expiry price > strike
Long call	Loss = premium	Gain/(loss) = (expiry price – strike price) – premium
Short call	Profit = premium	Gain/(loss) = (strike price – expiry price) + premium
Long put	Gain/(loss) = (strike price – expiry price) – premium	Loss = premium
Short put	Gain/(loss) = (expiry price – strike price) + premium	Profit = premium

3.6 FLEX Options

Learning Objective

1.1.7 Understand the trading mechanisms by which OTC and exchange-traded markets meet: block trades; EFPs/EFSs; Flex products

The FLexible EXchange option concept was pioneered by the Chicago Board Options Exchange (CBOE) in 1993. Since then a number of other options and derivatives exchanges have launched similar products. They are hybrid exchange-traded products which introduce some OTC features. OTC features are negotiated between the two parties to the contract, rather than standardised in the contract specification. The concept is to provide an exchange-traded product, which will offer greater flexibility by mixing the strengths of classic exchange-traded (ie, fully standardised) options with OTC (freely negotiable terms) options.

They differ from standardised exchange products in allowing users to specify certain parameters that are normally specified by the exchange within the terms of the contract. They give the ability to customise key contract terms like exercise price, exercise style and expiry date. For example, **FLEX options** are available on the FTSE 100 Index on ICE Futures Europe and investors can specify the exercise price and expiry day of the contract.

FLEX options have the added benefit of reducing the **credit risk** normally associated with OTC contracts. The credit risk is substantially reduced due to the exchange's use of a central clearing house.

For an explanation of block trades, **Exchange for Physicals (EFPs)** and Exchange for Swaps (EFSs), see Chapter 3, Section 2.

3.7 Options on Futures

Unlike an option on a physical asset, such as gold or a share, an option on a future gives the holder the right, but not the obligation, to become the buyer or seller (depending on whether the option is a call or a put) of a specified futures contract. All major derivatives exchanges offer options based on their futures contracts. In this way, they are a derivative of a derivative.

If an investor were to hold a call option on a December Euro Interbank Offered Rate (EURIBOR) future (see Chapter 2, Section 4 for a definition of EURIBOR), they would become the buyer of the futures contract upon exercise at, or before, expiry, depending upon the exercise style of the option. On exercise, the option seller would be **assigned** a short futures position.

Example 3

You sell two February calls on a Euronext, Paris rapeseed oil futures contract. If at expiration the corresponding future's contract is above the call's strike price, it will be automatically exercised and you will now be short two futures at the option's strike price.

4. Gearing

Learning Objective

1.1.4 Understand the significance of gearing to exchange-traded derivatives: how margin facilitates gearing; effect on derivative positions; reward versus outlay; reward versus risk

In the derivatives market, **gearing** is the measure of the amount of cash/initial investment spent on establishing a futures or options position, compared to the actual value of the underlying position.

At its simplest, gearing is the ability for the value of a derivative to rise by 100% in a very short timescale, when the underlying security has only risen by a far smaller amount, say 10%. The principle can be illustrated by looking at the gearing in the context of buying a house and taking out a mortgage.

Example 4 – Gearing Illustration

Assume a person buys a £100,000 flat by putting up £10,000 and taking out a mortgage for the remaining £90,000. If the flat increases in value by 10% to £110,000, and the individual still owes £90,000, their stake has risen to £20,000 – a 100% increase on their investment on a 10% increase in the underlying property.

Futures, options and **warrants** are all highly geared and the principle is the same as in the above illustration – a small change in the price of the underlying asset can result in a much bigger proportionate change in the value of the derivative position. This is due to the fact that the initial investment, such as the option premium, is relatively small compared to the face value of the underlying asset.

A warrant is a type of security that is similar to an option, in that it gives its owner the right to buy an asset at a set price. Warrants are often attached to or are part of a bond. Warrants can be separated from the bond and traded on their own.

4.1 Options Gearing

As the option premium is usually only a small fraction of the value of the asset, changes in the price of the underlying can produce disproportionate changes in the price of the option.

Example 5

You buy an XYZ plc 850 call for a premium of 20 when the share price is 800.

On expiry, the share price is 880. You would exercise the option and crystallise a net profit of 10, ie, (880 – 850) – 20. Your return on investment is 10 ÷ 20, ie, 50%.

However, if you had bought the share for 800 and later sold it for 880, your return on investment would have been 80 ÷ 800, ie, 10%.

Buying the call option might appear to be a more attractive reward than buying the share, but it is also more risky. If the share price only rises to, say, 808, you will lose 100% of your investment (the premium of 20), whereas holding the underlying share will have produced a profit of 8 ÷ 800, ie, 1%. The amount of gearing in an option is a direct function of the premium paid for it; the smaller the premium relative to the share price, the higher the potential gearing.

Options can also be volatile, offering high potential returns and losses (although the loss is limited to the initial investment) to investors. Time is also a factor, as options and warrants have limited lives and their value erodes as the expiry date approaches.

4.2 Futures Gearing

Gearing in a futures contract comes about through the margining system. When you buy a future, although you don't pay for the asset, you have to keep some collateral aside in case things go badly wrong. This collateral (**initial margin**) is a small fraction of the contract's face value, but when you make any profits or suffer any losses it is based on the contract's full face value. See Chapter 6, Section 3 for an in-depth explanation of the concept of initial margin.

The fact that exchanges and therefore brokers require only a small percentage of a contract's full value as an initial investment, in the form of initial margin, leads to the ability to gear futures trading positions.

Example 6

SGX's Japanese Government Bond (JGB) futures contract is based on a bond with a face value of JPY100 million. A broker normally requires only a percentage of the contract's full face value as initial margin – say, 20%. This means that their client will incur profits or losses on each contract based on JPY100 million, with only an initial payment of, say, JPY20 million. This is how gearing works.

Example 7

You go long a FTSE future at 7000. You will need to put aside, say, 300 points. Remember, each point is worth £10, which equals £3,000 of collateral.

Later you close your position for 7060, a profit of 60 points = £600, a return of 600 ÷ 3,000, ie, 20% on your collateral. In contrast, the index has only moved 60 points, which is less than 1%.

Exercise 2

If a call option with a premium of 10p gave the buyer the right to buy a share for 100p, what would be the gain (or loss) if at expiry the share was priced at:

a. 120p
b. 100p
c. 95p

The answers to this exercise can be found in the appendix at the end of this chapter.

The gearing on a future is simply because the buyers or sellers of futures only pay a small proportion of the price of the underlying asset as initial margin, and potentially gain from the whole movement in the underlying asset.

5. Liquidity

Learning Objective

1.1.5 Understand the principles and differences between the two major measures of exchange-traded liquidity (open interest and volume)

Liquidity is a term used to describe how easy it is to trade without incurring excessive costs. It represents the market's ability to absorb sudden shifts in supply and demand without dramatic price distortions. Liquid markets are alternatively described as deep. A security is said to be liquid if the **spread** between bid and ask price is narrow and trades of a reasonable size can be done at those quotes. In the market for shares, it represents the ease with which shares can be converted into cash.

In principle, derivatives markets are the same. Market prices will be established by the process of price discovery, with buyers and sellers stating their bid and offer prices. The difference between the bid and the offer is the bid/offer spread (or dealing spread); the tighter this spread, the more liquid the market. Furthermore, if there is a high volume of willing buyers and sellers either side of the bid/offer spread, any changes in demand will not move the price significantly. This is referred to as a low price elasticity of demand. A consequence of this is that it is cheaper to trade on liquid markets, as a dealer has to give up less value when agreeing a trade with the other side of the market because dealing spreads are close.

One of the main goals of derivatives exchanges is to have contracts that are liquid and easily traded. Liquidity encourages trading. This gives confidence that positions can be entered into and closed out (offset) without too much difficulty or expense. This creates a virtuous circle that encourages more investors, which further adds to liquidity.

The main elements of a liquid market are:

- many buyers and sellers
- small bid/offer spreads
- low commissions, and
- large amounts can be traded without causing major price movements.

Liquidity can be quantified by assessing the volume traded in a given period, or by looking at the number of cumulative open positions (the **open interest**).

Volume typically quantifies the number of contracts traded on a particular day, with each contract being counted once. It is, therefore, either the total number of short or long positions entered into during that day.

Open interest looks at the total number of long or short positions that remain outstanding at the end of a particular trading day. These are contracts which remain open and must, by definition, eventually be closed out (or settled by delivery if remaining open at the date of final maturity of the defined contract), hence open interest is a good indicator of the market's willingness to take and hold a position, and of long-term commitment to the market.

The higher the figures, the greater the liquidity.

There are two other measures of liquidity:

- **Immediacy** refers to the time needed to successfully trade a certain amount of a contract or asset at a specific cost.
- **Resilience**, the final dimension of liquidity, is the speed with which prices return to former levels after a large transaction. Unlike the other measures, resilience can only be determined over a period of time.

6. Exchange-Traded versus OTC-Traded Products

Learning Objective

1.1.6 Understand the main features and differences of over-the-counter (OTC) traded products in contrast to exchange-traded products: how an OTC-traded product is traded; standard versus bespoke OTC contracts; set maturity or expiry dates versus bespoke OTC contracts; margin requirements versus collateral; central clearing versus counterparty risk; liquidity from standard versus bespoke OTC contracts; risk profile of actively managed exchange-traded versus OTC hedging; market transparency versus confidential transactions

Derivatives can be entered into via standardised contracts provided on derivatives exchanges (such as ICE Futures Europe, the CME Group and the Osaka Exchange) or they can be negotiated and entered into away from any exchange, directly between the two counterparties. These contracts entered into away from an exchange are referred to as over-the-counter or OTC products.

The term future is exclusively used for exchange-traded obligations, with the equivalent OTC derivative being termed a forward. You probably recall that the sofa future encountered in the introduction was not traded on an exchange so, technically, it should have been described as a sofa forward.

The term option is used for both on-exchange transactions (exchange-traded options, or traded options for short) and OTC transactions.

Exchange-traded derivative (ETD) products, like futures, require their market participants to put collateral aside in the form of margin to mitigate the risk of one of the participants not fulfilling their obligations under the contract. The margin is administered by a **central counterparty (CCP)** (the clearing house, such as ICE Clear). The use of margin has become more common and structured for OTC transactions.Where the Basel Committee on Banking Supervision (BCBS) and the Board of the International Securities Organizations (BISC) have developed a standardised margin schedule for most OTC derivatives, that is being phased in by most market participants. The requirements for margin will be explored in more detail later in Chapter 6, Section 3.

The following table shows the fundamental points of comparison between exchange-traded and OTC derivatives:

	Exchange-Traded	OTC-Traded
Contract terms	Standardised, simple quality and quantity defined in the product specification.	Customised, specifically negotiated, totally confidential, flexible, large size possible.
Delivery	Standardised, under the exchange's product specification. Fixed dates.	Negotiable.
Liquidity	Excellent on major contracts, fast order execution. Largely an electronic environment.	Can be limited, varies dramatically depending on the underlying asset. Slower execution. Some markets may be made by fewer competing firms, perhaps only one.
Financial integrity	Existence of CCP means counterparty risk is removed. Daily mark to market (MTM).	While CCPs have become more common, the possibility of counterparty default possibility exists, hence the reason why credit ratings remain important.
Margin	Margin is always required, in the form of initial and **variation margin**.	While formal margin payments are not usually required, some contracts do require the payment or pledging of collateral. It is agreed on a case-by-case basis to secure the trade; it does not have a fixed payment, such as the margin payments associated with ETD trades.
Documentation	Standard and concise.	Tends to be one-off and more complex, although certain standard documentation is provided by trade associates, eg, the International Swaps & Derivatives Association (ISDA).
Regulation	Subject to significant regulation.	Under the European Market Infrastructure Regulation (EMIR) many types of trades are required to be cleared through a CCP. Market participants are also required to report trades to a warehouse (trade repository). See also Regulation in the table on the following page.
Price quotes	Highly transparent, public dissemination.	Limited. Need to shop around.
Transaction costs	Standardised, lower.	Individually priced, more expensive than exchange-traded like-for-like derivatives.

The following table highlights the **relative merits** of exchange-traded contracts compared to entering into similar contracts OTC:

Feature	Exchange-Traded	OTC-Traded
Standardisation and flexibility	The exchange standardises the expiry dates and underlying for each contract. As a result, the contracts are relatively inflexible.	Contracts are tailor-made between the participants, with expiry date and underlying agreed between the participants. Highly flexible.
Fungibility	Individual contracts (with the same expiry) are totally fungible.	The contracts are customised and are not as fungible.
Trading and liquidity	Contracts are easily traded on the exchange and therefore liquid. Trading can be conducted with any member of the market, and the fungible nature means that contracts can be opened with one member and closed with another.	Contracts are not standardised and are not easily traded, so liquidity can be restricted. The tailor-made nature of contracts means that closing the contract will involve negotiating with the original counterparty. However, some products (like interest rate swaps) are regularly traded between dealers in banks.
Counterparty risk	The counterparty in exchange-traded contracts is the CCP (the clearing house). The counterparty risk is relatively small.	The counterparty risk will be driven by the credit standing of the counterparty to the deal. However, some OTC products (eg, swaps and repos) can be cleared centrally through a clearing house, reducing counterparty risk.
Regulation	There is reasonable regulation for exchange-traded products.	Regulation has historically been very light for OTC products, but that is changing with the implementation of legislation such as the Dodd-Frank Act.
Public information	Trading activity and prices on the exchange are published on a real-time basis – trading details are revealed to the market, although the identification of the participants remains confidential.	There is little or no real-time publication of trading activity on the OTC markets – resulting in more confidentiality, but a lack of information on the competitiveness of quoted prices. With the introduction of the Commodity Futures Trading Commission (CFTC) and EMIR reporting, there is real-time reporting of OTC transactions.

Hedging	The standardised nature of contracts means that precisely hedging a particular position may not be possible due to the restricted contract sizes and expiry dates available.	The negotiation of the terms and conditions between participants can result in precisely hedging the underlying position.
Speculation	The available speculative exposures are restricted to exchange-traded products.	The availability to speculate is restricted only by the inability to find a suitable counterparty.

As mentioned in the table above, actively hedging a portfolio using either exchange-traded or OTC derivatives carries its own particular risks. While OTC derivatives contracts allow one to structure a hedge that exactly matches the underlying exposure (in amount, specific asset characteristics and maturity), these contracts do have counterparty risks and may have limited liquidity. In contrast, exchange-traded contracts do not have counterparty risk, but, given their standardised nature, risks may arise from any slight mismatch in maturity, contract size or slightly different asset characteristics. This should be taken into account when analysing the hedge's risk profile.

7. Markets and Participants

Learning Objective

1.1.9 Understand the main markets and stakeholders: foreign exchange, money markets, equity, fixed income, commodity; regulators in major markets; quote-driven versus order-driven; floor versus voice versus electronic; price givers – central banks, banks, major market corporates; price takers – central banks, banks, corporates, asset managers, insurance companies, private clients; buy-side; sell-side

Derivatives are based on a wide range of underlying markets. The main ones are:

- money markets/STIRs
- bonds – government and corporate
- equities (indices)
- FX
- commodities – **softs**, agricultural, energy and metals
- credit – credit default **swaps** and **swaptions**
- exotics – emissions, carbon credits.

As we will see in Chapter 2, the above-mentioned markets cover a wide range of products and, while they are structured differently, they do have a number of aspects in common. Most have some sort of regulator, whether it be the respective central bank, such as the Federal Reserve, Bank of England or European Central Bank (ECB), or a government agency, such as the **Financial Conduct Authority (FCA)** or Securities and Exchange Commission (SEC). In addition, all exchanges have authorities that set the minimum standards, such as trading hours, contract specification, margin requirements and delivery procedures. The following is a summary table of the main regulatory bodies for the main markets.

UK	Bank of England with its **Prudential Regulation Authority (PRA)** and Financial Policy Committee (FPC), and the Financial Conduct Authority (FCA)
EU	European Central Bank (ECB) European Banking Authority (EBA) European Securities and Markets Authority (ESMA) European Central Bank, respective country central banks and regulators such as: Autorité des Marchés Financiers (AMF) in France; Central Bank of Ireland in Ireland; Bundeszentrale für Finanzdienstleistungsaufsicht – Bundesbank and German Financial Supervisory Authority (BaFin) in Germany
US	Federal Reserve Bank (Fed) Securities and Exchange Commission (SEC) Commodity Futures Trading Commission (CFTC) Federal Deposit Insurance Corporation (FDIC)
Japan	Financial Services Agency (FSA) Securities and Exchange Surveillance Commission (SESC)
India	Reserve Bank of India (RBI) Securities and Exchange Board of India (SEBI)
China	China Securities Regulatory Commission (CSRC) China Insurance Regulatory Commission (CIRC) China Banking Regulatory Commission (CBRC)

Also, for the most part they have the same main participants, ie, the major global commercial and investment banks, fund managers, **sovereign wealth funds** and international corporations. In addition, most will also have local entities, which in the case of smaller or newly developing markets have links with international players, for either regulatory or customer reasons.

Electronic trading is widely used in both OTC markets, such as FX, as well as many exchanges. Some organised exchanges (often referred to as exchange-traded markets) have both screen-based trading and floor brokers, although more and more have moved to screen-based trading only, such as the Intercontinental Exchange – ICE (effective since 2005) and NYSE Liffe – (now part of ICE and effective since 2000). Exchanges that still have floor trading include the CME Group and LME (the only London-based exchange that still has ring trading).

Market makers are market participants who quote both a buy and a sell price for a financial instrument or commodity. They are found in OTC markets, such as FX; they are known as price-makers or -givers. They quote both sides of a price with the aim of making a profit by making the spread (the difference between their bid and offer prices). They also hope to increase their profits, since the positions that they hold after making a price are ones where they have not paid the spread to establish them. A market that relies on market-makers for its price is known as a price-driven market.

A price-taker is the market participant who either requests the price or deals via an intermediary on another participant's price. By doing so, they pay away the spread. That is, they deal on someone else's price.

Sell-side market participants are also sometimes called prime brokers. This usually refers to investment banks that sell securities and assets to money management firms (fund managers, pension funds and other funds) and corporate entities. They may be considered intermediaries that produce market research, whose aim is to generate trading ideas and then act as a counterparty to that trade.

Sell-side firms usually charge buy-side firms for the trade, through a commission or a charge that has been included in the trade's price. This charge is to cover the sell-side firm's costs of trading (trader's salary) and the cost of the research (analyst's salary). Many sell-side firms now delineate the cost of their products so that buy-side firms know they are paying an appropriate price for the best research and trade execution available.

On the other side, firms that buy securities and derivatives for their own account or their clients' accounts are said to be buy-side market participants. Most institutional investors, such as mutual funds, pension funds, hedge funds, private equity funds, trusts, insurance companies and proprietary traders, make up the vast majority of the buy-side.

The buy-side makes up one half of the financial market, and the sell-side makes up the other.

Firms on the buy-side are money managers that try to create value for their clients by purchasing securities that are underpriced. This usually involves taking on risk (for themselves or their clients) to generate a profit from these strategy-based trades.

The sell-side is made up of brokerage firms, investment banks and other entities that make buy/sell recommendations, upgrades, downgrades, target prices and research opinions which investors can use to make investing decisions. Since they normally act as intermediaries, most of their profit does not include trading risk.

Many market participants will find themselves as both price-makers and price-takers at any given time, depending on the circumstances and their positions. Liquidity in most markets comes from both market makers and order-driven prices from customer orders. While most participants are price-takers (see below), ie, fund managers, corporate clients, non-market making brokers, there are times when even market makers and central banks are also price-takers.

Example 8

Bank GHI might quote a two-way (bid/offer) price in spot GBP/USD to a client. If the client deals and the bank trader does not like the resulting position, they might call a few other banks for a spot GBP/USD price and deal on their price to regain the original position.

In the first case, Bank GHI is a market maker or price-maker, while in the second case it is a price-taker (since it is dealing on another bank's price).

In contrast, most exchanges operate on an order-driven or matched bargain basis. Such a system does not have designated market makers; instead, a deal is done when a buyer's bid meets a seller's offer. When this happens, the exchange's matching system will decide that a trade has taken place.

In summary, an order-driven market is one where the order flow determines prices. It displays all of the orders from both the buyers and sellers for each security, giving both the price and quantity of each security that is listed.

In a price- or quote-driven market, it is the market makers who determine the prices and the order flow. This type of market only displays the bids and offers of the designated market makers. The advantage of this type of market is the liquidity that the market makers provide, since they are required to meet their quoted prices. But a major drawback is that it lacks the degree of transparency of an order-driven market.

As new products are developed, the relationship between derivatives and their underlying assets and their markets will become more interdependent.

7.1 Different Market Participant Roles

Learning Objective

1.1.10 Understand the role of liquidity providers: intermediaries – IDBs; prime brokers; FCMs; executing brokers; clearing brokers

There is a wide range of roles and functions that different market participants fulfil to provide market liquidity. Some of these may seem to be far from the market maker's role as price-maker but, without these other services, most markets would not exist or be as liquid or efficient as they are:

- **Prime broker** – refers to the central trade processing, reporting, financing and servicing of the account activities of clients and traders that a broker may provide. These normally include:
  - clearance and settlement of trades in global markets
  - central custodianship of assets and using consolidated positions for the extension of leverage
  - financing in multiple currencies, as required
  - stock borrowing capabilities to support trade strategies
  - integrated web reporting of positions, activities and performance
  - hedge fund consulting services
  - facilitated communication between sales, trading and research.
- **Clearing broker** – a broker-dealer that acts as clearing agent in connection with a transaction. In addition to handling its own transactions, a clearing broker can provide clearing agent services to other broker-dealers, such as introducing brokers.
- **Introducing broker** – a broker-dealer that effects transactions with its customers through a clearing broker and does not hold customer funds or securities.
- **Executing broker** – a broker that finalises or executes an order on behalf of a client. That client could be another financial institution, a corporation, a hedge fund or a private individual.
- **Inter-dealer broker (IDB)** – acts as an intermediary between other market participants, such as brokers and/or market makers, who wish to buy or sell large quantities without revealing their identities. IDBs may also be able to deal in securities and derivatives that are not traded on exchanges.
- **Futures Commission Merchant (FCM)** – an individual or company that is registered with the CFTC, which solicits business from others for execution on a listed commodities exchange. FCMs can also extend credit to their customers.

Appendix

Answer to Exercise 1

The investor would have a profit of $42,000.

Index value sold	3400
Less index value at close-out	-3190
	210 index points

Profit = 210 index points x $10 per index point x 20 contracts = $42,000.

Answer to Exercise 2

a If the share was worth 120p, the buyer of the option would exercise and buy the share for 100p – making an immediate gain of 20p (120p – 100p), but having paid 10p as a premium. This represents a profit of 10p – a 100% return on the cash outlay compared to only a 20% return on the underlying. This is the essence of gearing.

b If the share was worth 100p, the buyer of the option would be indifferent as to whether to exercise or not; the share is no cheaper under the terms of the option than it is on the market. So, the buyer of the option would lose the 10p premium – 100% of the investment, when the underlying share did not rise or fall.

c If the share was worth 95p, the buyer of the option would not exercise; the share is cheaper on the market. Again, the premium has been paid upfront as required by the option contract. The buyer of the option would have paid the 10p premium – 100% of the investment, when the underlying share fell by just 5%.

End of Chapter Questions

1. What are contracts for differences?
   Answer reference: Section 2.3

2. Describe the activities of an arbitrageur.
   Answer reference: Section 2.5.3

3. What causes liquidity risk?
   Answer reference: Section 2.7

4. How would you describe an Asian option?
   Answer reference: Section 3.2

5. How do FLEX options differ from standardised exchange products?
   Answer reference: Section 3.6

6. In the derivatives market, what is meant by gearing?
   Answer reference: Section 4

7. What are the main elements of a liquid market?
   Answer reference: Section 5

8. What are OTC products?
   Answer reference: Section 6

9. Who are market makers?
   Answer reference: Section 7

10. What are prime brokers?
    Answer reference: Section 7.1

Chapter Two

Underlying Markets

This syllabus area will provide approximately 12 of the 100 examination questions

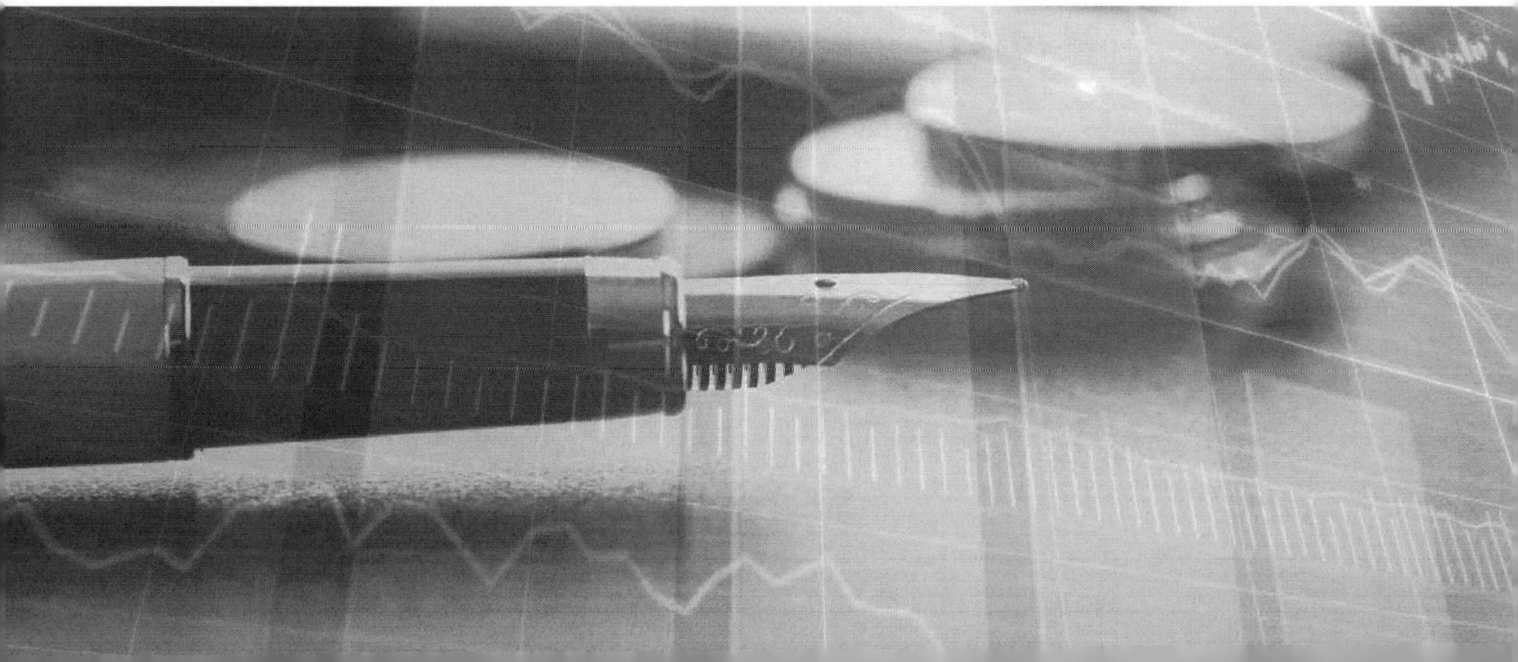

1. Introduction

This chapter outlines the underlying (or cash) markets and details the nature and type of the derivative products that are available. These include both financial and commodity-based markets, upon which wide ranges of derivative products are traded. While commodity-based contracts are where the derivative market first developed, trading in financial derivatives has become significantly greater in recent years.

2. Government and Corporate Debt

2.1 Government Bonds

Learning Objective

2.1.1 Understand the reasons for the government issuing bonds: public sector finance requirements; finance long-term debt; role of national debt in government finances

2.1.2 Understand the different categories of gilts and their special features (short, medium and long dated/undated/index linked/coupons and strippable)

2.1.3 Know the main overseas government bonds and their main features (T bonds/JGBs/Bunds/OATs): settlement; coupon; maturities; countries; spreads between different government bonds

A bond is a debt security, in which the authorised issuer owes the holders a debt and is obliged to pay interest (the coupon) at predetermined dates and repay the principal at a later date, termed maturity.

A bond is simply a loan, but in the form of a security, although the terminology used is rather different. The issuer is equivalent to the borrower, the bondholder to the lender, and the coupon to the interest. Bonds enable the issuer to finance long-term investments with external funds.

A government bond is a bond issued by a national government, which is most often denominated in the country's own currency. Governments issue bonds to finance their expenditures. They are used to finance the shortfall between its revenues and the spending that has been approved as part of its budget. Bonds fund or finance the national debt (the cumulative difference between government spending and income). The annual difference is formally known as the public sector net cash requirement (PSNCR), often referred to as the public sector borrowing requirement (PSBR). Bonds issued by governments in other currencies are called sovereign bonds.

UK government bonds are known as gilts, which is shorthand for gilt-edged securities. Gilts are issued by the Debt Management Office (DMO) on behalf of the government.

Most other governments also issue bonds. In the US, the Treasury is responsible for issuing T-bonds, while in Germany the Bundesbank issues Bunds. The following is a list of some of the international government bonds and their main features:

Country	Name	Coupon Frequency	Maturity	Trade Settled
US	Treasury bonds (T-bonds)	semi-annual	over ten years	T+1
France	Obligations Assimilables du Trésor (OATs)	annual	up to 30 years	T+2
Germany	Bund	annual	over ten years	T+2
Japan	Japan Government Bond (JGB)	semi-annual	long (ten years, most common), super-long (20 years)	T+2
UK	Gilts	semi-annual	up to 50 years	T+1
Italy	Buoni del Tesoro Poliennali (BTPs)	semi-annual	from three to 30 years	T+2 (primary market)/ T+2 (secondary market)

Like most bonds, each of the above international government bonds specifies a nominal amount (eg, £100), a coupon (which is an interest rate, eg, 2% per annum) and a maturity (or redemption) date (eg, 2025). The coupon for the majority of government bonds is paid in half-yearly intervals, so the 2% on the £100 nominal amount is paid in two instalments each year of £1.00, six months apart. This will take place throughout the life of the instrument; the final interest payment will be paid together with the redemption amount (the nominal) at maturity.

Government bonds are classified in a variety of ways, such as by the time remaining until they reach maturity and the government repays the debt:

- **short** – less than seven years remaining
- **medium** – seven to 15 years remaining
- **long** – greater than 15 years remaining.

Some bonds with no fixed maturity date are known as undated or perpetual bonds.

In countries with high inflation, some are index-linked, where both the coupons and the principal amounts are linked to increases in an inflation measurement index such as the Retail Prices Index (RPI) or Consumer Price Index (CPI).

Secondary market transactions in gilts are usually settled on the next business day (T+1).

2.1.1 Yield Spreads

In government bond markets, the **yield spread** or credit spread is the difference between the quoted rates of return on two different government bonds that have the same or very similar maturities. It reflects the market's view and is based on the market's/investor's perception of the different credit quality (or credit risk) between the two governments.

It is calculated by subtracting the yield of one government bond from the other.

The yield spread is a way of comparing any two financial products. In simple terms, it is an indication of the risk premium for investing in one government's bond over another government's bond. Therefore, the wider the yield spread between two bonds, the greater the risk premium associated with the bond that has the higher market yield. When the yield spread widens between two governments' bonds which have different quality or credit ratings, it implies that the market is factoring more risk of default on lower-grade bonds, ie, the bonds that have the higher yield.

An excellent example of this is what has been happening in the European government bond market since 2011. Since most investors view Germany, with its high credit rating and strong economy, as the safest of the euro government borrowers, it is usually the benchmark against which all other euro government bond yields are compared. For example, as investors lost confidence in the Greek government's ability to repay its debt, the yield spread on Greek government bonds over German government bonds (bunds) of the same maturity increased. During 2011 the yield spread between ten-year Greek government bonds and ten-year bunds widened from 29, before investors became concerned, to 4696 **basis** points (bps) in the first quarter of 2012. The increased risk premium demanded by investors to buy Greek government debt saw ten-year yields rise to a high of 48.6%, while bunds of the same maturity were trading at around 1.85%. While investor confidence in Greece helped this yield spread narrow to 7% in the middle of 2014, growing concern in relation to the Greek government that was elected in January 2015 has pushed the yield spread back to 1265 bps. Similar widening of spreads was also seen with Spanish, Portuguese, Cypriot and Italian government bonds in the past few years.

Note that, when analysing the yield spread between government bonds, they must have the same or very similar maturities and the same currency.

Remember: the yield spread between government bonds or any other bond or financial instrument is a measure of the relative risk premium demanded by investors to hold that bond/instrument.

2.1.2 Strippable Bonds

Certain government bonds have been designated as strippable by their issuer. Strippable means that the individual coupons and the principal amount can be separately traded. STRIP stands for Separate Trading of Registered Interest and Principal. By enabling investors to purchase an individual coupon, or principal cash flow, the strippable bonds can produce financial instruments that more precisely meet the investor's needs. For example, an investor might want to guarantee the receipt of £500,000 in 15 years to cover the repayment of a mortgage, and buying an individual strip could precisely meet this need.

2.1.3 Zero Coupon Bonds (ZCBs)

Zero coupon bonds (ZCBs) are bonds which do not pay periodic interest payments, or so-called coupons. ZCBs are purchased at a discount from their value at maturity. The holder of a ZCB is entitled to receive a single payment, usually of a specified sum of money at a specified time in the future. Some ZCBs are inflation-indexed, so the amount of money that will be paid to the bond holder is calculated to have a set amount of purchasing power rather than a set amount of money, but the majority of ZCBs pay a set amount of money known as the face value of the bond.

In contrast, an investor who has a regular bond receives income from coupon payments, which are usually made semi-annually. The investor also receives the principal or face value of the investment when the bond matures.

2.1.4 Yield Curves

Learning Objectives

2.1.4 Understand the relationship between return and maturity shown by yield curves: normal yield curves; inverted yield curves; flat yield curves

The yield of a bond is the rate of interest it provides based on the current market price. It is usually expressed as a percentage. A yield curve is a graph that shows the relationship between yields and maturities for a set of similar securities or deposits.

In most government bond markets there is a range of bonds available with various periods until maturity. By plotting the yields of these bonds on a graph, with yields on the vertical or Y axis and time remaining on the horizontal or X axis, a pattern emerges. The line of best fit across these points is the yield curve. It shows the yields available to investors in bonds over different time horizons.

The Normal Yield Curve

Typically, the shape of the yield curve is upward-sloping to the right, as shown here:

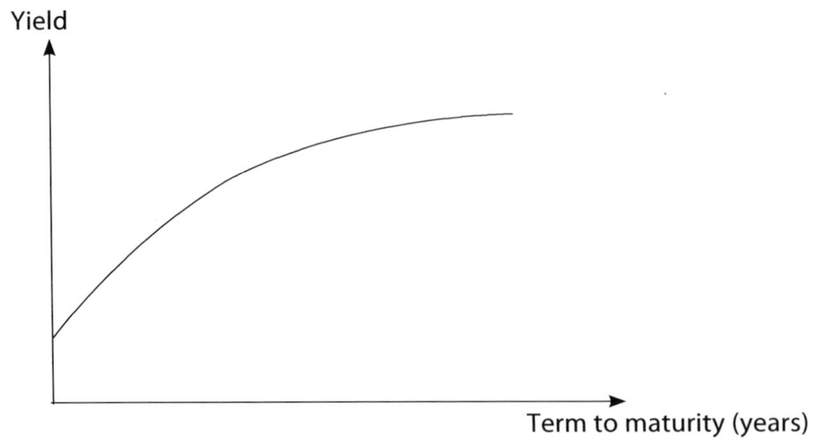

This is known as the normal yield curve, and its shape captures the fact that investors have a liquidity preference – they prefer more liquidity to less. As a result of this, they are willing to accept a lower yield on more liquid, short-dated bonds, and demand a higher yield on less liquid, longer-dated bonds. Investors are rewarded for lending their money for long periods by receiving a higher yield on instruments with longer maturities. Given the same coupon rate, the price of a short-dated gilt will be higher than that of a longer-dated bond, resulting in a higher yield for the longer-dated bond than for the equivalent shorter-dated bond. In other words, a normal yield curve represents investors' requirements to be paid a higher yield for longer maturities as compensation for the increased price risk associated with longer-dated securities.

The Inverted Yield Curve

Occasionally, the yield curve may not exhibit its normal upward slope. Instead, it might be downward-sloping – known as the inverted yield curve:

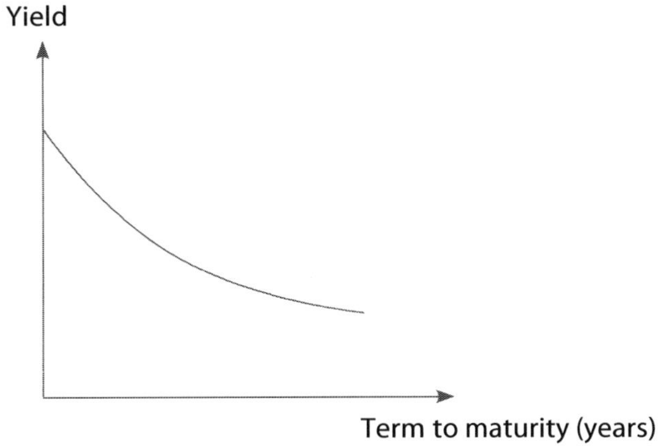

In an inverted yield curve, yields available on short-term bonds exceed those available on long-term bonds. This occurs when there is an expectation of a significant reduction in interest rates at some stage in the future. There is an inverse relationship between interest rates and bond prices. The consequence of this is, when investing in longer-term gilts that will be outstanding when the interest rates fall, the investor is willing to accept a lower yield. For shorter-term bonds that will not be outstanding when the interest rate falls, the investor is demanding a higher yield. The existence of an inverted yield curve does not remove any liquidity preference; rather, the impact of the anticipated interest rate fall outweighs the effect of the liquidity preference.

Horizontal Yield Curve

If short-term rates are the same as long-term ones, the curve is said to be flat or horizontal. This might happen if the government temporarily raises short-term rates while the market does not reflect this in higher long-term yields.

2.2 Other Bond Issuers

Learning Objective

2.1.5 Know the main features of the corporate bond market

2.1.6 Understand the relationship between government and corporate bonds: yield spread over government bonds; high grade and high yield bonds; bond ratings, transition and default

In addition to national governments, there is a wide variety of bond issuers. In many countries, regional, state and city governments also use the bond market to finance their budgets. International organisations, such as the World Bank, also issue bonds, to finance their projects.

A corporate bond is a bond issued by a corporation, as the name suggests. The term is usually applied to longer-term debt instruments, generally with a maturity date falling at least 12 months later. Corporate bonds can be issued in any currency. Corporate bonds are often listed on major exchanges (such bonds being described as listed bonds) and **electronic communication networks (ECNs)** like MarketAxess, and the coupon (ie, interest payment) is usually taxable. However, despite being listed on exchanges, the vast majority of trading volume in corporate bonds in most developed markets takes place in decentralised, dealer-based, OTC markets.

Compared to government bonds, corporate bonds generally pay a higher yield than the respective government bond. This is related to the higher risk of default (although this risk depends, of course, upon the particular corporations, the current market conditions and the credit rating of the company, which plays an important role). The reason corporate and most other bonds pay a higher yield than their respective government bond is the market's view that a government has the best credit and has the lowest risk of default in its own currency's domestic debt market. This is why government bonds are the benchmark yield in most markets.

As is the case for all markets, the entity's credit rating is a major factor in determining the coupon or yield that an investor demands to buy and hold a bond. The major credit rating agencies – Moody's, Fitch and Standard & Poor's – give each government and all other issuers a rating. A good example of how this works is the significant rise in yields/fall in the prices of Greek, Portuguese, Irish, Spanish and Italian government bonds in 2011 to 2015. Another more recent example is how Standard & Poor's downgrading of South Africa's government bonds, after the change of Finance Minister in April 2017, caused a sell-off by investors and a rise in yields. This reflects investors' increased concerns that these governments will not be able to fully repay their existing debt.

The higher the credit rating, the lower the yield required by investors to hold a specific bond/security.

The highest ratings are what the market considers investment grade; this allows securities to pay a lower yield, since investors see these securities as having a lower risk of default.

3. Foreign Exchange

Learning Objective

2.2.1 Understand the nature of the spot market and the trading and settlement of spot transactions: purpose of the market; what is the spot market; contract value dates; settlement periods and timescales

2.2.2 Understand the nature, characteristics, markets and uses of currency forward contracts: what is a currency forward contract including non-deliverable forwards; commercial and speculative uses; hedging uses in portfolio management; effect of time on open positions

2.2.3 Understand the factors that determine forward rates and how forward rates are quoted (in terms of premiums and discounts): what are premiums and discounts; what are forward points; how prices are quoted (may be tested by the use of simple calculations); effect of interest rate differentials; the relationship between the spot market and the forward market

2.2.4 Be able to calculate forward foreign exchange rates using interest rate differentials

The foreign exchange market (Forex, FX, or currency market) is a worldwide decentralised over-the-counter (OTC) financial market for the trading of currencies. Financial centres provide access to trading between a wide range of different types of buyers and sellers around the clock, with the exception of weekends. The FX market determines the relative values of all free-floating currencies.

The FX market is unique because of its:

- huge trading volume, leading to high liquidity
- geographical dispersion
- continuous operation: 24 hours a day except weekends, ie, trading from 20:15 GMT on Sunday until 22:00 GMT Friday
- variety of factors that affect exchange rates.

The spot FX market involves the exchange of one currency for another at an agreed rate, with spot settlement very soon after the date of transaction. For most currency transactions in the wholesale spot market this is T+2. For all FX trades, settlement requires that both domestic markets must be open. Therefore, in order for a EUR/JPY trade to settle, its value date must be when the banks in both the European Union (EU) and Japan are open.

The FX market is used by a wide range of participants, from companies and investors who need to exchange one currency for another as part of a trade or investment transaction, to the market makers and speculators who look to profit from providing liquidity and betting on one currency against another. Many commercial and investment banks provide spot FX quotes, in their role as market makers. This provides the FX market with liquidity, as they quote to other market participants and to their clients.

Remember that, in foreign exchange, one currency is quoted in terms of another currency. Therefore, in the quote GBP/USD = 1.2410/15, sterling (GBP) is the base currency while the dollar is being quoted in terms of sterling.

- 1.2410 is the **bid** for GBP – this means that the quoting bank will buy sterling and sell dollars at this rate, since it is cheaper: £1,000,000 costs $1,241,000.
- 1.2415 is the **offer** for GBP – here the quoting bank will sell sterling and buy dollars. At this rate sterling is more expensive: £1,000,000 costs $1,241,500.

Note that in most cases the amounts traded are also based on set amounts of the base currency.

Example 1

An American company has to pay an invoice issued by its German supplier. The German company has charged its American customer €15 million – this amount needs to be paid in two days. In order to pay this, the American company calls one of its banks and gets the following quote:

EUR/USD = 1.1005/10

The American company agrees to the rate and buys €15 million at 1.1010 and will pay its bank $16,515,000 (15 million x 1.1010) in two days' time. At the same time its bank will arrange the euro payment to its German supplier's account.

Example 2

But what could the same American company do if it gets an invoice in yen from a Japanese supplier, that is not due for two months?

In such situations, the American firm might consider entering into a forward contract. A forward contract is simply a deal between two participants to agree now the rate at which a certain amount of an international currency will be exchanged at some pre-agreed date in the future. These forward FX contract rates are quoted OTC by banks. The quotation is based on applying a margin to the spot quotes to arrive at a forward rate. For example:

USD/JPY	Bid	Offer
Spot	116.60	116.65
2mth forward points	0.65	0.60
2mth outright rate	115.95	116.05

In the second example above, the margin applied to the spot rate is a discount. The discount indicates that the base currency (the dollar, in the above example) is becoming cheaper relative to the yen. As a result, the forward points are deducted from the spot rate, so that in the forward deal, the dollar will buy fewer yen (the bid column), and the yen will buy more dollars (the offer column).

Remember that, since FX spot rates are quoted in terms of one currency versus another, when the base currency is at a discount, the traded currency must be at a premium. Therefore in this example, the US dollar is at a discount in the forward market, making the yen at a premium.

When quoting forward points, it is the market convention that when the forward points decrease, the bid decrease is greater than the offer decrease, as shown in the example above – 65/60 – and they would be subtracted from the spot rate. When the forward points quote increases, the base currency is more expensive in the forward market and the points would then be added to the spot rate. This is described as a premium for forward delivery. The banks will calculate the necessary premium or discount considering the relevant short-term interest rates (STIRs) of the two currencies.

The key advantage of forward contracts is certainty. The US firm could use the forward contract to lock into a rate of 116.05 today, rather than worry that the yen might strengthen over the next two months.

As well as commercial users, the forward market is used extensively by speculators, for example, hedge funds and the proprietary trading desks at investment banks. Since forward rates are based on the interest rate differential between the two currencies, the FX forward market is used to speculate on expected changes in the difference between these two interest rates. Speculators on the movements in spot rates mainly take spot or forward outright positions.

One final use of international currency forwards is in portfolio management. Suppose a UK asset manager has US investments expected to yield dividends and gains of 7% in the coming year. This could be reduced or even eliminated by international currency rate movements, assuming that the UK manager reports in GBP. Forward rates can be used to hedge this translation risk.

3.1 Forward FX Rates and Interest Rate Parity (IRP)

Learning Objective

2.2.4 Be able to calculate forward foreign exchange rates using interest rate differentials

We have seen that the forward rates of exchange are linked to the spot rate by applying a discount or premium. The factor that links spot rates is the relative interest rates between the two currencies.

The link between spot and forward rates is based on the principle of arbitrage. Put simply, if the forward rate quoted were not in line with relative interest rates, there would be an opportunity to make a guaranteed profit by borrowing funds and entering into a forward foreign exchange contract. This is the theory of interest rate parity (IRP). This is best illustrated by looking at an example.

Example 3

The spot FX rate for GBP/EUR is 1.2065, while the 12-month sterling interest rate is 1.5% compared to 0.5% for the euro.

Suppose the one-year forward FX rate for GBP/EUR is 1.1975. An arbitrageur could borrow €12.065 million at 0.5% and convert the euros into sterling in the spot market. This would give them £10 million to invest at 1.5% for one year. At the same time, the arbitrageur could enter into a one-year forward contract to sell the principal and interest from the deposit of £10,150,000 at 1.1975. The net result would be:

Borrowing €12.065 million at 0.5% results in a repayment of €12,125,325.

The deposit of £10 million at 1.5% receives £10,150,000 at maturity.

The one-year forward FX contract of selling £10,150,000 at 1.1975 produces €12,154,625.

The net result is an arbitrage profit of €29,300.

In order to avoid such arbitrage opportunities existing, the one-year forward rate must be based on the interest rate differential between the euro and sterling. In other words, the one-year GBP/EUR forward rate should be 1.1946. The arbitrage-free one-year GBP/EUR forward rate is based on the current interest rate differential, therefore from the information listed above, it is equal to €12,125,325/£10,150,000 or 1.1946.

The discount on sterling in the one-year forward FX rate is based on the difference between its one-year interest rate and the euro's interest rate. In this case, since sterling's rate is higher, it **must** be at a discount (ie, worth less in the forward market) to avoid any arbitrage opportunities.

The link between relative interest rates and the forward FX rate can be summarised as follows:

Higher interest rate currency = Discount in the forward foreign exchange market
Lower interest rate currency = Premium in the forward foreign exchange market

When calculating forward FX rates for periods of less than one year, we have to take into account the different day count conventions of the different currencies' money markets. For example, both the euro and dollar use an Actual/360 day count, while sterling uses Actual/365.

The following shows how to calculate a forward FX rate using the two currencies' interest rates:

$$\text{Forward rate} = \text{Spot rate} \times [1 + (n \times r_1)] / [1 + (n \times r_2)]$$

where:

r_1 = relevant interest rate for the traded or international currency.
r_2 = relevant interest rate for the base or domestic currency.
n = period in question.

Example 4

Given the following spot FX, spot and money market rates, what should be the theoretical six-month forward FX rate?

Spot EUR/USD rate = 1.0700

USD 6-month LIBOR (r_1) = 0.5%

Euro 6-month rate (r_2) = 0.2%

$$Fx_{fwd} = 1.0700 \times \frac{[1 + ((186/360) \times 0.0005)]}{[1 + ((186/360) \times 0.0002)]} = 1.0702$$

	Description	Sample Data
FX_spot	Spot price of underlying currency (domestic per 1 unit of foreign)	1.0700
r1	Traded currency's interest rate (for term of forward)	0.005
r2	Base currency's interest rate (for term of forward)	0.002
d_s	Trade date	1 May 17
d_del	Forward delivery date	3 Nov 17
acc_dom	Accrual method for domestic rate	Actual/360
acc_for	Accrual method for foreign rate	Actual/360

Result

The six-month forward EUR/USD rate is 1.1702.

The FX rate adjustment or fair basis, which is based on the interest rate differential, is $0.0002, ie, 2 **pips** (a pip is the smallest change that a given exchange rate can make).

The euro is at a premium versus the US dollar, since the US dollar has the higher interest rate.

3.1.1 Premiums and Discounts

The forward rates are closely related to the spot rates and interest rates of the two countries. A result of the IRP theory is that, for the country with the higher interest rate, its currency is weaker in the forward market than in the spot market. As shown in the previous example, the euro's interest rate was slightly lower than the USD interest rate, and the resulting theoretical forward rate is 1.0702 EUR/USD, compared with the spot rate of 1.0700.

The terms premium and discount refer to whether the forward rates are higher or lower than the spot rates. A premium means the forward price of the base currency is higher than the spot price and a discount means it is lower. In the paragraph above, the forward rate is therefore at a euro premium of 2 points.

In order to apply forward points to a spot rate to come up with an outright quote for the forward price, one needs to know whether the forward points are premiums or discounts. For premiums, bid forward points are added to bid spot prices and ask forward points are added to ask spot prices. For discounts, bid forward points are subtracted from ask spot prices, and ask forward points are subtracted from bid spot prices.

If all this seems confusing, just remember the rule that the bid/ask spreads of the forward price should always be greater than the spot price, and that the sum of the bid/ask spreads of the spot price and forward points should equal the spread of the forward price. The bigger spread in the forward market can be viewed as compensation for the increased risk the market maker takes in the forward market relative to the spot market.

3.2 Non-Deliverable Forwards (NDFs)

Learning Objectives

2.2.2 Understand the nature, characteristics, markets and uses of currency forward contracts: what is a currency forward contract including non-deliverable forwards; commercial and speculative uses; hedging uses in portfolio management; effect of time on open positions

A non-deliverable forward (NDF) is a cash-settled, short-term forward contract on a thinly traded or non-convertible international currency, where the profit or loss at the time of the settlement date is calculated by taking the difference between the agreed-upon exchange rate and the spot rate at the time of settlement, for an agreed-upon notional amount of funds.

All NDFs have a fixing date and a settlement date. The fixing date is the date at which the difference between the prevailing market exchange rate and the agreed-upon exchange rate is calculated. The settlement date is the date by which the payment of the difference is due to the party receiving payment.

NDFs are commonly quoted for time periods of one month up to one year, and are normally quoted and settled in USD (although EUR and GBP are also fairly common). They have become a popular instrument for corporations seeking to hedge exposure to other currencies that are not internationally traded.

As is the case with spot FX, forward FX contracts are used for a wide range of reasons. Since their prices are mainly based on the change in the relative difference between the two currencies' interest rates, those taking a speculative position are mainly betting on interest rate and not exchange rate movements. The latter is done using the spot FX market.

Other uses of forward FX contracts are for hedging, for commercial contracts, such as future trade-related payments, or future receipts from international operations to fund managers who use these contracts to hedge the FX risk associated with holding international assets within their fund. Unlike options, time does not affect the price of these contracts.

4. Money Markets

Learning Objective

2.3.2 Know the uses and requirements of inter-bank deposits: what are inter-bank deposits; why do they exist; determination of inter-bank offer rates; LIBOR, LIBID and EURIBOR, EONIA

While on the bond markets, the issuers (borrowers) and investors are seeking to raise and invest capital over the medium to long term, the money markets are geared towards short-term liquidity and providing a temporary safe haven for investment funds. Money markets are normally classed as covering cash and other instruments that mature within one year of the point of issue.

An interbank market for money exists simply because banks' balances with their central bank rise and fall as cash is received and paid. A bank with a shortfall will need to borrow from a bank with a surplus – hence there is an interbank market.

ICE **LIBOR** is a benchmark rate produced for five currencies with seven maturities quoted for each – ranging from overnight to one year, producing 35 rates each business day.

ICE LIBOR provides an indication of the average rate at which a LIBOR contributor bank can obtain unsecured funding in the London interbank market for a given period, in a given currency. Individual ICE LIBOR rates are the end product of a calculation based upon submissions from LIBOR contributor banks.

ICE Benchmark Administration maintains a reference panel of between 11 and 18 contributor banks for each currency calculated. IBA currently fixes in the following five currencies:

- CHF (Swiss franc)
- EUR (euro)
- GBP (pound sterling)
- JPY (Japanese yen)
- USD (US dollar).

ICE LIBOR was previously known as BBA LIBOR until 1 February 2014, the date on which the ICE Benchmark Administration (IBA) took over the administration of LIBOR.

What is ICE LIBOR used for?

ICE LIBOR has an essential role in the global financial system. Its importance to the financial sector and for other non-financial companies arises from the fact that most corporate debt and floating interest-rate-based instruments are 'LIBOR-based'. It is used as the floating rate for many financial contracts, from interest rate swaps to student loans, mortgages and corporate funding instruments. In total, hundreds of trillions of dollars' worth of interest rate exposure is tied to ICE LIBOR. Given its role as a global funding benchmark, ICE LIBOR is also frequently used for valuing existing positions.

ICE LIBOR determines the settlement prices for some of the most widely traded and most popular exchange-traded, STIR futures contracts. These contracts are used by companies around the world to hedge their interest rate exposure. They also provide private sector economists and central bankers with insights into market expectations of economic performance and interest rate developments. ICE LIBOR is also an important indicator used by some central banks when determining their official interest rate target.

For example, take a one-year sterling-denominated floating-rate note (or floater) that pays coupons based on three-month ICE LIBOR plus a margin of 35 basis points (0.35%). In this case, the ICE LIBOR rate used is the three-month sterling ICE LIBOR plus a 35 basis point spread. Therefore, at the beginning of each quarter, the coupon rate is reset in order to match the current three-month sterling ICE LIBOR, plus the predetermined spread (35bp). If on 1 June, the three-month ICE LIBOR is quoted as 0.59%, for that quarter this floating rate note's coupon will be 0.94% (0.59% + 0.35%).

ICE LIBOR is designed to reflect the short-term funding costs of the major banks that are active in the London market. Like most other financial benchmark rates, it is a 'polled' rate. It is calculated as follows:

Calculating ICE LIBOR

Definition

- Every contributor bank is asked to base their ICE LIBOR submissions on the following question: *'At what rate could you borrow funds, were you to do so by asking for, and then accepting, interbank offers in a reasonable market size just prior to 11.00 am London time?'*
- Therefore, submissions are based upon the lowest perceived rate at which a bank could go into the London interbank money market and obtain funding in reasonable market size, for a given maturity and currency.
- 'Reasonable market size' is intentionally unquantified; it would have to be constantly monitored and, in the current conditions, would have to be changed very frequently. It would also vary between currencies and maturities, leading to a considerable amount of confusion.
- All ICE LIBOR rates are quoted as an annualised interest rate. This is a market convention. For example, if an overnight pound sterling rate from a contributor bank is given as 2.00000%, this does not indicate that a contributing bank would expect to pay 2% interest on the value of an overnight loan. Instead, it means that it would expect to pay 2% divided by 365.

Calculation

- Every ICE LIBOR rate is calculated using a trimmed arithmetic mean. Once each submission is received, they are ranked in descending order and then the highest and lowest 25% of submissions are excluded. This trimming of the top and bottom quartiles allows for the exclusion of outliers from the final calculation.
- Details are shown in the following table. The remaining contributions are then arithmetically averaged and the result is rounded to five decimal places to create an ICE LIBOR rate. This is repeated for every currency and maturity, producing 35 rates every business day.

Number of Contributors	Methodology	Number of Contributor Rates Averaged
18	Top 4 highest rates, tail 4 lowest rates	10
17	Top 4 highest rates, tail 4 lowest rates	9
16	Top 4 highest rates, tail 4 lowest rates	8
15	Top 4 highest rates, tail 4 lowest rates	7
14	Top 3 highest rates, tail 3 lowest rates	8
13	Top highest rates, tail 3 lowest rates	7
12	Top highest rates, tail 3 lowest rates	6
11	Top highest rates, tail 3 lowest rates	5

ICE LIBOR is the world's most widely used benchmark for STIRs. It serves as the primary indicator for the average rate at which banks that contribute to its determination of LIBOR may obtain short-term loans in the London interbank market.

LIBOR or ICE LIBOR's primary function is to serve as the benchmark reference rate for debt instruments, including government and corporate bonds, mortgages, student loans, credit cards; as well as derivatives such as currency and interest swaps, among many other financial products.

For example, take a Swiss franc-denominated floating rate note that pays coupons based on LIBOR plus a margin of 35 basis points (0.35%) annually. In this case, the LIBOR rate used is the one-year LIBOR plus a 35 basis point spread. Every year, the coupon rate is reset in order to match the current Swiss franc one-year LIBOR, plus the predetermined spread.

If, for instance, the one-year LIBOR is 0.4% at the beginning of the year, the bond will pay 0.75% of its **par value** at the end of the year. The spread usually increases or decreases depending on the creditworthiness of the institution issuing debt.

Another prominent trait of LIBOR or ICE LIBOR is that it helps to evaluate the current state of the world's banking system as well as to set expectations for future central bank interest rates. This is based on the view that a dramatic spike in ICE LIBOR is caused by a significant rise in demand for short-term funding by the world's largest banks, which in turn could be an indication of a liquidity crisis.

4.1 Risk Implications

Learning Objective

2.3.4 Understand the risk implications of trading in the money market contracts: as a depositor; as a source of funding

One of the key aspects that allows the interbank money market to operate efficiently is confidence. Banks and other investors who lend their funds in the short-term market do so with little or no guarantee that the borrower to whom they are lending is creditworthy, ie, is financially strong enough to ensure that they will return their funds back at maturity. Most banks and other participants use internal guidelines or **credit limits** to determine how much they are willing to lend to another market counterparty. If the market loses confidence in a borrower or in the market structure overall, that funding will simply dry up. Should this occur, those in need of short-term funding must be willing to pay a higher rate to attract funding or seek funding from their respective central bank.

For borrowers who use the money market as a key source of funding, the lack of confidence which causes funding to dry up is a major risk, as was the case with Northern Rock, the building society that used this market in August 2007 for up to 75% of its funding. Despite the fact that it was willing to pay a premium over the prevailing interbank rate, once investors and lenders lost confidence, it faced a major funding crisis. This eventually led to its nationalisation by the UK government.

Another example of the sensitivity of the interbank money market can be seen in the more active role the ECB has played during the euro government bond crisis. The ECB has become an active source of funding of euros to a large number of European banks.

For depositors, the main risk is counterparty risk, ie, the risk that the borrower lent to will not be able to repay the funds at maturity. Again, given the nature of these contracts, it is the lender's internal guidelines and credit ratings that help the lender evaluate a borrower's financial situation and ability to repay.

4.2 Treasury Bills

Learning Objective

2.3.1 Know the basic characteristics of Treasury bills: term; how and when issued; issued at a discount; promissory note; redeemed at par

Treasury bills is the term given to the short-term debt that is issued by a number of governments. In the UK, the DMO makes new issues on a weekly basis on behalf of the UK government to cover its liquidity needs. They are typically issued with a maturity of 91 days (approximately three months), although some are issued with 182-day maturity (approximately six months). In the US, the Department of the Treasury also offers a weekly issue of new debt, with maturities of 28 days (one month) as well as three and six months like its UK counterpart. Several other governments also issue similar short-term debt instruments, which have the same characteristics.

Since T-bills (as they are known) are backed by the promise of their respective government, they are often referred to as promissory notes. The yield they offer provides a benchmark level of risk-free returns available on other short-term money market instruments in their respective markets. Treasury bills pay no coupon. They are issued at a discount to their nominal value, with the discount providing the return to the investor. Treasury bills are simply redeemed at their par value.

4.3 Certificate of Deposit (CD)

Learning Objective

2.3.3 Know the basic characteristics of certificates of deposit: term; how and when issued; issued at a discount/par; redeemed at par/premium

A certificate of deposit (CD) is a time deposit commonly offered to consumers by banks and other financial institutions. A CD is a promissory note issued by a bank or other financial institution. It is a time deposit that restricts holders from withdrawing funds on demand. Although it is still possible to withdraw the money, this action will often incur a penalty.

The most common maturities for CDs are three and six months. They are purchased at their face or par value and pay a specified interest rate at maturity. CDs usually pay a yield slightly higher than that of T-bills, reflecting their slightly higher credit risk. They can be issued in any denomination.

4.4 Commercial Paper (CP)

Commercial paper (CP) is a money market instrument that is issued by large financial and non-financial institutions, as a short-term borrowing facility. The debt is unsecured, but is normally backed by unused bank-based credit lines. Maturities normally range from two to nine months and are denominated in minimums of US$500,000 or similar amounts in other currencies.

While the US domestic CP market is the largest, similar markets also exist in the UK, Europe and Japan. The interest rate paid on CP depends on the market conditions, as well as the issuing company's credit rating.

5. Equities

Companies raise their initial capital – the money to carry on their activities – in two ways: through share capital and through loan stock. One important contrast to keep in mind is that people who hold loan stock are creditors of the company. The company owes them a debt, which they have to repay – but they have no ownership interest in the company. On the other hand, the people who own shares in a company are its owners. An individual may only have a few shares out of many thousands (or even millions) issued by the company – nevertheless, that individual still owns a small part of the company and has the rights that go with that ownership. This means that shareholders bear a fair amount of risk compared to investors in bonds issued by companies.

Bondholders expect to receive a certain sum in interest – no more, no less, no matter how well the company is doing. (The exception, as you should remember, is where the bond pays a variable rate of interest – but even then the interest is determined by a set formula.) In addition, the bondholder normally expects to receive a set amount of capital back on maturity; there is generally no additional profit or gain if the company is doing very well. The only real risk is that of the company running into difficulties that are so serious that it cannot repay its creditors – thankfully, not a very regular occurrence, although it can happen.

Shareholders, however, generally have a much greater exposure to the financial fortunes of the company they have invested in. If the company does well, they may receive a rising income stream, and the value of their shares can also increase substantially (giving them capital growth); but if a company does badly it may pay falling dividends – or no dividend at all. Its share price may also fall, potentially becoming worthless if the company gets into real trouble.

We will examine this concept in more depth as we progress through the chapter; for now, it is enough to remember that shares are generally characterised by relative insecurity of both income and capital over the short term (some types more so than others), but they offer a much higher probability of producing real growth over time than, for example, cash and bonds.

There are different types of share in a company, with different rights and investment risks attached to them; these risks are the main factors that determine the equity's valuation.

5.1 Ordinary Shares

Learning Objective

2.4.1 Know the principal features and characteristics of ordinary shares and non-voting shares: ranking in a liquidation, (for dividends); voting rights; partly paid shares and calls

As described at the start of this section, when investors buy a share in a company, they become a part-owner of that company. Under company law this brings an entitlement to certain rights. Some of these rights relate to the financial aspects of owning shares, and some relate to the communications between the company and the shareholder, including the actions they can take to make their views known on the company's performance and actions.

Ordinary shares, also known as common stock or common shares, are the most common form of share in the global equity markets. Often referred to as **equity**, ordinary shares are usually issued in registered form. Registered form is where the ownership is recorded in a register, often maintained by a registrar on behalf of the company.

This contrasts with bearer shares, where the issuer does not maintain a register and simple possession of the certificate is sufficient evidence of ownership. These are shares whose owners are not listed or registered; dividends are paid by clipping a coupon from the share certificate and submitting it to the paying agent. For bearer shares, the physical possession of the share certificate is the sole evidence of ownership. Bearer shares are negotiable (traded) without endorsement and are transferred on delivery.

5.1.1 Shareholders' Rights

A shareholder acquires a collection of rights and entitlements, and companies may issue different classes of share capital offering different rights. These rights are established when issuing the shares and are set out in the company's Articles of Association. An ordinary shareholder's principal rights will be:

- **dividends** – discretionary cash distributions paid out of profits earned by the company
- **capital repayment** – if and when the business is legally wound up, although as an ordinary shareholder they are the last category to be repaid and only when all other creditors have been repaid in full
- **voting rights** – the extent to which the shareholder can influence the conduct of the business, eg, appointment/removal of directors, the level of dividend payments and approval of a takeover bid;
- to receive advance notices of all **meetings** of the company and to attend, speak and vote at such meetings
- to be given the opportunity to **subscribe for a rights issue** on a pro rata basis (if this were not so, it would be easy for new shares to be issued to certain shareholders only, thus giving them effective control of the company). These are called **pre-emption rights**
- to **sell** their shares or **transfer** them without restriction. The London Stock Exchange (LSE), for example, insists on free transferability for listed company shares, although the Articles of Association of some unlisted companies may restrict the transfer of shares.

5.1.2 Voting and Non-Voting Shares

Normally, shares are voting shares, which confer the right to vote on company resolutions at annual and extraordinary general meetings. Non-voting shares do not confer such formal voting rights but do provide their holders with the same rights to receive dividends and capital return. They are sometimes called A or B shares (in some cases, B shares can have either no or less voting rights than A shares) or participation certificates. These non-voting shares exist to raise equity financing without diluting voting control from the remaining ordinary shareholders.

5.1.3 Partly Paid Shares

This occurs in an issue of shares where only a portion of the purchase price or capital sum due has been paid to the issuing company. The balance is usually payable in one or more instalments at predetermined future dates. The firm's directors normally have discretion as to when to require the payment of additional tranches.

5.2 Preference Shares

Learning Objectives

2.4.2 Understand the differences and principal characteristics of the following classes of preference shares: cumulative; participating; redeemable; convertible; valuation techniques given (eg, Gordon's Growth Model)

All companies that are quoted on the LSE must have ordinary shares, but they need not have preference shares. Preference shares are a separate class of shares that usually receive preference over ordinary shares as far as dividends and capital repayment are concerned.

Their rights are:

- **Dividends** – if any profits are available to pay dividends, they must firstly be used to pay preference dividends, since preference shares have a fixed dividend payment. In addition, any past unpaid preference dividends will take priority over ordinary share dividends. Any profits remaining belong, in full, to the ordinary shareholders. Preference shareholders, therefore, receive priority but are only entitled to a fixed rate of dividend, whereas ordinary shareholders own whatever is left, the equity.
- **Capital repayment** – if the business fails and the company goes into liquidation, preference shareholders are entitled to the repayment of their capital prior to ordinary shareholders but the amount repayable is restricted to the nominal value of the preference shares. Therefore, preference shareholders rank just behind other creditors (including debt holders) in a company's liquidation. Ordinary shareholders receive whatever is left after the claims of all creditors and preference shareholders have been met. Ordinary shareholders, therefore, own all of the reserves of the company.
- **Voting rights** – in the vast majority of cases, preference shares do not carry voting rights except when the company has failed to pay its preference dividend, ie, when the preference dividend is in arrears.

5.2.1 Types of Preference Share Capital

In addition to the general characteristics of preference share capital described above, a variety of refinements may be built into the terms of issue.

Cumulative or Non-Cumulative

A company may make insufficient profits to cover the payment of its preference dividend in a particular period. If the preference shares are cumulative, the company must pay in later years not only the current year's preference dividend but also the accumulated arrears of preference dividend from previous periods. This arrears of preference dividend must be paid before any ordinary dividend.

Participating

Preference shares are usually non-participating, in the sense that the fixed rate of dividend is the limit of their entitlement to participate in profits, and their nominal value is the limit of their entitlement to capital repayment.

If the shares are participating preference shares, the holders are also entitled to participate in surplus profits available for dividend after the fixed preference dividend has been paid.

If they are fully participating, they are also entitled to a share in capital repayment in excess of nominal value.

Redeemable

Companies may issue redeemable preference shares. The terms of issue enable the company to repay the shareholders at a predetermined price (often more than nominal value, ie, at a premium) on a future specified date or dates.

Convertible Preference Shares

Convertible preference shares offer the shareholder the usual preferential rights to dividend and capital repayment, plus the option to convert their holding into ordinary shares on predetermined future dates at specified prices.

In the past, convertible preference shares were popular in company restructurings; if the company had been in financial difficulties a lender might accept them in exchange for providing a loan. In the short term there were elements of reassurance in receiving a **preferential** dividend with the option of converting into equity if the company recovered and became highly profitable.

5.3 Warrants

Learning Objective

2.4.3 Understand equity warrants and equity options and know their differences: what is an equity warrant; what is an equity option; benefits to an investor or speculator; time to expiry; reasons to issue; who issues them; where traded; strike prices; effect of exercise; settlement; gearing against the underlying

2.4.4 Understand the effect of corporate actions on equity warrants: rights issues; bonus issues; stock splits; mergers and acquisitions

An equity warrant gives its holder the right to buy a company's shares over the life of the warrant at a fixed exercise price, which is usually at a premium over its current price at the time the warrant is issued. It is often issued by the company on which the warrant is based or another private party. Warrants are commonly attached to a corporate bond but, unlike **convertible bonds**, the bond itself continues to exist if the warrant is exercised. They can also be attached to preferred stock, to attract investors. The attachment of a warrant is seen as an inducement and usually allows the issuer to pay a lower coupon.

Equity warrants are very similar to equity options in that both represent the right to buy a set amount of a company's shares over a predefined time frame at a set price. They differ in that, while equity options are traded on a public exchange and the seller is usually not the issuing company, most warrants are traded privately and, as stated in the preceding paragraph, the company itself is the most common issuer.

Note that warrants are traded on some financial markets, such as the Deutsche Börse and the Hong Kong Exchange and Clearing (HKEX). But it should be noted that these exchanges do not trade equity options.

The lower coupon that is paid on a corporate bond with an equity warrant attached represents the premium the investor pays for the warrant (the equivalent of an option's premium). It allows the investor/speculator to take a view on the company's shares, and to profit if their price rises over the life of the warrant. Until the warrant is exercised, its holder is not entitled to receive any dividend that the company might pay.

Since the company issues equity warrants, it will include provisions to adjust the warrant's exercise price, or its number of shares in the case of share splits or bonus issues. Provisions for takeovers and mergers are more issue-specific.

Warrant certificates have stated particulars regarding the investment tool they represent. All warrants have a specified expiry date (the last day the rights of a warrant can be executed). Warrants are classified by their exercise style: an American warrant, for instance, can be exercised any time before or on the stated expiry date, and a European warrant, on the other hand, can be carried out only on the day of expiration.

The underlying instrument the warrant represents is also stated on warrant certificates. A warrant typically corresponds to a specific number of shares, but it can also represent a commodity, index or currency.

The exercise or strike price is the amount that must be paid in order to either buy the call warrant or sell the put warrant. The payment of the strike price results in a transfer of the specified amount of the underlying instrument.

The conversion ratio is the number of warrants needed in order to buy (or sell) one investment unit. Therefore, if the conversion ratio to buy an individual share is 3:1, this means that the holder needs three warrants in order to purchase one share. Usually, if the conversion ratio is high, the price of the share will be low, and vice versa. In the case of equity warrants, with any corporate actions such as rights issues, share splits, share buybacks and takeovers and mergers, the conversion ratio and strike price may be adjusted to reflect such activity. The reason for this is to ensure that listed products investors are not disadvantaged or do not gain undue benefit by equity adjustments.

Since most warrants are usually part of another financial instrument and are mainly traded on an OTC basis, the settlement process is very similar to that of any other OTC option (see Chapter 5).

5.4 Valuation Techniques

Calculating a share's/stock's value is not an exact science. There is a wide range of models that everyone from individual investors to large fund managers use when evaluating a share's price. Most are based on forecasts of the company's cash flow, future earnings and/or dividend payments.

One of the more widely accepted models is the Gordon Growth Model. The model attempts to determine a share's value based on the forecasts of its future dividend payments, using the assumption that they will grow at a constant rate. It uses a discount rate to calculate the present value of the future dividend payment stream, which then gives the share's value.

This model is not unique, in that most valuation techniques are based on the premise of calculating the present value of estimates of future profits a company will earn or dividends it will pay to its shareholders.

5.5 Major Stock Exchanges

The following is a list of the ten largest stock exchanges by their total market capitalisation as at 31 October 2015 (USD trillions):

New York Stock Exchange (NYSE) (US & Europe)	$18.33
NASDAQ OMX (US & North Europe)	$6.72
LSE	$6.10
Tokyo Stock SE Group	$4.45
Shanghai Stock Exchange	$3.92
Euronext	$3.14
Hong Kong Exchange (HKEX)	$2.93
Shenzhen Stock Exchange	$2.65
Toronto Stock Exchange (TSX)	$1.64
Deutsche Börse	$1.56

Source: World Federation of Exchanges (industry association)

The LSE is one of the world's leading equity exchanges and an international provider of services that facilitate the raising of finance and the trading of shares and debt securities. It is home to some of the world's most successful companies, giving them access to one of the deepest pools of capital in the world. The LSE offers both primary market activity, where issuers raise finance for the first time, and secondary market activity, where investors can use the exchange facilities to sell their shares to others. The LSE also provides a number of information products and services. Its Regulatory News Service (RNS) enables companies to meet their regulatory requirements easily when making announcements and financial communications. The LSE also provides market data via its **Infolect™** service, which provides information ranging from real-time data on individual share price movements to company announcements.

5.6 Emerging Markets

Equity trading has become truly global, as more countries have opened their markets to international investors. The following is a list of some of the largest emerging stock markets and the total value of shares traded on each of them in 2014:

Exchange	$bn
Bovespa – São Paulo Stock Exchange	824
Bombay Stock Exchange – Mumbai	1,642
Korea Exchange – Seoul	1,251
National Stock Exchange of India – Mumbai	1,642
Moscow Exchange	278

Source: World Federation of Exchanges (industry association)

Two instruments that have helped the movement of investment capital from investors in developed economies to emerging markets are **American depositary receipts (ADRs)** and **global depositary receipts (GDRs)**.

An ADR represents ownership of shares in a non-US company (usually one whose main listing is an emerging equity market) that are traded on a US market. The shares of many non-US companies trade on US exchanges through the use of ADRs. ADRs enable US investors to buy shares in non-US companies without undertaking cross-border transactions. ADRs are priced in US dollars, pay dividends in US dollars and can be traded like the shares of US-based companies.

Each ADR is issued by a US depositary bank and can represent a fraction of a share, a single share, or multiple shares of the non-US companies. An owner of an ADR has the right to obtain the international stock it represents, but US investors usually find it more convenient simply to own the ADR. The price of any ADR is close to the price that the international share is trading at in its home market, once there has been an adjustment to take into account the ratio of ADRs to international shares.

GDRs are the global version of ADRs. While they are structured in the same way, they trade on non-US exchanges, such as the LSE.

6. Commodities

A commodity is a raw, or primary, product – for example, commodities include agricultural products (such as livestock, grain and fruit), energy products (such as oil and gas) and metals (such as copper and aluminium). Commodity derivatives are based on commodities, as distinct from financial derivatives based on financial instruments or financial data. The commodity derivatives markets provide market participants with similar instruments to those available in the financial markets (eg, futures and options), and many commodity products pre-date the financial derivatives market, which only commenced in the 1970s and 1980s. The Chicago Board of Trade (CBOT), which was established in 1848, lays claim to being the oldest futures exchange in the world, but although it is where the modern form of the futures market originates, the trading of commodities contracts has been going on for many centuries within Europe and Japan. The London Metal Exchange (LME), founded in 1877, traces its roots back to 1571 and the opening of the Royal Exchange.

The concepts covered in Chapter 1 apply equally to both financial and commodity derivatives markets. However, further factors may need to be taken into account when dealing in the commodity derivatives markets; for example, agricultural markets are heavily affected by the growing cycle of the crop and by the weather.

Some of the main global commodity derivatives markets, with examples of some of their contracts, are:

- **CME Group** – the CBOT for agricultural and soft commodities, gold, metals and ethanol, and the CME for energy – products including gas oil, crude oil and natural gas.
- **Euronext Derivatives** – soft commodities, eg, cocoa, sugar, coffee, and agricultural commodities, eg, wheat, corn, barley.
- **Dubai Mercantile Exchange** – crude oil.

- **ICE (Intercontinental Exchange)** – crude oil, refined energy products, natural gas, and soft commodities, such as cotton, cocoa, coffee and wood.
- **LME** – base metals, steel rebar, some precious metals, minor metals (cobalt and molybdenum).
- **Tokyo Commodities Exchange** – base metals, oil and rubber.
- **Shanghai Metal Exchange** – base metals.
- **Multi Commodity Exchange of India (MCX) Mumbai** – soft and agricultural commodities, gold, ferrous and base metals, and energy.
- **New York Mercantile Exchange (NYMEX)** – metals and energy contracts.
- **European Climate Exchange (ECX)** – environmental contracts.

6.1 Softs and Agriculturals

Learning Objective

2.5.1 Know the main softs and agriculturals and the influences on supply: coffee, cocoa, white sugar, soya bean, wheat, rape seed oil, grains, livestock; change in demand; change in production, weather; holding cost

Softs is a label for a particular set of commodities that includes cocoa, sugar and coffee. Agricultural commodities include grains, such as wheat and soya beans, as well as livestock and seed oils.

The price influences on soft commodities (ie, coffee, sugar and cocoa) and agricultural products (ie, wheat, soya beans) can be summarised as supply and demand factors. Supply is the amount of the particular commodity that is being provided to the market. Obviously, this will be driven, inter alia, by such factors as the amount of land that is given over to producing a crop, weather conditions over the growing season and the impact of any other factors such as disease or insect activity, the application of better technology and the availability of transport and warehouse facilities. For example, the extremely hot and dry weather that parts of Russia and Central Asia experienced in 2010 had a significant effect on global markets by reducing the supply of wheat which sparked higher prices. Furthermore, the greater the number and diversity of sources for a particular soft or agricultural commodity, the more stable the supply. For example, if cocoa is grown in multiple locations, harmful weather in any one location will have less impact.

Demand will be driven by whether nations have a deficit of the particular commodity, rather than a surplus. Moreover, the wealth of the population, economic and industrial growth, consumer tastes and habits and tax incentives, are important factors.

Example 5

ICE trades a variety of commodity products, including cocoa, robusta coffee and white sugar. Some examples of contract details that are relevant to the examination are contained in the table below:

Product	Contract Size (tonnes)	Tick Size (per tonne)	Tick Value (per contract)
Cocoa	10	$1.00	$10.00
Robusta coffee	10	$1.00	$10.00
White sugar	50	$ 0.10	$10.00

These commodity products can be traded on ICE Connect.

There are options available on the futures. The options are American-style (see Chapter 1, Section 3.2).

The option premiums are not paid upfront, but are paid futures-style. These soft commodity futures are all physically delivered and use LCH.Clearnet SA as central counterparty (CCP).

For those futures contracts that reach delivery, the **exchange delivery settlement price (EDSP)** is broadly the price at which the future traded at the end of the trading period on the **last trading day**. The sellers choose where to deliver, based on the exchange's specified delivery points (eg, for Euronext Paris' corn futures, delivery is made to a listed European port; for Euronext's corn futures, a listed international port; and for futures, an approved grain store). The delivered commodities are matched to buyers by LCH.Clearnet SA.

For options on the futures, the options expire in the month before the delivery month, eg, March corn options that enable the buyer to enter into a March cocoa future expire on the last business day of February.

Similar to financial assets, commodities also have their own version of a carrying cost. But, in the case of commodities, it is referred to as their holding cost. This refers to the costs associated with keeping any commodity inventory, which may include warehousing, spoilage, obsolescence, interest and taxes. For soft and agricultural commodities, spoilage is a key concern, since many of the commodities in the category may have a limited product life. When calculating the profits and losses from a commodities trade, holding costs must be taken into account.

6.2 Base and Precious Metals

Learning Objective

2.6.1 Know the main base and precious metals and the influences on supply: copper, nickel, aluminium, zinc, tin, lead, gold and silver; change in demand; change in production; marginal costs of mining; changes in industry; political or strategic; holding cost

There are numerous metals produced worldwide and subsequently refined for use in a wide variety of products and processes. Derivatives products have been introduced on some of the major metals. Trading is concentrated on two exchanges: the LME and the COMEX division of NYMEX in New York.

However, these two exchanges do not compete on all metals, with only copper and aluminium trading on both exchanges.

As with soft commodities, metal prices are influenced by supply and demand. Factors influencing supply include the availability of raw materials and the costs of extraction and production. A producer will measure the cost of extraction against a metal's price: when the marginal cost of mining rises above a metal's current price, production will stop. This follows the basic economic principle that marginal cost must be less than the price in order to contribute to the other costs incurred, and potentially provide a profit. Such costs may be affected by political stability and environmental legislation.

Demand comes from underlying users of the commodity, for example, the growing demand for metals in rapidly industrialising economies, including China and India. It also originates from investors such as hedge funds, who might buy metal futures in anticipation of excess demand or incorporate commodities into specific funds. Producers use the market for hedging their production. Traditionally, the price of precious metals such as gold will rise in times of crisis – gold is seen as a safe haven.

All metal commodities, like softs, have holding or warehousing costs associated with taking delivery and holding the commodity. As with all other costs of carry, the longer one holds the asset (commodity), the higher the holding cost.

Finally, metals used in packaging, for example, are influenced by the cost of alternatives such as glass and plastic, and by consumer/government concerns about sustainable resources and recycling.

The major metals can be subdivided into base metals and precious metals. The major metals and their uses are summarised in the following table:

Metal	Major Uses
Base	
Copper	Electrics, electronics, building
Aluminium	Aerospace, packaging, kitchen equipment, windows, car manufacture, buildings, canning
Zinc	Galvanising, production of brass
Nickel	Production of stainless steel and other alloys
Lead	Batteries, petrol additive, buildings
Tin	Packaging, power
Precious	
Gold	Jewellery, dentistry, computers, electronics, investments
Silver	Jewellery, ornaments, photography, dentistry, electronics

6.3 Energy Products

Learning Objective

2.7.1 Know the main energy products and the influences on price (crude oil and natural gas): change in demand; change in production; marginal costs of production; delivery costs; political or strategic; OPEC

The energy market includes the market for refined oil products and natural gas products. Like the market for any other product, the price influences can be summarised as supply factors and demand factors. Supply is finite, and countries with surplus oil and gas reserves are able to export to those countries with insufficient oil and gas to meet their requirements. Prices could be raised by producers restricting supply, for example, by the activities of the major oil producers in the Organisation of the Petroleum Exporting Countries (OPEC). Demand for oil and gas is ultimately driven by levels of consumption, which in turn is driven by energy needs (for example, from manufacturing industry and transport). ICE is Europe's largest energy exchange, listing a wide range of crude and refined oil and natural gas contracts.

Prices can react sharply to political crises, particularly in major oil-producing regions of the world, such as the Middle East. Furthermore, since the level of demand is directly determined by the consuming economies' growth, economic forecasts and economic data also have an impact on energy prices.

Prices also react quickly to changes in supply resulting from bad weather and accidents, such as oil spills from offshore sources. The 2010 spill in the Gulf of Mexico might have a longer-term effect on prices, if environmental concerns delay or block any future licences for offshore drilling in a number of regions.

Oil includes both crude oil and various fractions produced as a result of the refining process, eg, naphtha, butane, kerosene, petrol and heating/gas oil.

Crude oil is defined by three primary factors:

- field of origin, for example, Brent, West Texas, Dubai
- density, ie, low density or **light**, high density or **heavy**
- sulphur content, ie, low sulphur or **sweet**, high sulphur or **sour**.

6.4 Exotics

Learning Objective

2.8.1 Know the main products and the influences on price: freight; emissions; weather

Recent developments have seen the expansion of derivatives trading into a wide range of exotic contracts. These include weather, emissions and freight, to name a select few.

A weather derivative is a contract that obligates the buyer to purchase the value of the underlying weather index – measured in heating degree days (HDDs) or cooling degree days (CDDs) – at a future date. The settlement price of the underlying weather index is equal to the value of the relevant month's HDD/CDD multiplied by $20. Weather futures can enable businesses to protect themselves against losses caused by unexpected shifts in weather conditions.

As expected, one of the main influences on price is the short- and long-term weather forecast. Contract prices are also subject to shock when unexpected weather events happen, such as hurricanes and snowstorms. This is an aspect that they have in common with many agricultural contracts.

Growing environmental concerns have prompted several exchanges to start trading several different types of emissions contracts. Exchanges in Europe, Asia and North America have listed several types of futures contracts for carbon dioxide, sulphur dioxide, methane and nitrogen dioxide emissions. These contracts set a price for a set amount of emissions allotment, with the goal of getting emissions to a predetermined level, such as those set by the Kyoto Accord. Those entities that are heavy polluters buy these to offset what they produce. As regulations get stricter and pollution targets are reduced, prices are expected to rise.

Freight derivatives, which include forward freight agreements (FFAs), container freight swap agreements and options, are financial contracts that are based on the future levels of freight rates, for dry bulk carriers, tankers and container ships. These instruments are settled against various freight rate indices, which are published by the Baltic Exchange (for dry and most wet contracts) and Platts (Asian wet contracts).

FFAs are often traded OTC (through broker members of the Forward Freight Agreement Brokers' Association – FFABA), but recently screen-based trading is becoming more popular. Trades can be given up for clearing by the broker to one of the clearing houses that support such trades. Currently, there are four clearing houses for freight: NOS Clearing, ICE Futures Europe, NYMEX and SGX. Freight derivatives are primarily used by ship-owners and -operators, oil companies, trading companies and grain houses as tools for managing freight rate risk.

Recently, with commodities now standing at the forefront of international economics, the large financial trading houses, including banks and hedge funds, have entered the market.

A property derivative is a financial derivative whose value is based on the value of an underlying real estate asset. Since real estate prices are sometimes subject to market inefficiencies and are hard to price accurately, property derivatives are often based on a real estate property index. In turn, the real estate property index attempts to reflect price movements in the aggregate real estate market to provide a more accurate representation of underlying real estate assets' performance.

Trading or taking positions in property derivatives is also known as synthetic real estate.

Property derivatives usually take the form of a total return swap, forward contract or futures, or can adopt a funded format where the property derivative is included as part of a bond or note structure. Under the total return swap or forward contract, the parties will usually take contrary positions on the price movements of a property index.

Hybrid derivatives basically combine two different types of derivatives in one contract. They do this by incorporating two or more types of risks into a single derivative. One of the most widely used examples is a swaption = swap + option.

Hybrids very often combine features and risks from different markets. For example, a hybrid derivative could be a contract that gives its owner the right to sell a bill paying LIBOR + 200 bps for an individual share at specified prices when a specific share index reaches certain points. The option involves two markets: the money market and the equity market.

Any multi-asset derivative whose components don't belong to the same asset class can be considered to be a hybrid derivative. In general, financial derivatives can be divided into basic derivatives and hybrid derivatives, where the latter results from combining a host contract with an embedded derivative.

Example 6

Hybrid derivative = Host contract + Embedded derivative

Hybrid derivative = A GBP 1.52 put versus the USD that depends on the price of gold reaching USD 1,200 per ounce.

Hybrid derivatives allow investors, speculators, and hedgers to take a view on combinations of asset classes in a single contract. For example, a fund manager with multi-asset exposures can use hybrid derivatives as a hedging tool.

End of Chapter Questions

1. What is a bond?
   Answer reference: Section 2.1

2. Why do corporate bonds pay a higher yield than government bonds?
   Answer reference: Section 2.2

3. Why is the FX market unique?
   Answer reference: Section 3

4. What is an NDF?
   Answer reference: Section 3.2

5. Why does the interbank money market exist?
   Answer reference: Section 4

6. What is commercial paper?
   Answer reference: Section 4.4

7. How do bearer shares differ from ordinary shares?
   Answer reference: Section 5.1

8. What is an equity warrant?
   Answer reference: Section 5.3

9. What are softs?
   Answer reference: Section 6.1

10. How are weather derivatives used?
    Answer reference: Section 6.4

Chapter Three

Exchange-Traded Futures and Options

This syllabus area will provide approximately 9 of the 100 examination questions

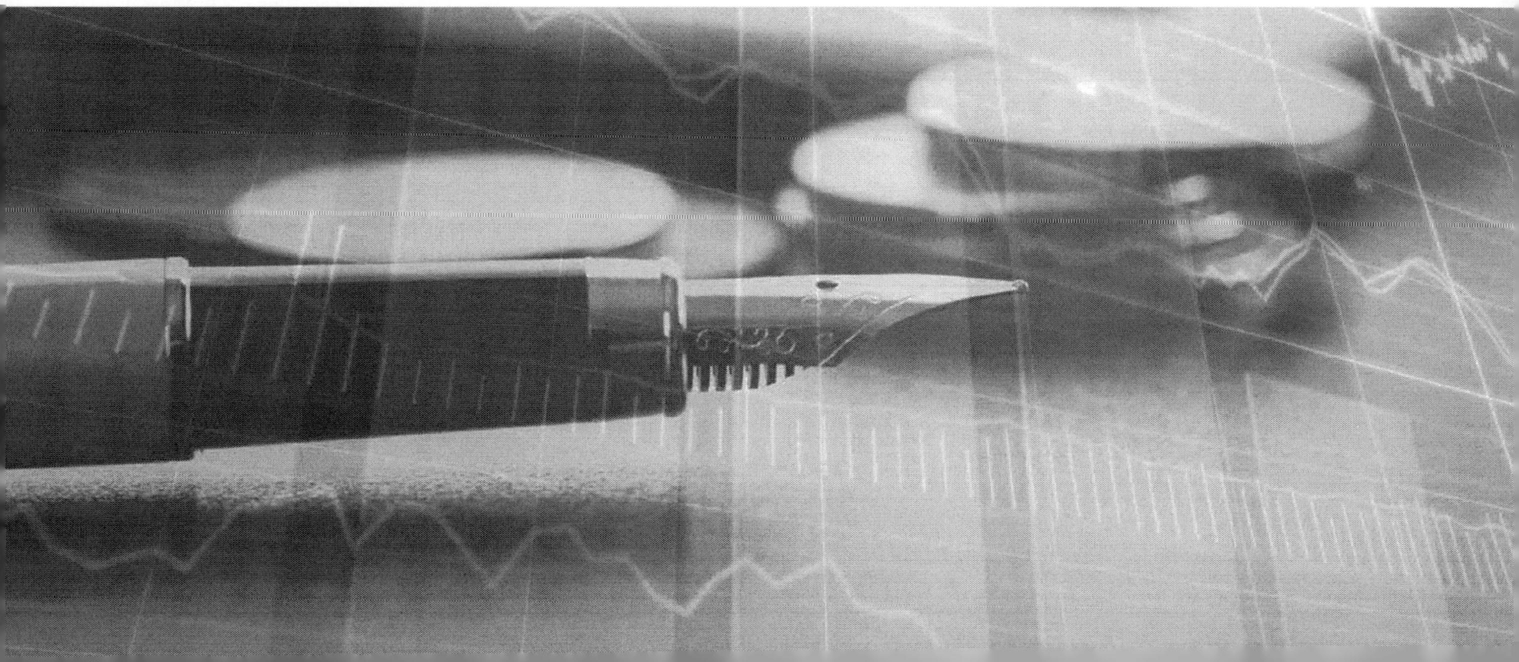

1. Derivatives Exchanges

1.1 Introduction to Derivatives Exchanges

Learning Objective

3.1.1 Know the structures, physical and electronic trading processes, clearing mechanisms and main products of the following exchanges: Euronext, LME, ICE Futures, Turquoise Derivatives, Eurex, MEFF, BClear; PHLX, CBOE, OneChicago, NYBOT (ICE), CME Group; SGX, Osaka, TSE, KOFEX; BSE, NSE, MCX

A derivatives exchange is an exchange which provides a marketplace where one can buy and sell futures, options and other contracts of specific quantities of a commodity or financial instrument at a specified price with delivery set at a specified time in the future.

In providing the marketplace, the exchange will have established a trading mechanism or platform, ie, trading can take place using the traditional pits or floor trading, or electronically via computer screens using a trading platform. Some exchanges, for some contracts, use both.

UK	
Euronext Derivatives	Euronext group's global derivatives market. Electronic trading via the Universal Trading Platform (UTP). Trades futures and options on currencies, equities, exchange-traded funds (ETFs), indices and commodities. Some of its main contracts are GBP/USD, EUR/USD, as well as universal stock futures and track options. All trades are cleared via LCH.Clearnet SA.
London Metal Exchange (LME)	Both **ring** physical trading, and electronic via LMEselect and inter-office on the telephone. Trades futures and options on: aluminium, copper, nickel, tin, zinc, lead and steel, plus aluminium alloy, and its own metal-based index.
ICE Futures Europe	All trading is done electronically. Trades futures and options on a wide range of energy products, such as Brent Crude, West Texas Intermediate (WTI), gas oil, electricity, coal and natural gas. It also trades a range of index and **single stock futures**, as well as short-term interest and bond futures, such as Long Gilts. Trades are cleared via ICE Clear Europe.
London Stock Exchange (LSE) Derivatives	All trading is done electronically. Trades standardised and flexible futures and options of the shares and indices on the FTSE 100, FTSE Super Liquid (largest 35 shares) and the Norwegian OBX index. It also has contracts linked to the most liquid Russian shares and indices. Trades are processed, cleared and guaranteed by CCP Clearing with LCH.Clearnet.

Euronext is Europe's second largest exchange, spanning Amsterdam, Brussels, Lisbon and Paris, referred to respectively as the Amsterdam, Brussels, Lisbon and Paris markets. These are linked to Euronext's London market via the Universal Trading Platform (UTP), which in effect creates one pan-European securities market.

Bclear, which is accessible via ICE Block Reported Trade Service, covers a wide range of global equity markets. It combines the flexibility of over-the-counter (OTC) markets with the benefits of exchange-traded and cleared contracts. Bclear offers options on a wide range of individual companies' shares, UK, and European index futures and options, Universal Stock futures and variance futures on the AEX, CAC 40 and FTSE 100 indices. Bclear can also be used by member firms to process OTC derivatives business, to help reduce their operational risk and manage the contractual counterparty risk.

NASDAQ Group is a US-based company that owns and operates the NASDAQ stock market and eight European stock exchanges in Armenia, the Nordic and Baltic regions. Given the wide range of exchanges, the group has several different trading systems to fit each market and product traded; these include the Genium INET trading platform, CONDICO – which is used for commodities trading and clearing – and CLICK XT. The group trades a wide variety of futures and options on a range of underlying assets that include shares, indices, interest rates and commodities. The group's two main clearing systems include Genium INET Clearing and SECUR.

NASDAQ Options Market (NOM) is one of NASDAQ OMX Group's two electronic options markets. All trading is run on NASDAQ's INET technology. The NOM is a US-based options market, that trades a wide range of NASDAQ and PHLX options. NOM uses the same clearing systems as its parent.

US	
Chicago Board of Trade (CBOT) – part of the CME Group	Both **open outcry** physical trading and electronic via EOS Trader and CME Direct. Trades futures on a wide range of agricultural products, gold, silver, interest rates (US notes, bonds, swaps), the Dow Jones indices, and has a joint trading agreement with SGX to trade several of its contracts. All trades processed under the JADE agreement. All trades processed by the Front End Clearing (FEC) System and Front End Clearing Plus (FEC+), which are based on CME Direct.
Chicago Board Options Exchange (CBOE)	The CBOE is the largest US options exchange, established by the CBOT in 1973. It was the first exchange to list standardised, exchange-traded stock options and its contracts are cleared by the Options Clearing Corporation (OCC).
Chicago Mercantile Exchange (CME)	Both open outcry physical trading, and CME Globex electronic trading platform. Trades futures on a wide range of commodities, short-term interest rates, FX, US economic data, **equity indices**, weather and real estate. All trades processed via CME Direct system.
New York Mercantile Exchange (NYMEX) – part of the CME Group	Both open outcry physical trading, and via CME Globex and NYMEX ClearPort, for OTC transactions; also after-hours trading on CME Global electronic trading platform for futures only. Trades futures and options on a wide range of metals, energy products and options on spreads between different grades of oil such as the Brent/WTI spread. All trades are processed via the exchange's clearing house.
OneChicago	The OneChicago match engine is accessible from either the CBOEdirect or CME Globex systems. An electronically traded market via both CBOEdirect and Globex systems. Trades single stock futures (known as security futures), as well as futures on narrowly defined share indices and exchange-traded funds. Trades are processed through either CME Clearing or OCC depending on membership.
NASDAQ (PHLX)	Combination of floor trading and PHLX XL, the exchange's electronic trading platform. Trades stock, index, equity sector and currency options. Both offer standardised and FLEX options. All trades are processed via the exchange's clearing house.

Europe	
Eurex	An electronically traded market and Europe's largest derivatives exchange. Trades a wide range of futures and options on: STIRs, equities, index and single stock futures, volatility index, credit derivatives and exchange-traded funds. Also FLEX options. All trades processed via Eurex Clearing AG.
Euronext exchanges (Amsterdam, Brussels, Lisbon and Paris)	Electronic trading can be carried out via Optiq and the Universal Trading Platform (UTP). Trades futures and options on currencies, swaps, equities and commodities. All four exchanges use LCH.Clearnet SA to process their trades.
MEFF – Spanish Exchange for Financial Futures and Options	All trading is done via the MEFF Derivative Trading Platform. Trades futures and options on interest rates, bonds, the IBEX 35 index and leading Spanish shares. Trades are processed directly from the MEFF Derivatives Trading Platform by the exchange's clearing house.

Asia	
Singapore Exchange (SGX)	All trading is done electronically via the SGX QUEST system. Trades futures and options on interest rates, bonds and regional equity indices. Main contracts include JGB, Eurodollar and Euroyen, Nikkei 225 contracts. All trades are processed and cleared via SGX Derivatives Clearing (SGX-DC).
Osaka Securities Exchange	A physical and electronic market. Trades futures and options on the Nikkei 225 index, as well as individual Japanese shares. Trades processed via the exchange's clearing house.
Tokyo Stock Exchange (TSE)	An electronic market that trades futures and options on several TOPIX and TSE indices, as well as individual shares and government bonds. Trading is done via the Tdex+ system.
Korea Exchange (KRX) Futures Market Division	The KSE, KOSDAQ and KOFEX markets have been consolidated and now all derivative products are traded on the futures market division of KRX. On KOFEX, all orders are processed via the exchange's automatic trading system. KOFEX trades futures and options of several Korean and US indices as well as gold and certificates of deposit (CD) interest rate futures. All trades are processed via the KRX's clearing house.

Emerging Markets	
Brazilian Mercantile & Futures Exchange (BM&F)	Some agricultural contracts are traded physically; all other contracts are traded electronically via NSC screen trading system. Trades futures on a range of agricultural products. Futures and options on gold, coffee, corn, soybeans, USD, the Bovespa share index and a range of domestic interest rates. Trades are cleared through the three BM&F clearing houses for the respective contract product.
Dubai Mercantile Exchange (DME)	A fully electronic exchange. Trades an Oman Crude Oil future and two spread futures, Brent/Oman Crude and WTI/Oman Crude. Trades are cleared through the NYMEX clearing house.
National Commodities & Derivatives Exchange (NCDEX) Ltd (India)	Trading is done on the exchange's automated trading system. Trades futures on agro products, precious, base and ferrous metals, energy products and polymers. Trades are processed via the exchange's clearing house, with physical delivery through its depository clearing system, while margin payments and **cash settlement** processed are via an approved clearing bank.
South African Futures Exchange (Safex) – part of the Johannesburg Stock Exchange (JSE)	Trading is done electronically using the JSE's TALX system, also accessed via the SETS trading system. Trades a wide range of futures contracts on agricultural products, gold, interest rates, FX, the JSE index and single stock futures.
Shanghai Futures Exchange (SHFE)	Trading takes place on its trading floor and via its electronic trading system. Trades futures contracts on a number of metals (aluminium, copper, zinc), rubber and fuel oil. Trades are processed via the exchange's clearing system, with physical delivery using any of its approved warehouses.
China Financial Futures Exchange (CFFEX)	All trading is done electronically, using the CFFEX's system, which is also linked to the exchange's clearing house. CSI 200 index futures are currently the only contract traded.
Bombay Stock Exchange (BSE) (India)	A fully screen-based exchange, using the exchange's derivatives trading and settlement system (DTSS) system, as well as internet-based trading. Trades a range of individual equity, equity index and currency-based derivatives. Uses its internal system for clearing and delivery.
Multi Commodity Exchange of India Ltd (MCX)	A fully electronic exchange. Trades futures in a wide range of commodities, including bullion, energy, ferrous and non-ferrous metals, oil, seeds, spices and plastics. Trades are cleared and delivered via the exchange's Demat system.

1.2 Membership Structure and Trading Rights

Learning Objective

3.1.2 Know the membership structures (brokers, dealers and broker-dealers, general clearing, individual clearing and non-clearing) and their principal rights: executing trades for third parties; executing trades for their own account; executing trades for other members; capacity as broker; capacity as dealer; capacities of clearing members

Access to most exchange markets is via membership. Firms may join in a number of different membership categories:

- **Brokers** – may only trade for third parties (including clients and other members).
- **Dealers** – may trade for their own account. They can also trade for other members providing that they are authorised by the appropriate regulatory body.
- **Broker-dealers** – are entitled to trade both for third parties and their own account.

The forms of membership also depend on whether the firm wishes to clear business traded on the market and for whom the contracts will be cleared.

All exchanges have a clearing house, which serves as the central counterparty (CCP) to all trades executed on the exchange between clearing members. Remember that one of the key attractions of exchange-traded contracts is that there is no counterparty risk: the clearing house guarantees the delivery of all contracts.

Exchanges have different types of membership that determine the types of trading services a firm can execute, and the same is true of clearing services.

Clearing members can be general clearing members (GCMs), which enables them to clear their own principal trades, on behalf of their clients and on behalf of other non-clearing members. Or, they can be individual clearing members (ICMs), only able to clear their own principal trades and trades on behalf of their clients.

Also, non-clearing members may be party to a maximum of two clearing agreements, one in respect of commodity contracts and one in respect of other exchange contracts.

Most clearing houses require that their GCMs have a higher level of financial resources than they require from ICMs.

Each and every contract (transaction) traded on the exchange will be supported by a clearing member in whose name the transaction is registered.

2. Trading Platforms

Learning Objective

3.2.1 Know the essential details of the trading mechanisms: open outcry, telephone and electronic platforms; whether quote- or order-driven; how the trading host matches orders; the order types accepted by the markets; the trading strategies that are recognised; record-keeping

3.2.2 Know the essential details of wholesale trading facilities: block trades and basis trades; exchange for physical, exchange for swaps; Flex facilities

3.2.3 Understand the significance, implications and uses of wholesale trading facilities

Pit trading or open outcry (called ring trading at the LME) is the original trading method. It is a quote- or price-driven system, where traders quote the prices for which they are willing to buy or sell specific contracts. The LME is one of the few European exchanges that operates both ring trading during its most liquid times and LMEselect, an electronic platform, for extended trading. The LME has four five-minute ring trading sessions per day for each of its major metal contracts. These take place at different times during the main trading day and are limited to the specific contract during its allotted time.

The other markets that also use this pit trading are found in the US: the CBOT and the CME. But even on these exchanges, screen-based trading is becoming increasingly more popular.

A key aspect of the LME's ring trading is its ring dealing membership category. Each ring dealing member is allowed to trade during each ring dealing session, in addition to the 24-hour inter-office trading that takes place on the LME. Note that seats on open outcry markets are normally more valuable given the limited number of seats due to capacity limitations. This results in waiting lists for seats and an open market for seat sales and leases.

Telephone trading is exclusively limited to trades and orders between clients and their executing brokers. This is most often the case when a client calls their broker who has a direct line to their trader who quotes a price. If the client deals on it, the trader will trade on the market price. Electronic trading systems have replaced telephone trading in most of the main exchanges.

Most exchange trading is purely electronic via an electronic system, which is an anonymous, order-driven system, where traders are unaware of their actual counterparty, both pre-trade and post-trade. To access the system, an order is submitted into the central order book by, or via, an exchange member.

On the LME trading takes place both on the ring trading or its LMEselect system, while ICE trading takes place via applications that are embedded in ICE Connect that includes both online and mobile trading. Examples of other electronic trading systems are CME Globex and CME Direct, which are used for several of the agricultural contracts trading on the CME Group. Many exchanges in developing markets such as the SHFE and the NCDEX also use electronic trading systems.

Once the order has been received, the system stores the order on the central order book. Orders are matched on the basis of price, and then time priority. After the trades have been executed, trade details are fed to a trade registration system, such as the Universal Clearing Platform (UCP) as used by the Euronext exchanges.

In the case of ICE Futures Europe, once trades have been registered using its trading position, they are passed automatically to ICE Clear Europe. The trade then novates and ICE Clear Europe becomes the CCP to the buying and selling clearing members. (Novation is covered in more detail in Chapter 6.)

As with all electronic trading systems, the UTP accepts a variety of order types:

- **Normal limit orders** – to be executed at the stated price or better.
- **Market orders** – to be executed at the best price immediately available.
- **Market on open orders** – these may be submitted prior to the opening of the day's trading with the intention of being executed at the opening price for the day.

Some order types can be given certain periods of validity, such as good 'til cancelled (GTC). Furthermore, they can be given certain quantity requirements, such as immediate and cancel (do as much as possible now and cancel any remaining), complete volume (do the whole order or none at all) or minimum volume (only do the order if a certain minimum can be achieved).

Where permitted by the exchange rules, cross trades (where a match has been established by negotiation prior to entry in the system) are allowed as long as they are entered into the system as separate buy and sell orders.

The strategies that are recognised by most exchanges are many and varied. Among the acceptable strategies are all of the strategies covered in the syllabus, ie, spreads, **straddles**, **strangles** and **synthetics** (more detail on derivatives strategies can be found in Chapter 8).

In addition, most exchanges recognise two types of wholesale trades: block trades and basis trades.

A block trade is a large transaction made between an exchange member and a wholesale client. The exchange specifies the size of the transaction that is required before it becomes a block trade. Block trades are allowed to be negotiated away from the central order book as long as they are reported into the exchange once they are agreed.

The block trade facility allows members and their wholesale clients (those with sufficient knowledge, expertise and understanding) to transact business as bilaterally agreed transactions without delay and with certainty of price and execution. The block trade facility complements the central markets, which continue to be the primary method for trading.

Each exchange determines which products can be block traded. The transaction sizes required to be classified as a block trade vary. For example, ICE Futures, London has set a minimum of 100 contracts for short sterling and gilt futures, while for FTSE futures it is 500 contracts. Block trades must be reported within five minutes and are denoted by the letter K. The Hong Kong Exchanges and Clearing (HKEx) defines the minimum number of contracts in a block trade for its stock index futures and options as 100 contracts, while for individual stock options it is 500 contracts. Once reported, these trades are denoted by INT on the HKEx in the ticker window to differentiate them.

A basis trade is the simultaneous exchange of a financial asset or instrument (eg, a government bond or a basket of shares) together with an appropriate offsetting number of futures contracts, in a privately negotiated transaction between two parties. Similarly to block trades, the exchange allows the futures part of the basis trade to be executed outside the central order book. As with block trades, basis trades are reported into the exchange once they are agreed.

The FLEX facility, such as the one offered by ICE Futures, London for FTSE 100 index options, gives any exchange member the freedom to customise the trades with respect to the strike/exercise price and expiration date. The FLEX facility is one that combines the flexibility of the OTC market with the clearing and other advantages of exchange trading. The FLEX concept was originally introduced by the CBOE. See Chapter 1, Section 3.6, FLEX Options.

Some FLEX facilities offered by exchanges are another way to increase trading volumes based on advances in risk management and systems.

On most exchanges, wholesale trading facilities enable participants to enter off-order-book trades into the exchange's system. With these facilities the participants can benefit from the flexibility of customised trading and the advantages of standardised clearing and settlement. Most facilities are pure OTC trade entry facilities, with bilateral agreement of price and quantities.

Two aspects of wholesale trading facilities are:

- **Exchange for Physical (EFP)** – an off-market transaction that involves the swapping (or exchanging) of an OTC position for a futures position. In order that an EFP transaction can take place, the OTC side and futures components must be **substantially similar** in terms of either value and/or quantity.
- **Exchange for Swap (EFS)** – similar to EFP, in that it involves the swapping (or exchanging) of an OTC swap with a series of futures contracts. The OTC interest rate swap must have a price correlation so that the futures are a suitable instrument for hedging the cash market transaction.

EFP transactions have a number of benefits for market participants, which explain their existence. These are:

- Counterparty credit exposure can be reduced when an existing OTC position is reversed and replaced with a futures position. In so doing, an EFP allows counterparties to release **credit**, clearing their credit limits for further OTC trading.
- Reduced balance sheet and margin requirements – by **netting** OTC positions against offsetting futures positions, margin and credit limit requirements can be reduced.
- 24-hour trading – EFP transactions can normally be negotiated around the clock but must be registered during exchange business days between explicit time brackets.

3. Clearing Mechanisms

Learning Objective

3.3.1 Understand the matching and clearing arrangements: trade capture processes/order matching processes; how contracts are delivered and settled; physical or cash; establishment of settlement price; options into futures; sellers initiate delivery

3.3.2 Understand how the physical delivery methods for commodities operate and where they differ from other derivatives: warehouses, warrants and good delivery; large position reporting; price discovery – official and closing prices

3.3.3 Know the main exchanges and contracts that have common settlement prices and links and the extent to which these allow investors to transfer open positions from one exchange to another: CME Group; SGX

Every exchange uses a clearing house, which clears all trades and supervises the processing and delivery of all trades executed on that exchange. The process by which the clearing house becomes counterparty to all trades is novation.

Each contract, as part of its specification, has details of its settlement procedure. While most contracts are closed out before maturity, each has a settlement/delivery process that the clearing house supervises to ensure that both sellers and buyers receive proper payment or delivery of the underlying asset.

The physical settlement approach is part of the mechanism which ensures that price convergence of futures to cash market prices will occur.

Cash settlement (often known as a **contract for difference**), which is another final settlement mechanism, is straightforward, since it requires the net cash payment of the difference between the value at the final position's closing price and the value based on the previous day's closing price. This is due to the fact that all contracts are marked to market at the end of each trading day and the clearing house either receives or pays that day's variation margin.

The details of physical delivery are set out as part of the contract's details. The specifications of each contract clearly define the details of what is an acceptable asset that can be delivered. Since exchange-traded contracts have standard amounts, they also have specific standards of what can be delivered. This is particularly the case for commodity contracts.

It is the seller who initiates the delivery process. Once advised, the clearing house will assign a buyer at random and advise them that delivery will take place. For most financial futures, the delivery process is straightforward, since, with the exception of long-dated government bond contracts, most have a single underlying asset that can be delivered. For government bond contracts, such as gilts or T-bonds, the exchange will have a list of bonds that are eligible for delivery and each bond will have a price factor, on which the final invoice payment is based.

For options, it is the buyer who initiates delivery by exercising the option. In the case of options on futures, upon exercise the exchange will automatically replace the exercised option position with the corresponding future at the option's strike price.

With commodities, the delivery process is a little more involved, since, depending on the contract, there might be a choice of acceptable grades of the commodity that can be delivered. Also, the exchange will have a list of authorised warehouses or agents where the seller can deposit/deliver the commodity. In some cases, such as with the LME, the exchange will have a network of authorised warehouses that can issue warrants (as warehouse receipts), which are recorded and held within their **LMEsword** delivery system. LMEsword, which was launched in 1999 as SWORD, is a secure transfer system for LME warrants which can be held in a central depository; it acts as a central database, holding details of ownership, and is subject to stringent security controls. This assures the buyer that the metal that they have purchased is of the correct deliverable quantity and grade and that he will have ownership upon payment.

3.1 Mutual Offset

CME Group and the SGX allow common settlement or offset for four of the contracts that are traded on both exchanges. A wide range of contracts is included in this agreement such as the yen-denominated and USD-denominated Nikkei 225 future, Eurodollar and Euroyen TIBOR contracts.

4. Calculating the Profit/Loss on Futures and Options

Learning Objective

3.3.4 Be able to calculate profit/loss on delivery/expiry of futures and options

The syllabus requires that candidates are able to calculate the profit (or loss) on the delivery of equity index futures and options. This is best achieved by studying the following examples and then attempting the exercises.

Example 1 – The FTSE 100 Index Future

An investor buys five FTSE 100 futures at 6720 and holds them to delivery. The EDSP, which is the official price at the expiry of the contract, is 7423.

The contract size for the ICE Futures Europe future is the index x £10 per point, the tick size is 0.50 index points and the tick value is £5 per tick.

The profit/loss is calculated by taking the number of ticks moved x tick value x number of contracts.

The investor's position has moved into profit by 763 index points (they have agreed to buy at 6720 something that now costs 7423).

Since each index point represents two ticks, that is a movement of 763 x 2 = 1526 ticks.

The investor's total profit = 1526 x £5 x 5 contracts = £38,150.

While £38,150 is the investor's total profit of this position, the final payment will be based on the difference between the previous day's closing price and the contract's official price at expiry, 7423. This is due to the exchange's daily margin payments.

Example 2 – SHFE Natural Rubber Future

A manufacturer buys ten SHFE July natural rubber futures at CNY (yuan) 19650. One month ahead of its maturity, the position is closed out at CNY 20250.

The contract specification is as follows: contract size is 5 ton, quotation is in yuan per ton and the tick size is 5 yuan.

The profit/loss is calculated by obtaining the difference between the opening and close-out prices and then multiplying this by the contract's size and then by the number of contracts.

The manufacturer's position moved in their favour by CNY 600 (the futures were bought at CNY 19650 and sold at CNY 20250).

On each contract a profit of CNY 3000 (CNY 600 x 5 ton, the contract size) has been made.

The total profit for the position = CNY 30,000 (CNY 3000 per contract x 10 contracts).

Example 3 – FTSE 100 Index Option

An investor buys three FTSE call options with a strike of 6900 for a premium of 12. At expiry, the cash index stands at 6910.

The investor's options are worth exercising because the value of the underlying (the cash index) exceeds the strike price at expiry. The gain on exercise will be ten index points (6910 – 6900), but the investor has incurred a premium cost of 12 index points. So, the overall position is a loss of two index points per contract.

The investor's overall loss is two index points x £10 x 3 contracts = £60.

(Remember that the options' contract size is the same as that of the underlying futures contract.)

You will see in Chapter 6 that all losses are paid by market users to, and from, their brokers. Brokers settle via clearing members who in turn settle via the clearing house. Some of the above loss may have already been paid through the margining system.

Exercise 1

An investor buys six FTSE 100 contracts on ICE Futures, London at 7205. At expiry the EDSP is 7251. What is the investor's gain or loss?

The answer can be found in the appendix at the end of this chapter.

Exercise 2

An investor buys seven FTSE put options with a strike of 7047 for a premium of 15. At expiry, the cash index stands at 6927. What is the gain or loss to the investor?

(Remember that the option's contract size is the same as that of the underlying futures contract.)

The answer can be found in the appendix at the end of this chapter.

Exercise 3

A fund manager sells 20 LMEX put options with a strike of 4180 and receives a premium of 18. At expiry the index stands at 4170. What is the fund manager's profit or loss?

The answer can be found in the appendix at the end of this chapter.

Appendix

Answer to Exercise 1

The investor has gained 7251 – 7205 = 46 index points on each contract.

46 x 2 = 92 ticks.

92 ticks x £5 = £460 per contract.

£460 x 6 contracts = £2,760 gain.

Note: The contract specification of FTSE 100 index futures is that the tick size is equal to 0.5 index points. Therefore in the above exercise, the gain of 46 index points is equal to 92 ticks of the futures contract. Therefore, while the value of one index point is £10, the contract's tick value is £5.

Answer to Exercise 2

The put options will be worth exercising, each gaining 7047 – 6927 = 120 index points. However, the investor's option cost 15 index points, so the overall gain is 120 – 15 = 105 index points.

105 index points x £10 x 7 contracts = £7,350

Answer to Exercise 3

While the put will be exercised against the fund manager, since the index is 10 points lower than the strike price, the fund manager still has a profit of 8 per option (18 – 10).

8 index points x $10 x 20 puts = $1,600.

End of Chapter Questions

1. What is Euronext?
   Answer reference: Section 1.1

2. Describe the three main types of exchange membership.
   Answer reference: Section 1.2

3. What is one of the key attractions of exchange-traded contracts?
   Answer reference: Section 1.2

4. Describe pit trading.
   Answer reference: Section 2

5. What is a block trade?
   Answer reference: Section 2

6. What is good about the FLEX facility?
   Answer reference: Section 2

7. Describe EFP.
   Answer reference: Section 2

8. What happens when novation occurs?
   Answer reference: Section 3

9. With options, who initiates delivery?
   Answer reference: Section 3

10. Which exchanges allow mutual offset?
    Answer reference: Section 3.1

Chapter Four

Principles of Exchange-Traded Futures and Options

This syllabus area will provide approximately 16 of the 100 examination questions

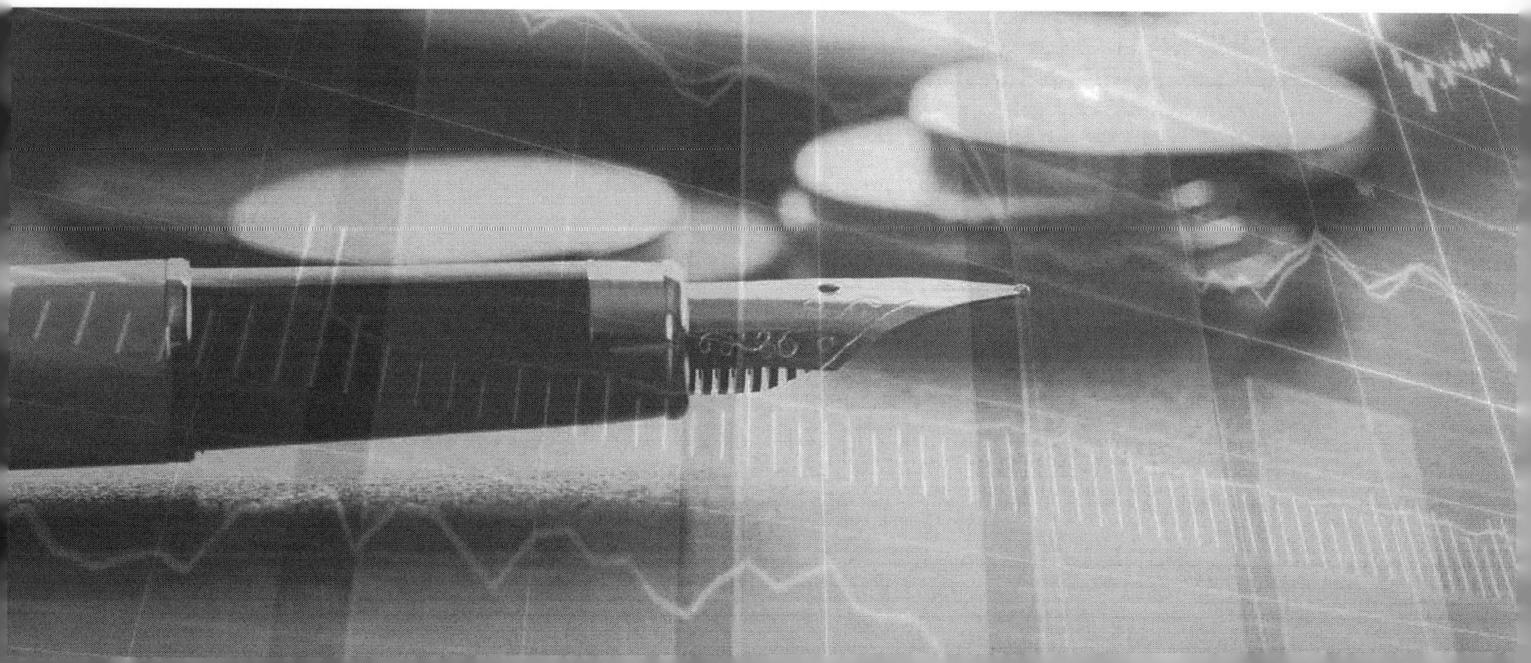

1. Futures Pricing

Learning Objective

4.1.1 Understand the mechanisms for futures pricing and the relationship with the underlying cash prices together with the significance of contributing factors: contango and backwardation; price convergence at maturity; the concept of fair value according to IAS

1.1 Futures Pricing Relationships

We already know that a future is a derivative. It is derived from the underlying asset, and the price of the future will be derived from the price of the underlying asset in the cash market, plus the net cost of holding the position over the term of the contract, such as any financing associated with owning the underlying asset.

However, it is normal to find that the cash price is different from the price for various deliveries in the future. Why? Well, it is tempting to think that the future's price is the market's perception of what the price of the underlying asset will be at the time of delivery, but this is not the case.

The price of the future is NOT the market's perception of what the price of the asset will be at the time of delivery.

Although prices in both markets are set by the interaction of buyers and sellers, there is a mathematical relationship that binds them together. It is important to understand the nature of this relationship. The following comments are based on this simple example:

Example 1

Cash price (January) = 400

March futures price = 417

June futures price = 433

Why should anyone want to pay 417 in March for an asset that is only worth 400 today?

The price relationship between the cash asset and the same asset in the future is based on an arbitrage principle.

1.2 Cost of Carry

Learning Objective

4.1.2 Understand the implications of the cost of carry and what may be included in these: what is cost of carry; interest rates and asset yields; storage costs, insurance and interest costs

It is January, and an investor who wants a particular asset in March has two choices:

- go long the March future and lock in the buying price for the asset at 417, or
- buy the asset today for 400 and store it until it is needed in March.

However, by buying the asset today, the investor is forgoing the interest which could be earned on the funds until March. Furthermore, there may be costs associated with storing the asset until it is needed (in the case of a commodity). The result is that anyone wanting delivery of the asset in March will be willing to pay the higher price because they are earning interest on their funds, in the meantime, and not incurring any storage costs.

Similarly, the person holding the asset will require a higher price for future delivery to compensate for the costs involved.

These are referred to as costs of carry.

The main components of costs of carry are:

- finance costs (interest) over the period
- storage costs, and
- insurance.

As mentioned above, **cost of carry** can be significant for all commodity futures, and therefore will cause a major difference between the current cash and futures price. As would be the case with the three-month LME lead futures contract, given the contract's size of 25 tonnes, the combination of storage and insurance costs for this amount of lead, in addition to any financing costs (which also apply to financial futures) is a major factor in determining that contract's **fair value**.

As will be seen in Section 1.4 below, there may also be benefits of carry, such as dividend yields when equity derivatives are considered.

1.3 Fair Value (Arbitrage-Free Value)

Knowing what the cash price of an asset is, and how much it will cost to carry the asset up to the moment of delivery, it is possible to calculate a futures price that will be fair to both the buyer and seller of the contract. This is known as the fair value of the future.

If the differential between the cash price and futures price is less than the cost of carry, the investor would be better off buying the future rather than buying the asset and holding it.

If the differential is greater than the cost of carry, an investor would be better off buying the asset and holding it.

It is only when the differential exactly reflects the cost of carry that the buyer is indifferent as to whether to buy in the cash market or the futures market.

Therefore:

Fair value of the future = cash price + cost of carry

1.3.1 Calculating the Fair Value

Learning Objective

4.1.3 Be able to calculate the fair value of a future from relevant cash market prices, yields and interest rates

To calculate the fair value of a particular future, simply take the cash price, calculate the interest for the period and calculate the other costs involved. The total of the cash price plus the interest plus the other costs equals the fair value.

Example 2

The cash price of a commodity is £1,250, the interest rate is 6% pa, and the storage costs are 1% pa.

The fair value of a future with 90 days to delivery is:

Cash price	£1,250.00		
Finance	£1,250 x 0.06 x (90/365)	=	£18.49
Storage	£1,250 x 0.01 x (90/365)	=	£3.08
Fair value	£1,271.57		

Note, this is the method that should be used in the exam.

Exercise 1

If the cash price of a particular asset is £750, the prevailing rate of short-term interest is 3% pa and the estimated storage costs (including insurance) for the asset are 0.5% pa, what is the fair value of a futures contract with 45 days to expiry?

The answer can be found in the appendix at the end of this chapter.

1.3.2 Calculating the Fair Value for Equity Index Futures

In calculating the fair value of an equity index future, only the net finance costs need to be considered, as the other costs are negligible.

Net finance costs = interest – present value of dividends

This is because, by holding the underlying, the investor forgoes the interest on the funds invested in the shares, but receives dividends from those shares.

The pricing of all stock futures takes this into account, such as the Cathay Pacific futures traded on the Hong Kong exchange, the pricing of which will be based on the net difference between the net cost of financing to buy the shares less the share's current dividend.

Example 3

The S&P 500 index is currently 2100, the one-year US interest rate is 0.55% and the index's dividend yield is 2.25% pa. The fair value of a future with 182 days to delivery is:

Cash index	= 2100
Interest rate	= 0.55%
Index dividend yield	= 2.25%
Fair value of cash index	= 2100 x (1 + (0.0055 x (182/360))) – cash price x interest rate.
	= 2105.84

Dividend yield conversion:

S&P 500 dividend yield	= 2.25%
Conversion to dividend points	= 2100 x 0.0225 = 47.25
	= 47.25 points per year x (182/360) = 23.89 points
Fair value of the future	= 2105.84 – 23.89 = 2081.95

Exercise 2

The FTSE 100 cash index is 6990, interest rates are 0.8% pa and the dividend yield on the index is 3.6% pa. What is the fair value of a FTSE 100 future with 91 days to run?

The answer can be found in the appendix at the end of this chapter.

1.3.3 International Accounting Standards Board (IASB) Definition of Fair Value

The International Accounting Standards Board (IASB) defines the fair value of a future or any other derivative instrument as the amount or price at which the future/instrument can be exchanged/traded between two market participants at a given time, as an arm's length market transaction.

In other words, the IASB's definition of a future's fair value is its current market price. For market participants, the IASB requires at least a daily **mark to market** (MTM) valuation of all futures positions.

1.4 Contango and Backwardation

In markets where there is a net cost of carry in holding the asset to delivery, futures prices are higher than cash prices, and the market is said to be in contango, ie, a **contango** market.

For equity futures, the cost of carry very much depends on the specific share, based on its dividend yield compared to the level of current interest rates.

In markets where there is a net benefit in holding the asset to delivery, futures prices are lower than cash prices, and the market is said to be in **backwardation**, ie, a backwardation market.

Backwardation is most common in both the bond and short-term interest rate (STIR) markets when long-term interest rates are higher than short-term rates. Backwardation can also occur within commodities markets when there is a very steep premium for material available for immediate delivery, indicating a perception of a current shortage in the underlying commodity.

Example 4

The cash price of a bond is £110.50. The interest rate available on 30-day deposits is 0.25% pa and the bond yields 1.6% pa.

The fair value of a one-month future is:

Cash price	= £110.500
Finance costs £110.50 x (0.0025 – 0.016) x (1/12)	= –0.00124
Fair value	= £110.376

ie, the futures price is lower than the cash price.

Exercise 3

The approximate cash price of the notional long gilt is £104.30. The interest rate available on two-month deposits is 0.25% pa and the bond yields 1.5% pa. What is the fair value of the long gilt future with two months to expiry?

The answer can be found in the appendix at the end of this chapter.

1.5 Convergence

The cost of carry determines the differential between cash and futures prices and is the cost associated with holding the asset from now until expiry. It follows that, as the point of expiry approaches, the costs of carry diminish and the differential must narrow. At expiry, the cost of carry is zero, so the cash and futures prices must converge over the life of the future until they meet at expiry.

1.6 Basis

Learning Objective

4.1.4 Understand the importance of basis: behaviour at expiry; significance of changes; basis risk

Basis is a measure of the difference between cash and futures prices.

Basis = cash price – futures price

This is also sometimes referred to as crude basis.

The term basis can also be used to describe the difference between two futures prices (eg, March futures price versus June futures price).

In contango markets, the futures price is greater than the cash price, so the basis will be a negative number. Basis is negative in contango markets.

In backwardation markets, the futures price is less than the cash price, so the basis will be a positive number. Basis is positive in backwardation markets.

Because of convergence, in both types of market the basis must narrow to zero as the contract moves towards expiry.

In a perfect market, the basis should reflect the cost of carry and the future would always trade at its fair value. However, as markets are not perfect, the actual difference between two prices will be influenced by short-term supply and demand pressures. It is unlikely that the future will be trading exactly at its fair value at any moment in time. Basis can change as a result of changes:

- in supply and demand
- to the cost of carry, eg, interest rates, insurance costs, dividend yields
- in time remaining to expiry (convergence).

Movements in basis can adversely impact hedging strategies, and correctly anticipating the changes in basis can provide trading opportunities.

1.6.1 Changes in Basis – Terminology

Strengthening of Basis

When basis moves in a positive direction it is said to be strengthening. This is the expected situation in a contango market – as the future moves towards expiry, and the cash and futures prices converge, the basis becomes less negative. The strengthening basis narrows the gap in prices in a contango market, as price differentials become less significant. This is shown in the following illustration:

	March futures price	June futures price	Basis
Today	417	433	–16
Tomorrow	410	420	–10

In contrast, a strengthening of basis in a backwardation market results in a widening gap between the two prices. This is because basis is already a positive number and any movement in a positive direction will increase the difference between the two prices. This is shown in the following illustration:

	March futures price	June futures price	Basis
Today	110.15	110.02	+0.13
Tomorrow	111.00	110.75	+0.25

Weakening of Basis

When basis moves in a negative direction, it is said to be weakening. A weakening of basis in a contango market widens the gap in prices, with the negative price differential increasing. This is shown in the following illustration:

	March futures price	June futures price	Basis
Today	417	433	–16
Tomorrow	410	429	–19

A weakening of basis in a backwardation market narrows the gap between prices because the positive basis moves in a negative direction to become less positive. This is shown in the following illustration:

	March futures price	June futures price	Basis
Today	110.15	110.02	+0.13
Tomorrow	111.00	110.92	+0.08

In summary, due to the convergence of futures and cash prices as a contract nears maturity, the following is expected:

- In **contango** markets (eg, equity index), the basis **strengthens** towards expiry.
- In **backwardation** markets (eg, STIR and bond futures), the basis **weakens** towards expiry.

1.6.2 Changes in Basis – The Trades

Whenever the basis is expected to strengthen (irrespective of whether the market is in contango or backwardation), a trader should buy the spread. This involves buying the near-dated instrument and simultaneously selling the far-dated instrument, eg, buy March future and sell June future.

This is shown in the following example:

Example 5

Assume that a trader is anticipating a strengthening of basis between the March and June FTSE 100 futures. At present, March is trading at 6950 and June is trading at 6960 – a basis of minus 10. The trader buys the spread by buying 500 March FTSE 100 futures and simultaneously selling 500 June FTSE 100 futures. Two days later, the basis has strengthened, with the March FTSE 100 still trading at 6950 and the June contract trading at 6958. The trader closes out his positions.

The outcome:

March FTSE 100 contracts	bought 500 at	6950
	sold 500 at	6950
	result = no gain/loss	
June FTSE 100 contracts	sold 500 at	6960
	bought 500 at	6958
	result = gain of 2 index points	

Overall gain 2 points x £10 per point x 500 contracts = £10,000.

Whenever the basis is expected to weaken (irrespective of whether the market is in contango or backwardation), a trader should sell the spread. This involves selling the near-dated instrument and simultaneously buying the far-dated instrument, eg, sell March future and buy June future.

Example 6

Currently the March futures price is 417 and the June futures price is 433. A trader expects a weakening of basis over the next week. He sells the spread today. The following week, the March future is still trading at 417, while the June future is trading at 439. The price difference has widened, so the trader's anticipated weakening of basis was correct. The outcome is as follows:

March futures	sold at	417
a week later	purchased at	417
	no gain/loss	0
June futures	bought at	433
a week later	sold at	439
	gain	6

Overall gain = 6 = the amount of the change in basis.

1.6.3 Summary of Basis Changes and Trades

Market	Gap	Basis	Action
Contango	Narrowing	Strengthening	Buy the spread
Contango	Widening	Weakening	Sell the spread
Backwardation	Narrowing	Weakening	Sell the spread
Backwardation	Widening	Strengthening	Buy the spread

1.6.4 Basis Risk

Basis risk is defined as the risk that a futures price will move differently to that of its underlying asset.

There is a number of reasons why a futures price differs from that of its underlying asset. But there is a relationship between the two, which means that a futures price should broadly follow the price movements of its underlying asset. Further, the difference between the two should become less as the future approaches its expiration (convergence).

Other factors can occasionally influence the futures price and have a lesser effect, if any, on the cash market, or vice versa. When this happens, the basis will change. However, this basis risk is significantly less than the risk associated with price changes of the underlying asset.

The only foolproof method of eliminating basis risk would be to hold a futures contract to its expiration. At expiry, the futures price and the cash price will converge.

1.7 Arbitrage Trades

Learning Objective

4.1.5 Understand the principles of cash/futures arbitrage: what should be included in arbitrage calculations; cash and carry arbitrage; when arbitrage opportunities exist; arbitrage possibilities; arbitrage risk

The term arbitrage refers to a trader's attempt to profit by exploiting price differentials between identical, or similar, financial instruments that are trading on different markets, or in different forms. The examples considered above, of buying or selling the spread, could be described as arbitrage trades because they attempt to exploit pricing differentials between futures on the same underlying asset with different maturities.

However, there is also the potential to arbitrage mispricings between the underlying (cash) instrument and the futures available on that instrument. Such arbitrage opportunities exist when the future is not trading at its fair value.

The following two subsections (1.7.1 and 1.7.2) consider firstly how to arbitrage when a future is above its fair value and, secondly, how to arbitrage when a future is trading below its fair value.

1.7.1 Cash and Carry Arbitrage

If the future is currently trading above its fair value it means that it is expensive relative to the price of the underlying asset.

The appropriate arbitrage trade is to buy the relatively cheap underlying asset and simultaneously sell a future. This is known as a cash and carry trade because the underlying cash asset is carried to satisfy the sale of the future. This is illustrated in the following example:

Example 7

Current cash price	Fair value for future	Current futures price
1450	1485	1497

The trader buys the underlying for 1450. He incurs a further 35 in costs of carry over the period, giving an effective buying price of 1485. However, by selling the future, the trader is guaranteed a selling price of 1497, thus locking in a profit of 12.

The trader can either hold the position to expiry and realise the profit of 12, or wait for an opportunity to close out before expiry if the basis changes earlier.

1.7.2 Reverse Cash and Carry Arbitrage

If the future is currently trading below its fair value it means that it is cheap relative to the price of the underlying asset.

The appropriate arbitrage trade to exploit this mispricing is to sell the relatively expensive underlying cash asset and to buy the relatively cheap future. This is known as a reverse cash and carry trade. A reverse cash and carry trade is illustrated in the following example:

Example 8

Current cash price	Fair value for future	Current futures price
1450	1485	1477

The trader sells the underlying for 1450, releases funds which can be placed on interest and saves storage costs over the period. This gives an effective selling price of 1485. However, by buying the future, the trader is guaranteed a buying price of 1477, thus locking in a profit of 8.

The trader can either hold the position to expiry and realise the profit of 8, or wait for an opportunity to close out before expiry if the basis changes earlier.

1.7.3 The Arbitrage Channel

In the examples above, the fact that trading incurs expenses by way of commissions and fees, as well as bid and offer spreads, has not been considered. The effect of these trading costs is to make arbitrage unprofitable if they outweigh the achievable arbitrage profits.

Therefore, the futures price can move away from its fair value without there being any arbitrage activity, as long as the movement is less than the trading costs that would be incurred. This creates what is referred to as an arbitrage channel – the range of prices within which there will be no possibility to arbitrage owing to transaction costs outweighing any potential benefits.

If, however, the futures price moves beyond the limits of the channel, arbitrage becomes profitable. The arbitrage activity forces the futures price back into the channel and ensures that the futures price does not move too far away from fair value. This explains the strong correlation between cash and futures prices.

The Arbitrage Channel

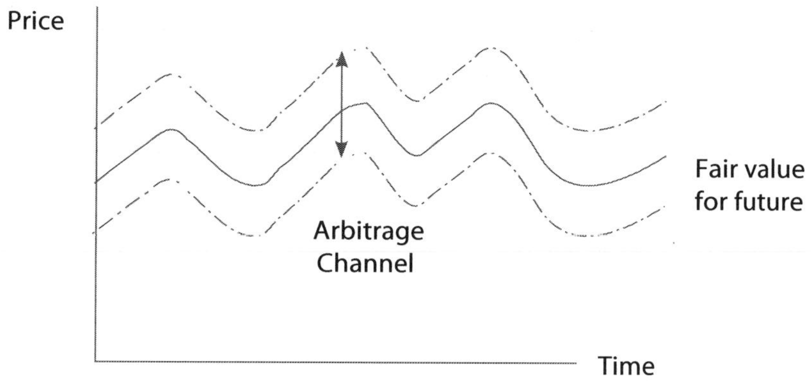

1.8 Hedging and Basis Risk

An unhedged position is at risk from changes in the price of the asset held. Futures can be used to offset this risk, with the underlying cash position being mirrored by an opposite position in the futures market.

Although the cash and futures prices are strongly correlated, there is, as we have seen, some flexibility in that relationship. Basis changes will affect the performance of the hedge.

The future might not have been trading at its fair value at the time the hedge was undertaken. This will, in time, be rectified by market pressure or convergence, and will therefore lead to some profits/losses on the hedge.

Basis might have changed from the time the hedge was placed to the time it was offset, thus resulting in profits/losses on the hedge. The hedge might over- or underperform due to changes in basis. However, the risk of significant underperformance is small because arbitrage will keep the futures price close to its fair value.

2. Options Pricing

Learning Objective

4.2.1 Understand the factors of options pricing: option premium; time value; intrinsic value; what affects time and intrinsic values; in-the-money, out-of-the-money and at-the-money

Unlike a futures contract, where both parties enter into an obligation to deliver the asset (for the seller) or agreed sum (for the buyer), an options contract allows one of the counterparties a choice – the holder has the right to exercise the option, but not the obligation. The writer is obliged to meet the delivery obligations if the option is exercised.

Clearly, the writer requires compensation to take on the risk and the holder is willing to pay for the flexibility that the option allows. This payment takes the form of a premium.

2.1 The Premium

The premium is the price of the option – the price paid. The level of the premium is determined by buyers and sellers trading in the market and is the cost of the option. Option buyers must pay the agreed premium to the option sellers. It is non-returnable.

There are a number of factors that determine the level of the premium. Changes in these factors will result in a change in the option's premium.

The two most obvious factors are the strike (or exercise) price and the time to run until the option expires. These are illustrated in the following example:

Example 9

ABC plc shares are currently trading at 550, and the following call options are available, conferring the right to buy at the various strike prices:

Strike price	Premium for March expiry	Premium for April expiry
500 call	70	85
525 call	49	61
550 call	37	46
575 call	25	39
600 call	19	28

The various strikes and expiries have different premiums reflecting the risks involved in holding/selling those options. The longer-dated expiries are more expensive than the near months, and the lower strike price options have higher premiums.

The premium is made up of two broad elements: intrinsic value and **time value**:

Premium (PM) = intrinsic value (IV) + time value (TV)

2.1.1 Intrinsic Value (IV)

The intrinsic value (IV) of an option is the difference between the strike price and the underlying asset's price. Call options have IV when the strike is lower than the underlying asset price. Put options possess IV if the strike is greater than the underlying's cash price. IV can never be negative; it is either positive or zero.

There has to be some IV for an option to be worth exercising. An option with zero IV is not worth exercising at expiry. IV can also be thought of as the minimum value that an option can have. An option either has or does not have IV. From the above example, for ABC plc the 500 calls have an IV of 50p – they must be worth at least 50p because they enable 550p shares to be purchased at 500p.

In the above example, both the 500 and 525 strikes have IV. If the price remained at 550p at expiry, holders of both those options would exercise them because they allow the holders to buy the asset at a cheaper price than the current market price.

All options that have IV at expiry will be exercised. As the premium is not refundable, the amount paid for the option is not a factor in determining whether to exercise. The holder will realise any IV that will then be used to offset the cost of the premium. If the IV is greater than the premium paid, the holder will make a net profit and the writer will make a net loss.

An option with IV is described as being in-the-money (ITM). An option with no IV is described as being out-of-the-money (OTM). An option with an exercise price that equals, or is close to, the underlying asset price is described as being at-the-money (ATM). Sometimes options that are significantly ITM are described as deep in-the-money options. Similarly, options that are significantly OTM are described as far out-of-the-money options.

Exercise 4

Here is a summary of the terms for a call option:

Status of a call option	Definition
In-the-money	Market price > exercise price
At-the-money	Market price = exercise price
Out-of-the-money	Market price < exercise price
Break-even point	Market price = exercise price + premium

Try to complete the same table for a put option:

Status of a put option	Definition
In-the-money	
At-the-money	
Out-of-the-money	
Break-even point	

The answers can be found in the appendix at the end of this chapter.

2.1.2 Time Value (TV)

In the ABC plc example, the 550, 575 and 600 strikes have no IV, yet a premium still has to be paid. The 500 and 525 strikes have IV, but the premium exceeds the IV.

The time value (TV) is simply the excess above the option's IV, ie, the difference between the premium and IV:

$$TV = PM - IV$$

Why should an option buyer pay more than its IV? The answer is simply that the price of the underlying can move during the lifetime of the option. There is always a possibility that the price can move beyond any given levels by the time of expiry, resulting in potential profits, or losses, for traders. The TV reflects the possibility, or probability, that the price can move beyond any given strike, thus making it worth exercising, and is the price paid for that uncertainty.

The following example illustrates the IV and TV of ABC plc options.

Example 10

ABC plc's current share price is 550p. The premium for March options, and their IV and TV, are as follows:

Strike	Call PM	Call IV	Call TV	Put PM	Put IV	Put TV
500	70	50	20	18	0	18
525	49	25	24	23	0	23
550	37	0	37	35	0	35
575	25	0	25	47	25	22
600	19	0	19	67	50	17

The call IV is the share price minus the strike, and the balance is the TV.

The put IV is the strike minus the share price, and the balance is the TV.

Exercise 5

If a call option has a strike price of 234p, the current price of the underlying share is 256p and the option premium is 40p, calculate the IV and, thus, the TV of the option.

The answers can be found in the appendix at the end of this chapter.

2.1.3 Main Determinants of an Option's Premium

Learning Objective

4.2.2 Understand the factors determining option premiums: volatility; interest rates; strike or exercise price; time to expiry; underlying asset price; dividends/coupons

The two elements that make up the option premium are IV and TV. The IV can be determined quite simply: the difference between the underlying price and the strike price for ITM options, or zero for OTM options. The price of the underlying asset is a major influence because it determines the amount of IV.

The TV can be calculated as that part of the option's premium that is not IV. So, the TV reflects the uncertainty (probability) of an option being exercised. But who or what determines how much TV there should be at any moment?

There are three major factors that determine the amount of TV – all of them are to do with uncertainty. The greater the uncertainty, the greater the TV.

1. Time to Expiry

A longer-dated option will have more TV than a near-dated one with the same strike. The price of the underlying can move over a greater range in one year than in one week. This means that there is more uncertainty associated with an option with one year to expiry, so the TV will be greater. Looked at another way, the holder has more time for the option to work in their favour and will be prepared to pay more, while the writer is at risk for a longer time and will need to be paid more for that risk.

If an option with one year to expiry must have more TV than one with one week to expiry, it stands to reason that the TV in an option gradually leaks away as expiry approaches (traders usually talk about the erosion of time value, or time decay). As expiry approaches, there is generally less uncertainty about whether a particular option will be worth exercising. On expiry, there is no uncertainty left. At that stage, either the option will be exercised, or it will not. If the option is OTM at expiry, IV=0 and TV=0, then it will not be exercised. If it is ITM, the holder will exercise to realise the IV, and there is no possibility of making any more, so TV=0.

The rate at which the TV erodes over the life of the option is not linear (see graph below). The erosion speeds up as expiry approaches.

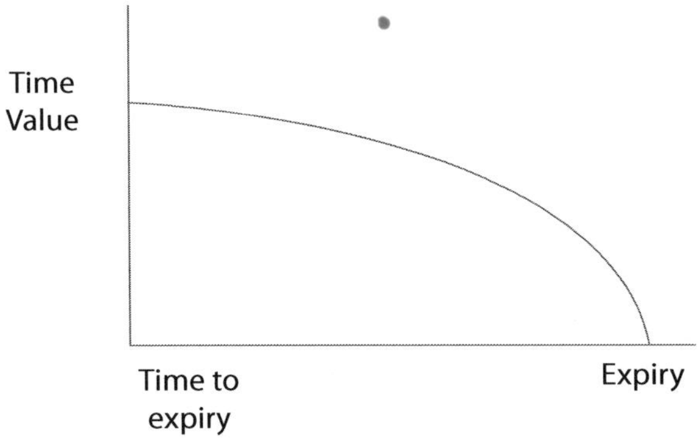

Erosion of TV works against the holder. If an investor buys an option today, and other factors (such as the underlying price and volatility) remain constant, it will be worth less next week. If the investor closed next week, they would crystallise a loss. Erosion must, therefore, work in favour of the writer. Providing that other factors remain constant, an option writer could sell an option today and close out next week at a lower price, crystallising a profit.

2. The Distance Between the Strike and the Underlying

Remember that the TV reflects the uncertainty about whether an option is likely to be exercised on expiry.

- **ITM options** (especially deep ITM options) have a high probability of exercise. There is less uncertainty about the outcome, so there is less TV.
- **OTM options** (especially far OTM options) have a high probability of being abandoned. There is less uncertainty about the outcome, so there is less TV.
- **ATM options** must, therefore, **have the highest amount of TV** because that is the strike where most of the **uncertainty exists.**

3. Volatility

The more volatile the price of an asset, the greater the uncertainty, so the higher the TV and, hence, the premium. If the price of an asset is prone to large movements, holders have a higher chance of making a profit and writers are at greater risk. Volatility, therefore, has a major impact on the option premium because of its effect on the TV and the price of an option.

However, there are three types of volatility to be considered:

1. **Historic volatility** – this represents how volatile the asset has been in the past, and can be measured accurately because we know what the price movements have been. It is only of limited value in pricing an option, because there is no guarantee that the same volatility will prevail in the future.
2. **Future volatility** – in pricing an option, or deciding whether an option is worth buying or selling, it would be incredibly useful to know what the volatility of the asset was going to be. Unfortunately, nobody can predict future volatility perfectly.
3. **Implied volatility** – as it is impossible to predict future volatility, traders must effectively take a view on it. This is implicit when options are traded. If volatility is a component of an options premium, by buying and selling options, the market forms a collective view about what is likely to happen in the future.

The actual figure for implied volatility is derived from options pricing models. Perhaps the best known of these is the Black-Scholes model, named after its authors, Fischer Black and Myron Scholes, two American economists who created the algorithm in 1973. Inputs such as volatility, strike price, underlying price, time to expiry and cost of carry are needed by pricing models in order to compute the premium. If the current option premium is known, the volatility figure can be adjusted (the others being fixed at any moment in time) until the premium calculated by the model is the same as the current price in the market. In other words, by working backwards through the model, it is possible to calculate the volatility implied by the premium.

Different option pricing models are better suited to differing requirements. For example, the Black-Scholes model can only be used to price European exercise options. Another, known as the binomial pricing model, is more appropriate for pricing American-style options.

A third type of pricing model is the Stochastic Alpha, Beta, Rho (SABR) pricing model, which is based upon a different premise, one that uses different levels of implied volatility to price options on the same underlying asset. Its pricing basis is the volatility smile, which states that the implied volatility (the one that is used to price an option) is greater for options with strike prices that are well ITM and very much OTM. That is when the option's strike price is very different from the underlying asset's cash price.

Adjustments to models will also need to be made to take into account the differences between options on futures and options based upon actual underlying assets, and to take into account dividends when addressing equity-based assets.

2.1.4 Other Factors Determining the Option Premium

For some types of options, the prices of calls and puts are affected by interest rates and dividend yields.

An example of an option on a physical would be an option on an individual company's shares. If the interest rate rises, the buyer of a call, who effectively keeps his money in the bank, earns more interest. The call writer, who has his money in the shares, is disadvantaged. It is only fair that writers should charge more if rates rise.

From this it is a simple step to see the impact of dividends. If dividends rise relative to interest rates then call writers can afford to charge slightly lower premiums.

For the writers of puts, who hold cash as cover, higher interest rates mean they can charge slightly lower premiums.

2.1.5 Summary: The Impact on Option Prices as Determinants Change

Now that we have seen the factors that affect the option premium, we can summarise the impact of a change in those factors on call and put premiums. The following table is a summary of how call and put prices change as the factors that affect the premium option vary:

Factor	Call premiums	Put premiums
Price of underlying rises	Rise	Fall
Time to expiry rises	Rise	Rise
Volatility rises	Rise	Rise
Exercise price rises	Fall	Rise
Interest rate rises:		
Options on physicals	Rise	Fall
Options on futures Note	Generally unchanged	Generally unchanged

Obviously, the opposite reaction applies to decreases!

Note: If interest rates rise, the cost of carry rises, impacting the futures price as well as the incentive to hold cash.

2.2 The Put/Call Parity Theorem

Learning Objective

4.2.3 Be able to calculate the put/call parity theorem: what is the put/call parity theorem; identifying arbitrage opportunities; risk-free interest rate

While there is no absolute fair value for an option's premium, there is a connection between the call and put premiums for the same strike on the same underlying asset. Call and put premiums must be fair in relation to one another (for any given price of the underlying), otherwise arbitrage opportunities present themselves.

The **put/call parity theorem** defines the relationship between call and put prices and the price of the underlying asset.

The following put/call parity formula applies to all options at expiry and to options on futures at all times:

$$C - P = S - K$$

where:

C	=	Call premium
P	=	Put premium
S	=	Underlying price (Spot or caSh price/futures price if the option is on a future)
K	=	StriKe price

Example 11

If the futures price is 100.95, the strike price is 100 and the call option on the future's premium is 1.07, the price of the put option on the future can be calculated:

C – P	=	S – K
1.07 – P	=	100.95 –100
1.07 – P	=	0.95
P	=	1.07 – 0.95
P	=	0.12

As long as three of the variables are known, the value of the missing variable can be calculated by simply rearranging the formula.

Exercise 6

If the futures price is 101.5, and the premium for a call with a strike of 110 is 12, what is the premium for a put with the same strike?

The answer can be found in the appendix at the end of this chapter.

For options on futures, the underlying asset is the future itself (the right to buy/sell a future on the asset). Costs of carry do not need to be taken into account because the futures price already includes them. However, the formula for put/call parity needs to be adjusted to take account of the costs of carry for options on the underlying asset when it is not a future or forward and therefore has a possible income flow (such as a share dividend or bond coupon payment) that is paid before the option expires.

The formula becomes:

$$\mathbf{C - P = S - \frac{K}{(1+ r)^\wedge t}}$$

where:
C, P, S and K are the same as above
r = annual risk-free interest rate
t = time to expiry (in years).

This is the formula used for individual equity options and equity index options.

Example 12

ABC plc's share price is 600. The put premium for the 500 strike is 7. The option expires in three months and risk-free interest rates are currently 6% pa.

The call premium for the 500 strike should be:

$$C - P = S - \frac{K}{(1+r)^\wedge t} \text{ where } r = 0.06 \text{ and } t = 0.25 \text{ years}$$

$$C - 7 = 600 - \frac{500}{(1 + 0.06)^\wedge 0.25}$$

$$C - 7 = 600 - \frac{500}{1.014674}$$

$C - 7 = 600 - 492.77$

$C - 7 = 107.23$

$C = 107.23 + 7$

$C = 114.23$

Note that at expiry t = 0, so the formula becomes C – P = S – K.

Exercise 7

If shares in XYZ plc are currently trading at 410p, and the premium for the 400p call option that expires in two months is 25p, what is the premium for the 400p put that expires at the same time? Interest rates are currently 3% pa.

The answer can be found in the appendix at the end of this chapter.

The above formulae are more accurate for European-style options than for American-style options. This is because American-style options have the added complication that they can be exercised early.

If the call and put premiums are not consistent with put/call parity, they are mispriced and arbitrage is possible. The key arbitrage trades are (assuming that the options are options on futures):

- **If the call is relatively cheap, buy the call, sell the put and sell the future**. The combination of buying the call and selling the put creates a synthetic long futures position. This is closed out by selling the future to lock in an arbitrage profit. This trade is termed a **reversal**.
- **If the put is relatively cheap, buy the put, sell the call and buy the future**. The combination of buying the put and selling the call creates a synthetic short futures position. This is closed out by buying the future to lock in an arbitrage profit. This trade is termed a **conversion**.

2.3 Delta (Δ)

Learning Objective

4.2.5 Be able to calculate the sensitivity of the option premium to changes in price by applying delta values to cumulative positions: what is delta; uses of delta

One of the factors which can change the premium during the lifetime of an option is movement in the price of the underlying. However, the premium does not always move by the same amount as the underlying asset.

The **delta** of an option is a measure of the sensitivity of the option's price to changes in the price of the underlying asset. Simplistically, it can be calculated by measuring the change in an option premium brought about by a small change in the price of the underlying. This would be done using option pricing models such as Black-Scholes.

$$\text{Simplistically, delta } (\Delta) = \frac{\text{change in option premium}}{\text{change in price of underlying}}$$

The delta will lie somewhere between 0 and 1. For example, if the change in price of the underlying was 20p, and perhaps the option increased by 12p, this would give a delta of 12/20 = 0.6.

A delta of 0 means that the premium is totally insensitive to small changes in the price of the asset. This will be the case for options that are far OTM.

A delta of 1 means that the premium will change by exactly the same monetary amount as the underlying. This will be the case for options that are deep ITM.

The sign of the delta enables us to distinguish between calls and puts:

- **Call deltas are positive** because the premium will rise when the price of the underlying rises.
- **Put deltas are negative** because the premium will fall when the price of the underlying rises.

Example 13

ABC plc's share price is 575. The 625 call has a delta of 0.30 and a premium of 26. The 525 put has a delta of –0.30 and a premium of 24.

If the share price rises to 585, using delta we can approximate the new call and put premiums.

The share price has risen by 10.

The delta of the call is 0.30, so the change in premium will be 10 x 0.3 = 3 (ie, the call premium will rise from 26 to 29).

The delta of the put is –0.30, so the change in premium will be 10 x (–0.30) = –3 (ie, the put premium will fall from 24 to 21).

As seen, the delta for a deep ITM call option will be +1, and for a deep ITM put will be –1.

The delta for a far OTM call or put will be zero.

Generally, an ATM option will have a delta of approximately 0.5, +0.5 for a call and –0.5 for a put.

Furthermore, the underlying physical asset and long futures will always have a delta of +1 and short futures will have a delta of –1.

As an out-of-the-money option approaches its expiration, its delta will approach zero. The longer to expiration, the slower the decline, but, as an option's expiry date gets closer, the change in delta will increase.

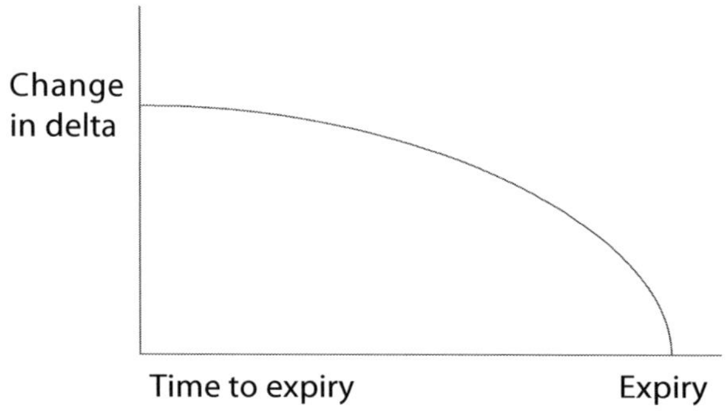

Summary of Deltas

Instrument	Delta
Physical asset or future of a deep ITM call	+1
ATM call	+0.5
Far OTM call or a far OTM put	0
ATM put	–0.5
Deep ITM put	–1

2.3.1 Delta Value of Cumulative Positions

Deltas can also be used to measure the sensitivity of a portfolio containing futures/underlyings, calls and puts. The delta calculated for a portfolio of positions is known as the cumulative delta.

In order to measure the cumulative delta of a combined portfolio, the deltas of the individual positions within it need to be added together. The cumulative delta gives the overall sensitivity and directional bias of a portfolio. The directional bias is obtained by taking account of long and short positions (+ for long and – for short).

This is best illustrated by looking at an example.

Example 14

Investor A is short an ATM put.

The net delta position is (–1) x (–0.5) = +0.5

This is arrived at by taking the number of positions (1) and assigning a negative to it because it is a short position. This –1 is then multiplied by the delta of an ATM put of –0.5.

The result is that if the price of the underlying rises by 10, Investor A's position improves by 5. The price of the put will have decreased, thus showing a profit on the trade. Obviously, a decrease in the underlying price will show a loss.

Example 15

Investor B is long five ITM calls with a delta of 0.7.

Investor B's net delta is (+5) x (+0.7) = +3.5

If the price of the underlying rises by 1, Investor B's position improves by 3.5. The price of each of the calls will have gone up by 0.7 and she has 5 of them.

Example 16

Investor C has the following portfolio on the same underlying:

Position	Delta	Comments
Long 10 futures	1.00	
Short 3 calls	+0.30	OTM call
Long 4 puts	–0.65	ITM call
Short 5 puts	–0.15	OTM put
Long 8 calls	0	Far OTM call

The cumulative delta is:

(+ 10)	x	(+1.00)	=	+10.00
(–3)	x	(+0.30)	=	–0.90
(+ 4)	x	(–0.65)	=	–2.60
(–5)	x	(–0.15)	=	+0.75
(+8)	x	(0)	=	0.00
				+7.25

A very **bullish** position – currently equivalent to being long over seven futures.

Cumulative deltas can be useful to gauge what is required to hedge a portfolio. A portfolio that has a cumulative delta of 0 is insensitive to price movements in the underlying asset – it is a hedged position, often referred to as delta neutral or delta hedged.

Taking Example 16 above, the cumulative delta was +7.25. In order to delta hedge, positions with a cumulative delta of –7.25 need to be added, eg, sell seven futures and buy a put with a delta of 0.25.

It is also useful to note that such delta hedging only hedges against price risk; other risks associated with time decay, volatility and basis still remain. Delta is also a dynamic measure so, as time passes, or the price of the underlying asset changes, the delta will change.

Exercise 8

You have the following position in the same underlying asset:

Short 4 futures
Short 3 ATM calls
Long 6 deep ITM puts

What is your cumulative delta?

The answer can be found in the appendix at the end of this chapter.

2.4 Other Greek Measures

Learning Objective

4.2.4 Understand the qualitative characteristics of the following Greeks and their uses: delta; gamma; theta; vega; rho

In addition to delta, which was explained in Section 2.3, there are several other Greeks measuring the relationship between an option's price and changes in the price of the underlying asset, as well as over time.

2.4.1 Gamma

Gamma is the measure of how delta changes (the rate of change of delta) with respect to movements in the price of the underlying. It is small when the option is either deep ITM, or far OTM. It is at its greatest when the option is ATM, especially when the option is close to expiry. Traders will monitor the impact of gamma on the premiums of options. Short-dated ATM options are more volatile than longer-dated ones, and these differences may present an opportunity for trading profits. Asset managers also use gamma in their dynamic hedging strategies. As stated in Section 2.3.1, a portfolio can be delta neutral. The delta will have to be monitored and perhaps rebalanced because of the impact of gamma on the portfolio delta.

Since gamma is the measure of changes in delta, it represents the required adjustments to any hedges associated with a single option's position or a portfolio of options. It represents the size of these adjustments.

For option holders, the changes in gamma usually correspond to profitable trades, ie, the required adjustments to the delta hedge of the underlying asset will result in a profit. For example, if an investor has a long position on a call option on an individual share, as the share's price rises, the option's delta will increase, as measured by gamma, and the investor will sell the adjustment or change to delta at a higher price. Therefore, when one has a long position in an option or a net long position in an option portfolio, one is said to have a positive gamma indicator, or simply, positive gamma. The opposite is true when one is an option writer or holds a net short option portfolio.

2.4.2 Vega

Vega is a measure of how a 1% change in implied volatility affects an option's price. Vega is always positive for long options positions – both calls and puts. It is greatest for ATM options. The further an option goes ITM or OTM, the smaller vega will become. Time increases the effect of changes in volatility upon an option's value. Therefore, vega is higher for long-dated options than short-dated options, and falls as an option approaches its expiration date. Vega can change even if there is no dramatic change in the movements of the underlying asset's price; it is affected by any change in expected volatility.

Vega is useful since it measures an option's or option portfolio's sensitivity to both market sentiment (expected volatility) and current market conditions. Many traders/investors use vega as the key measure of profitability of their options positions, since if they are delta neutral they are trading on an asset's volatility and not on a specific direction; therefore, vega tells them how well their positions are performing relative to current market conditions.

2.4.3 Theta

Theta is the measure of the rate of decline of an option's value due to the passage of time. Theta represents how much an option's value will change as one day passes and its underlying asset's price remains steady. Theta can also represent the time decay on the value of an option. If all other factors are held constant, an option will lose value as time moves closer to its maturity.

The measure of theta quantifies the risk that time imposes on options, since they have an expiration date and in most cases are only exercisable for a certain period of time. Time has importance for option traders on a conceptual level more than a practical one.

Theta and Option Positions

- **Long calls** and **long puts** always have **negative theta**.
- **Short calls** and **short puts** always have **positive theta**.

Theta is highest for ATM options and gradually decreases as an option moves further ITM or OTM.

Theta increases sharply as an option approaches its expiration and can severely undermine a long option holder's position, particularly if volatility is also decreasing at the same time. This is because theta is higher when either volatility is lower or there are fewer days to expiration.

Theta is used as a factor in combination with gamma and vega in determining trading strategies, since it represents the change in an option's fair value per day. As a percentage of an option's value, theta increases as expiration gets closer. Therefore, if vega is falling, a trader is more likely to sell an option that is a few days from expiration rather than one that is six months away.

2.4.4 Rho

Rho is the measure of changes in an option's value due to a change in interest rates. Rho measures how much an option's value will change from a 1% change in market interest rates. Rho is the least used of the Greek measures, since the relationship between an option's price and interest rates is fairly stable. Also, the chances that an option's value will change dramatically, due to a rise or fall in interest rates, are very low.

The impact of interest rates on an option's price is based on the cost of carry associated with holding the underlying asset relative to the option. The interest cost of buying the underlying asset is priced into the option's premium. While other Greek measures, such as delta, are 0.5 for an ATM option, rho is normally in the range of 0.04–0.02 for the same option.

An increase in interest rates will increase the value of calls and decrease the value of puts, while a drop in interest rates will have the opposite effect. The longer the time to expiration, the higher an option's rho. ATM and ITM options have relatively higher rho.

2.5 Premium Payment

Learning Objective

4.2.6 Know the requirements of, and process for, premium payment: when paid, immediately or marking to market; the roles of the clearing house and broker; what the seller receives

For the majority of options contracts, the buyer of the option is requested to pay the premium immediately. The seller of the option will receive the premium into their broker's account on the morning of the next business day.

At the point of trading, the seller's broker becomes liable for any margin required by the clearing house. This is collected when the market value of the underlying instrument moves against the seller (known as marking to market). Both the broker and the clearing house make the margin collection, with respect to the selling client and broker respectively. For example, if the MTM shows the option to be further ITM, the seller will need to deliver margin to their broker and on to the clearing house to represent the worsening of their position.

However, the margining of options positions is made more complex because some option premiums are payable futures-style. Such premiums are not payable immediately, but are paid during the life of the contract through margining. Certain financial options on ICE Futures and Euronext exchanges, such as bond and interest rate options, are futures-style.

The following table summarises the margin requirements for options positions:

Position	Initial margin	Variation margin
Equity Index and Single Stock Options		
Long positions	No	No
Short positions	Yes	No
Bond and STIR Options		
Long positions	No	Yes
Short positions	Yes	Yes

3. Open Outcry versus Screen Trading

In an open outcry market, the exchange floor is split into designated sections, traditionally known as pits, where individual futures or options products are traded.

Orders are initially received by a floor booth belonging to the broker and are transmitted to the trader in the pit. Traders stand in their pits and trading takes place face to face. To maintain price transparency, orders are shouted out (backed up by hand signals) so that all participants have an equal opportunity to trade.

In a screen-based market, orders are placed directly onto an electronic order book via traders' computer terminals. This obviously eliminates the need to have a trading floor. Orders will take their place in the relevant buy/sell queue (determined by price and time of placement) where they will await a matching transaction, or they will match against orders that are currently in the system. Depending on whether they are market or conditional orders, they may be executed immediately or remain stored in the queue. The order will move up or down the queue as a result of trading and the placing of other orders.

European exchanges are now generally screen-based, whereas open outcry floors still exist in the US; however, all the major American exchanges have adopted electronic trading in parallel with open outcry.

3.1 Trade Execution and the Nature of Orders

Learning Objective

4.3.1 Know the principles of order flow: how clients, brokers and exchange members are linked; electronic and open outcry markets; audit trail

4.3.2 Know the definition, significance of and differences between principal and agency orders (ie, of dual capacity versus agency orders): dealing as a principal; cross trading; advantages to the client

3.1.1 Principles of Order Flow

In a traditional open outcry system, customer orders specify:

- the asset
- whether it is a buy or sell order
- the size of order (number of contracts or lots)
- the expiry month, and
- price conditions (if any).

The order is passed by telephone or electronic means to the edge of the trading floor, where a booth clerk passes or signals it to the trader in the pit. Many pit traders execute orders for clients as well as for their own institution.

The details of any trade executed are then passed back by the trader to the clerk, who confirms back to their office and enters details of the trade onto a matching system; this allows trades to be matched with the floor counterparty so that any discrepancies can be resolved before the trades are registered at the clearing house.

For screen-traded systems (eg, CME Direct), order flow is more straightforward. Orders are input and then executed and reported by the system. There is no need to match trade details afterwards with a counterparty, as the trades are already matched when the order book links together a buyer and a seller.

3.1.2 Principal and Agency Functions

Exchange members can execute a trade in one of two capacities, either as principal or as agent.

Acting as principal means that the member is carrying out the trade on their own behalf and will be subject to profits and losses on those trades. In other words, when dealing as a principal, the member firm is dealing for its own account and therefore it will benefit from, and incur, any profits or losses from that position itself.

Acting as agent means that the firm is carrying out the trade on behalf of clients, ie, acting as broker. So an agency order is one arranged by a brokerage on behalf of its client. This may give the client the advantage of anonymity in the arranged transaction. The trade will be registered in a client account (see notes on trade registration in Section 4 of this chapter) and the client will be responsible to the member for profits/losses resulting from it.

The ability of the member to act as either principal or agent in any transaction is known as dual capacity. In other words, a member is allowed to trade for both its own account and execute its clients' orders. It is argued that clients benefit from this, since it allows the member firm to obtain better prices when executing market orders for clients, in addition to the extra insight that members can pass along as advice to clients. But some would argue that it also increases the possibility of a conflict of interest, when both client and member are looking to trade the same instrument at the same time.

Cross trading is when a brokerage firm matches a buy order of one customer against the sell order of another, when one is non-competitive (that is, the customer has not specified a specific price). On US exchanges, this practice is permissible only when executed in accordance with the Commodity Exchange Act, Commodity Futures Trading Commission (CFTC) regulations and the rules of the exchange. See Section 3.1.6 of this chapter.

3.1.3 Opening Trades

Opening trades create a position in the market and so incur rights or obligations. They are subject to profits/losses arising from subsequent price movements. They can be opening purchases or sales.

3.1.4 Closing Trades

Closing trades are trades that offset an existing long/short position (established through an opening purchase/sale) in the market. They extinguish any existing rights or obligations. A closing transaction is the point at which profits/losses on the contract are crystallised. They can be closing sales or purchases.

3.1.5 Volume and Open Interest

Both of these are measures of a derivatives contract's liquidity.

- **Volume** is usually reported for each product and its expiry month; it shows the cumulative number of contracts traded so far each day.
- **Open interest** shows the total number of contracts for any delivery month that remain open. Open positions are contracts that will either be closed out before expiry or taken to delivery. As most contracts will be closed out before expiry, it is an important indicator of the contract's liquidity.

NB: Open interest is the sum of all open long positions **or** the sum of all open short positions, **not** the sum of both.

3.1.6 Cross Trades

As noted in Section 3.1.2 of this chapter, a member of an exchange is said to have dual capacity if they are able to trade as a principal and arrange trades as an agent. This dual capacity will enable the member to enter into cross trades, sometimes referred to as matching orders. A cross trade is a situation where the member:

- has a buyer and a seller for the contract at a given price, or
- is willing to deal with a client as principal.

The member can effectively conduct the transaction without taking the trade into the market. However, for the purposes of price transparency and to allow other traders the opportunity to trade at the given price, the order needs to be executed within the market.

There are strict rules that need to be adhered to prior to the exchange accepting a cross order; for example, in an open outcry market, cross trades must be verified and signed off by exchange officials (pit observers) when the order is executed. An exchange's rules will state whether cross trades are permitted and what reporting conditions apply.

3.1.7 Audit Trail

An audit trail is a record of a transaction. To assist in the resolution of disputes and to promote confidence in an exchange, it is important to be able to trace a trade from start to finish and vice versa.

As a result of the increase in screen-based and electronic trading/orders, most exchanges now require that their members have an Order Audit Trail System (OATS) in place that is able to track all orders and ensure a clear resolution of any disputes.

3.2 Order Types

Learning Objective

4.3.3 Understand the range of types of orders, their uses and effects: market order; limit order; market if touched order; opening and closing orders; good 'til cancelled; immediate or cancel/ fill or kill order; stop order; stop limit order

While particular exchange systems have specific names for the types of orders they accept, the following types of order are typical of those placed in derivatives markets.

They can be used on their own or combined with others as appropriate.

- **Market Order** – this is an order to buy/sell immediately. It does not stipulate a price and will be executed at the best price currently available in the market. A buy order will **hit** the ask price, a sell order will **hit** the bid. A market order is used when certainty of execution is a priority over price of execution.
- **Limit Order** – such an order stipulates a required price level. If the trade can be executed at a better price than stated, the client will be **filled** at the improved price. The broker is not allowed to take the difference. Execution is not guaranteed, as the market may not reach the required price.
- **Spread Order** – the simultaneous purchase and sale of futures or options is executed for a specified price difference.
- **Scale Order** – a **stepped** order when a gradual entry/exit from a position is needed.
- **Market if Touched (MIT)** – a combination of a limit order and a market order. Initially, the trade specifies a limit. If the market trades at or through the price, the order becomes a market order and will be executed at the best prevailing price.
- **Opening Order** – an order, with or without a stipulated price, which is to be executed during the official opening period of the market, usually the first two minutes of trading. If the order cannot be filled during that period, it is cancelled.
- **Closing Order** – as above, but executed towards the end of the day.
- **Limit or Market on Close (MOC)** – will be executed at the stipulated price during the day, or else it will be executed at the best available price towards the end of the day, usually within the last five or ten minutes of trading. It is guaranteed to be filled.

- **Stop (Loss) Order** – this is designed to limit trading losses. A stop is primarily used to close out a position if the price moves against the trader. The stop is triggered when the market trades at the stipulated price. However, there is no guarantee that the order will be filled at the stop price. In volatile markets it may not be possible to obtain that price, so it can be filled at any price once it is triggered.
- **Stop Limit Order** – as above, but this order stipulates two prices within which the stop order operates. Once the stop price is reached, a stop limit order becomes a limit order that will be executed at a specified price (or better).
- **Guaranteed Stop** – a facility offered by some brokers that guarantees the stop price to a client (perhaps the firm is willing to take the position at that price). The broker will probably charge more for this service.
- **Good 'til Cancelled (GTC)** – this is really an instruction accompanying an order and defines the period of validity for the order. A GTC order is firm until the client specifies otherwise. In the real world, most orders are **Good For the Day (GFD)** and will be cancelled if the order remains unfilled at the close of trading.
- **Fill or Kill (FOK)** – this means execute the whole quantity of the order if market conditions permit, otherwise cancel the whole order if the former cannot be achieved. They are often referred to as **immediate or cancel** orders.
- **Day Order** – an order to buy or sell a security that automatically expires if not executed on the day the order was placed. A day order is an order that is good for that trading day only.

When brokers enter client orders they will occasionally make mistakes. Some exchanges allow members to correct genuine mistakes by requiring the brokerage firm to submit a correction declaration. Depending on the exchange's policy and rules, the erroneous trade may possibly be reversed. The exchange will check to ensure that the client is not disadvantaged.

4. Trade Registration

Learning Objective

4.4.1 Know the processes involved in trade registration, trade input and trade matching and differing requirements of electronic and open outcry markets

Once a deal has taken place, the position needs to be allocated to the relevant account. The trade may have been executed for the firm itself (and may, therefore, be allocated to the firm's principal account), or on behalf of a client (and may, therefore, be allocated to a client account).

The details of the trade will be reported into the administration system that is used by the exchange, such as CME Direct for the CME Group or, in the case of the Dubai Mercantile Exchange (DME), its DME Direct system. These systems will ensure that the trade inputs are matched; in other words, that both a purchase and a sale exist on the same terms. This process is particularly important when the exchange uses open outcry, where there is scope for more human error than in an electronic order matching system.

4.1 Client Accounts

Learning Objective

4.4.3 Understand the use of different types of accounts: use of house accounts; customer accounts – segregated and non-segregated

As mentioned in Section 3.1.2 of this chapter, trades may be executed by the firm for itself or on behalf of a client. As a result of this, the trades will be assigned to one of three types of account:

1. **House** – for all proprietary trades of the clearing member.
2. **Segregated** – for trades that the member firm is registering on behalf of a segregated client. In the event of the member firm's default, these positions will be protected against having to meet the defaulting firm's liability.
3. **Non-segregated** – client trades that are not segregated and therefore are not protected in the event of the firm's default.

Note that most exchanges and major market regulators require their member firms to ensure that all client assets are placed in segregated accounts. The client benefits from such accounts in that, should the member firm have financial problems, their funds will be protected and can only be used to meet their commitments. Member firms cannot use funds from segregated accounts to meet any of their own, or other, client margin or other financial commitments.

The decision as to whether to use a non-segregated account, when permitted by the exchange or market regulators, is the client's and not the member firm's.

4.2 Pre-Registration/Allocations/Give-Ups

Learning Objective

4.4.2 Understand the purpose and importance of give-ups/allocations: reasons to allocate a trade to an account; use of give-up agreements; risk implications

Pre-registration involves a member firm indicating that a deal it is doing should be allocated or 'given-up' to a second member. This is also described as an **allocation**.

Give-ups are the sending of a trade to another member of the exchange. The member to whom the trade is given up is said to be performing a give-in.

Both of the parties to an allocated transaction run the risk that the other will not fulfil its obligations. A give-up trade is allocated to the give-in on Euronext; this is done by the Universal Clearing Platform (UCP).

Give-up trades are mainly performed in order to separate the execution and the clearing function. Hence, a customer might wish to trade (execute) through one exchange member but state that the trade should be given up to the customer's usual clearing broker. This keeps one clearing relationship between the customer and the clearing broker. In addition, give-ups are sometimes undertaken because of shortages of trading staff at a give-in firm, or to preserve anonymity where a give-up firm is helping another member build up a position.

Example 17

Member firm ABC executes, confirms and matches a trade which it pre-registers, notifying the system that the trade should be allocated to another member firm (DEF).

ABC gives-up the trade to DEF. In turn, DEF will claim the trade, which will be registered to DEF as a house, segregated or non-segregated transaction.

Appendix

Answers to Exercise 1

The fair value of a future with 45 days to delivery will be:

Cash price		£750.00
Finance	£750 x 0.03 x (45/365)	2.77
Storage	£750 x 0.005 x (45/365)	0.46
Fair value		£753.23

Answer to Exercise 2

The fair value of the FTSE 100 future with 91 days to delivery will be:

Cash index = 6990

Interest rate = 0.8%

Dividend yield = 3.6%

Fair value = cash price x interest rate (1 + (0.008 x (91/365))) – dividend points (see below).

Dividend yield conversion: FTSE 100 dividend yield = 3.6%

Conversion to dividend points = 6990 x 0.036	= 251.6
	= 251.6 points per year x (91/365) = 62.74 points
Fair value of the future = 7003.94 – 62.74	= 6941.20

Answer to Exercise 3

Cash price	=	£104.30
Finance costs £104.30 x (0.0025 – 0.015) x (2/12)	=	(0.22)
Fair value	=	£104.08

Answer to Exercise 4

Status of a put option	Definition
ITM	Market price < exercise price
ATM	Market price = exercise price
OTM	Market price > exercise price
Break-even point	Market price = exercise price – premium

Answer to Exercise 5

The option allows the investor to buy a share at 234p that is currently trading at 256p. This is equivalent to saving 22p, and this is the IV.

Premium = IV + TV

Given the premium of 40p and the IV of 22p from above:

40p = 22p + TV

Rearranging this equation gives:

TV = 40p – 22p = 18p

Answer to Exercise 6

Using C – P = S – K

12 – P = 101.5 – 110

12 – P = –8.5

P = 12 + 8.5

P = 20.5

Answer to Exercise 7

The put premium can be found by solving the following equation:

$C - P = S - \frac{K}{(1+r)^t}$ where r = 0.03 and t = 2/12 or 0.16667 of a year

$25 - P = 410 - \frac{400}{(1+0.03)^{0.16667}}$

$25 - P = 410 - \frac{400}{1.004939}$

25 – P = 410 – 398.03

25 – P = 11.97

25 – 11.97 = P

P = 13.03

Answer to Exercise 8

				Δ
Short 4 futures	–4	x	1	–4
Short 3 ATM calls	–3	x	0.5	–1.5
Long 6 deep ITM puts	+6	x	–1	–6
Cumulative delta				–11.5

End of Chapter Questions

1. Name the main components of cost of carry.
   Answer reference: Section 1.2

2. What is the fair value of a future?
   Answer reference: Section 1.3

3. How do you calculate the fair value of a future?
   Answer reference: Section 1.3.1

4. What is contango?
   Answer reference: Section 1.4

5. What is the arbitrage channel?
   Answer reference: Section 1.7.3

6. In the options market, what is the premium?
   Answer reference: Section 2.1

7. Describe the order flow for screen-traded systems.
   Answer reference: Section 3.1.1

8. What is OATS?
   Answer reference: Section 3.1.7

9. Name the three types of client accounts.
   Answer reference: Section 4.1

10. What are give-ups?
    Answer reference: Section 4.2

Chapter Five

Principles of OTC Derivatives

This syllabus area will provide approximately 16 of the 100 examination questions

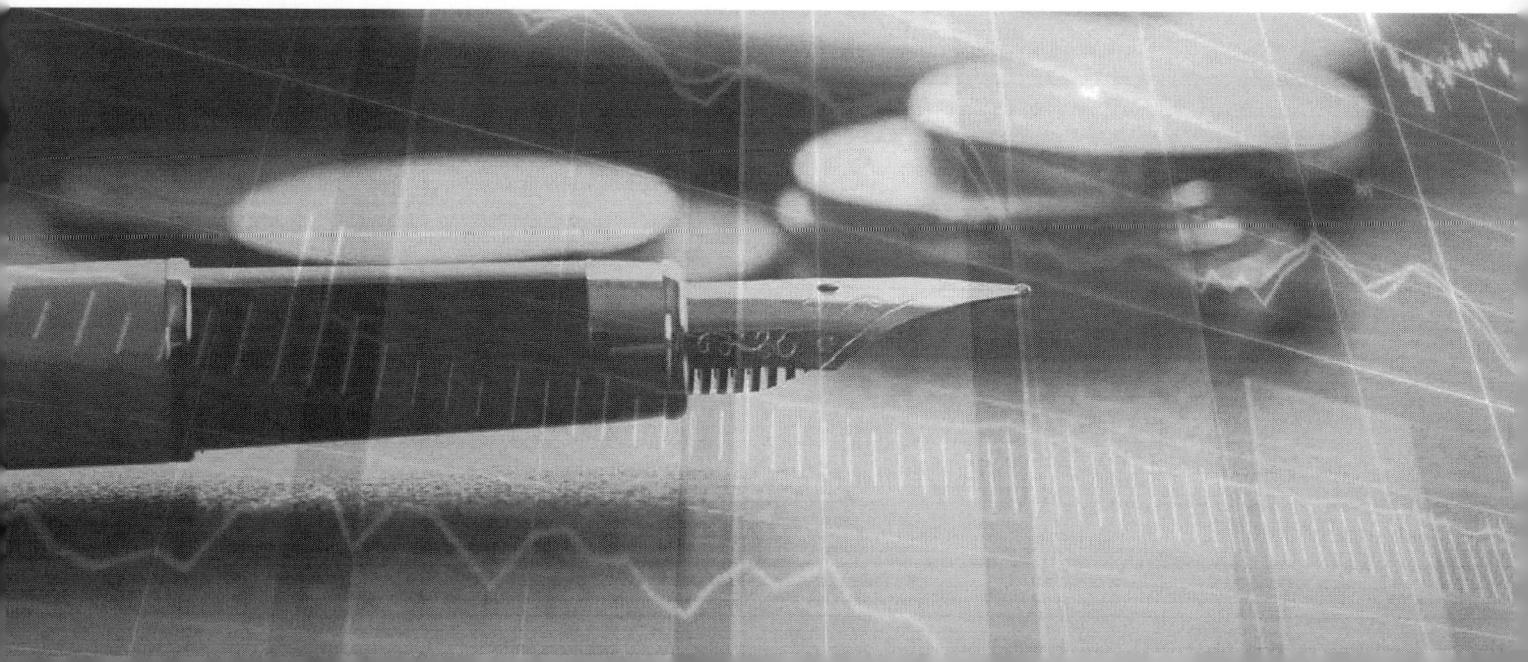

1. General Introduction

So far the focus has been on exchange-traded derivatives (ETDs) rather than over-the-counter (OTC) or off-exchange derivatives. OTC derivatives have been extremely popular for hedging, speculation and arbitrage, principally because their contracts are not standardised and therefore can be constructed around the unique needs of their users. This is despite the fact that a central counterparty (CCP) and trade reporting (TR) procedure have only recently been established for these contracts. The European Market Infrastructure Regulation (EMIR) (see Section 3.2 of Chapter 9 for more details of this) was created to provide greater stability in the European Union (EU) derivatives market.

Exchange-traded derivatives have standardised contract specifications that may not precisely meet the hedging or speculative needs of the investor. In the OTC market, the derivatives can be precisely tailored to the needs of the investor.

The OTC markets also provide confidentiality, in that the only market participants aware of the deals that have been completed are the two counterparties, plus anyone else they care to inform. By comparison, the exchange-traded derivatives markets are much more transparent, with the exchanges providing details of all prices and volumes traded in order to assist in the price formation process and to build confidence and liquidity.

The value of underlying instruments traded in the OTC markets is much larger than that traded on exchanges. Major OTC products include swaps and swaptions, **forward rate agreements (FRAs)**, **caps**, **floors**, **collars** and a range of credit derivatives.

2. Forwards and Contracts for Differences (CFDs)

Learning Objective

5.1.1 Understand the basic concepts and fundamental characteristics of: forwards, FRAs

5.3.1 Understand the mechanisms for OTC derivative pricing and the relationship with the underlying cash prices together with the significance of contributing factors: forward and forward/forward rates; cash flow analysis and the zero curve; the role of interest rates and yields; other factors affecting pricing

2.1 Forwards

A forward contract is an OTC transaction in which delivery of the commodity/asset is deferred until a date in the future that is specified in the contract. Although the delivery is made in the future, the price is determined on the initial trade date.

Forward contracts are traded on a wide variety of assets such as currencies, commodities and equities.

The forward price that is agreed by the buyer and seller is determined by a number of factors, such as the interest rate differential between the two currencies, in the case of an foreign exchange (FX) forward. For commodities, these factors will include the current interest rate, the cost of financing should the commodity be purchased today and storage costs. Equity forward prices take into account the differential between the current interest rate and the equity's dividend yield.

These factors are key to reducing arbitrage opportunities, in the same way as in futures prices.

Example 1

A French company has a series of future yen payments over the next 12 months and is concerned that the euro will weaken against the yen, thus making its materials more expensive. In order to lock in its cost now, the company can enter into a series of EUR/JPY forward contracts that will allow it to set the exchange rate today for its future payments. This is done through FX forwards contracts where the company buys yen against the euro, for specific future dates at rates that are agreed today.

Since this is an OTC transaction, the company can arrange the amounts and dates to match exactly the payments it has to make to its Japanese supplier. The forward contracts' rates will be based on the current FX spot rate and the interest rate differential between euros and yen. Since euro interest rates are slightly lower than yen rates over the period, the euro will be at a slight premium to the yen, thereby making it less expensive at that forward date.

Example 2

A food company is concerned that the forecasts of a drought will result in a significant reduction in this year's cocoa harvest. Since the company has several key production dates, exchange-traded cocoa futures are not an option. Therefore, it calls its broker and arranges a series of cocoa forward contracts, where it agrees to buy set amounts at set dates at prices agreed upon today. The cocoa forward's price will be determined by today's market price of a tonne of cocoa, plus any adjustment for storage costs and the current interest rate for the forward's duration.

Forwards are similar to futures contracts as they are legally binding agreements to make or take delivery of a specified quantity of a specific asset at a certain time in the future for a price that is agreed today. They are usually traded off-exchange (OTC) but can also be traded on-exchange, eg, the London Metal Exchange (LME) lists forward contracts. They may not be marked to market daily or, if they are, the resulting profits are not paid out until maturity, and any losses must be paid to the exchange clearing house and if they are cleared by an exchange's clearing house any losses must be paid to that clearing house. Forwards are, therefore, settled only on the delivery date.

Most forwards, however, are OTC contracts, usually with banks. Outright forwards are a common product traded in the FX market. Corporations, institutional investors and banks themselves use forwards to manage their FX transaction risks. If an organisation is importing or exporting goods (or investing) in another currency, it can use forwards to protect against adverse currency movements. Forward contracts are also used to lock in the price of physical commodities, such as energy, metals and foodstuffs (see Example 2 above).

In the physical markets, an airline might use forward prices on jet fuel to lock in one of its major costs. They will agree a price today for delivery in a future month.

Forwards are derivatives – the future price agreed for a forward is based on the spot price of the underlying asset; in the case of a currency it will be adjusted for the interest rates in the relevant currencies.

2.2 Contracts for Differences (CFDs)

Learning Objective

5.1.9 Understand how spread betting differs from other contracts for differences

5.1.11 Understand the basic concepts and fundamental characteristics of CFDs

Contracts for differences (CFDs) allow investors to benefit from the capital gains from a particular underlying index, stock, currency or commodity without having to actually physically own or pay for it. The investor enters into an agreement with a CFD provider – usually a stockbroker or a firm offering an online dealing service – to settle the difference between the opening price of a particular investment when the agreement is made and its price when the agreement is ended. The profit or loss is determined by the difference between the prices at which the investor buys and sells the contract and the contract amount. The investor can profit from predicting the correct movement in the underlying asset's price, either up or down, without having to buy or sell the actual asset.

The key difference between CFDs and more traditional trading is that CFDs do not buy or sell the underlying asset, but trade on its price movement.

Investors using CFDs have one key decision to make – do they think the underlying asset is going to go up or down? If they get it right, they will win; if they get it wrong, they will lose. The key feature of CFDs is that they do not have a set maturity and, since they are OTC contracts, the contract's specification ranges from the asset to the amount negotiated between the buyer and seller.

CFDs are cost-efficient, in that an investor buying a CFD on a share does not have to pay stamp duty, nor the broker's fee that is normally associated with share transactions. CFDs also allow investors who are **bearish** on a share an easier way to profit from the fall in a share's price, rather than physically going short a share.

CFDs are based on margin trading, so an investor can leverage their position. Most brokers require a margin deposit of 10–30% of the contract's value. This allows investors to increase their risk, based on the size of their initial investment. But many contracts include an automatic **stop-loss** order as part of the contract, which minimises the risk of a large loss. Most CFD trades are normally intra-day trades, since each time this type of position is held open overnight it incurs an interest charge.

CFDs do not have an expiry or maturity date like options or futures. As opposed to an expiry date, a CFD is effectively renewed/rolled over at the close of each trading day if desired. An investor can keep their position open indefinitely, as long as there is enough margin in their account to support the position.

Example 3

An investor is bearish on company ABC plc shares. They are currently trading at 145p. The investor decides to sell a CFD on 5,000 shares at that price. The investor's broker requires a 15% margin or £1,087.50.

5,000 x 145p = £7,250

£7,250.00 x 0.15 = £1,087.50

Just before closing, ABC's shares have fallen to 137p. The investor decides to end the CFD, realising a profit of £400.

5,000 x 137p = £6,850

£7,250 – £6,850 = £400

This is a return of 36.8% on the investment.

The two key differences between spread betting and CFDs are that the latter do not have a fixed maturity/expiration date and that spread betting in the UK is considered gambling and therefore is treated differently as far as tax is concerned, since CFDs are subject to capital gains tax.

3. Foreign Exchange (FX) Forwards and Swaps

Learning Objective

5.1.3 Understand the basic concepts and fundamental characteristics of FX and currency forwards, swaps and swaptions: FX forward (outright quotes verses pips); FX and currency swap/swaption

---

The FX spot market involves the exchange of two currencies very soon after the date of transaction. For most currency transactions in the wholesale market this is T+2.

The market is used by customers with a need to exchange one currency for another. This will often be because of an underlying transaction – for example, the import or export of goods or services, or the purchase or sale of investments.

Suppose that the GBP/USD spot rate is 1.2400/10.

The size of the spread between the bid price ($1.2400) and the ask or offer price ($1.2410) will depend on the size of the transaction and the importance of the customer relationship.

Small clients might face a spread wider than two cents. On deals with large corporates or in interbank transactions, the spread might be as low as five pips or 0.0005 of a dollar. A pip is the smallest price increment in a currency. It is similar to ticks in the futures markets. In the above example, in GBP/USD, a move from 1.2400 to1.2401 is one pip. Thus, for interbank deals, the GBP/USD spot prices might be quoted as 1.2400/05.

Spot FX facilities are provided by most commercial banks.

Remember that in FX, one currency is quoted in terms of another currency. Therefore, in the quote shown above, sterling is the base currency – the first currency quoted, by FX market convention is the base or action currency – while the dollar is being quoted in terms of sterling.

- **1.2400 is the bid for GBP** – this means that the quoting bank will buy sterling and sell dollars at this rate, since it is cheaper: £1,000,000 costs $1,240,000.
- **1.2405 is the offer for GBP** – here the quoting bank will sell sterling and buy dollars. At this rate, sterling is more expensive: £1,000,000 costs $1,240,500.

Note that in most cases the amounts traded are also based on set amounts of the base currency.

Take the case of a UK consultancy firm that has a contract in Europe and will be receiving payments in euros over the next six months. It might want to **lock in** the exchange rate for these payments now by entering into a forward contract. A forward contract is simply a deal between two participants to agree now the rate at which a certain amount of an international currency will be exchanged at some pre-agreed date in the future. These forward contract rates are quoted OTC by banks. The quotation is based on applying a margin to the spot quotes to arrive at a forward rate. Any FX contract that matures one day beyond the normal spot date (T+2) is considered a forward deal. For the major currencies, forwards, or outright forwards as they are known, can have maturities of five or ten years. But note that the longer the maturity, the less liquid the market.

Example 4

Spot GBP/EUR is	1.1700/1.1705
one month is	1.1680/1.6900
three months is	1.1630/1.1645
six months is	1.1605/1.1625

In the above example, the margin applied to the spot rate is a premium to the traded currency – EUR. A premium indicates that the base currency (sterling, in the above example) is becoming less expensive relative to the euro. As a result, the forward points are subtracted from the spot rate, so that in the forward deal the pound will buy less euros (the bid column), and the euro holder will have to pay less to get the same number of pounds (the ask column). Again the reason for this is based on the fact that sterling interest rates are higher than the corresponding euro interest rates.

When quoting forward points, it is the market convention that, when the forward points decrease, the bid increase is more than the offer's increase as in Example 4 above – the one-month forward points would be quoted as 20/15, then they would be subtracted from the spot rate. Remember, in this case, it indicates that the base currency, GBP, is at a discount and the traded currency, the euro, is at a premium, based on their interest rates.

When the forward points quote increases, the base currency is at a premium in the forward market and the points will then be added from the spot rate. This is described as a forward delivery premium.

The banks will calculate the necessary premium or discount considering the relevant short-term interest rates (STIRs) of the two currencies.

The key advantage of forward contracts is certainty.

As well as commercial users, the forward market is used extensively by speculators, eg, hedge funds and the proprietary trading desks at investment banks. Since forward rates are based on the interest rate differential between the two currencies, the FX forward market is used to speculate on expected changes in the difference between these two interest rates. This is done using FX swaps, which entail buying one currency spot and selling it at a future/forward date at the same time. Therefore, any movements in the forward points, which are based on the interest rate differential between the two currencies, will be the basis for any profits or losses on such a trade.

Speculators on the movements in spot rates mainly take spot or outright forward positions.

3.1 Interest Rate Parity

The forward rates of exchange are linked to the spot rate by applying a discount or premium. The factor that links spot rates is the relative interest rate between the two currencies.

The link between spot and forward rates is based on the principle of arbitrage. Put simply, if the forward rate quoted were not in line with relative interest rates, there would be an opportunity to make a guaranteed profit by borrowing funds and entering into a forward FX contract. This is the theory of interest rate parity.

The link between relative interest rates and the forward FX rate can be summarised as follows:

Higher interest rate currency = discount in the forward FX market
Lower interest rate currency = premium in the forward FX market

When calculating forward FX rates for periods of less than one year, we have to take into account the different day count conventions of the different currencies' money markets. For example, both the euro and dollar use an Actual/360 day count, while sterling uses Actual/365.

3.2 Currency Swaps

Currency swaps were one of the earliest types of swap. One of the first examples was between the World Bank and IBM in 1981. IBM wanted to borrow US dollars and the World Bank wanted to borrow Swiss francs and German marks. However, because the World Bank was already a frequent issuer of European currency debt and IBM was not, the rarity value meant IBM could borrow Swiss francs and German marks more cheaply. So, IBM borrowed Swiss francs and German marks, the World Bank borrowed US dollars and they entered into a swap – the result being that they both saved money on their borrowings.

Currency swaps have continued to develop. It is possible to enter into currency swaps that exchange:

- fixed interest in one currency for floating interest in another currency
- fixed interest in one currency for fixed interest in another currency, or
- floating interest in one currency for floating interest in another currency.

An illustration of the potential benefit of a currency swap is provided below:

Example 5

A UK company expects to receive a stream of US dollars over the next five years from exports. It needs to convert US dollars into sterling. Rather than use a series of separate forward FX transactions to achieve this, it could instead use a currency swap. The series of US dollar flows are considered as a package and, in the swap, the company agrees to pay these flows to a counterparty over the five years, in return for a series of sterling cash flows. This would be a fixed currency swap without principal exchanges. The UK company has protected itself against its UK income being eroded by exchange rate movements depreciating against the US dollars. Conversely, if exchange rates improve, it will see no benefit.

As seen in Example 5, the uses of currency swaps include potentially reducing the cost of borrowing and replacing future cash flows that are unpredictable (due to exchange rate movements) with predictable cash flows agreed in a swap.

4. Interest Rate Swaps and Swaptions

Learning Objective

5.1.1 Understand the basic concepts and fundamental characteristics of swaps

5.1.2 Understand the basic concepts and fundamental characteristics of interest rate swaps and swaptions: underlying (fixed/fixed, fixed/floating, floating/floating); interest calculation (compared to bond markets)

5.5.2 Know the common interest rate swap instruments and their relationships to other markets: inflation; amortising; accreting; rollercoaster; forward start

A swap is an OTC derivative where two counterparties exchange one stream of a cash flow against another. These payment streams are called the legs of the swap. The cash flows are calculated over a notional principal/asset amount.

For example, a straightforward interest rate swap (a so-called plain vanilla swap) involves one party exchanging a floating interest rate obligation for another party's fixed-rate obligation. The floating rate will be determined on the swap's reset date.

For example, for a fixed versus six-month floating swap, the reset date will be every six months. Once the floating rate is determined, the swap will start accruing interest as of its effective date.

The plain vanilla interest rate swap, based on an agreed notional principal sum, will specify a particular start date and run for a set period. The swap will specify particular periods at the end of which the cash flow exchanges will take place; this is known as the swap's payment date.

With the agreement of both parties, and after an evaluation or mark to market of the swap's value, either party can initiate action to cancel or end the swap after an agreed payment. When this happens, all calculations of **accrued interest** are based on the swap's termination date. This is the date that the swap officially ceases to exist.

For example, a three-year plain vanilla interest rate swap might be arranged with quarterly payments based on a principal sum of £6 million, effective from 1 January 2011, exchanging a fixed interest rate for a floating interest rate based on ICE LIBOR. The first payment under the swap will be at the end of March 2011, the second at the end of June 2011 and so on.

At each payment date, a net payment will be made between the two participants based on the difference between the floating rate (such as ICE LIBOR or the Fed Funds rate) and the fixed rate on the underlying principal sum for the quarter. If ICE LIBOR exceeds the fixed rate, the difference will be paid to the party that is due to receive ICE LIBOR and pay the fixed interest. The payments will be made in the opposite direction if ICE LIBOR is less than the fixed rate.

A swaption is an arrangement where a buyer pays an upfront sum for the right to enter into a swap agreement by a pre-agreed date in the future. In other words, the buyer of a swaption has the option to enter into a swap. The concept is the same as for options.

Large corporations and other institutions use these interest rate swaps and swaptions to manage risk and, potentially, take advantage of cheaper and more appropriate funding. The arrangements are facilitated by financial institutions. It is a wholesale market not open to the private investor.

As they are OTC instruments, swaps come in a variety of forms. In addition to fixed-for-floating swaps (as illustrated above), there are also floating for floating swaps, alternatively referred to as basis swaps. As well as these interest rate swaps that are based on a single currency, there are also currency swaps (where there is an exchange of currency, as well as interest; see Section 3.2 of this chapter) and equity index swaps.

In an equity swap (or index swap), two counterparties agree to exchange the return on an equity index, or a specified basket of shares, for a fixed or floating rate of interest. This enables the creation of a synthetic portfolio of shares without the need to buy all of the individual underlying shares and incur the transactions costs for doing so. See Section 6.10 of this chapter.

A fixed/floating swap (the plain vanilla swap described above) is also known as a coupon swap. An alternative is a floating/floating swap, known as a basis swap, in which each of the two payment streams is based on a floating rate.

For example, an organisation might pay three-month ICE LIBOR and receive six-month ICE LIBOR. A basis swap might also be a currency swap (see below) – for example, paying three-month ICE LIBOR in one currency and receiving six-month ICE LIBOR in another. The term basis swap, therefore, covers a range of possibilities.

For example:

- single-currency swap from one period ICE LIBOR to another period ICE LIBOR
- single-currency swap from ICE LIBOR to an overnight interest rate
- single-currency swap from ICE LIBOR to another interest rate, such as a commercial paper (CP) rate
- cross-currency swap from a floating rate in one currency to a floating rate in another currency.

5. Caps, Floors and Collars

Learning Objective

5.1.1 Understand the basic concepts and fundamental characteristics of: caps; floors; collars

Various OTC option-based products are offered by banks to their customers, some of which can be constructed from straightforward options. Caps, floors and collars are commonly employed with regard to interest rates.

- A **cap** is an option product which can be used to protect the cost of a floating-rate borrowing over a series of settlement periods. Suppose that a borrower has a five-year GBP loan which they roll over every three months at the three-month ICE LIBOR then current. They can buy a five-year cap which will put a maximum cost on each of the rollovers. Whenever the rollover rate exceeds the cap strike rate, they receive the difference. Suppose the strike rate on the cap is 1% and ICE LIBOR is set at 1.2%. Then, at the end of the three-month interest rate period, the purchaser of the cap will receive 0.2% accrued over the three-month period. Whenever the rollover rate is lower than the cap strike rate, nothing is paid or received. The settlement for a cap is paid at the end of the interest period, exactly as for a swap.
- **Floors** are options that enable the buyer to demand a minimum rate of interest paid on a deposit, regardless of a fall in the prevailing rate of interest. Floors can be used to protect the income on a floating-rate investment by putting a minimum return on each rollover. Whenever the rollover rate is lower than the floor strike rate, the buyer receives the difference. Whenever the rollover rate is higher than the floor strike rate, nothing is paid or received. The settlement mechanics for a floor are analogous to those for a cap.
- **Collars** are contracts that incorporate both a cap and a floor. For a borrower, a cap provides a fixed worst-case level of interest but allows the customer to pay the market rate if this turns out better. A collar allows the customer to pay a better market rate in the same way, but only down to a certain level. Beyond that level the customer must pay interest at another fixed best-case level. In return for this reduced opportunity, the customer pays a lower premium for the option.

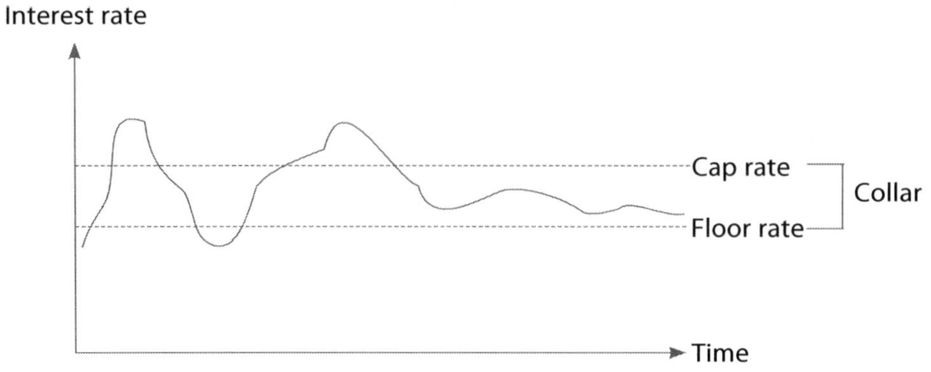

Collars can be constructed so that the two premiums – the premium paid to buy the cap and the premium received when a floor is sold – net zero. This is referred to as a **zero cost collar**.

Example 6

Suppose City plc is a floating-rate borrower that fears rates rising.

It has borrowed £100 million for three years at ICE LIBOR plus 0.25%. City plc can buy a cap (an OTC option) so that, if rates go above its specified rate (say 6%), the bank from whom it bought the cap (Cap Bank plc) will pay City plc compensation. If it had capped the whole £100 million and in year two rates were 8%, City plc would pay 8% + 0.25% (£8.25 million) to its lending bankers but receive 8% – 6% (£2 million) from Cap Bank.

During the term of the cap, the worst rate that City plc can pay is 6% plus 0.25%.

If the premium City plc were quoted was too high, it might finance this by selling a floor to Cap Bank plc or to another bank.

Caps, floors and collars tend to be the preserve of wholesale market participants and are arranged by the large banks.

6. Other Types of Swaps

Learning Objective

5.1.6 Understand the basic concepts of total return and asset swaps

5.5.2 Know the common interest rate swap instruments and their relationships to other markets: inflation; amortising; accreting; rollercoaster; forward start

There are several types of swaps in common use other than interest rate and currency swaps. Here we will describe the variety of products and types of swaps that are traded in the OTC market. At the end of the chapter, some of the operational complexities that arise are considered.

6.1 Asset and Total Return Swaps

An asset swap is a swap that can be used to change the interest rate exposure or currency exposure of an investment. The swap itself can be straightforward. The term asset swap is used to denote the reason for doing the swap, and is also used for the whole package of the asset and the swap together.

An investor might, for example, buy a floating-rate note (FRN) and also transact a swap to receive a fixed interest rate and pay ICE LIBOR. The result will be a synthetic fixed-rate investment. Or, in reverse, they might create a synthetic FRN by buying an underlying fixed-rate investment while paying fixed and receiving floating in the swap.

The advantage of such a structure is that the investor is able to choose the underlying asset according to such criteria as availability, credit quality, liquidity and competitive pricing. The choice of whether to invest in fixed or floating rate can be separated from the choice of asset.

5

Example 7

An investor wishes to buy a ten-year FRN issued by the government (because they want the highest credit rating possible) but no such issue exists. They can instead buy a ten-year government fixed-rate bond and swap it.

Even if such an FRN does already exist, it might be that the synthetic structure using the swap achieves a slightly better yield, if the two markets are not exactly in line.

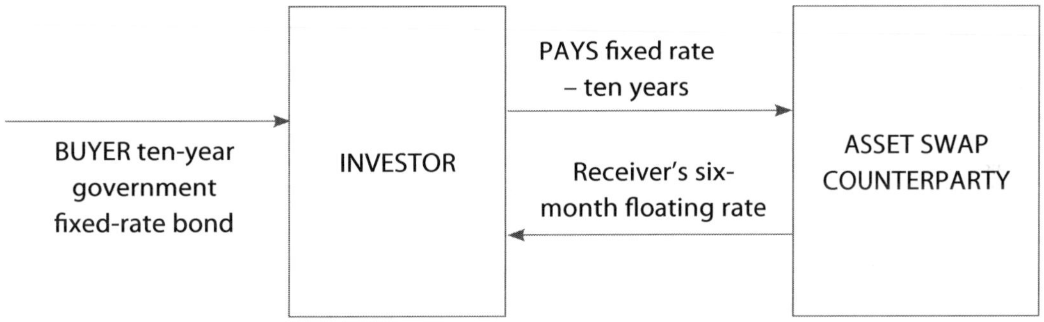

In a total return swap, one of the legs pays the total return on a particular financial asset, ie, the total benefit that would have arisen from holding that asset, including all interest payments, fees and capital appreciation. This amount could be negative if the security's value has fallen rather than risen.

For example, the swap could be linked to the value of a particular bond. In this case, one party will pay the other the total increase in value of the bond from the start of the swap to the end of the swap (or receive the total fall in value) and also pay the value of any coupons received on the bond over the life of the swap. The other leg of the swap will typically be a floating-rate interest such as ICE LIBOR.

Example 8

A UK pension fund wishes to invest in eurozone shares quickly.

One way to do this is to become the receiver of a total return swap (TRS) that has a portfolio of eurozone shares as the underlying instrument.

The price of the TRS will be roughly the same as the cost of a long position of the underlying share portfolio for the pension fund, the TRS buyer.

The pension fund will receive any increase in the value of the eurozone share portfolio (underlying asset), while the seller will receive any fall in the share portfolio's value, ie, the pension fund will pay the seller if the portfolio decreases in value.

6.2 Amortising, Accreting and Rollercoaster Swaps

An interest rate swap is often used by a company to convert the interest rate risk on a borrowing, eg, from floating-rate to fixed-rate.

Suppose that an underlying borrowing arrangement with a bank involves paying the loan back in instalments during its life (an amortising loan). In this case, the swap needs to be amortising also, to match the loan pattern; the notional principal on which the swap payments are based will decrease over the life of the swap.

Other patterns could also be used. For example, the notional principal in the swap might be designed to increase (an accreting swap) rather than decrease. Or it might rise and fall repeatedly, in line with seasonal borrowing requirements (a rollercoaster swap).

6.3 Inflation Swaps

An inflation swap involves an exchange of cash flows, with one or both of its legs calculated with reference to an inflation index. It provides investors with protection against rising prices on a notional principal or an asset's future value. An investor who wants protection from rising prices agrees to pay a fixed amount based on the expected rate of inflation.

The swap payments are based on benchmarks such as the Retail Prices Index (RPI) in the UK, the eurozone's Harmonised Index of Consumer Prices (HICP), or the US Consumer Price Index (CPI). Maturities normally range from five to 30 years for inflation swaps.

6.4 Constant Maturity Swaps (CMSs)

A constant maturity swap (CMS) allows the purchaser to fix the base of received flows on a swap.

The floating leg of a basic interest rate swap is typically reset against a published index, such as ICE LIBOR. The floating leg of a CMS, however, is fixed against a point on the swap curve on a periodic basis.

It is an interest rate swap where the interest rate on one leg is reset periodically, but with reference to a market swap rate rather than ICE LIBOR. The other leg of the swap is generally ICE LIBOR but may be a fixed rate or, potentially, another constant maturity rate.

CMSs can either be single currency or involve two currencies. The prime factor for a CMS, therefore, is the shape of the forward implied yield curves.

6.5 Arrears Swaps

In a plain vanilla interest rate swap, the floating interest rate is observed at the start of a period and paid at the end of that period. In an arrears swap, however, the floating rate is observed and paid at the end of the period. For example, in an ICE LIBOR-in-arrears swap with semi-annual resets, the six-month ICE LIBOR rate from time t_i to t_{i+I} is used to calculate the coupon payment at time t_i.

6.6 Forward Start Swaps

A forward start swap is one that is agreed today, but the exchange of funds takes place at a future date. It is often priced as two partially offsetting swaps – both starting today, but one ending on the deferred start date of the forward swap. For example, a one-year swap and a five-year swap could partially offset to create a four-year swap, starting in a year's time. Forward start swaps are also known as deferred start swaps or delayed start swaps.

6.7 Overnight Index Swaps (OISs)

An overnight index swap (OIS) is a fixed/floating swap (or basis swap) where the floating index (or at least one of them) is an overnight interest rate, eg, a swap to pay 0.5% fixed for three months and receive the overnight interest rate recorded each day.

In this case, the overnight benchmark interest rate used is not, say, overnight ICE LIBOR, which is the rate at a particular time of day. Instead, the benchmark used is a published overnight index, such as Fed funds effective for USD. This is the average of the overnight interest rate throughout a given day, weighted by the volume of business transacted in the market at that rate. The equivalent published indices for sterling and the euro are the Sterling OverNight Index Average (SONIA) and the Euro OverNight Index Average (EONIA) respectively. Some OISs use a 'tom/next' interest rate rather than an overnight interest rate (by buying or selling a foreign amount settling tomorrow and then doing the opposite – selling or buying it back, settling the day after).

In order to avoid the expense and administration of many payment transfers, the floating-rate payment is not physically paid each day. Rather, it is accumulated and paid, say, each month. Because this effectively delays the payment, the daily interest rate fixings are compounded to calculate the actual payment, rather than simply added together.

An OIS might be used, for example, by a bank that lends money for three months at a fixed rate but funds itself in the overnight market. The swap described above – pay 0.5% fixed for three months and receive the overnight interest rate – would hedge the interest rate risk.

Although OIS means overnight index swap in general, it usually refers to a USD OIS in particular. Similarly, although TOIS means 'tom/next indexed swap' in general, it usually refers to a USD TOIS in particular.

The OIS market has grown dramatically in volume. Some of the instrument's various advantages and uses are as follows:

- Liquidity requirements and interest rate risk can be managed separately. Suppose, for example, that a bank wishes to borrow for one year to ensure liquidity but would prefer to fund itself overnight from the point of view of interest rate risk. It can take in a one-year borrowing and transact a one-year OIS to pay the OI and receive one-year fixed.
- An OIS can be used in arbitrage strategies. For example, a dealer might borrow funds repeatedly in the overnight market, lend for, say, a three-month term, and pay fixed/receive the OI in an OIS.
- Credit risk can be reduced significantly. Rather than lend money for one year, a dealer can transact an OIS to pay the OI and receive one-year fixed, and at the same time lend money for only one day in the overnight market and then roll over this overnight cash loan repeatedly for a year. The credit risk on the rolling overnight loan is far smaller than the credit risk would be on a one-year loan. This separates the interest rate decision from the balance sheet decision. The same could be done with a traditional term swap, say for one year against three-month LIBOR, but an overnight credit risk is clearly less than a three-month one and leaves the dealer with greater flexibility in their lending decisions.
- Conversely, an investor can use an OIS for an asset swap, whereby they invest in an attractively priced long-term investment but swap the income to the overnight rate (receive the OI and pay the fixed in the OIS).

6.8 Mark to Market (MTM) Swaps

An MTM swap is one where settlements are calculated by revaluing the swap (ie, marking it to market) regularly and paying or receiving the MTM loss or gain since the previous settlement. The benefit of this is that it removes, at each settlement date, any credit risk that has built up.

The effect is the same as closing out the existing swap, settling its current value, and putting in place a new swap at the current swap rate for the remaining life of the original swap. This can be done for a single currency swap or a cross currency swap (an FX resettable swap).

An FX resettable swap has the characteristics and structure of a basic currency swap and an MTM swap. This includes the fact that all payment dates must be set so that they are business days for both currencies, to avoid any mismatch of payments. Also, as is the case with most basic FX swaps, there will be an exchange of principal at the beginning and end of the swap.

6.9 Commodity Swaps

Learning Objective

5.1.5 Understand the basic concepts and fundamental characteristics of commodity forwards, swaps

5.6.2 Know the basic purpose of the following: commodity swaps

A commodity swap involves paying or receiving a cash flow that is determined by the price or returns of a specific commodity. This type of swap has become increasingly popular given the significant volatility in both the supply and demand for most commodities. The users of this type of swap are interested in hedging their risks. This ranges from airlines, who want to lock in one of their major costs – jet fuel – to farmers and other agricultural producers looking for a stable income flow from their production.

A fixed-for-floating commodity price swap is one whereby one party periodically pays to the other the cash value of an agreed quantity of the underlying commodity multiplied by a fixed price, and the other party in return periodically pays the cash value of an agreed quantity multiplied by a floating price, indexed to current commodity prices. With this swap there is no exchange of the commodities. This is analogous to a fixed floating interest rate swap.

Example 9

An aluminium producer makes regular sales of aluminium and receives the market price for his sales of aluminium. They believe that the aluminium price is going to fall over the next 12 months and wishes to hedge against this risk. He therefore undertakes a swap to receive, from a swap counterparty, an agreed fixed aluminium price each month, based on an agreed quantity of aluminium. At the same time, they agree to pay that counterparty each month the market price for aluminium, which is then current, based on the same quantity. They will continue to sell aluminium to their customers in the usual way, as the swap is a completely separate transaction from the underlying physical aluminium sales.

The net effect is that the producer will receive an approximately fixed price for their aluminium sales. The two swap parties will need to agree on an aluminium price index for the purpose of the swap settlements. This index will not necessarily be exactly the same as the price received by the producer from his customers from time to time, such that they will be left with a basis risk, but the two should move closely in line. The timing of the swap settlements might also not be exactly the same as for the physical sales, but again, the producer will be better protected than if they had not hedged at all.

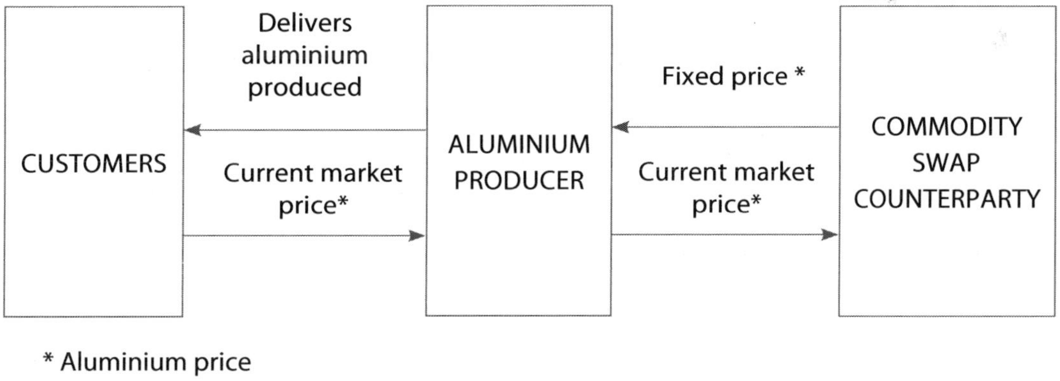

A commodity price-for-interest swap is one whereby the value of a fixed amount of the specified commodity is exchanged for a floating-rate interest payment (usually related to LIBOR) or a fixed-rate interest payment.

Commodity swaps can involve any commodity if, for example, a producer wishes to fix the net price he will receive over time, a user wishes to fix the net price he will pay over time, or a speculator wishes to take a view on the price over time. Some particular areas in which such swaps are transacted are:

- bullion swaps (gold, silver, platinum and palladium)
- energy swaps (crude oil, natural gas and gasoline).

6.10 Equity, Volatility, Variance and Dividend Swaps

Learning Objective

5.1.4 Understand the basic concepts and fundamental characteristics of equity forwards, swaps and swaptions: equity baskets/index; equity forwards; equity swaps/swaptions

5.5.1 Know common equity swap instruments and their relationship to other markets and products: total return; volatility; variance; dividend swaps

Equity swaps are swaps whose payments on one or both sides are linked to the performance of equities or an equity index. They are sometimes used to avoid withholding taxes, obtain leverage, or enjoy the returns from ownership without actually owning equity.

This type of swap allows an investor or fund manager to exchange the returns on an equity investment (an individual share, a basket or index) for a return on another non-equity or equity-based investment. Its returns are strictly based on the relative volatility of an individual share or index.

Example 10

The simplest type of equity swap is a bullet swap in which all payments are made at maturity.

Investor A swaps $10 million at ICE LIBOR + 0.05% (ICE LIBOR + 5 basis points) against the return of the Hang Seng index over six months. Investor A will receive from investor B any percentage increase in the Hang Seng applied to the $10 million notional. If the Hang Seng declined over the year, not only will investor A receive nothing from investor B, but investor A will have to pay investor B the value of the fall in the index, thus synthesising an actual investment in that index.

Let's assume that in six months' time ICE LIBOR is 5.5% and also assume a swap tenure of precisely 180 days. If that is the case, then the floating leg payer/equity receiver (investor A) will owe (5.5% + 0.05%) x $10,000,000 x 180/360 = $277,500 to the equity payer/floating leg receiver (investor B).

If over the same period the Hang Seng rose from 23,100 to 25,250 or 9.3%, investor B would have to pay investor A 9.3% of $10 million = $930,000. But if over that same period the Hang Seng fell to 22,100 or by 4.3%, investor A will have to pay investor B a total of $707,500 ($430,000 due to the drop in the index and $277,500 for the ICE LIBOR leg of the swap).

Equity basket swaps are swaps where one or both of the underlying assets is/are a non-index basket of shares. The shares in this basket often have similar characteristics to exchange-traded equity index derivatives, but are always traded OTC, since the basket of shares used is not standardised as an equity index.

The shares that are included in these baskets are normally used for correlation trading; that is, they are included in the basket to fulfil the objective that one of the counterparties requires. The fact that these baskets are specific for each swap is the main reason why these are traded on an OTC basis.

A variance swap takes the concept of an equity swap beyond the movement in equity prices. A variance swap allows an investor to hedge or speculate on the future price movements of an underlying asset, which can be a currency, interest rate, commodity or index. In a variance swap, one side's payment will be linked to the realised variance – the price movements of the specific asset over the life of the swap. These prices are recorded on a daily basis and are most commonly based on the asset's closing price. The other side of the swap will pay a fixed amount, which is agreed upfront.

The main attraction/advantage of a variance swap is that it provides pure exposure to the volatility of the underlying asset's price as opposed to straight call or put options, which may require delta hedging. It is for this reason that variance swaps are more widely used in the equity markets than volatility swaps. The profit/loss of a variance swap depends solely on the difference between implied and actual volatility.

A dividend swap is a swap that allows one to swap fixed payments, for example, ones which might be based on current interest rates, with dividend payments from an individual share or group of shares or an equity index. Unlike other equity-related swaps, dividend swaps are based solely on the actual dividend payments, without taking into account the underlying share price or index level.

The holder of the fixed leg will pay their counterparty a predesignated fixed payment at each interval. The other party – the holder of the floating leg – will pay their counterparty the total dividends that were paid out by a selected underlying, which can be a single company, a basket of companies or all the members of an index. The payments are multiplied by a notional number of shares, which is agreed when the swap is first entered into.

Like most swaps, the contract is usually arranged such that its value at signing is zero. This is accomplished by making the value of the fixed leg equal to the value of the floating leg – in other words, the fixed leg will be equal to the average expected dividends over the term of the swap. Therefore, the fixed leg of the swap can be used to estimate market forecasts of the dividends that will be paid out by the underlying.

An equity forward contract is an OTC contract between two parties to buy or to sell an individual share, basket of shares or equity index at a specified future time at a price agreed upon today.

Forward contracts on an equity basket or index work in the same way as on an individual share. Instead of entering into separate contracts for each of the individual shares in the basket, the investor can give a list of securities in the portfolio to their broker, who will quote the price for which the dealer will purchase or sell the securities in the basket at a future date.

It is important to remember that dividends do have an effect on forwards; however, when you compare the effect from a risk management perspective for a basket or equity index, dividends have a minor impact when compared to the price movements in the shares that make up the index or basket.

Most equity forwards do not pay dividends except for forwards that are total return forwards. Total return forwards take into consideration the payments and reinvestment of any dividends paid on any shares that are included in the index. This is in addition to the return on the index itself.

6.11 Property and Environmental Swaps

Learning Objective

5.6.2 Know the basic purpose of the following: property swaps, environmental swaps

Environmental swaps (also known as debt for nature swaps) are usually debt swaps, which allow the debtor country (usually a less developed country) to have the amount of its debt reduced by the amount that it spends on key environmental projects. These swaps can be structured on a bilateral or tripartite basis. In the bilateral type of swap, the borrower has its debt reduced directly by the creditor for the amount that has been spent on the pre-agreed environmental issue. In a tripartite-based swap, a third party, such as an international organisation, pays the creditor for the amount that the borrower has spent on the environmental project. One of the main purposes of this type of swap is to reduce the debt problems of poorer countries while promoting conservation/environmental issues.

Property swaps are a variation on a TRS, where the return/payment of one side is linked to the returns (rental income and/or appreciation in value) of a specific property or group of properties or a development. In return the buyer of the property return will pay a pre-agreed interest rate.

While most property swaps are used by investors to gain exposure to the property sector, without the cost of physically buying the properties, this type of swap has become popular as a way of making houses affordable in a rising property market.

6.12 Zero Coupon Inflation Products

Learning Objective

5.1.7 Understand the basic concepts and fundamental characteristics of zero coupon inflation products

A zero coupon inflation product is a standard derivative product based on an inflation rate. The underlying asset is a single price index (inflation measure) such as the CPI in the US or the RPI in the UK.

It is called a zero coupon product or swap because there is only one financial flow, at the end, without any intermediate coupon. At the maturity date there is a swap of a fixed amount against a floating amount.

This type of product allows market participants to:

- hedge against/speculate on future inflation fluctuations
- evaluate inflation-linked securities, including asset swapping **Treasury Inflation Protected Securities** (TIPS) and other securities
- hedge against central bank credit tightening policies (due to the fact that central banks will tighten monetary policy to fight rising inflation).

7. Credit Derivatives

Learning Objective

5.1.8 Understand the basic concepts and fundamental characteristics of credit derivatives and the main credit events: default events; ratings transitions

An area of derivative products that has grown significantly in recent years is that of credit derivatives. These are instruments whose value depends on agreed credit events relating to a third-party company, for example, a credit rating downgrading of that company, or an increase in that company's cost of funds in the market, or a default, or bankruptcy. The purpose of such derivatives is to enable an organisation to protect against unwanted credit exposure, by passing that exposure on to someone else. Credit derivatives can also be used to increase credit exposure, in return for income.

7.1 Credit Default Swaps (CDSs)

Learning Objectives

5.4.1 Know the common credit derivative instruments and their relationships to other markets and products: credit default swaps; credit linked notes

5.4.2 Understand the mechanisms for pricing credit derivatives and the relationships with asset swap prices

In a credit default swap (CDS), the party buying the credit protection makes a periodic payment (or pays an upfront fee) to the other party. In return, it receives an agreed compensation if there is a credit event relating to some third party or parties.

Credit events are typically defined to include a material default, bankruptcy, a significant fall in an asset's value or debt restructuring for a specified reference asset. If such a credit event occurs, the seller makes a predetermined payment to the buyer, and the swap then terminates.

What can be considered a credit event?

- **Default** – failure by the reference asset(s) to make specific debt or other reference payments as defined in the default swap agreement (see below).
- **Significant fall in asset price/value** – most common in basket-based swaps, the swap contract will have a clearly defined valuation level for a specific asset or basket of assets. Once its/their value falls below this level, the buyer can trigger the swap payment agreement.
- **Bankruptcy** – once the reference asset files for, or is forced into, bankruptcy, most default swaps are automatically triggered for final payment.
- **Debt restructuring** – if the reference asset or its creditors initiate debt restructuring that will change the status or priority of the default swap buyer's asset, if included in the swap agreement, the buyer will receive payment.

- **Merger or demerger** – any change in the owner status or independence of the asset or company is considered a credit event, as is any significant change in the asset ownership structure.
- **Governmental intervention.**

The definition of a credit event is determined in the agreement made between the counterparties to the transaction at the time of the trade. The agreement, which is usually based on the International Swaps and Derivatives Association's (ISDA's) master agreement (see Section 10 of this chapter), will also clearly define the responsibilities and process for notification of a credit event; this is normally done by the buyer or its agent. It also includes the details of the settlement procedures. This is, in effect, an option, and the periodic payments are effectively an option premium.

There are three types of CDS:

- **Basic** – based on a specific asset as reference to the credit event. The reference asset is usually the asset or at least is the pricing guide to the obligation that can be delivered, if that is part of the swap agreement.
- **Basket** – based on the default of a basket of securities, such as a portfolio of several airline debts. The terms of this type of CDS could be based on the first to default, or any number within the basket, to trigger the credit event. The number of securities in the basket can range from three to 20. The greater the number in the basket, the higher the initial premium, given the wider insurance provided.
- **Index** – based on the movements of an index, either a debt-related or equity/market-based index; the buyer will most likely purchase protection if the underlying index falls below a certain level. This type of CDS is closely related to a total return swap (see Section 6.1 of this chapter).

If a default should occur, the agreed **compensation** is settled by a cash payment or physical delivery.

- **Cash settlement** – this is effected by paying a sum of money in compensation. This might, for example, be determined by the level at which a reference asset (such as a bond issued by the underlying third party company) trades after the default.
- **Physical settlement** – this is where the buyer of the risk pays the full value of the principal against delivery of the defaulted asset. This could be a specific asset agreed in advance (reference asset or obligation) or any financial obligation of the given issuer, eg, a bond, a derivative contract.

Every CDS includes the trigger points and notification procedures, such as who has the right to notify, time limits and payment schedules. In most cases, the buyer has exclusive notification/exercise rights, while some swaps have an automatic notification trigger, under certain predefined events. As with all other OTC products, these can be customised to meet the buyer's demands or the nature of the reference asset or assets.

Most CDSs are priced using the reduced-form pricing approach, in which the credit event process is modelled directly into the swap's price, based on the probability of the credit event occurring. The most widely used measure of the probability is what is known as the default swap or asset swap spread, which is basically the premium being paid to investors over ICE LIBOR or another reference rate to hold the asset. The ongoing premium payments made by the purchaser of the default swap are based on this spread and will most likely change on an ongoing basis over the duration of the swap.

Example 11

Bank ABC has a portfolio of airline leases and is concerned that higher fuel prices will hurt airline profits. It buys a basket CDS that is based on a portfolio of aircraft leases for five airlines from a hedge fund. The terms of the basket swap define a trigger credit event when the second of the airlines applies to restructure its leases. When this occurs, Bank ABC notifies the hedge fund of the trigger; it receives the remaining payments due from all of the leases and the hedge fund now owns the leases and is directly exposed to the five airlines.

7.1.1 Credit Linked Notes (CLNs)

A credit linked note (CLN) is a form of funded credit derivative. It is structured as a security, with an embedded CDS allowing the issuer to transfer a specific credit risk to credit investors. The issuer is not obligated to repay the debt if a specified event occurs. This eliminates the need for a third-party insurance provider. Under this structure, the coupon or price of the note is linked to the performance of a reference asset. It offers borrowers a hedge against credit risk, and gives investors a higher yield on the note for accepting exposure to a specific credit event.

Example 12

A bank lends money to a company, and at the time it issues a CLN, which is bought by investors. The interest rate on the note is determined by the credit risk of the company. The funds the bank raises by issuing the note are invested in high-quality, low-risk bonds.

If the company remains solvent, the bank is obliged to pay the note in full. But, if the company goes bankrupt or is unable to repay the loan, the note holders/investors become the company's creditors and take on the original loan. The bank in turn gets compensated by the returns on less risky bond investments funded by issuing CLNs.

7.2 Credit Spread Options

In a credit spread option, a credit spread is first defined as the difference between the yield on a particular asset (eg, the yield on a particular bond issued by a company) and some agreed benchmark (eg, a swap rate or government Treasury bond yield for the same maturity as the bond).

A strike rate is then set for this spread. In the case of a put option, the option buyer then pays a premium upfront and receives any difference between the actual spread and the agreed strike if the spread rises above that strike.

Example 13

Bank A lends cash to Company XYZ for five years and then wishes to protect against the credit risk of Company XYZ. Bank A purchases a credit spread put option, where the credit spread is defined as the difference between the yield on a particular bond issued by Company XYZ and the yield on a Treasury bond. If the spread rises above an agreed level (the strike), Bank A receives an agreed compensation from Bank B to offset the deterioration in its own asset (its loan to Company XYZ).

Credit spread options are designed to hedge against (for the buyer) or capitalise on (for the seller) changes in credit spreads, ie, differences in their respective yields. A reference security is selected and strike spread and maturity are set. The pay-off is based on whether the actual spot or market spread at the exercise date is over or under the spread on the reference security. The transaction may be either based on changes in a credit spread relative to a risk-free benchmark (eg, LIBOR, gilts or US Treasuries) or changes in the relative spread between two credit instruments.

Credit spread options may be structured as American or European options.

The buyer of a credit spread option is looking to protect or hedge against widening of the spread between the two securities. If a fund manager holds a large position in a non-EU government debt, they might buy a credit spread option with EU government debt as a reference to protect the portfolio from a deterioration in the fund's holding debt's price in the short term, if elections are expected shortly.

Example 14

A fund manager has a €50 million position in a ten-year non-EU government bond that yields 7%. The manager is confident that the position has good long-term potential, but is concerned that the upcoming elections may cause short-term spreads to widen. Currently, ten-year EU government debt is yielding 4.75%.

The fund manager can buy a three-month €50 million spread option on the 7% non-EU government debt versus a 4.75% EU government bond; the fund's bond is currently trading at a 2.25% spread to its EU benchmark.

The fund manager can lock in the 2.25% spread by buying the credit spread option. It is a European-style option. In three months' time, if the spread has widened beyond 2.25%, the fund will receive the equivalent payment that will effectively lock in that spread.

7.3 Option-Adjusted Spreads (OASs)

As discussed earlier, we know that any bond's yield is typically comprised of two components:

1. The risk-free return on a similar benchmark security, such as government bonds.
2. A premium above the yield on that benchmark security that compensates an investor for that specific bond's associated credit risk.

This premium is referred to as its 'yield spread' or simply 'spread'. For bonds with embedded options (callable or puttable bonds, for instance), this spread must be adjusted to account for the fact that the embedded option may change the expected cash flows of this bond.

For example, if a bond is repaid before it matures, its interest payments cease and principal is returned earlier than the bond's maturity. This option-adjusted measure is referred to as an option-adjusted spread (OAS).

An OAS is the yield spread which has to be added to a benchmark yield curve to discount a security's payments to match its market price, using a dynamic pricing model that accounts for these embedded options.

The OAS helps investors compare a fixed-income security's cash flows to reference rates, while also valuing embedded options against general market volatility. By separately analysing the security's two components – the bond and the embedded option – analysts can determine whether the investment is worthwhile at a given price. The OAS method is more accurate than simply comparing a bond's yield to maturity to a benchmark.

The OAS takes into account two types of volatility facing fixed-income investments with embedded options: changing interest rates (which affect all bonds) and prepayment risk. The shortfall of this approach is that estimates are based on historical data, but are used in a forward-looking model. For example, prepayment is typically estimated from historical data, and does not take into account economic shifts or other changes that might occur in the future.

OASs are model-dependent. This concept can be applied to a mortgage-backed security (MBS), or any other bond that has an embedded option (such as being callable or that allows for early repayment), or any other interest rate derivative or option.

In the context of an MBS or callable bond, the option relates primarily to the borrower's right to refinance the debt at a lower interest rate. These securities must therefore pay higher yields than any non-callable debt, and their values are more fairly compared by OAS than by yield. OAS is usually measured in basis points (bps).

7.4 Credit Default Options and Other Instruments

Learning Objective

5.4.1 Know the common credit derivative instruments and their relationships to other markets and products: CDOs/CBOs; synthetic CDOs

A credit default option is an option to buy protection (payer option) or sell protection (receiver option) on a CDS based on a specific reference credit with a specific maturity. The option is usually a European-style option, meaning that it is exercisable only at one date in the future at a specific strike price defined as a coupon on the CDS.

Credit default options on single credits are extinguished upon default without any cash flows, other than the upfront premium paid by the buyer of the option. Therefore, buying a payer option does not provide protection against an actual default, but only against an increase in the credit spread (higher interest rate/lower price for that single credit). This may explain why these options are very illiquid and therefore less popular. Another key feature is that their prices are usually based on very high implied volatilities. A put option that makes a pay-off if the issuer of a specified reference asset defaults is called a default option.

Collateralised debt obligations (CDOs) are a type of structured asset-backed security (ABS) whose value and payments are derived from a portfolio of fixed-income underlying assets. CDOs' securities are split into different risk classes, or tranches, where senior tranches are considered the safest securities. The interest and principal payments are made based on seniority; therefore, the junior tranches pay a higher coupon payment (and interest rate) and are quoted at lower prices to compensate for their higher default risk.

CDOs vary in structure and underlying assets, but the basic principle is the same. A CDO is a type of ABS. To create a CDO, a corporate entity is constructed to hold assets as collateral and to sell the packages of cash flows to investors.

The following is an example of how a typical CDO is constructed. A special purpose entity (SPE, more commonly referred to as a special purpose vehicle or SPV in European markets) acquires a portfolio of underlying assets. Common examples of the types of these underlying assets include mortgage-backed securities, commercial real estate bonds and/or corporate loans.

The SPE then issues bonds (CDOs) with different tranches, and the proceeds are used to purchase the portfolio of underlying assets. The senior CDOs, since they pay a higher price, are paid from the cash flows from the underlying assets before the junior securities and equity securities. Losses are first borne by the equity securities, next by the junior securities, and finally by the senior securities.

The risk and return for a CDO investor depends directly on how the CDO and its tranches are defined, and only indirectly on the performance of the underlying assets. In particular, the investment depends on the assumptions and methods used to define the risk and return of the tranches. CDOs, like all other ABSs, allow the originators of the underlying assets to pass credit risk to another institution or to individual investors. Thus investors must understand how the risk for CDOs is calculated. The issuer of the CDO, typically an investment bank, earns a commission at time of issue and earns management fees during the life of the CDO.

A few analysts and investors are concerned that CDOs, other ABSs and other derivatives spread risk and uncertainty about the value of the underlying assets more widely, rather than reducing risk through diversification. The onset of the 2007/08 credit crunch gave substantial support to this point of view. In fact, before the credit crunch, all of the credit rating agencies failed to adequately account for these large risks (this can be seen in the case of the nationwide collapse of housing values) when rating CDOs and other ABSs.

A collateralised bond obligation (CBO) is a derivative security that creates an investment grade bond from a pool of junk bonds (high-risk). These junk bonds are typically not investment grade, but, because a CBO includes a pool of several types of credit-quality bonds together, they offer enough diversification to be considered investment grade.

In other words, a CBO is a type of ABS that is composed of the receivables/payments from junk bonds. Issuers of CBOs package and sell their receivables on bonds they own to investors in order to reduce their default risk. Returns on CBOs are considered to be a lower risk than the individual bonds backing them. This is based on the view that it is unlikely that all or even most of the junk bonds will default. They are similar in structure to a collateralised mortgage obligation (CMO), but different in that CBOs represent different levels of credit risk, not different maturities.

A synthetic CDO is a form of CDO that invests in CDSs or other non-cash assets to gain exposure to a portfolio of fixed income assets, as opposed to a basic (or cash flow) CDO, which is backed by a portfolio of underlying assets. As with basic CDOs, synthetic CDOs are typically divided into credit tranches based on the level of credit risk assumed. Initial investments into the CDO are made by the lower tranches, while the senior tranches may not have to make an initial investment. All tranches will receive periodic payments based on the cash flows from the CDSs. If a credit event occurs in the fixed income portfolio, the synthetic CDO and its investors become responsible for the losses, starting from the lowest rated tranches and working upwards.

Synthetic CDOs can offer extremely high yields to investors. However, investors can also be responsible for much more than their initial investments if several credit events occur in the reference portfolio.

Synthetic CDOs were first created in the late 1990s as a way for large holders of commercial loans to protect their balance sheets without actually selling the loans and potentially harming client relationships. They have become increasingly popular because they tend to have shorter lifespans than cash flow CDOs.

8. Over-the-Counter (OTC) Options

An option is defined as a contract whereby one party has the right to complete a transaction in the future (at a previously agreed amount, date and price) if they so choose, but is not obliged to do so. This party is known as the buyer of the option, or option holder. The counterparty, the option seller or writer, has no choice; therefore, they must complete the transaction if the first party wishes, but they cannot do so otherwise.

For the buyer, an option is, therefore, similar to a forward deal, with the difference that they can subsequently decide whether or not to exercise or complete the transaction.

For the seller, it is similar to a forward deal with the difference that they do not know whether or not they will be required to fulfil their obligations. Clearly, the contract will be delivered only if it is advantageous to the option buyer.

In return for this flexibility awarded to the option buyer, the buyer must pay an upfront premium to compensate the option seller for the latter's additional risk.

As with other derivative contracts, such as forwards, options can be used to hedge an existing position or future commitment, as well as for speculation.

8.1 OTC Options Products

Learning Objective

5.7.1 Know the common OTC option products: European, American, Bermudan, Asian; lookbacks and variants; ratchets/cliquets

5.7.2 Understand the mechanisms for option pricing and the relationship with the underlying cash prices together with the significance of contributing factors: structure; arbitrage restrictions; valuation inputs; SABR model; Black-Scholes model; Binomial model

5.7.3 Know the requirements of, and process for, premium payment: when paid; credit exposure; collateral process

The three most popular exercise styles of options that are available:

- European
- American, and
- Bermudan.

With a European option, the holder can exercise the option only on the expiry date. With a three-month option, for example, they can choose only at the end of three months whether or not to exercise.

An American option, however, allows the holder to choose to exercise at any time between the purchase of the option and expiry. The premium is normally higher for American options, if all other specifications of the option are the same. European and American options are both available everywhere; the terms are technical, not geographical.

Bermudan options lie between European and American (as Bermuda lies between Europe and America). A Bermudan option can be exercised on any of various specified dates between original purchase of the option and expiry. Bermudan style is also occasionally known as mid-Atlantic or pseudo-American style.

With both American and Bermudan options, it is possible for the option to allow for partial exercise on a number of occasions within the total amount of the option.

There are also some more exotic OTC options structures:

An Asian option (or average rate or average price option) is a cash-settled OTC option that pays the difference between the average rate of the underlying (calculated on predetermined fixings of an agreed reference rate) and a predetermined strike rate. The volatility of an averaged rate is lower than the volatility of the rates from which the average is calculated and so average-rate options are cheaper than standard European options.

An average strike option is one whose strike price is set at the expiration date to be the average rate of the underlying over the life of the option. This is compared with its final value at expiry. The option can be exercised for physical delivery, or cash settled against the underlying price at maturity.

As with an average rate option, average strike options are cheaper than standard European options.

A cliquet or ratchet option is a series of ATM options, with periodic settlement, resetting the strike value to the price level at that time. The option locks-in the difference between the old and new strike and pays it out as profit. The profit can be accumulated until final maturity, or paid out at each reset date.

A lookback option is a call or put option whose strike price is not determined until the option is exercised. At the time of exercise, the holder can exercise the option at any underlying price that has occurred during the option's life. In the case of a call, the buyer will choose the lowest price, and, in the case of a put, the buyer will choose the highest price. The premium on such options tends to be high, since they give the buyer great flexibility, and the writer has to take on a lot of risk.

The two most widely used and accepted models for option pricing are the Black-Scholes and binomial models. The key factors that both use in calculating an option's premium are:

- strike price
- underlying asset's price
- time to expiration
- underlying asset's volatility or implied volatility
- risk-free interest rate.

An option's premium rises:

- as its time until expiration increases
- as the volatility of the underlying asset rises
- the greater its IV (ie, for calls: the lower the strike price versus the asset's current market price and for puts: the higher the strike price versus the asset's current market price).

The following, known as the Greeks, are measures of the changes in an option's premium over its life:

- **Delta** is the ratio comparing the change in the price of the underlying asset to the corresponding change in the option's price or value. It is sometimes referred to as the **hedge ratio**. The closer an option is to being ITM, the closer delta is to one. Delta has a range of zero to one. Delta reflects the change in value of option position/change in value of the underlying. Note that, while delta for calls is positive, it is negative for puts.

Example 15

A call on BP shares has a delta of 0.6: if BP shares fall by 50p in a trading day, the corresponding call will lose 30p from its premium/value, owing to the fall in the underlying shares.

Example 16

A EUR put/USD call with a delta of –0.3 will see its value rise as the EUR falls. Therefore, if EUR/USD falls by 0.5% in a day, the put's value will rise by 0.15% due to the movement in the spot rate.

- **Gamma** is the rate of change for delta with respect to the underlying asset's price. Mathematically, gamma is the first derivative of delta and is used when trying to gauge the price of an option relative to the amount by which it is ITM or OTM. When an option being measured is deep ITM or OTM, gamma is small. When the option is near-the-money, gamma is largest. Gamma is most extreme for short-dated (those close to expiration), near-the-money options. Gamma reflects the change in delta of option position/change in value of the underlying.
- **Vega** is the change in an option's value for a 1% change in implied volatility. Vega is positive for long calls and put positions. It is also greatest for longer and ATM options.
- **Theta** is a measure of the rate of decline in the value of an option due to the passage of time. Theta can also be referred to as a measure of the time decay on the value of an option. If everything is held constant, the option will lose value as time moves closer to the maturity of the option. The measure of theta quantifies the risk that time imposes on options, as options are only exercisable for a certain period of time.

For more on this subject, see Chapter 4, Sections 2.3 and 2.4.

A major drawback of the Black-Scholes model is that it is based on the assumption that the volatility of the underlying asset is a constant input into the option's price. But in times of high volatility and for certain types of assets (particularly financial assets) and strike prices, those trading options observed that this assumption that implied volatility is constant does not hold true.

Those pricing options observed that there is a one-to-one relationship between its implied volatility and the option's price. In many cases options with strikes prices that are very far OTM or ITM appear to have higher implied volatilities, since their market prices were higher than expected, if the asset's implied volatility remained constant. The result is that an option's implied volatility is dependent on its strike price and therefore is not constant, but forms what is called the volatility smile or volatility skew.

The SABR model is a stochastic volatility model which is based on the premise that the asset's price and volatility are correlated. The name refers to the parameters of the model. The SABR model is widely used by financial options traders, especially those in the interest rate derivative markets.

Volatility smiles are implied volatility patterns that arise in pricing financial options. In particular, for a given expiration, options whose strike price differs substantially from the underlying asset's price command higher prices (and thus implied volatilities) than what is suggested by standard option pricing models. These options are said to be either deep ITM or deep OTM and the SABR model is currently the best pricing model for markets where this pattern occurs.

While OTC options lack the central clearing house and settlement/payment process that exchange-traded options have, the market does have a standard procedure for premium payments. The general rule is that the buyer will pay the premium on either the next business day or T+2 at the latest (the latter being the general rule for OTC FX options).

Since the sole credit risk exists for the option holder/buyer, in certain cases banks/brokers who have purchased options from clients may require collateral payments as the option moves closer ITM (ie, its value increases). An accepted benchmark for these payments is related to the option's delta.

8.1.1 Flexible Exchange (FLEX) Options

Learning Objective

5.1.10 Understand the basic concepts and fundamental characteristics of flex options: how they differ from standard exchange traded options; how they differ from OTC options

FLexible EXchange (FLEX) options combine the benefits of customisation of an OTC product with the advantages of being listed on an exchange.

FLEX options allow investors to customise key contract terms, including expiration date, exercise style, and exercise price, and to take advantage of expanded position limits.

FLEX options differ from standard ETD options since they offer a wide degree of flexibility. FLEX options, unlike ETD options, do not have standardised strike prices, expiration dates or contract sizes.

While they provide the same degree of choice, FLEX options do not have the same credit/counterparty risk associated with other OTC options. Since they are listed on an exchange, they have the same clearing house protection as any other ETD product.

8.2 Structured Products

Learning Objective

5.6.1 Understand how structured products utilise embedded derivatives to achieve a risk/return profile: convertible bonds; index-linked notes; capital protected products; callable/puttable bonds

Options are written on a vast range of underlying instruments, including bonds. A straightforward bond option is thus a call or put on a particular bond. For example, a fund manager or bond dealer might use a call or a put to take a view on a bond, in the same way as they might by buying or selling the bond in the cash market.

A callable bond is a bond with a call option embedded in it. The call can be exercised by the issuer of the bond. Certain circumstances defined for that particular bond – for example on certain dates (such as coupon dates) and at a certain strike price (often higher than par) – allow the issuer to buy back the bond. This in effect allows the issuer to redeem the bond early, which it might do if interest rates fall so that it can issue a new bond instead, to finance itself more cheaply.

A puttable bond is a bond with a put option embedded in it. The put can be exercised by the holder of the bond, again under certain circumstances defined for that particular bond – on certain dates, and at a certain strike price (often lower than par). This, in effect, allows the holder to insist on early redemption of the bond, which it might do if interest rates rise so that it can buy a new bond at a higher yield.

A convertible bond is a bond with an option exercisable by the bondholder to convert the bond into something else, usually equity in the issuing company. Again, there will be conditions attached: certain dates on which this will be exercisable and a fixed number of shares for a given face value of the bond. The holder will exercise this right if the shares become sufficiently valuable.

Example 17

ABC plc requires £15 million in ten-year funding for an expansion project. It has decided to raise this amount by issuing a convertible bond. In doing so, it can reduce the yield required by investors, owing to the fact that the bond will include an option or warrant that will allow the bondholders to convert the bond into ABC's shares at a predefined price. It also avoids having to issue new shares and diluting current shareholders' stake in the company.

Today ABC's shares are trading at 105p, and ten-year bond yields on corporate bonds of similar credit standing are 2.5% (which is 95 bps above the ten-year UK government bond).

ABC's convertible bond will have a 2.35% yield along with a conversion clause that allows bondholders to convert this bond into the equivalent amount of ABC shares at a conversion rate of 130p, after five years.

The net result is that the company is able to save 15 bps on its interest payments, whilst bondholders are able to profit if the company is successful and its share price rises.

When valuing convertible callable and puttable bonds, you must remember that you must value both the bond itself and its embedded option or warrant. In most cases, a call allows the bondholder to exchange the bond for the company's shares or demand repayment before its maturity, whilst a put allows the borrower to repay the bond early. How this can be valued was discussed in Section 7.3 of this chapter.

An index-linked note is an instrument whose return is determined by a specific index. This index could be an equity index, which can be based on the performance of a single share, or a basket of shares, or a market index, such as the FTSE 100 or S&P 500 index or, for a bond/debt instrument, an inflation index such as the CPI or the RPI. For example, for UK-issued index-linked gilts in 1981, both the semi-annual coupon payments and their redemption value were linked to the UK retail prices index.

An equity-linked note is a debt instrument whose yield is determined by the performance of an equity product. A company might link the return of its debt to the performance of its share price as a method of lowering the base interest rate.

A capital protected product (which is also known as a capital protected borrowing) is generally associated with the purchase and holding of shares or other financial securities, such as single warrants. This type of financial product allows an investor to borrow money or obtain credit to purchase shares or other types of financial securities. These shares and financial securities purchased then become security for the loan. Under the terms of the financial product, if the shares or financial securities fall in value below their purchase price, the purchaser can transfer the shares or securities back (a put option), or surrender them to the lender to meet all outstanding obligations under the loan (a limited recourse loan). Therefore, the purchaser/investor is guaranteed a minimum price/value for the shares/securities that are part of the capital protected product. In effect, it is a loan with an embedded put option for the financed securities.

Capital protected loans, generally, have higher interest rates and/or additional fees. Capital protected borrowings include arrangements where an investor uses shares or other financial securities as security for borrowing money or obtaining credit, and those shares or other financial securities are protected from a fall in their value.

9. Market Transparency, Trade Transparency, Trade Reporting and Monitoring

9.1 Trade Reporting

Learning Objective

5.8.1 Know the purpose and requirements of trade reporting in markets: information to be reported; process for reporting; responsibility for reporting

In order to regulate the activities of their member firms satisfactorily, derivatives exchanges need to know what trades have been executed by their members. To this end, they may require members to trade report the transactions they have been involved in. The exchanges specify the time limits within which these trade reports must be submitted, and the member firms could be subject to disciplinary action if they fail to adhere to these limits.

The electronic nature of trading systems provided by exchanges such as ICE Futures means that trade reporting is largely performed automatically by the electronic system. It is only block and basis trades that need to be reported into the exchange. On ICE Futures, block trades must be reported to the exchange within five minutes of verbal agreement being reached, under normal market conditions. Those block trades that are dependent on the execution of a transaction in another instrument or when market conditions are considered exceptional, must be reported within 15 minutes. All basis trades must be reported within 15 minutes of the time the trade was organised.

9.2 Price Transparency

Learning Objectives

5.8.2 Know the advantages and main sources for exchange price feeds: price transparency; current bids and offers; trade prices; high/low prices; last night closing price; traded volume

In order for investors to have confidence in the exchange, they must know that prices are determined fairly. For an exchange, investor confidence is vital because its income is primarily derived from fees charged on the contracts traded.

Price transparency is a central part of investor confidence and refers to the availability of up-to-date trading information for anyone who wishes to receive it. This transparency is generally provided by the exchange feeding the prices to members and to quote vendors such as Reuters and Bloomberg.

9.2.1 Constituents of Exchange Price Feeds

The exchange disseminates the trade reporting information through a price feed to its members. Real-time price and trade information via the feed is made available to quote vendors (eg, Reuters and Bloomberg) and directly to its members, such as Euronext's Exchange Data Publisher, so that investors at large can see the information on their price screens. The price screens will generally include the following information:

Buying and Selling Prices

The best buying price (bid – often shown by the letter **B**) and offer price (selling price – often shown by the letter **A** for ask) will constitute the bid/offer spread in the market.

The screens are designed to report all data that traders and investors wish to know. This will include volume traded and open interest (as at the close of the previous business day), plus price information showing the opening price, the closing price (again, as at the close of the previous business day), the price of the last trade, and the day's high and low prices, all shown by delivery month. This data is made available both via real-time price feeds and on a delayed basis.

Delivery Month Codes

Each futures expiry month has its unique identifier.

January	F	April	J	July	N	October	V
February	G	May	K	August	Q	November	X
March	H	June	M	September	U	December	Z

For example, Z 4245B 4246A = current bid/ask for December future.

9.3 Monitoring Volume and Open Interest

Learning Objective

5.8.3 Understand the importance of monitoring volume and open interest information and settlement: purpose of monitoring open interest; breach of credit limit; guarantee in the event of settlement failure; effect of client's failure to monitor open interest

It is important for any exchange to publish accurately its open interest so that all market observers and investors can make judgements in respect of their positions and trading strategies. To this end, markets such as ICE Futures Europe and Eurex set down procedural rules as to how members of the market should report open interest on a daily basis back to the exchange(s). In the case of Euronext this is effected by the use of the UTP, through which all members report their holdings in respect of their ongoing client positions. These details are provided to interested parties via information vendors.

This is separate from the open interest that may be recorded in omnibus accounts at the clearing houses. It falls to every client to be aware of their position(s) where they are holding long or short contracts, and to instruct their clearing brokers carrying their positions where contracts are to be closed, matching purchases against sales. Sometimes systems will exist operationally to effect these close-outs automatically.

If a client fails to manage the open interest on their account properly, it may lead to unwanted delivery situations.

If the client's position were to become excessive, there is a danger of the client breaching their credit limit with the broker when prices move against him. However the clearing system provides a mutual guarantee structure.

10. Documentation and Collateral

10.1 Master Agreements

Learning Objective

5.2.1 Know the main ISDA documents supporting OTC derivative activities: master agreements; credit support annex documentation; confirmations; ISDA protocols

6.4.3 Understand the mechanisms of collateral management: Credit Support Annex (CSA): thresholds; haircuts; minimum transfer amount

The recognition by swap participants of the need for a means to reduce potential disagreements by developing standardised documentation was instrumental in ISDA becoming chartered in 1985.

Generally, the aims of the ISDA documentation are to:

- provide standard market terms to encourage growth and confidence in OTC products
- minimise the administration needed to support transactions
- help to facilitate cross-border trading.

A master agreement provides a single umbrella framework within which all relevant OTC deals between two parties can be transacted. A key advantage of this is that all individual transactions can be brought together to form part of the master agreement. This means that, in the event of a counterparty becoming insolvent or going into default, it is possible to close out all transactions covered by the master agreement rather than relying on cross-default or other provisions to close out transactions individually.

Once the master agreement is in place, each deal still needs to be confirmed in the usual way. It is not necessary to repeat the legal terms and conditions when confirming each transaction, as these have already been covered in the master agreement. Most importantly, the master agreement allows for all the deals to be netted in the event of a default, rather than considered separately. This is important to provide protection for the non-defaulting party against selective default and termination.

The master agreement is negotiated between the two parties on the basis of a standard printed contract, and is legally binding once signed by both parties. It provides mutual protection for both parties. No specific references are made in the agreement to individual transaction terms. To enable a degree of flexibility, there is a schedule to the master agreement to allow for specific provisions to be determined by the counterparties.

The most important of the issues dealt with by the master agreement are:

- **termination events**, ie, generally external circumstances outside the control of the parties, eg, changes in tax law or illegality, which can allow deals to be terminated early by one of the parties affected
- **events of default**, ie, events which are generally the fault of one of the two parties, eg, failing to pay an amount due or bankruptcy, which can allow all outstanding deals to be terminated early by the other party
- **netting** (important for credit risk and, as explained in Chapter 9, for capital adequacy purposes). The master agreement covers two types of netting:
    - **payment netting** (netting of amounts due in the same currency on the same day in the ordinary course of business), and
    - **close-out netting** (netting of all amounts due between the parties upon early termination by valuing all transactions and converting amounts due to a single termination currency for settlement). This is a key part of the documentation. When negotiating documentation with a counterparty, it is vital to ensure that close-out netting will in fact be supported by the courts. In some legal jurisdictions, this is not necessarily the case. Banks must therefore seek legal opinions from all relevant jurisdictions when negotiating.

The specific terms of each deal are set out in a supplement to the master agreement, called a confirmation. Each confirmation refers to the master agreement and is governed by the terms agreed between the parties in that contract. This enables the confirmation to be considerably shorter than it otherwise would be. If there is a conflict between something contained in the confirmation and the master agreement, the confirmation takes precedence for that deal.

If a master agreement has not yet been agreed and signed between the parties, the general terms of the published contract (ie, without any variations as may be agreed in the schedule) apply. This will generally protect both parties as to how their rights and obligations will be legally interpreted. There is some risk, however, that in the event of default this interpretation may depend on the legal jurisdiction of each party. It is, therefore, best practice to have the master agreement negotiated and signed between the parties as quickly as possible.

10.1.1 Credit Support Annex (CSA)

In response to the growing concern over the counterparty credit risk associated with longer-term OTC derivative contracts, the ISDA has included, as part of its documentation procedures that allow counterparties to periodically reduce this exposure, a credit support annex (CSA) as part of an ISDA agreement.

For example, Company A enters into a ten-year interest rate swap, as a fixed-rate payer, with one of its main banks. As market rates fall, in favour of the bank and against Company A, the MTM profit on the swap represents a loss to Company A and a profit for the bank. This in turn increases the bank's risk exposure to the company, since it has a loss on this swap position. One way that the bank can reduce its risk exposure created by the swap is to enter into a CSA or collateral support document (CSD), which contains the details of the conditions and procedures by which collateralisation will occur.

A CSA is a legal document that regulates and defines the criteria for collateral payments (credit support) for OTC derivative transactions. It is one of the four parts of an ISDA contract. A CSA defines the rules and conditions under which collateral is transferred between the counterparties to the derivative contract. Its main aim is to mitigate the credit risk arising from the OTM or MTM loss of a derivatives position. The CSA defines the timing (how often), the minimum transfer allowed and the type of collateral accepted for these transfers. All CSAs require an ISDA agreement to be in place.

In addition to setting the timing of the MTM, the CSA will also include key procedural details, setting:

- the **threshold amounts** – the unsecured credit exposure that one counterparty is prepared to accept before making a collateral request, usually set at a relatively low level, in order to reduce credit risk
- **minimum transfer amounts** – the minimum amount of a collateral request; any collateral transfer below this amount is not permitted. It is designed to prevent frequent and unnecessary calls of collateral, as well as to avoid the costs involved with small transfer payments
- the valuation percentage or **haircut** – the discount that is applied to the collateral's market value; this protects the collateral receiver from falls in the collateral's value in the period between collateral calls. The higher the quality of the collateral, the lower the haircut.

The CSD is very similar to a CSA, in that it contains the timing and procedure for the MTM of the contract. Once the new valuation has been agreed, the counterparty with the negative MTM valuation will transfer the change in value to the counterparty with the positive MTM.

10.1.2 Protocols

A protocol is the term used to describe the set of documents, such as master agreements, that are widely used by market participants and that define the procedures associated with specific financial transactions and the responsibilities of each counterparty. They are useful, in that these agreements set out all the legal requirements and are regularly updated when necessary. For example, the ISDA set out several protocols after the euro was introduced, to ensure an easy transition for those existing transactions such as currency swaps that were originally denominated in euro members' old national currencies, so that euro-based settlement could take place.

These protocols cover a wide range of transactions. The use of these is not restricted to the ISDA. The Federal Reserve has also issued them, when required.

There are protocols that define the most basic aspects, such as the particular nature of a swap. The specific definition of each type of swap can be found earlier throughout this chapter.

10.2 Collateral Management

Learning Objective

5.10.1 Know the importance of accurate and timely settlement processes for OTC products: deal tickets and term sheets

5.11.1 Understand the potential impact of credit exposures on OTC positions: nature of OTC contracts; mark-to-market and potential exposures; term of OTC derivatives; credit support agreements; acceptable forms of collateral (certainty and currency of asset); the collateral process (mark-to-market, hurdle, minimum cashflow, parties involved)

Collateral is something of value. Collateral is held against the risk of default by a counterparty. It is important that the collateral is an asset that is easy to liquidate in the case of default. The main types of collateral that are accepted include cash, bank guarantees, CDS, government bonds and negotiable (ie, tradeable) securities. However, some major exchanges only accept cash or high-grade government bonds. See also Chapter 6, Section 4.1.

Collateral management is the process that allows market participants to reduce the counterparty credit exposure that arises from longer-maturity OTC derivative contracts, such as swaps and options.

If a bank considers that the credit risk incurred by trading with a particular counterparty is too great, or has already reached the credit limit in place, it may ask for collateral from the counterparty in order to continue trading with it. Cover for initial margin can also be provided using collateral rather than cash (see Chapter 6, Section 4).

A bank ensures that it has the most up-to-date and accurate measure of its credit exposure to a counterparty by ensuring that its operations area processes all deal tickets and term sheets on a timely basis. A term sheet is a non-binding agreement which sets out the basic terms and conditions under which an investment or trade will be made; a term sheet is usually used as a template to develop a more detailed legal document.

The bank assesses the size of the risk it is taking in making the transaction and requires that the counterparty places collateral to that value with it, either at the same time as dealing or beforehand. Typically, the arrangement will allow for the bank to ask for more collateral subsequently (this is known as the delivery amount) if the value of the existing trade or collateral falls during the life of the deal. It might also return some collateral if the value of either the collateral or the trade rises; this is known as the return amount.

The amount associated with either normally has a pre-agreed minimum, the minimum transfer amount. This is useful in reducing the cost and number of transfer payments between the bank and its counterparty during the contract's existence.

The bank ensures that the amount of collateral reflects both the current risk associated with the counterparty's possible default to the transaction, and the current value of the collateral it holds by having its operations area conduct regular MTM valuations of both the transaction and the collateral it currently holds. This enables the bank to manage its exposure to the counterparty, since the counterparty's potential loss is the cost that the bank would incur if the counterparty defaulted and it had to close out the transaction in the market. This will ensure that, at any given time, the bank has the amount of risk collateral required; this is referred to as the threshold amount for the transaction.

If either the risk increases and/or the value of the collateral falls, the counterparty will be required to deposit more collateral with the bank. As an extra insurance, most banks will require more collateral than the current risk requires to ensure that it is fully covered at all times. This practice is similar to the amount of margin that exchanges require. For example, suppose that a bank transacts a straightforward interest rate swap with a counterparty, whereby the bank is paying fixed and receiving floating. At the time of the transaction, there is no immediate credit risk. This is the same as saying that the MTM value of the swap at that moment is zero – the threshold amount. Ignoring transaction and legal costs, if the counterparty were to go bankrupt immediately, the bank could instantly replace the transaction by an identical transaction with another counterparty.

However, if the market moves so that swap fixed interest rates rise slightly, the bank could only replace the transaction at a slight loss if the counterparty defaulted. At this point, if the bank has an arrangement in place to do so, it can ask the counterparty to transfer some collateral to it – the delivery amount. Depending on the agreement with the counterparty, this will be a specified percentage of the potential loss, the maximum percentage being 100% of the loss.

Any collateral called by a bank will normally be held in a third party account and not the company's own account. This is to protect the depositing counterparty's assets from being used to meet any liabilities of the holding bank (eg, in the case of bankruptcy). If the counterparty then goes bankrupt, the bank can try to use this collateral to offset the loss. In practice, the extent to which it can do so depends on the documentation governing the transaction and the collateral (this is known as the dispute resolution clauses), the law governing each, and the legal jurisdiction of each of the two parties. The bank is nevertheless generally in a stronger position than it would be without the collateral.

Collateral of this nature is often called margin, and asking for collateral, or more collateral, is making a margin call. It may be that the bank subtracts or assigns a reduced value to the collateral's market value. This is known as a haircut. The size of the haircut reflects the bank's perceived risk of holding the specific asset. In other words, it is applied to protect against any potential movements in the market and potential changes in the collateral's value which might arise before there is time for extra collateral to be transferred from the counterparty. The size of this haircut is directly related to the minimum threshold amount and the price volatility of the collateral.

Depending on the transaction's agreement, collateral or a margin might be called for by either party (ie, by whichever party is currently in MTM profit from whichever party is currently in loss) or by the higher credit-rated party. The agreement may be that margin calls can be made daily, weekly or monthly, or only at the time of an event such as an interest settlement.

The quality of collateral varies. The best is cash in the currency of the risk, which will not vary in value. The next best is generally a government security in that currency; although the value of it will vary with the market (thereby requiring margin calls to be made) there is generally no significant credit risk.

It is important to note that it is the bank's/broker's decision as to what types of securities are acceptable as collateral. Their relationship with the client and the specific regulatory rules they are subject to are major factors. Also, the types of acceptable collateral vary among different clearing houses. Generally speaking, lower-quality assets, such as junk bonds and illiquid shares/equities, are not acceptable forms of collateral.

In general, the issues to be considered regarding the quality of collateral are the volatility in its value, its creditworthiness, and its liquidity (ie, the ease with which it can be sold if necessary in the event of a counterparty default).

Swaps are sometimes transacted on the basis of mutual collateralisation. This involves both counterparties depositing collateral at the start of the transaction. A party is then obliged to add further collateral subsequently, either because of an increasing loss, or because its credit rating falls.

There must be a benchmark pricing source agreed for marking the transaction to market. For convenience, this benchmark might be an exchange-traded price or accepted market published price, such as LIBOR. For example, a swap involving an equity index might use the closing futures market price for the index.

In summary, management of collateral requires that the bank does the following:

- marks the transaction to market on a regular basis
- monitors the value of the collateral (if necessary, converted to the same currency as the MTM value of the transaction)
- makes margin calls and returns as appropriate
- checks that margin calls have been received
- makes transfers to the counterparty in response to any margin calls it makes against the bank
- pays interest on any cash collateral according to whatever has been agreed.

11. Trade Processing Services

Learning Objective

5.9.1 Know the trading mechanisms and platforms for common OTC derivatives along with processing requirements and platforms: Markit Wire/Markit SERV; DTCC Deriv/SERV and TIW; SwiftNet FpML; TriOptima; ICE LINK; DTCC AffirmXpress

The derivatives markets have seen a significant increase in both trading volumes and the number of different types of products traded. One of the key developments that has helped volumes increase, while limiting costs and making deal processing more efficient, is electronic processing. This covers a wide range of electronic trading platforms to a number of electronic processing and clearing services.

Some electronic processing platforms have direct links with a number of trading platforms, which allows trade execution direct feeds to straight-though processing (STP) tools.

Regulators are greatly concerned about the operational as well as the legal, regulatory and financial risks posed by the growing use and complexity of OTC derivatives. This was highlighted during the credit crunch and was focused upon with great interest by regulators subsequently. There is therefore a great deal of scope to apply superior electronic processing and confirmation processes to improve the post-trade and downstream processes attached to OTC derivative instruments.

For example, the very large global custodian banks whose clients include both traditional and hedge fund managers are institutions that are very exposed to operational risks in this field. Therefore they are now leading efforts to improve the processing, servicing and valuation of OTC derivatives of all kinds. They, together with investment banks, have embarked upon building derivative-processing platforms.

Many specialist trade confirmation services, such as the Depository Trust and Clearing Corporation's DTCC Deriv/SERV and others, have been adopted throughout the industry.

The following are brief descriptions of the better-known electronic services that are currently available in the derivatives market.

11.1 MarkitSERV

MarkitSERV is a company that combines IHS Markit's (MarkitWire) and the DTCC's electronic trade confirmation and workflow platforms to provide a single gateway for OTC derivative trade processing. The strategic partnership was first announced in July 2008 and received regulatory approval in September 2009 from the UK Financial Services Authority (FSA) (now replaced by the FCA) and the US Department of Justice.

Jointly owned by DTCC and IHS Markit, MarkitSERV combines the DTCC Deriv/SERV and MarkitWire trade confirmation platforms to cover all major asset classes including credit, interest rate, equity, FX non-deliverable forwards (NDFs) and commodity derivatives. It connects multiple market participants and execution venues to downstream processing platforms such as DTCC's trade information warehouse (TIW) for CDSs. It also connects to various central counterparty platforms for interest rate swaps and CDSs, in collaboration with the DTCC TIW.

MarkitSERV also connects dealers and their clients to central clearing counterparties (CCPs), trade repositories and third-party administrators and buy-side institutions.

MarkitSERV's main aim is to increase greater co-operation within the industry over infrastructure to accelerate the adoption of electronic trade confirmation and reduce risk in the OTC derivative markets.

11.2 SwapClear

SwapClear was launched in September 1999 to provide clearing for basic interest rate swaps and was the first service designed by LCH.Clearnet to meet the needs of the OTC derivatives market. In clearing swaps, LCH.Clearnet becomes the central counterparty to each half of the OTC trade.

In effect, SwapClear provides the clearing house function to the OTC derivatives markets. It offers the interbank swap market a facility to free up credit lines, reduce risk and use capital. SwapClear also gives banks the ability to net multiple OTC swaps in an efficient multilateral agreement, as LCH.Clearnet becomes the central counterparty.

SwapClear is not an STP system. Before a swap is registered with SwapClear, the bank must have already confirmed and processed the swap with its original counterparty. The benefits of the system are realised after the swap has been received, since SwapClear provides an automated facility for MTM swaps and collateral, and allows for net payment of margin requirements per currency.

The service is for clearing members of SwapClear. If one of the original parties is not a clearing member, the chain is longer. For example, if neither party is a clearing member, each original contract is replaced by two new contracts: one between that original party and a clearing member, and another between the clearing member and LCH.Clearnet. The clearing member takes collateral from the non-clearing dealer on whose behalf it has cleared, in the same way that LCH.Clearnet has taken margin from the clearing member.

To be a SwapClear clearing member (SCM), an organisation must:

- be an LCH.Clearnet shareholder
- contribute to LCH.Clearnet's default fund
- meet minimum resource requirements
- make regular financial reports to LCH.Clearnet
- maintain adequate systems and records and employ operations staff with adequate expertise in swaps.

To be a SwapClear dealer, other than a clearing member, an organisation must:

- be a principal in wholesale market transactions
- be a SWIFT user
- have (or be a fully guaranteed subsidiary of an entity that has) a credit rating of BBB or better.

Both counterparties to a swap transaction must be SwapClear dealers for the transaction to be registered through SwapClear.

Confirmations between the two parties are matched through Accord (SWIFT's own confirmation matching system) or another compatible matching system. Once both parties have agreed the transaction and agreed to clear it through SwapClear, the details are submitted to LCH.Clearnet via SWIFT. LCH.Clearnet will only accept confirmed transactions, which encourages the use of automatic matching facilities.

The products cleared through SwapClear include a wide range of swaps and FRAs:

- Interest rate and zero coupon, single currency basis, compounding swaps:
  - EUR, USD and GBP swaps up to 50 years
  - AUD, CAD, CHF, JPY, SEK up to 30 years
  - CZK, DKK, HKD, HUF, NOK, NZD, PLN, SGD and ZAR up to 20 years.
- Overnight interest rate swap – CHF, EUR, USD and GBP up to two years.
- Variable notional swaps – EUR, USD and GBP swaps up to 50 years.

The benefits of SwapClear are:

- a reduction in credit risk through effective multilateral netting and margining of exposures, freeing up bank credit lines for further business
- a reduction in regulatory capital requirements through the Capital Requirements Directive (CRD) Annex II exemption, removing the need for banks to calculate counterparty risk requirements
- initial margin offsets between swaps and interest rate and government bond futures and options positions traded on Euronext
- a reduction of operational risk through the centralisation and standardisation of processes providing post-trade STP
- a reduction in operational and administrative costs.

11.3 The Depository Trust & Clearing Corporation (DTCC)

The DTCC provides a matching service (Deriv/SERV) for OTC derivatives, which is used in post-trade processing. The service requires mainframe-to-mainframe connections between the DTCC and each firm.

Deriv/SERV is a global service offering, focused on automating the entire life cycle of OTC derivatives. This includes front-office trade affirmation, automated confirmation and matching, payment processing, and a trade warehouse. The service offered includes:

- **Omgeo OASYS** is a screen affirmation platform that allows traders and front office staff to affirm credit derivative trades from multiple inter-dealer brokers (IDBs) at the point of trade. The platform allows immediate trade affirmation of brokered transactions. It also supports credit derivatives, including single-name and index CDSs, and tranched index swaps.
- **Omgeo Central Trade Manager (Omgeo CTM)** provides a platform for the central matching of cross-border and domestic transactions, automating the trade confirmation process across several asset classes, such as equities, fixed income, repurchase agreements (repos), exchange-traded derivatives and synthetic equity swaps.
- **Payments** – Deriv/SERV provides payment matching and bilateral netting services, providing greater accuracy and STP.
- **Trade information warehouse (TIW)** – the warehouse maintains the most up-to-date record of each contract and automates the servicing of contracts, which can extend over five years or more. The warehouse comprises a comprehensive database containing the most up-to-date record of each contract, as well as a processing component that standardises and automates **downstream** processing over a contract's life cycle.

In addition, the DTCC (which is currently the largest global securities processing service), through its subsidiaries, provides post-trade clearance, settlement, custody and information services for a wide range of cash market and derivatives equities. The National Securities Clearing Corporation (NSCC) subsidiary, which acts as a central counterparty, provides trade guarantees, netting and risk management services for equity and debt transactions from all US stock exchanges and markets. The Depository Trust Company (DTC) subsidiary has custody of, and provides asset servicing for, millions of securities issues of issuers from the US and over 60 other countries. The DTC serves as a major clearing house for institutional post-trade settlement.

Many market participants have designed direct links between their internal MIS systems to the DTCC to increase efficiency, reduce operational risk and provide better service for their clients.

11.4 SWIFTNet FpML

SWIFT, the financial industry's co-operative payment system, has developed SWIFTNet FpML, which allows users to send and receive secure messages and OTC derivative trade confirmations and advice via their SWIFTNet system. This is a real-time matching and exception service for handling FX, money market and OTC derivative confirmations. Its main goal is to enhance the efficiency of the user's STP of OTC derivative contracts.

SWIFTNet FpML is accessible via SWIFT's secure IP network. It also provides a long-term archival service for all trades processed through the system, which will be held for one year after their maturity. FpML is widely recognised as the standard of choice among ISDA members for communicating information electronically. The service is geared to work with users' existing processing systems and is available to all SWIFT members.

Its key benefits are:

- reducing operational risk
- lowering costs
- ease of access via graphical user interface (GUI) and application programming interface (API)
- increasing STP
- reducing **settlement risk**.

11.5 NEX TriOptima

TriOptima is a financial software and service technology company that has developed products that help its users reduce the capital, credit, and operational costs, and centrally manage counterparty risk associated with their OTC derivative portfolios.

Its core services provide a wide range of OTC derivative portfolio management that range from the reduction swap inventory and counterparty risk to managing disputes and automatic margin management.

Currently, TriOptima's core services meet current and anticipated regulatory regulations for OTC derivatives compression and reconciliation.

11.6 Financial products Markup Language (FpML)

Financial products Markup Language (FpML) is an open source industry-standard protocol developed for the electronic dealing and processing of OTC derivatives communications. It is based on extensible markup language (XML), the standard meta-language for describing data shared between software applications. The purpose of FpML, which is available free, is to automate the flow of information across the entire derivatives network, independently of the underlying software or hardware infrastructure supporting the activities related to these transactions.

FpML provides the standard data content and structure to exchange derivatives transactions electronically. While it is an open data standard, it is not an application nor an electronic dealing or processing service. It is the standard used by many of the services cited in the previous section, and also by most participants in the derivatives markets.

The following is a list of the main products that are currently covered by FpML applications:

- **Interest rate derivatives** – interest swaps, swaptions, FRAs, caps and floors, inflation swaps, and bullet payments.
- **FX** – swaps, spots, forwards, and options.
- **Credit** – single-name CDSs, CDS indices and baskets.
- **Equity** – equity swaps, equity options, variance swaps, and total return swaps.

11.7 ICE Link

ICE Link (formerly known as T-Zero) is an electronic credit derivatives trade matching and processing services provider. It provides trade information and novation of credit derivative transactions on a T+0 basis, which meets industry targets set by the ISDA Board Oversight Committee (IBOC).

11.8 EurexOTC Clear

EurexOTC Clear is a transaction management service for OTC swaps provided by the Eurex Group. Its goal is the reduction of counterparty risk, margin and collateral requirements, as well as the clearing for OTC interest rate swaps, FX and zero-coupon inflation swaps.

12. Settlement and Processing of Over-the-Counter (OTC) Contracts

Learning Objective

5.10.1 Know the importance of accurate and timely settlement processes for OTC products: trade confirmations; reconciliation processes (internal and external); cashflow/asset movement instructions and control processes; close out or maturity instructions; the implications of spreadsheet environments

5.10.2 Understand the main control process: banks/brokers; investment managers; front to back office reconciliation; trade validation; profit and loss reporting

12.1 The Importance of Controls

The efficient administration of all transactions is essential. In the case of derivatives, the risks arising from inefficiency are potentially greater because derivatives are geared, therefore the full risk of any trade can be significantly more than the initial transaction. There is no set structure that organisations apply for the administration of their derivatives business.

For example, the structure in a bank will generally be different from that within a fund management company.

There will be many factors involved, including:

- **volumes of transactions** – the market players will undertake many more transactions, particularly if they are market makers, so they will tend to have more specialist areas within the overall operations area
- **range and complexity of products** – an end-user, such as a fund manager, is likely to be involved in a narrower range of products, so will require a narrower range of expertise
- **valuations and risk monitoring** – both market makers and end-users need to have efficient systems that value all existing positions, as well as measure all of their associated risks
- **reporting** – while the regulatory reporting requirements for the fund manager may be less onerous and less frequent than for a bank, both will have to report their respective positions on a regular basis.

In some organisations the structure of the operations area is along product lines; in others it cuts across product lines and is organised along process lines instead, eg, by domicile of the counterparty or by complexity of the deal. Within derivatives operations, particularly in major market participants, there is also often a split between OTC and exchange-traded instruments. Within a bank, there is often a front office, a middle office, an operations department (what used to be called the back office) and a risk management area. Which processes are performed in which area can vary from bank to bank. Hence it is better to concentrate on the processes themselves. No matter how the operations area is organised, the key objectives are efficiency, flexibility, security and control.

12.2 The Process Flow

The process an OTC derivatives transaction follows has many steps that are common to all financial transactions.

12.2.1 Trade Capture and Verification

Since most trades are automatically input into the system in the dealing room, the details of the transaction must be verified by the middle office by the end of the trading day. Trade entry must follow the deal immediately, because any delay means that market risk and credit risk are not being monitored correctly, and because, in turn, it delays the confirmation and settlement process. The same problems arise if trades are booked incorrectly. For example, if the sale of an equity index call is booked as a purchase, not only will the trader's position be incorrect, so will the bank's risk report. This type of error will also result in the bank paying the premium, as well as not being able to monitor that it has in fact received the premium from its counterparty. The error will also cause a failed settlement.

The late or incorrect booking of trades, particularly where exacerbated by poor controls, can result in a wide range of potential problems including:

- inaccuracies in evaluating risk, managing positions and investment decisions
- late settlement-related interest payments and fees owed to counterparties
- operational losses through funding and timing difficulties, eg, late receipt of sales proceeds can create knock-on delays in settling other trades
- poor-quality client servicing, eg, inaccurate or late reports
- rule breaches, leading to fines or disciplinary action taken by exchanges and/or regulators
- reputational loss, including loss of trading/research opportunities with certain counterparties, and negative impact on client and stakeholder relationships.

Similar risks can arise through over-reliance on spreadsheets, which are very accessible and familiar to many people, but nevertheless proven to distort our perceptions of efficiency, accuracy and utility. When replaced by expertly programmed and tested software designed to work as part of a bigger system, spreadsheets are often found to be much slower to run, and highly susceptible to bugs and human error.

12.2.2 Position Keeping and Profit and Loss Analysis

Positions must be monitored for risk control and the profit and loss calculated. The extent to which position keeping is a responsibility of the front office or of the operations area varies between organisations. Clearly it is of prime importance to the dealer to monitor their own position, as that is what gives rise to their profit or loss. Most dealers are now able to monitor their current position using a real-time position system.

However, the role of checking for risk management purposes should fall outside the dealing area. Most major houses have a product control team or similar unit that performs this function. Again, using electronic position keeping, this area is able to ensure that each dealer and the trading area as a whole remains within their respective individual, product and area limits at all times. Any positions that are above their limit should be reported. Failure to maintain up-to-date and reconciled end-of-day positions between the dealing room and product control team could result in losses from unreported transactions or positions in excess of risk management limits.

12.2.3 Confirmation and Documentation

The details of the trade and any documentation to be used are agreed. It is important that these be agreed between the operations areas of the two parties, independently of the dealers, to reduce the risk of either fraud or unauthorised dealing on the part of the dealer.

A confirmation sets out the terms and conditions of an individual transaction at the point of trading; it is a written representation of the verbal contract (the trade) and is evidence that the transaction has occurred. Once it has been signed by both parties, there is no possibility of dispute over the trade's terms and conditions. It is important that there is a reference on the confirmation to the date of the master agreement. The confirmation incorporates the ISDA definitions appropriate to that trade.

Historically, the key difference between the administration of OTC transactions and that for exchange-traded contracts concerns the documentation relating to the trades. As there are no standard terms for OTC contracts, unlike for a listed product on an exchange, both counterparties to an OTC transaction were required to ensure that the trade was recorded on the terms that both dealers agreed at the time of the trade. However, for those counterparties with high mutual trading, a master confirmation can be agreed upon. This provides a general framework for the confirmation of each type of transaction. Its use improves the speed of the confirmation process, thus avoiding later settlement and risk management problems that arise when incorrect position records are encountered or with late or missed payments.

The financial crisis of 2008 highlighted the problem of counterparty credit risk in the OTC derivatives market. In response to this, in order to ensure that government funds would not again be used to bail out the financial industry, and in order to prevent a further market collapse, the EU introduced a series of regulations that require all OTC derivative trades are reported to a trade repository (TR) as well as a central counterparty, thus reducing counterparty credit risk and operational risks.

The details of all trades must be reported no later than the working day following the conclusion (modification or termination) of the contract.

The reporting obligation applies to derivatives contracts, which are entered into on or after the date of entry into force (16 August 2012) of EMIR and to those contracts that are already outstanding on that date.

EMIR reporting requirements do not apply to individuals nor do they extend to non-EU counterparties. However, in the case of an EU counterparty under EMIR dealing with American counterparties (or from other jurisdictions), the equivalent Dodd-Frank or other OTC derivative reporting requirements will apply to the other side of the transaction.

A master confirmation represents the market consensus as to how a product is expected to work and sets out the standard definitions and terms for that product on either a global or regional basis. It allows thereafter for the exchange of what is called a transaction supplement, which has only the trade- specific details of the individual transaction. The transaction supplement merely has to reference the fact that it is written under the terms of the master confirmation and so in most cases it is shorter than a normal confirmation.

Similarly IHS Markit has been responsible for achieving consensus in the credit market in the same way as ISDA and, by publishing standard terms has allowed market participants to reference those terms, in much the same way as if they had executed a specific master confirmation.

Any disagreements must be identified, reported and resolved immediately, and if a confirmation, or acknowledgement of a confirmation, is not received from the counterparty within a prescribed time, escalation procedures must be in place.

12.2.4 Settlement

At the time of the trade and/or subsequently, there will be one or more settlements to be made, which must be monitored, calculated, netted if appropriate, and settled.

The settlement process in OTC derivatives is more complex than with cash instruments. With cash instruments there is often only one fixed settlement date; the amount to be settled is fixed, and this amount can be calculated as soon as the deal has been transacted. With OTC derivatives, apart from the premium paid upfront for an option, this is often not the case.

For example:

- A cap has a series of potential settlement dates; all, some or none may involve a settlement.
- An American option can be exercised at any time until expiry.
- The settlement amount on a fixed/floating swap cannot be calculated until the floating rate has been set.
- The fact that a payment is necessary and the specific amount related to a CDS is determined should the predefined credit event occur.

Timely trade processing can help avoid the risks that can arise through late settlement.

12.2.5 Reconciliation

All the cash flows passing across the bank account which arise from the transaction must be compared with the expected cash flows and any discrepancies investigated.

12.2.6 Collateral Management

If collateral is required on one or both sides to the deal, its market value must be monitored frequently as must the current value of the deal, so that the collateral requirement can be adjusted accordingly. The reference prices that are used in any MTM valuation should be agreed as part of the original deal, in order to avoid any disagreement.

12.2.7 Risk Management

The trade will give rise to both market risk and credit risk. Although the responsibility for monitoring these does not usually fall within the operations area, the operations area is a vital link in ensuring that the data used for the risk analysis is updated both quickly and accurately.

End of Chapter Questions

1. What is a forward contract?
   Answer reference: Section 2.1

2. How soon does delivery generally take place in the FX spot market?
   Answer reference: Section 3

3. What is a swaption?
   Answer reference: Section 4

4. How do collars relate to caps and floors?
   Answer reference: Section 5

5. What are inflation swap payments based on?
   Answer reference: Section 6.3

6. What is a credit linked note?
   Answer reference: Section 7.1.1

7. Describe a Bermudan option.
   Answer reference: Section 8.1

8. What is a puttable bond?
   Answer reference: Section 8.2

9. How is collateral used?
   Answer reference: Section 10.2

10. Name the conditions for being a SwapClear clearing member.
    Answer reference: Section 11.2

Chapter Six

Principles of Clearing and Margin

This syllabus area will provide approximately 10 of the 100 examination questions

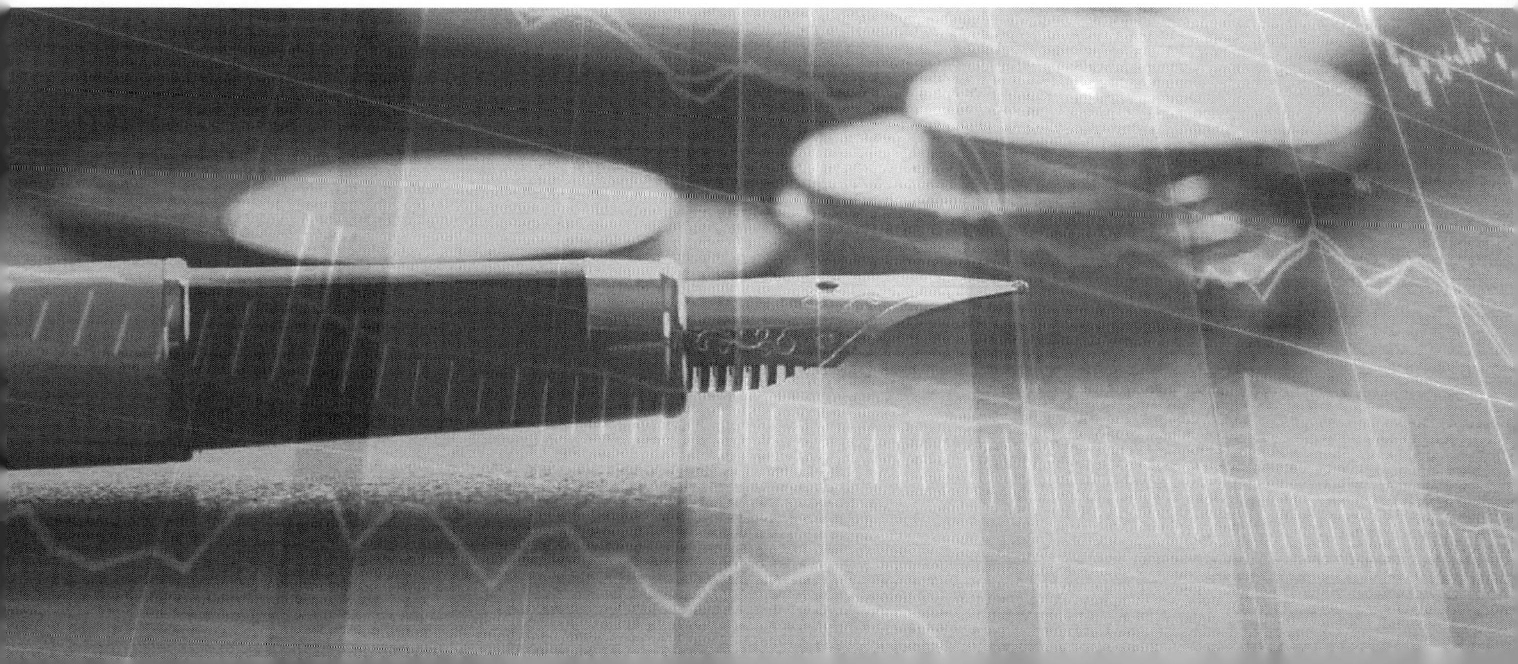

1. The Definition and Purpose of Clearing

1.1 Clearing and Risk

Learning Objective

6.1.1 Understand the purpose of clearing and the function of novation: mutual offset system; principal to principal; broker's position

6.1.2 Understand the risks usually associated with the clearing process and the implications of default: settlement risk; counterparty risk; currency risk

Clearing is the process by which derivatives trades are confirmed and registered. Registration is with a clearing house that becomes legal counterparty to every transaction. The legal process whereby the clearing house becomes the counterparty to all trades is called novation. This involves substituting the clearing house as the buyer to every seller and the seller to every buyer. Hence every original exchange contract becomes two new contracts; the original contract no longer exists.

Any currency risk that exists for clearing members with regard to settlement is minimal, since as a member of a clearing house and exchange it must maintain an account in the clearing house's currency. Any currency risk that does arise from the clearing process arises from the exchange rate movements between the member's home currency and that of the exchange's, for the amounts of their net daily margin payments.

This central counterparty structure removes almost all counterparty risk (credit risk) from all clearing members operating within the market. The only counterparty risk faced by clearing members is with the clearing house itself, not with each other.

In addition, the clearing house will monitor all open positions and will facilitate the settlement process by acting as the intermediary with respect to the close-out and delivery of futures contracts and the exercise and assignment of option contracts. In the rare case of default, the clearing house faces one day of market risk, since all members must pay a daily margin payment which is based on their net position's profit/loss relative to the previous day's price movement.

For the rare occasion that the margin payments do not cover the net position's loss, all clearing houses, such as LCH.Clearnet or ICE Clear Europe, maintain a default fund, which is cash that is paid in by its members. In order to ensure that the fund is sufficient, the clearing house runs a wide range of stress tests, so that the fund's size meets worst-case estimates of the market's volatility. Note that this fund only covers default by members directly to the clearing house.

One of the major advantages of having such a clearing system, therefore, is that it greatly reduces counterparty risk. The clearing house guarantees the financial performance of the contract and, as long as the clearing house is backed by substantial financial resources, and is thus highly creditworthy, market users and investors can have a high degree of confidence in the system. Another advantage is that contracts become very easy to trade, with the clearing house making it easy to close out a trade by taking an equal and opposite position – because both long and short positions are novated to the clearing house as central counterparty, the previous position is effectively closed.

Settlement risk – the risk that an expected payment of cash or a security will not be made on time or at all – is another risk associated with the delivery/clearing process. The establishment of a netting system/agreement is an effective method of minimising this kind of risk.

One extension of the clearing process is a mutual offset system. This is an agreement between two exchanges that allows trades executed on one exchange to be booked and cleared through another. Such an agreement exists between the CME and the SGX for a few of the contracts that are traded on both. Two of these contracts are the eurodollar and the JGB contracts.

In a principal-to-principal system, such as that operated by ICE Clear Europe, the clearing house guarantees the performance of trades executed by its members on the exchanges that it serves. The guarantee does not extend to members' clients or non-clearing exchange member firms. As a result, it will implicate the broker as long as the broker is an ICE Clear Europe member.

Major Exchanges	Clearing Houses
Euronext Derivatives	LCH.Clearnet SA
LME	LME Clear
LSE Derivatives	LCH.Clearnet ltd
ICE Futures Europe	ICE Clear Europe
CME Group (CBOT, CME and NYMEX)	CME Clearing
OneChicago	CME Clearing or Options Clearing Corporation (OCC) depending on membership
NASDAQ (PHLX)	Clearing Trade Interface (CTI) via NASDAQ OMX
Eurex	Eurex Clearing AG
Euronext Europe	LCH.Clearnet SA – moving to ICE Clear
Mercado Español de Futuros Financieros (MEFF)	Exchange's clearing house
Singapore Exchange (SGX)	SGX-DC (exchange's clearing house)
Osaka Securities Exchange (OSE)	Exchange's clearing house
Brazilian Mercantile & Futures Exchange (BM&F) Bovespa	Trades are cleared through the BM&F **Bovespa** clearing house
Dubai Mercantile Exchange (DME)	CME Clearing
National Commodity & Derivatives Exchange Ltd (NCDEX) (India)	Trades are processed via the exchange's clearing house, physical delivery through its depository clearing system, while margin payments and cash settlement are via an approved clearing bank
South African Futures Exchange (Safex), part of the Johannesburg Stock Exchange (JSE)	Exchange's clearing house
Shanghai Futures Exchange (SHFE)	Exchange's clearing house

Recently there has been a similar shift to establishing a central counterparty and a formal trade reporting procedure for OTC derivative contracts. The main reason for this is to provide greater stability in the market, by reducing counterparty credit risk and better risk management. The EMIR is the regulatory legislation for this clearing and margin structure for the EU derivatives market.

1.2 The Structure of the Clearing System

Learning Objective

6.1.3 Understand the role played by the clearing house in the clearing process: clearing house relationship with members in settlement; transfer of payments

6.1.5 Understand the relationship between clearing members and non-clearing members: clearing versus non-clearing member; use of general clearing members to clear trades

The different tiers that make up the clearing system at the exchange level are the clearing house, the clearing members (of which there are two types) and the non-clearing members. The clearing members themselves can be general clearing members or individual clearing members, which means respectively that they clear either for themselves and/or:

- for direct clients and for other exchange members, or
- for direct clients only.

The clearing house is typically owned by its members or by the exchange whose contracts it clears, or both. There are different models. For example, in the case of the OCC in the US, the clearing corporation is jointly owned by several exchanges. On the other hand, the CME's clearing house is a division of the exchange itself. ICE Clear Europe's parent is Intercontinental Exchange Holdings.

The tiers are:

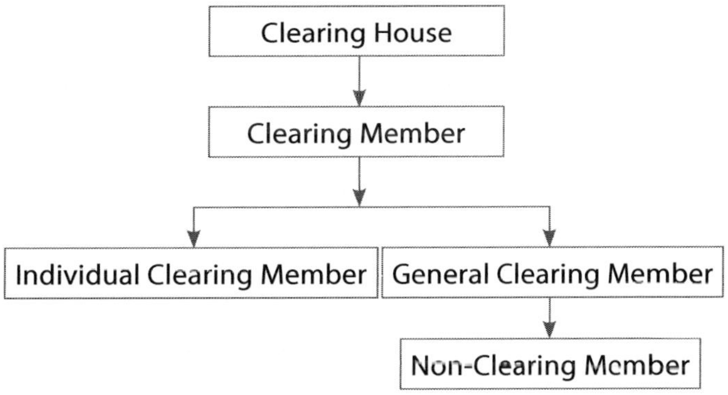

To illustrate its different tiers and the clearing process, it is useful to look at a typical trade and the individual steps involved. The futures example that follows highlights the systems and procedures that are used when a trade initiates on ICE Europe, for which ICE Clear Europe acts as the clearing house.

As mentioned in Chapter 4, Section 4, the first part of the clearing process is trade reporting or registration. For most exchanges, such as ICE Futures Europe, its electronic trading system automatically reports a trade, once it happens, to the universal clearing platform (UCP). Once this takes place, the clearing process begins.

Example 1

Step 1. The trade
Mr X. Ample is a client of ABC Ltd, a member firm of ICE Futures. He places a market order. ABC Ltd will act as broker, executing the trade on the ICE Futures exchange. ABC Ltd is not a member of ICE Clear Europe.

Any trade executed needs to be reported to and registered with the clearing house (ICE Clear Europe). The trade will need to be registered via a clearing member, and ABC Ltd has an agreement with a general clearing member, KMM Ltd, a firm which is a member of both the exchange and ICE Clear Europe.

Step 2. Confirmation and matching
ABC Ltd will pass details of the trade to KMM Ltd (its clearing member) who will input the details into the confirmation and matching system (known as UCP, used by ICE) where it will wait until the counterparty to the ABC Ltd trade enters the equal and opposite details into the system.

Step 3. Registration
Once matched, KMM Ltd registers the trade with ICE Clear Europe (via UCP), giving details of the type of account the trade is assigned to. The account will either be in a segregated, **client** account, or within the non-segregated **house** account.

Step 4. Novation
At the point of registering the trade with ICE Clear Europe the contract is novated, resulting in ICE Clear Europe becoming counterparty to two new transactions – one with KMM Ltd and the other with ABC Ltd's original counterparty. The original contract between ABC Ltd and its counterparty no longer exists.

In effect, ABC Ltd (a non-clearing firm) has committed KMM Ltd (its clearing member) to a transaction with ICE Clear Europe (the clearing house).

ICE Clear Europe guarantees the performance of the contract to its immediate counterparty, the clearing member – KMM Ltd in the above example. This is known as a principal-to-principal guarantee.

ICE Clear Europe will call on KMM Ltd for any subsequent payments (margin) on the contract as necessary. KMM Ltd, as a clearing member, will pay any margin due through the Assured Payments Service (APS) – a system used by ICE Clear Europe in conjunction with several leading banks, which will automatically debit members' bank accounts. KMM Ltd will collect any payments from ABC Ltd, its customer. ABC Ltd will in turn call on any payments from its customer, Mr Ample. Each party has a principal-to-principal relationship with the other.

When Mr Ample decides to close the position, the same process takes place. Note that ABC Ltd will not have to go back to the original counterparty because the original contract no longer exists. As the contract is standardised, the offsetting trade simply cancels out the trade previously registered with the clearing house, thus cancelling any delivery obligations.

Note also that the clearing house does not give any guarantees to Mr Ample, the client. Mr Ample and his broker (ABC Ltd) have a risk on each other defaulting, as does ABC Ltd and the clearing member (KMM Ltd). So, although the system substantially reduces the risk of default, it does not eliminate it along the whole system.

1.3 Guarantee

Learning Objective

6.1.4 Understand the backing arrangements in place in the event of a member default: novation; guarantee of performance of the contract; default fund; members' contributions; principal to buyer and seller; control of funds to clearing members' accounts, requirement for members to use an approved bank

6.1.6 Understand the principles of mutual and independent guarantees: mutual guarantees versus independent guarantees; purpose of the guarantees; funding of the default fund at the clearing house

Clearing houses operate a principal-to-principal guarantee based on a mutual guarantee structure. There are many clearing houses and their models differ.

As an example, the supporting financial resources pertaining to ICE Clear Europe in London are provided as follows:

- **Initial margins** are collected from clearing members in the form of cash (in various prime currencies) and acceptable securities and other collateral.
- In the event of a **member default**, the clearing house will first utilise the **margin monies and collateral placed by the defaulting member**.
- The major tranche of financial support which is next in line is the **member default fund**, which is a pool of units and to which every clearing member contributes in cash (interest-bearing) according to the volume of its clearing activities. The amount that members are required to deposit is reviewed and normally every three months. See Section 1.5.1 of this chapter. Hence, for example, a member default occurring in swaps clearing is also supported by the fund provided by those firms involved in futures or equity clearing. As a result of this, the system is known as a **mutual guarantee system**. An **independent guarantee system** would not have a collective default fund.
- The next level of support is provided by an **insurance policy** from an insurance company.

In the event of a clearing member defaulting on its obligations, the following sources are drawn upon to cover the losses arising on the default:

- Firstly, the default member's margin held by the clearing house is used.
- Then the default fund contributions of that member are used.
- Then the default fund contributions of other clearing member firms are used.
- Then the insurance policy is called upon.

This process is called 'waterfall'.

1.4 Prime Brokers

Learning Objective

6.1.7 Understand the services offered by prime brokers as they relate to derivatives: borrowing and lending securities; financing positions; providing custody and safekeeping of assets; clearing and settling trades; administering onshore and offshore funds; corporate actions; capital introductions; risk management; regulation of prime brokers

A prime broker's role in relation to derivatives is that it is primarily responsible for the following:

- Efficient and best execution of all trades.
- Ensuring confirmation of client trades through the required trade documentation.
- Settlement of trade cash flows, to provide cash financing or securities lending as pre-agreed and when needed.
- Providing custody and safekeeping of all assets, as well as any risk management systems that the client may require.
- Keeping clients aware of all issuer correspondence, such an annual meetings and corporate actions.

A prime broker can provide a number of services for its client; these include:

- Clearing and settlement of trade in global markets.
- Central custodianship of assets, and using consolidated positions for the extension of leverage.
- Financing multiple currencies, as required.
- Stock borrowing capabilities to support trade strategies.
- Integrated web reporting of positions, activities and performance.
- Hedge fund consulting services.
- Facilitating communication between sales, trading and research.

In addition, certain prime brokers provide additional **value-added** services which may include:

- **Capital introduction** – a process whereby the prime broker attempts to introduce its hedge fund to qualified hedge fund investors who have an interest in exploring new opportunities to make hedge fund investments.
- **Office space leasing and servicing** – certain prime brokers lease commercial real estate and then sublease blocks of space for hedge fund tenants. These prime brokers, typically, provide a suite of on-site services for clients who utilise their space.
- **Risk management advisory services** – the provision of risk analysis technology, sometimes supplemented by consulting by senior risk professionals.
- **Consulting services** – a range of consulting and advisory services, typically provided to **start-up** hedge funds, and focused on issues associated with regulatory establishment requirements in the jurisdiction where the hedge fund manager will be resident, as well as in the jurisdiction(s) where the fund itself will be domiciled.

Given the wide range of services and different types of clients prime brokers deal with, from large hedge funds and companies to individual investors, the regulation of prime brokers is the responsibility of a number of agencies. In the UK, they are regulated by the FCA and **MiFID (Marketing of Financial**

Instruments Directive). The latter is expected to remain key in post-Brexit UK, since its scope is the entire EEA and, therefore, goes beyond the EU. In the US both the Federal Reserve and the **SEC** monitor their activities.

1.5 Exchange-Cleared OTC Products

Learning Objective

6.1.8 Know which exchanges/clearing houses offer OTC clearing arrangements and for which major products

6.1.9 Understand how OTC products can be centrally cleared: eligibility and credit standing of counterparties; constraints placed upon contract terms; the margin processes; advantages and uses of centralised clearing of OTC products; setup of the clearing fund

6.1.10 Understand how centrally cleared products are executed

The increased concern over counterparty risk combined with exchanges' desire to expand and diversify has led to exchanges offering clearing facilities and guarantees to a range of OTC derivatives.

One such clearing facility is ICE Futures Europe, LCH.Clearnet. Once an OTC trade is agreed, its details can be submitted into LCH.Clearnet and the OTC trade is replaced with an exchange contract. LCH.Clearnet provides clearing for a wide range of individual and index equity, commodity and other LCH.Clearnet financial futures and options. These include contracts on all of the major European indices and a few key US indices, plus many individual equities, as well as bond and short-term interest products. One of the few restrictions on the OTC contracts that can use LCH.Clearnet is based on volume or trade size. This varies for specific contracts, but most have a minimum trade size to use LCH.Clearnet.

The CME Group's Clearing360 provides a similar if somewhat more restricted service for OTC interest rate derivative contracts and FX option block trades. Access to Clearing360 is restricted to firms that act as principal or agent for the OTC trades. These include hedge funds, major banks, prime brokers and proprietary trading firms.

Rather than simply clearing the OTC trades, Clearing360 substitutes the OTC FRAs and interest rate swaps with corresponding futures contracts.

Eurex also provides clearing of OTC block trades, EFP, EFS and Vola trades (bilateral volatility trades which involve OTC options and the off-exchange purchase or sale of the underlying futures contract) using its EurexOTC Clear system.

The main advantage of having an OTC derivative cleared or substituted by an exchange's clearing house is that it eliminates any counterparty risk. This is particularly attractive for longer-term contracts. Once the OTC contract is cleared it is subject to the same requirements, such as margin payments and delivery procedures, as any other exchange-traded derivative.

Centrally cleared OTC products are executed and delivered in a similar process to exchange-traded products. For any type of delivery to take place, both counterparties must be exchange members and have either a direct or indirect clearing relationship with the respective clearing house.

Unlike exchange-traded contracts, the clearing house does not assign or match buyers to sellers, but it does monitor and guarantee that delivery is made on both sides of the trade. The trades are executed between two counterparties and delivery takes place using the respective clearing system.

1.5.1 Clearing Fund

A clearing fund is a fund composed of assets contributed by market participants (clearing members) in a central counterparty (CCP) or by providers of guarantee arrangements that may be used to meet the obligations of a defaulting CCP participant. In certain circumstances, it may also be used to cover losses and liquidity pressures resulting from such defaults. A clearing fund serves as insurance against unusual price movements not covered by the margin calculation in the event of a member defaulting.

Every clearing member is required to contribute to the clearing fund. The required amount is based on a risk assessment using each clearing member's level of uncovered risk, which is based upon the trading activity. This risk-based payment is reviewed on a regular basis. For example, LCH.Clearnet recalculates each clearing member's payment on a monthly basis; other exchanges reassess these payments on a quarterly basis.

The clearing fund will be used should a clearing member default in the delivery process. The fund is used only after any margin or other related funds have been utilised.

The main types of collateral that are accepted by these clearing funds are:

- cash (EUR, USD, GBP, CHF, JPY, SEK, DKK, NOK)
- bonds to be deposited with the clearing house, valued at market; haircuts applied upon maturity.

UK	Gilts
US	Treasury bills and bonds
Germany	Bunds
France	OATs, BTFs (bills of up to one year to maturity), BTANs (1–6-year notes)
Italy	BOTs (bills of up to one year to maturity), BTPs (bonds), CCTs (floating rate notes)
Japan	JGBs

2. Price and Position Limits

Learning Objective

6.2.1 Understand price limits and position limits and the effects of their application: price limits; what are position limits; who imposes limits; purpose of price and position limits; action in the event of breach

2.1 Price Limits

These are circuit breakers imposed by the exchange that place limits on absolute price movements on the contract on any day. If the limit is breached (limit up/limit down), trading in the contract halts for a few minutes. The idea is that, at a time when markets are subject to extreme price movements, a trading halt gives participants time to calm down and take a more reasoned view about trading conditions. However, it does not always work.

While some exchanges do not have any standing price limits on most derivatives contracts, others do. Eg, on ICE there are no price limits for long gilt contracts, while there are for their JGB futures (of JPY2 from the TSE closing price).

Others have scaled price limits. The CME Group has several 'down-price' limits on most of its equity index futures, starting at 5% down to 20% down (each requiring a longer time before trading can resume). Also CME Globex has a 5% either-direction price limit on all of its equity contracts.

The NCDEX also has scaled daily price limit rules. While the price limit depends on the specific contract and ranges from +/– 4% for its gold futures to +/–6% for several of its agricultural/soft contracts, such as robusta coffee. Once that limit has been breached, trading resumes after a 15-minute cooling-off period, and the price limit is increased by 50%. So for example, the new price limit for gold would be +/–6%. But if that limit is broken, trading will be ended for that day.

An exchange's electronic systems also operate price limits to make sure that orders entered onto the system are within an allowed spread, around the prevailing market price. If orders are entered outside this price spread, they are rejected. This should lessen the possibility of errors on entry.

2.2 Position Limits

It is always possible for someone to try to corner the market in any asset by building up large derivatives positions. This would give them the power to manipulate short-term price movements to their advantage. Position limits attempt to prevent this from happening.

With this in mind, many exchanges do have position limits when contracts approach their maturities. For example, the CME Group has established a limit during the last ten days of trading for Treasury futures and the last five days for their wheat contracts. Less liquid markets have established stricter limits, such as in Kuala Lumpur, where the KLSE has a position limit of 10,000 contracts per open position for its composite index future, for the future's entire life.

Similarly, for credit risk reasons, a clearing house or broker may impose position limits on a clearing member firm or client respectively, such that only a position of a certain size may be carried. An example of this is MEFF's open position limit (OPL), which limits a member's open position to one that will require a theoretical extraordinary margin that is 20% of the member's shareholder's funds. Such a position limit is based on credit risk, rather than market manipulation concerns.

3. Margin

3.1 Introduction

Learning Objective

6.3.7 Understand how a firm deals with margin payments for its own positions and for clients' positions through its books: use of house accounts; use of client segregated accounts; use of client non-segregated/pooled accounts

6.3.8 Understand the difference between the clearing house's margin and that of the broker and the collection/payment process: amounts paid by clearing member and its clients; flow of margin

In guaranteeing contracts, the clearing house is taking on a substantial risk, especially on those contracts which have a **contingent liability**, such as futures contracts and written options. (A contingent liability is one where a loss might arise but it is not possible to be certain of its amount – the outcome is contingent upon the price of the underlying asset.)

In order for any clearing house to protect itself, there are a number of steps that it might take.

- It only permits firms that meet (and continue to meet) its membership and financial criteria to become clearing members. This is the first line of defence – the quality of its membership.
- It only deals directly with clearing members, all of whom have the most onerous financial resources requirements.
- The next line of defence is its margining system, where margin is best defined as the cash (or equivalent) deposited with the clearing house to cover the risk of the clearing member defaulting on its position.
- It relies on its own financial resources and perhaps operates inter alia a default fund; it has lines of credit with a consortium of major banks; and it has insurance policies.

The underlying reason for requiring margin payments is to support the guarantee provided by the clearing house, in other words to reduce or eliminate any counterparty credit risk. This is the underlying purpose of an efficient margin system.

Margin is collected in two ways: initial margin is largely collected when a position is first established, and then variation margin may be collected as that position worsens. Margin is demanded by the clearing house separately for the house accounts maintained by the clearing member (which will include any non-segregated client positions) and the segregated client accounts. As an example, ICE Clear Europe will demand margin from each type of account separately, on the basis of the net positions in that account.

SPAN, which stands for **Standard Portfolio ANalysis of risk**, is the leading system used to calculate daily margin requirements, and has been adopted by most of the leading futures and options exchanges. It uses a set of algorithms to determine a portfolio's daily risk. The SPAN margining system measures and determines the risk and therefore the daily margin requirement based on the entire portfolio, rather than on each specific open position. It allows both futures and options to be included together when calculating a portfolio's risk.

SPAN has the capacity that allows for both inter-maturity and inter-commodity spreads.

One of the first exchanges to use SPAN was the CBOT, which is now part of the CME Group. SPAN's ability to measure across a wide range of products and contracts allows clearing members more efficient use of their capital, as it often implies lower margin requirements.

Placing client positions within the house account as non-segregated clients may provide a cash flow benefit to the clearing firm, because any credit positions will effectively offset any debit positions. These benefits would be lost if the client's account were segregated. However, the client is obviously facing an additional risk if they are non-segregated. If the firm were to default they would potentially lose out.

These margin demands are made of the clearing member, and for ICE Clear Europe any cash payments are drawn directly from a bank account held by that member. This process (mentioned in Section 1.2 of this chapter) is known as the PPS, and the accounts are referred to as PPS accounts. Note that no cash call will be made for initial margin if the clearing member is covering initial margin requirements by an acceptable form of collateral and sufficient value of that collateral is already in place.

For the clients of the clearing member, the financial rules set by the FCA require the margin demanded by the clearing member to be at least as much as that being demanded by the clearing house, in order to avoid the need to retain more financial resources.

The concept and protection provided by margins has started to be applied to a select group of exchange-cleared OTC products. The two types that have been most popular to date have been CFDs (which are mainly cash-settled) and certain types of energy contracts. In both cases, the clearing house will swap the OTC contract with an exchange-based equivalent. It can then apply its standard margin requirements to the position, and normal payments and procedures are then followed.

3.2 Types of Margin

Learning Objective

6.3.1 Understand the differences between initial and variation margin and the significance of marking to market and withdrawal of variation margin profits: marking to market; trigger levels; offsetting long and short positions; when paid

6.3.6 Know methods of margining for centrally cleared OTC products and their implications: how exposure is calculated; what margins are applied; how and when margin payments are made

As stated in Section 3.1 of this chapter, there are basically two types of margin: **initial** and **variation** margin.

3.2.1 Initial Margin

Learning Objective

6.3.3 Understand the nature and use of offsets for spread/spot month margining: purpose of offsets; what is spot month margin; purpose of spot month margins; purpose of spread margins

6.3.4 Understand why the clearing house might call intra-day margin: purpose of intra-day margin; when is intra-day margin paid

Initial margin is a good faith deposit (perhaps in the form of collateral rather than cash), lodged with the clearing house against potential liabilities on an open position. It is returned when the position is closed out.

Initial margin is calculated by the clearing house in respect of clearing members' positions using whatever system it has adopted (see the notes on SPAN margining in Section 3.1). The clearing member similarly calculates margin with respect to its clients, and may demand a higher rate of margin (known as broker margin) from its client.

Once a client's trade has been executed, the clearing member or broker that holds the client's account will put the trade in the client's segregated or non-segregated account (depending on its relationship with the client), and at the same time collect the initial margin that is required.

Note that if the new trade was the purchase of an option, no initial margin is collected; instead the premium payment will be collected from the client's account. The reason for this is that buying an option is not a contingent liability transaction. The maximum loss an option buyer will have is the upfront premium payment.

Initial margin seeks to protect the clearing house (and in turn the broker) from the worst-case loss a position could potentially incur in one day. The actual initial margin rate per contract will be set by looking at the recent price volatility of the contract and will be determined by the clearing house following consultation with the exchange.

Example 2

For example, by continually monitoring market prices, ICE Clear Europe calculates that the most the price of the FTSE futures contract could move in one day is 300 points. Given the tick size and tick value, this could mean a potential loss of £3,000 per contract on the day on long/short open positions. So the initial margin rate will be set at £3,000 per contract for both the buyer and seller of a future. If the volatility changes up or down, the initial margin requirement may be changed.

Initial margin is recomputed every business day and effectively called first thing in the morning before markets open.

After the market has opened, if there is a sudden jump in the volatility, and the clearing house is no longer comfortable with the amount of initial margin held – indeed, if the initial margin amount is exhausted – it can call for an extra intra-day margin which is taken immediately from the clearing members via their PPS accounts.

Initial margin can be provided in cash or covered by acceptable non-cash collateral. Clearing houses have different rules on the forms of acceptable collateral they will accept. As one might expect, the lists of collateral published by ICE Clear Europe, OCC and the CME Group are rather longer than those of smaller clearing houses. See Section 4 of this chapter.

As stated in section 3.1 of this chapter, the system used to calculate initial margins for futures and options positions is known as SPAN. Other clearing houses may use methods other than this, some risk-based and some self-developed. Another well-known method is the **Theoretical Intermarket Margining System (TIMS)**, which was invented and used by the OCC. However, in August 2006 the OCC implemented its new STANS system (System for Theoretical Analysis and Numerical Simulations), which is more sophisticated. All three systems are portfolio approaches that examine the risk of futures and options positions in the same portfolio and work out the worst scenario from a standard set of scenarios in order to fairly reflect the risk of the clearing house. See Section 3.3 of this chapter for more on SPAN, TIMS and STANS.

Spreads involve more than one position across different delivery months in the same contract (a trader perhaps being long a June FTSE 100 future and short a September FTSE 100 future). The initial margin will be substantially lower than normal in this case because the two positions largely offset each other, and the price movements of each month, although not perfectly, do tend to correlate in their movement. These are known as intracommodity spreads.

Spreads also exist between different instruments that always exhibit correlation in their price movements. These are called intercommodity spreads and apply to such contracts as ICE Futures Europe Gas Oil and ICE Futures Europe Brent Crude Oil.

Therefore, most exchanges take into account the offsetting nature of these positions when setting the margin requirements. The net result is a reduction in the margin required for the two spreads mentioned above. For example, CBOT has a comprehensive list of the offset that is applied to spreads margin due to their reduced risk. It depends on the particular contract and varies from $25 to as much as $110 per contract.

As a contract nears its expiry date, its volatility can increase. If physical delivery is required in final settlement of the contract, then only those position holders who wish, or may wish, to take delivery should maintain their open contracts in the market. Others should close out or roll their positions forward to later delivery months. Therefore, as delivery for that product draws near, the clearing house may wish to minimise the speculative and delivery pressures by increasing the initial margin (this is known as a spot month margin). This occurs in order to ensure that those position holders contemplating taking the contract to delivery either have the underlying asset to deliver or have allocated adequate funds to effect settlement. It will also force any less well capitalised speculators out of the market, thereby reducing short-term speculative pressures.

3.2.2 Variation Margin

Learning Objective

6.3.2 Know the means by which exchanges establish settlement prices: what are settlement prices; closing ranges/prices

Exchanges establish settlement prices every business day in order to provide the price yardsticks for calculation of MTM variation margin and valuation of positions at the end of the day. This procedure is normally conducted at the end of the trading period, so the daily settlement price is also referred to as the closing price. However, some markets do not use the closing price, particularly those that have a global pricing influence (such as the LME), or markets that are in operation for most of the 24-hour day.

The closing range is a measure of the range or spread of prices that are quoted during a specified time just before daily trading ends. Each exchange has its own criteria for determining the closing range; most have different time frames for different contracts and they are usually longer for commodity contracts compared to financial contracts.

Example 3 below explains the standard criteria used by LCH.Clearnet on its futures contracts to arrive at daily settlement prices for each delivery month.

Example 3

A time is specified at which the daily settlement price is calculated (eg, the close of trading for that day), and the two minutes up to this time are known as the settlement range. The first 90 seconds of the settlement range allows the market supervision department to monitor spread levels. Generally, the daily settlement price is then simply the weighted average traded price during the final 30 seconds of the settlement range. However, market supervision has the flexibility to adjust the daily settlement price if the calculated price is not deemed to be a fair reflection of the market price.

At the close of each trading day all positions are marked to market based on the daily settlement price. The profit/loss on the day is measured and must be paid to/received from the clearing house as variation margin by the following day by the clearing members. The same procedure applies between clearing members and their customers by exactly the same process in turn. In this way, profits and losses accruing to positions are accounted for every day.

Variation margin, which must be paid in cash (cleared funds) in the currency of the contract, is calculated as:

Variation margin = ticks moved on the day (today's closing price – yesterday's closing price) x the contract's tick value x number of contracts of the open position.

Exercise 1

A trader goes short five FTSE 100 futures at 7140 and, at the end of the day, the daily settlement price is 7175. What is the variation margin payable?

The answer can be found in the appendix at the end of this chapter.

Each clearing member has at least one bank account to which ICE Clear Europe has access via a direct debit system so that variation margin payments can be transferred. These are the PPS accounts.

Exercise 2

A trader has a position of being long 20 LME three-month tin futures at $19,950 and at the end of the day the daily settlement price is $19,980. What is the variation margin flow for this position?

The answer can be found in the appendix at the end of this chapter.

3.2.3 Maintenance Margin

This is an arrangement between member and client and is not operated by the clearing house. Usually a member firm will expect a client to deposit more than the initial margin. This provides a safety cushion for the member and allows for the payment of some variation margin without referring back to the client every day. Once the credit breaches a preset limit (trigger/maintenance level), the member will issue a margin call (trigger margin), expecting the client to replenish the account to the original amount. This practice is common in the United States. For example, if the initial margin for a long gilt futures contract on ICE Clear Europe is set at £5,000 per contract, a broker/clearing member might require that its client deposit an additional 25% of that amount as a maintenance margin. This will ensure that the member is protected from any possible losses, should the client be unable to meet any variation margin payments, particularly in volatile markets.

The level of maintenance margin is usually set at 25–50% of the initial margin payment of any new positions.

3.3 Methods of Determining a Margin

Learning Objective

6.3.5 Know methods of margining involving delta and SPAN and their implications: use of delta; use of SPAN; effect of price change in the underlying; use of net liquidation value

Exchanges have developed several different programmes to calculate the initial and variation or daily margin requirements for all new and existing futures and options positions. The two most common are SPAN and TIMS.

The level of variation/daily margin required for an existing position is determined by the change in the price of the underlying asset.

For futures, there is a direct relationship, therefore a 3% rise in the price of gold in the cash market will have a similar effect on the margin required for those short gold futures, since the future's price will rise at least that amount.

For options, the relationship between price changes in the underlying and its effect on an option's value is more complex, given the characteristics of an option. As explained in Chapter 4, Section 2.3, an option's **delta** is used to measure the sensitivity of an option's price to changes in the price of the underlying asset. Since an

ATM option has a delta of 0.5, a 3% rise in the price of its underlying asset will result in an approximate 1.5% rise in the value of the option. Remember, however, that this is only one of the factors that will influence the option's price; any changes to its volatility and time decay will also be taken into account.

3.3.1 Standard Portfolio Analysis (SPAN)

SPAN is a scenario-based risk programme used for calculating daily margins. It was originally developed by the CME Group, which then permitted LCH.Clearnet (previously used by NYSE Liffe) to adapt its specifications to produce London SPAN. It has also been licensed by the CME Group for use by many other clearing houses.

Essentially, SPAN looks at the impact on a position of futures and options contracts if the price and volatility of the underlying asset changes by set amounts. Its parameters include the initial margin rate (known as the scanning range) and the percentage volatility movement.

SPAN is based on the estimation of the liquidation value of a position or portfolio using several scenarios representing changes in market conditions. There is a set of scenarios for each contract, which is updated on a daily basis, to reflect current market conditions.

SPAN scenarios include the following factors:

- possible changes of the underlying asset's price
- changes in the underlying asset's price volatility
- the impact of time on an option's value.

Although it draws heavily upon complex options pricing theory, SPAN itself is based upon an extremely simple set of arithmetic equations, and it is this simplicity that is perhaps the key element of the programme's success. SPAN considers a total of 16 risk scenarios, when estimating the maximum loss that might be incurred from one position from one trading day to another. This is the basis for the clearing house's initial and variation margin requirements.

It separates the total position of the clearing member into individual portfolios, eg, all gilt futures and options in one portfolio, and FTSE 100 futures and options in another.

For each portfolio, the clearing house will set its maximum scanning range; for the FTSE 100 – say, a 300-point price movement, up and down – as well as a change in the volatility – say, a 30% rise or fall. It then applies 16 scenarios with price and volatility moving up and down by varying degrees and measures the impact on the position, eg, price up 1/3 of range and volatility up 30%.

A charge for inter-month spreads is added, as delivery months within one instrument do not exhibit perfect correlation between each other. A credit is given for inter-commodity spreads (where permitted by the clearing house), recognising the correlation of price movements between different contracts because gains in one instrument will often offset losses in another. SPAN also recognises the additional risk of spot delivery months and adds a charge for this. Finally, it chooses the largest resulting negative number. This then becomes the initial margin requirement.

In a futures contract there are only price movements to consider, so the initial margin tends to remain the same unless the scanning range is changed.

Options positions (and combined futures and options positions) will be affected by changes in volatility as this is the most important element in pricing options, so the initial margin needed to maintain a position is likely to change daily. For options positions, SPAN uses deltas to calculate the equivalent number of futures to quantify any potential offset.

SPAN produces an overall initial margin requirement for the member, covering all of the contracts registered in the member's name at ICE Clear Europe. If a member has registered positions in both house and client accounts, it must simultaneously meet a separate requirement for each account.

3.3.2 Theoretical Intermarket Margining System (TIMS) and System for Theoretical Analysis and Numerical Simulations (STANS)

The Theoretical Intermarket Margining System (TIMS) was launched in 1986 and has been approved for use by the OCC and is also used by several other exchanges. TIMS uses a portfolio-based margining methodology and is particularly well suited for measuring the risk of mixed portfolios (those containing physicals, futures and options).

TIMS uses an option pricing model to identify the risks of options on a specific underlying asset which have different strike prices and maturities, and provides for offsets between positions in different, but highly correlated, underlying assets.

It bases its total margin calculation for each position on calculating two margin components: the premium margin and the risk margin. The sum of these is the total margin. The premium margin is the market value of a particular position at the close of trading. It represents the daily change or price movement. The risk margin uses an option pricing formula to measure the potential change in the position's value, assuming the assessed maximum probable intra-day price movement (using forecasts of implied volatility).

TIMS is a more complex methodology than SPAN, but one that is considered to be well suited for use in these mixed portfolios, given its use of the option pricing model, stress testing, implied volatility and correlation modelling.

As noted in Section 3.2.1 of this chapter, in August 2006 the OCC implemented STANS – a proprietary risk margining system based on a more modern approach to measuring risk. This new approach requires more sophisticated statistical methods, more complex calculations and greater computing power than TIMS; it addresses certain shortcomings of the TIMS model, particularly with respect to correlations in price movements and the modelling of extreme events.

STANS generates a set of 10,000 hypothetical market scenarios that incorporate information extracted from the historical behaviour of each individual security, as well as its relationship to the behaviour of other securities. Scenarios are generated for more than 7,000 risk factors, including a broad range of individual equities, exchange-traded funds, stock indices, currencies and commodity products.

Although the OCC continues to use TIMS for several risk management functions, it relies on STANS for the critically important purpose of assessing clearing member margin requirements. According to the OCC, the STANS model provides margin calculations that are more precise, more realistic, and more consistent across portfolios, which should improve the financial stability of the derivatives markets and produce capital efficiencies beneficial to investors.

Both SPAN and TIMS were designed to measure the market risk associated with derivatives.

3.3.3 Net Liquidation Value (NLV)

Because margin requirements are based on the net positions held by the member firm, and there may be a variety of positions held at a given time, the calculation of the total margin amount due or to be received is based on the net liquidation values (NLVs) of the constituent parts of the portfolio. This allows for the profits showing on a portion of a member firm's positions to offset the losses of other positions in its portfolio, resulting in one net payment.

4. Collateral and Credit

4.1 Acceptable Collateral

Learning Objective

6.4.1 Know the definition, purpose and uses of collateral and the types of acceptable collateral (cash versus non-cash)

Cover for initial margin can be provided using collateral rather than cash. The following is the full list of assets that some of the major clearing houses accept as payment for initial margin from their members:

- **Cash** in most major currencies (sterling, euros, US dollars, Swiss francs, Swedish krona, Danish krone, Norwegian kroner and Japanese yen). Most national exchanges accept cash deposits at approved banks in their local currency.
- **Bank guarantees** from an approved bank in an approved form.
- **Certificates of deposit** (denominated in £ sterling and US dollars).
- **Government debt** (bills, bonds and notes) from the following 14 countries: the UK; Germany; Italy; the Netherlands; Sweden; Austria; the US; France; Spain; Belgium; Canada; Australia; Finland; Denmark.

However, it is important to note that:

- undated bonds are not acceptable
- the bonds must be denominated in the currency of the issuing country
- Swiss bonds are not acceptable
- collateral is also marked to market daily and is subject to a published 'haircut', which means that the full market value is not credited; this has become more common after the downgrading of several government bonds on the list
- the securities that are used as collateral are lodged with depositories and custodians that are acceptable to the specific clearing house.

4.2 Credit Lines

Learning Objective

6.4.2 Understand the significance of credit lines: purpose of credit lines; what credit lines cover; deals in excess of a credit line; significance of collateral

Although it is uncommon, some exchanges allow their members to extend credit to their clients to cover margin requirements. Deals requested in excess of a specified credit line will be rejected by the exchange member firm. These so-called credit lines will be subject to the regulatory rules specifying the circumstances in which lending money to clients is acceptable. For example, the FCA has rules on customer borrowing; under FCA rules, credit may be extended for up to five days without a formal written loan agreement.

Credit lines, which are used by customers to finance their derivatives trading, are not allowed by the ICE markets for their financial products.

Collateral is the assets that are used as a guarantee or as security for the credit line or loan. Collateral reduces the exchange member's credit risk from the client to whom they have extended the credit line.

4.3 Collateral Management

Learning Objective

6.4.3 Understand the mechanisms of collateral management: valuation and pricing; Credit Support Annex (CSA); thresholds; haircuts; minimum transfer amount

Collateral management is the process that allows market participants to reduce the counterparty credit exposure that arises from longer-maturity OTC derivative contracts, such as swaps and options.

Example

Company A enters into a 10-year interest rate swap, as a fixed rate payer, with one of its main banks. As market rates fall, in favour of the bank and against Company A, the MTM profit on the swap represents a loss to Company A and a profit for the bank. This, in turn, increases the bank's risk exposure to the company, since it has a loss on this swap position.

One way that the banks can reduce the risk exposure created by the swap is to enter into a CSA or CSD, which contains the details of the conditions and procedures by which collateralisation will occur. See Chapter 5, Section 10.1.1.

This process is very similar to the daily margin process that all exchange clearing houses go through with their members. In addition to reducing counterparty risk, collateral management can also improve capital usage, increase the potential number of transactions that can be undertaken with an individual counterparty, and reduce dealing spreads.

Most CSAs and CSDs that a bank or dealer would enter into with counterparties that are other banks or clients are two-way agreements. This means that both sides of the trade are subject to the terms of the agreement that ensures that both will be able to meet their respective obligations to the OTC trades. But most sovereign, supranational and agency (SSA) counterparties do not agree to this and in most cases the bank is subject to a one-way CSA.

A one-way CSA means that the bank or dealer is required to post the required amount of collateral with its SSA counterparty when the trade moves in the SSA's favour, but the SSA is not required to reciprocate and post the collateral when the trade moves in favour of the bank/dealer.

Appendix

Answers to Exercise 1

Sold at	7140
Less: current cost of purchase	(7175)
Loss in index points per contract	(35)

Variation margin payable = 35 index points x £10 per index point x 5 contracts = £1,750.

Answers to Exercise 2

Bought at	$19,950
Daily settlement price	$19,980
Profit	$30

Variation payable to the trader = $30 per tonne x 5 tonne contract size x 20 contracts = $3,000.

End of Chapter Questions

1. How does the process of clearing work?
   Answer reference: Section 1.1

2. What is used to minimise settlement risk?
   Answer reference: Section 1.1

3. A prime broker's role in relation to derivatives is primarily responsible for what?
   Answer reference: Section 1.4

4. In what way is clearing fund paid for?
   Answer reference: Section 1.5.1

5. What is the purpose of price limits?
   Answer reference: Section 2.1

6. In what way is margin collected?
   Answer reference: Section 3.1

7. What is SPAN?
   Answer reference: Section 3.1

8. How is initial margin used?
   Answer reference: Section 3.2.1

9. How is variation margin for a future's position calculated?
   Answer reference: Section 3.3

10. What is the closing range?
    Answer reference: Section 3.2.2

Chapter Seven

Delivery and Settlement

This syllabus area will provide approximately 7 of the 100 examination questions

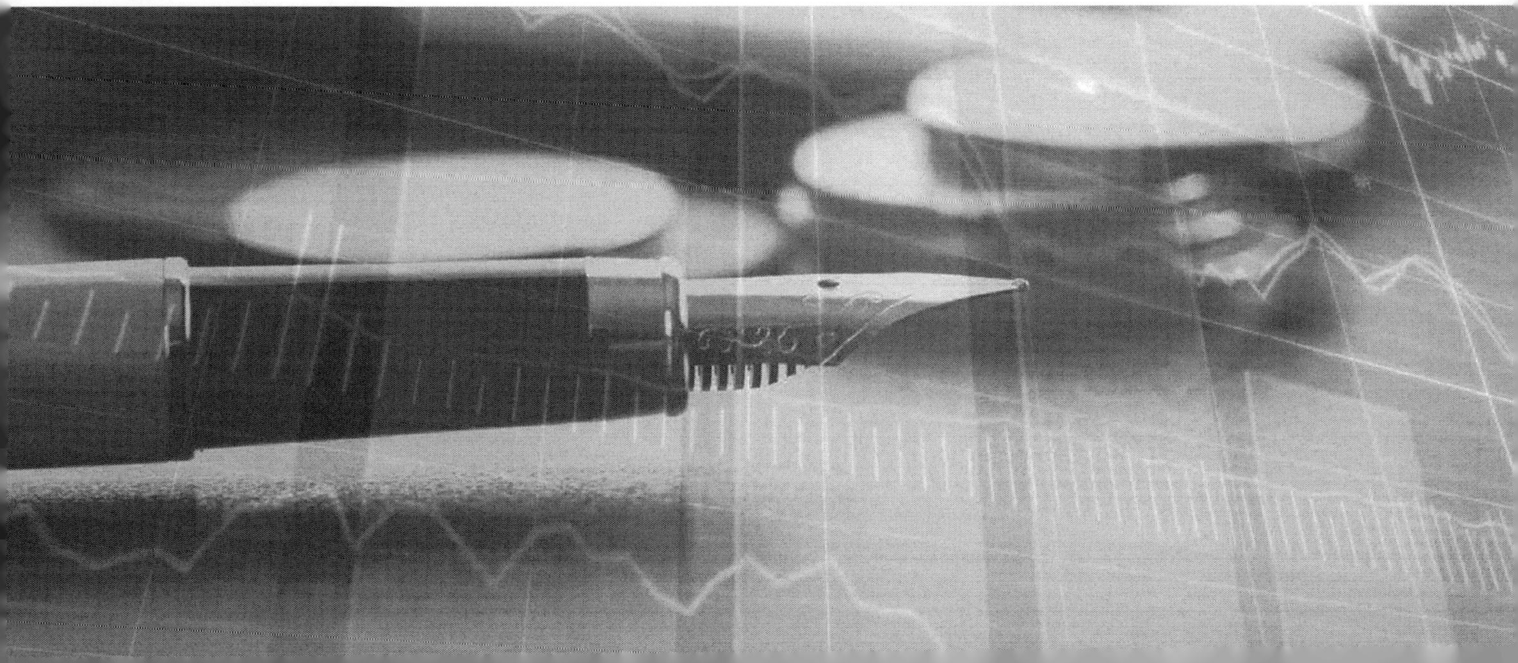

1. Delivery and Settlement – Futures

1.1 Introduction

Learning Objective

7.1.5 Know the role of the clearing house as counterparty in delivery: when the clearing house becomes the counterparty; role of the clearing house as counterparty; role of the clearing house as guarantor; counterparty risk; assignment; use of warrants in delivery

Even though most futures positions are closed out before expiry, the conceptual basis of these contracts is that delivery can take place. Hence mechanisms must be in place to ensure that this can happen. The clearing house will manage and define rules and procedures, in conjunction with the exchange, to govern the delivery process.

As seen in Chapter 6, Section 1.1, the clearing house becomes the legal counterparty (via the process known as novation) after the trades have been confirmed and registered. The clearing house guarantees the performance of the trades carried out by its members and substantially reduces counterparty risk.

As buyer and seller to each contract, when a futures contract proceeds to delivery, the clearing house manages the contract delivery of open contracts between clearing members and may enable the delivery of documents to represent the underlying assets (such as warrants used in the metals market operated by the LME).

For example, each LME warrant represents one lot of a specific type/grade of metal. The buyer of the metal (or holder of the warrant) presents this to an LME listed warehouse and, upon receipt of the warrant, it will deliver to the holder the precise amount and grade of metal that it represents.

1.2 Closing Contracts

Learning Objective

7.1.6 Understand the purpose and uses of LME closing contracts

Holders of futures contracts have three choices:

1. to close out the contract before expiry, or
2. to roll the position forward by closing out the existing position and simultaneously establishing a new position in a new quoted month, or
3. to proceed to delivery.

Closing the contracts before delivery will avoid the need to make or take delivery and enable the holder to realise any profit or loss arising on the position.

While any gains or losses will be realised when a contract is closed out or delivered, the decision to close it out provides the holder/seller with more flexibility, since he can do it at any time up to its maturity. Also it may be cheaper, since it allows the holder/seller to realise any profits or losses, without incurring any delivery/storage charges that would occur if the contract went through its delivery process.

In order to relinquish any obligations in the market, a close-out instruction must be given by the client. This instruction determines which long position (or part-position) to close out against which short position (or part-position).

For clients holding various positions in a particular contract (ie, both long and short positions held gross), there are various common methods for performing close-outs:

- **First-in, first-out (FIFO)** – close out the oldest long position against the oldest short position.
- **Last-in, first-out (LIFO)** – close out the most recent trade (long or short) against the oldest position (long or short).
- **Maximum profit** – close out an equal number of long and short positions to realise the maximum amount of profit.
- **Maximum loss** – close out an equal number of long and short positions to realise the maximum loss.

Positions can be designated to be left open, for instance if they are part of a specific strategy.

There are other close-out methods that are used, and it is also possible to provide manual instructions to close out specific positions. A position which has been closed out and effectively no longer exists is described as being flat.

If a position is closed out incorrectly or in error it is possible to bust the settlement. This is the term used for reversing the closing action and reopening a position.

1.3 Alternative Delivery Procedures (ADPs)

Learning Objective

7.1.3 Know the role of alternative delivery procedures (ADPs) in physical delivery

In the event that the seller and buyer (once the two have been allocated by the clearing house) agree to make delivery other than as specified in the exchange's rules and regulations for that contract, both parties must advise the clearing house of their agreement. The clearing house will then liquidate the contracts at the agreed settlement price, in fulfilment of all its obligations under the delivery contract. This agreement is known as an **alternative delivery procedure (ADP)**.

ADPs are used when changing the delivery details has an impact on one of the party's financial investments. All ADP agreements must be agreed by both the seller and buyer.

An ADP may take place at any time during the delivery period, once the long and short futures positions have been matched for the purpose of delivery. ADPs are almost exclusive to commodity contracts, and are accepted by a wide range of major exchanges, such as ICE, CME and Euronext.

Example 1

For an ICE Gasoil Futures contract, if the buyer and seller agree to a delivery procedure that is outside of the ICE Futures Europe rules, both parties must advise the clearing house using the form 'ICE gasoil futures: confirmation of agreed ADP'.

If an ADP is agreed, the clearing house will settle the relevant contracts at the settlement price agreed between the buyer and seller; this fulfils its obligations under the contract in respect of delivery. If the agreed price is not the one at which the positions were placed under tender, the difference between the two prices will be debited or credited to the clearing members' accounts and an invoice or credit note will be issued. This detail must be reported to the clearing house.

If the confirmation of agreed ADP form is received by the clearing house after 15:00 GMT, it will be deemed to have been received on the next business day.

A reduced delivery fee is charged for ADPs agreed at least two days prior to the first day of the delivery range.

If an ADP is agreed, once the clearing members' accounts have been amended by the clearing house as described and delivery has been completed, the counterparties and the clearing house are automatically released from all their rights, liabilities and obligations in respect of the affected contract or contracts.

1.4 Physical Delivery or Cash Settlement

Learning Objective

7.1.2 Understand the differences between cash settlement and physically delivered contracts and the final payment process: what is cash settlement; what is physical delivery; factors used in ascertaining the invoice amount; who calculates the invoice amount; differences between financial and commodity products

7.1.4 Understand the importance and implications of the delivery of open contracts at expiry and the significance of the short position: purpose of open contracts; physical versus cash delivery; financials versus commodities; avoidance of delivery – reasons & methods; advantages and disadvantages of cash delivery; asset delivery to the clearing house; seller's choice of delivery time and method; relevance of first notice day, last notice day & delivery day or period

As seen in Section 1.3 of this chapter, the rationale for closing out a contract is to avoid the need to take or make delivery of the underlying asset. For those contracts that have not been closed out and remain open at expiry, the exchange rules define what assets, in terms of quality and quantity, may be delivered in final settlement of exchange contracts.

For example, the LME defines in its rules the brands, origins and warehouses that are acceptable as good delivery against each of its metals contracts, and ICE Futures similarly defines delivery points and deliverable grades for its deliverable gas oil contract.

The LME uses a warrant-based system that allows for easy delivery, since its approved warehouses are located around the world. This system is known as LMEsword. It allows the LME to accommodate metal producers that have excess supply at times. In this aspect, it becomes the market of last resort.

LMEsword is a secure electronic transfer system for LME warrants which are to be held in a central depository. All LME warrants are produced to a standard format with a barcode. Warehouse companies issuing these warrants ensure that the details are known to LMEsword, which acts as a central database, holding details of ownership and is subject to stringent security controls. The ownership of LME warrants can be transferred between LMEsword members in a matter of seconds and all rent payments are automatically calculated.

LMEsword brings a number of benefits, particularly in administrative efficiency, by removing the physical transfer of warrants and simplifying the manual operations involved. It also reduces the number of times a warrant has to be passed by hand, as warrants no longer need to be physically transferred from owner to owner every time the material is bought or sold. Warrants are immobilised in a depository.

For physically deliverable futures contracts, the underlying asset changes hands. The exchange stipulates the last trading day for the contract, at the end of which the closing price is established. In the case of the ICE Futures Europe markets, this is known as the EDSP. At expiry, the exchange rules define what assets, in terms of quality, quantity and location, may be finally delivered.

The delivery process then begins for all open positions.

Futures sellers give notice declaring their intention to deliver the asset to the clearing house. This is known as a tender notice – they are tendering for delivery. It then assigns those assets to futures buyers, usually on a random basis. If there is any flexibility allowed in the contract, the futures seller has the choice of what, where and when to deliver – this is referred to as seller's choice.

The timetable for the tender process varies between contracts. Sometimes there is only one notice day and tenders are all processed together (an example is the euro-bund future on Eurex). On other contracts, there may be a longer period starting with a first notice day and ending with a **last notice day** (such as the long gilt, cocoa and robusta coffee futures on ICE Futures, London). The underlying asset is then delivered on the delivery day.

These are the first two steps of four main stages that are part of ICE's delivery procedure:

1. The seller or holder of the short futures position advises ICE Clear Europe of their intention to deliver the underlying asset.
2. ICE Clear Europe then matches sellers to buyers on a random basis. UCP is also used for trade and position management following the transaction providing daily position management. But it then feeds the positions and margin requirements to ICE Clear's Extensible Clearing System (ECS).

The next two steps in the delivery process are discussed in the following sections of this chapter:

3. ICE Clear Europe calculates the **invoice amount** and notifies the seller and buyer.
4. The seller delivers the underlying asset, as instructed, to the clearing house and receives the invoice amount. The buyer makes the invoice payment to the clearing house and receives delivery of the underlying asset.

Whether the physical delivery is for a financial or commodity contract, the process can be significant. For both, the seller must ensure that, whether it is 30-year US Treasury or South American soya beans, they must deliver the correct quantity and quality, as specified in the contract. But, as the LMEsword system shows, that for the most part, the delivery process for commodities can be more involved and sometimes more expensive.

For both, however, the delivery process ensures that the buyer receives what was paid for and that it is available to them, whether it be JGBs deposited in their Tokyo brokerage account, or a warrant giving them access to a metal, such as copper.

1.4.1 Invoice Amount

For physically delivered contracts, the futures buyer(s) will receive an invoice for the asset and have to pay the amount stated in the invoice. The formula is:

EDSP x scale factor x number of contracts

The scale factor converts the price quote to reflect the total value of the assets being delivered, as in the following example.

Example 2

The EDSP for Brent Crude is $55.00 per barrel. Contract size is 1,000 barrels. Because the price is quoted in barrels, and each contract is for 1,000 barrels, the scale factor is 1,000.

The invoice amount for five contracts might be:

$55.00 x 1,000 x 5 = $275,000

The EDSP is unlikely to be the price originally agreed. Suppose the buyer went long at $56.00. By paying $45.00, he is paying less than the agreed price. But remember that the buyer will already have had to pay variation margin over the lifetime of the contract and that loss will be in his account. So, in net terms, the actual price paid is the agreed price of $56.00 per barrel.

As seen earlier in Chapter 3, the invoice amount for a bond futures contract is slightly more involved. It is given by the following equation:

(EDSP x price factor x scale factor x number of contracts) + accrued interest

There are two additional elements in this equation. The price factor is used to convert the EDSP based on the notional bond to the equivalent EDSP for the bond actually being delivered. The accrued interest reflects the fact that the EDSP is quoted clean (ignoring the accrued interest implicit within the bond at the point of delivery).

Exercise 1

What will be the invoice amount for the following delivery of ICE London's long gilt future?

Five contracts when the EDSP for the contract is £98.50, the price factor of the bond being delivered is 1.12142 and the bond has accrued interest of £4.54 per £100 nominal. The scale factor is 1,000.

The answer can be found in the appendix at the end of this chapter.

1.4.2 Cash Settlement – Contracts for Difference (CFDs)

With cash-settled contracts there is no exchange of the underlying asset. There is an exchange of funds representing profits and losses on the contract.

The key advantage of cash settlement over physical delivery is that cash settlement avoids the need for the asset to be delivered and the consequent need for precise specification of quantity, quality and location. Cash settlement also allows contracts to be based on non-deliverable underlying assets, such as STIR deposits, or the FTSE 100 and S&P 500 equity indices.

As variation margin payments will already have been made/received daily throughout the life of the open position, the only element required to settle the trade is the payment of the last day's variation margin against the EDSP (being the final price for the contract month); this satisfies the delivery obligations.

But in some cases, cash settlement is seen as a disadvantage. This is the case in some bond index futures, such as ICE London's EuroMTS government bond index future, which is based on the price of several euro government bonds and does not provide for pricing factors that allow for delivery of a specific bond that is a component of the index. This is due to the fact that this future is exclusively cash-settled but, as mentioned in the next paragraph, there is a possibility that its price is vulnerable to manipulation.

There is concern that cash settlement for this contract, since it is based on an index, may be vulnerable to manipulation by market participants in some cases. In addition, it also carries risks, in that trading activity on the underlying market during the EDSP period is likely to be affected by the activity of particular market participants who are seeking to obtain price convergence at the EDSP between offsetting bond and futures positions. Such participants might typically seek to achieve this by unwinding their bond positions during the EDSP period at prices which they anticipate will contribute to the calculation of index figures, which will, in turn, be used to determine the final EDSP.

1.5 Exchange Delivery Settlement Price (EDSP)

Learning Objective

7.1.1 Understand the purpose of the Exchange Delivery Settlement Price (EDSP) and the factors affecting it: purpose of EDSP; auction process; factors included in calculating the EDSP value; reasons for exchange to set the EDSP; no EDSP on the last notice day

The exchange delivery settlement price (EDSP) is the ICE Europe market's term for a future's closing price.

The EDSP (or equivalent on other exchanges) is very significant, as it is the sole price at which all outstanding futures (bought and sold) will be closed. In setting the EDSP, the exchange must use an openly declared mechanism that will prevent any price manipulation. The resulting price must be fair, and truly representative of spot prices.

Note that many contracts are cash-settled and, by definition, physical delivery does not apply (examples are STIR and stock index futures and options). The EDSP process is still of fundamental importance, however, as the EDSP effectively becomes the final price at which variation margin changes hands. Some exchanges have contracts which offer the option of cash settlement instead of settlement by physical delivery (eg, ICE Futures Europe Brent Crude oil).

The EDSP could be subject to manipulation and needs to be a fair reflection of the underlying asset at expiry. As a result, the exchange will endeavour to avoid manipulation by following the procedures, outlined in Chapter 6, Section 3, for establishing the daily settlement prices.

ICE Futures uses a variety of techniques across its various contracts. The flagship contract, the ICE EURIBOR STIR future, depends upon an EDSP price that is supplied by the European Banking Federation (ie, the price view of some 40+ banks). Whatever technique is used to determine the EDSP by an exchange, it must be fair and reflect as accurately as possible the price status in the underlying market. It must also be free from manipulation. Exchanges keep such matters under close supervision, together with the regulators. For example, the procedure for establishing the EDSP for the FTSE 100 futures and options contracts on ICE Futures (when it was NYSE Liffe) London was changed for the November 2004 expiry. Previously, a price-averaging system, based on actual trades over the last 20 minutes of trading on the morning of the last trading day, was used. This was replaced by a system that derives the EDSP from an intra-day auction.

The new system ensures that, at expiry, potentially substantial trading activity in the underlying shares is channelled into a mechanism where there is opportunity for aggregate supply and demand to be matched efficiently. Every share in the FTSE is included within parallel auctions, all of which last for no more than 15 minutes. By doing this, the exchange knows that the EDSP is being based upon the very latest information from the market as to where each share price (and hence the overall index itself) lies. Similar approaches are used by derivatives markets in Germany and the US.

ICE Futures Europe uses a completely different technique for its long gilt futures contract. The EDSP of this contract is the market price of the contract at 11.00am on the second business day prior to settlement, unless notice is given on the last notice day, when it is the price prevailing on the last trading day. The invoice amount with respect to the deliverable gilt is calculated by a price factor system, with an adjustment for any coupon interest accruing as at the settlement day.

2. Delivery and Settlement – Options

Learning Objective

7.2.1 Understand the significance and implications of the exercise of options, the assignment of obligations, abandonment and expiry: purpose of assignment of obligations; instigating an assignment notice; receiving an assignment notice; abandonment; which options are most likely to be exercised before expiry; exercise at expiry; European, American and Asian options; action upon exercise; reasons for assignments; effect of assignment; advantages to the investor; probability of assignment

Assignment is the process of obliging option sellers to perform their obligations. For example:

- A seller of an equity call is obliged to sell the shares at the option's strike price.
- A seller of a bond call will, potentially, become the short to a bond future at the option's strike price.

2.1 Exercise of Physically Deliverable Options

A European-style option can only be exercised at expiry, whereas an American-style option can be exercised over a set period up to the expiry date. However, remember that even American-style options are unlikely to be exercised until the expiry date approaches, because the holder will prefer to sell the option and realise the time value that adds to the option's premium.

Furthermore, an option holder will only exercise an option if it is ITM, with the exercise itself either realising a profit or reducing the loss on the open trade.

If the option holder decides to exercise a profitable (ITM) option, he notifies his broker. The broker will then fill in an exercise notice that is delivered to the clearing house (by the deadline) via the clearing member. Notice how with options, unlike futures where the seller commences the delivery cycle, it is the buyer (holder or owner) who exercises his right and starts the process.

On receipt of the exercise notice the clearing house will select (assign), at random, an option writer (seller or short) and send them an assignment notice. The assignment notice is the formal notification that the terms of the contract must be fulfilled. The transaction then becomes a cash market transaction and is subject to the normal trading costs, such as commissions.

Example 3

On exercise of an ICE Futures Europe equity call option contract on the shares of a UK company, both the holder and the writer will receive contract notes, and the holder will have to pay commission on the value of the shares, as well as stamp duty reserve tax (SDRT) and Panel on Takeovers and Mergers (PTM) levy. The trade will settle through the UK equity cash market settlement mechanism (Euroclear UK & Ireland Ltd) on the normal equity settlement timetable of T+3.

2.2 Exercise of Cash-Settled Options – Contracts for Differences (CFDs)

The process is effectively to transfer the IV of the option from the writer to the holder.

Example 4

If an investor exercises one FTSE call option with a strike at 6800 when the EDSP is 7050, since the contract size is £10 per point he will receive:

$$(7050 - 6800) \times £10 = £2{,}500$$

Remember, for options which have futures-style premium payment (as with all Euronext markets), variation margin will have accounted for most of this, and only the final day's variation margin will change hands.

But if this were an OTC option, the option holder would most likely receive the full amount upon its exercise.

2.3 Exercise of Options on Futures

If these are exercised, the process is as above, except that the holder and writer will be assigned a long/short futures position at the strike price. As a result of the option being exercised, the open interest in the underlying futures contract will increase by the number of exercised options.

2.4 Abandonment and Cabinet Trades

If the holder decides not to exercise, the option lapses and the writer's obligation ceases.

Holders tend to wait until the last possible moment before abandoning the option. They will abandon options that are OTM, or slightly ITM but not worth exercising when transaction costs are taken into account.

Sometimes traders prefer to close out the position for a nominal amount – a cabinet trade – in order to crystallise a loss for tax or accounting purposes. If an investor wants to set losses against current or future capital gains, documentation is required.

2.5 Automatic Exercise

Learning Objective

7.2.2 Understand the significance of automatic exercise: purpose of automatic exercise; options that may be subject to automatic exercise; reasons for clearing houses to adopt automatic exercise; benefits to members and holders of long positions; prevention of automatic exercise

ICE Clear Europe operates an automatic exercise facility (ICE Futures) whereby it will automatically exercise any option that is sufficiently ITM at expiry. This reduces the paperwork and also means that participants need not worry about forgetting to exercise.

The trigger for automatic exercise is when the price of the underlying asset is at or above a certain level for a call or at or below a certain level for a put – in other words, when the option is ITM at its expiration enough to cover any delivery cost associated with exercising the option.

Capped-style options are ones that are subject to automatic exercise. They have an established profit cap; once the underlying asset's price has moved beyond that cap and the option is ITM at expiration, it will be subject to automatic exercise.

Note, there are exercise fees to be paid, so, if an investor does not want the option exercised, a suppression notice must be filed with the clearing house.

2.6 Early Exercise of Options

It is possible to exercise American-style options before their expiry. The decision to exercise early is the responsibility of the holder and not the clearing house. The clearing house will assign the contracts to writers at random.

Normally, it is not rational to exercise an option before its expiry. Exercising realises the IV of the option and not its TV. It makes more sense to sell the option to capture the TV as well. However, for some types of options (eg, equity-based) there are times when it will be feasible to exercise early. This requires three criteria:

1. **American-style** – European-style options cannot be exercised before expiry.
2. **Deep-ITM** – the option must have IV.
3. **Close to expiry/short-dated** – there must be very little TV left.

With equity options there are sometimes good reasons to exercise early, because the owner can then take up dividend rights pertaining to a stock, or be able to obtain voting rights.

Appendix

Answer to Exercise 1

The invoice amount is given by the equation:

(EDSP x price factor x scale factor x number of contracts) + accrued interest

where:

EDSP	=	£98.50
Price factor	=	1.12142
Scale factor	=	1,000 (the long gilt contract has a notional value of £100,000 nominal and with the EDSP based on £100 nominal it must be scaled up by 1,000)
Number of contracts	=	5
Accrued interest	=	£4.54 x 1,000 x 5 = £22,700 (the accrued interest must reflect £100,000 nominal per contract)
Invoice amount	=	(98.5 x 1.12142 x 1,000 x 5) + 22,700 = £574,999

End of Chapter Questions

1. How would an LME warrant be used in the delivery process?
   Answer reference: Section 1.1

2. What three choices do holders of futures contracts have?
   Answer reference: Section 1.2

3. What is meant by 'bust the settlement'?
   Answer reference: Section 1.2

4. What is an ADP?
   Answer reference: Section 1.3

5. What is the key advantage of cash settlement over physical delivery?
   Answer reference: Section 1.4.2

6. What is the EDSP?
   Answer reference: Section 1.5

7. Describe the main difference between European-style and American-style options.
   Answer reference: Section 2.1

8. How is an assignment notice used?
   Answer reference: Section 2.1

9. What is a cabinet trade?
   Answer reference: Section 2.4

10. What triggers the ICE Clear Europe operates an automatic exercise facility?
    Answer reference: Section 2.5

Chapter Eight

Trading, Hedging and Investment Strategies

This syllabus area will provide approximately 16 of the 100 examination questions

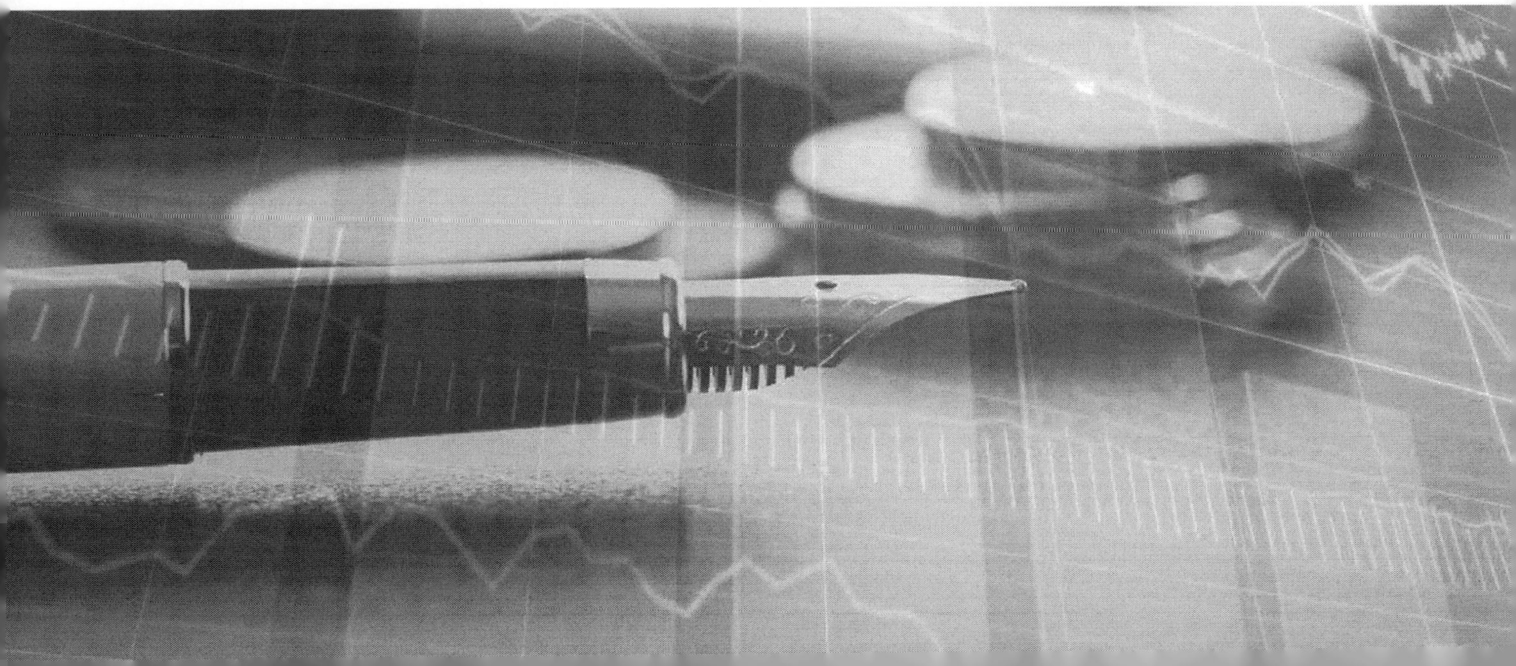

1. Introduction

Learning Objective

8.1.1 Understand the categories of users of derivatives and structured products and their respective use of derivative products: hedger; speculator; arbitrageur

A structured product, also known as a market-linked product, is generally an investment strategy that is based on derivatives, such as futures, options and, to a lesser extent, swaps.

Given the variety of products that are considered to be structured products, there is no single, uniform definition of the term. They can include a combination of an underlying asset and a single derivative or a strategy that includes a number of different contracts or derivatives, such as a range of options or series of futures contracts.

As such, structured products were created to meet an investor's specific needs that cannot be met from the standard or underlying financial instruments available in the markets. Structured products can be used as an alternative to a direct investment, as part of the asset allocation process to reduce risk, to increase one's exposure to an asset or market, or to take advantage of any mispricing that may occur.

In this chapter we will look at how the different types of structured products (a combination of these contracts) can be used.

Remember that hedging involves reducing the risk of adverse price movements on an underlying position, arbitrage activities take advantage of mispricings and speculators are placing bets on the direction of the price of the underlying asset by taking on new or extra risk.

2. Futures Spreads

Learning Objective

8.2.1 Know the distinctions between intra-market spreads and inter-market spreads and the scenarios in which they may be appropriate: use in differing market conditions; situations resulting in profitability/loss

A futures spread trade involves simultaneously buying and selling futures contracts.

Note that in all types of futures or options spreads, or even **combination** trades, it is always possible to leg in to the strategy by undertaking one half of the trade now and completing the second leg at a later date. Clearly, until the second leg is completed, the trader will be exposed to price risk.

2.1 Intramarket Spreads

These are trades based on the simultaneous buying and selling of futures with different expiry dates, but on the same underlying asset. For example, selling the June long gilt contract (ie, the long-dated gilt future) and buying the September long gilt contract.

The motivation for entering into these intramarket spreads can take a number of forms:

- Anticipating changes in basis – it could be that the basis is expected to strengthen or weaken.
- Reducing risk – intramarket spreads are less risky than taking an outright position (basis risk is smaller than price risk, but profits will be smaller too).
- Arbitrage – where the same underlying product is traded in two different markets and there are price differences; for example, buying SGX Nikkei 225 futures (traded in Singapore) and selling OSE Nikkei 225 futures (traded in Osaka).
- To roll over an existing hedge so that it continues further into the future – as would be the case of selling the June natural gas on ICE, to close out an existing long futures position, and then buying the December natural gas future, to continue the hedge for another six months.

2.2 Intermarket Spreads

These trades are based on simultaneously buying and selling futures on different underlying (but probably correlated) assets: for example, buying September short sterling contracts and selling September long gilt contracts.

The motivation for these trades is often that the price relationship between two correlated products has temporarily broken down or has moved outside its normal range. The trade anticipates a re-establishment of a more normal relationship.

They are very popular in interest rate markets where traders take a view on the relationship between long-term and short-term interest rates (the yield curve). The example quoted above is a trade that anticipates a steepening of the yield curve.

These trades are also used as a means of changing asset allocations within a portfolio. A fund manager may be long equities and be looking to reduce the exposure by selling some shares and using the funds to buy bonds. By using the futures market (selling FTSE 100 futures and buying long gilt futures), it is possible to produce the same effect without the need to trade the actual securities. It is usually much faster and less expensive. In the meantime, the fund manager can continue to benefit from dividend income until the securities are sold as needed, and will unwind the futures positions only when he has the required physical portfolio in place.

NB: in differentiating between intra- and intermarket spreads, it is the underlying asset that is important and not the physical location of the futures product.

- Intra (**within**) = underlying assets are the same.
- Inter (**between**) = underlying assets are different.

Example 1

An international equity fund manager holds the view that UK shares will outperform US shares over the next few months.

To take advantage of this view, they will sell S&P 500 futures contracts and, at the same time, buy the FTSE 100 futures for the same maturity and for the same amount.

By using this intermarket spread the fund manager has reallocated the fund's investments from US to UK equities to take advantage of the view that the UK market will outperform the US market.

3. Hedging Using Futures

Learning Objective

8.4.1 Know the characteristics and implications of long and short positions

Remember that unhedged positions are at risk from changes in the price of the underlying asset. The unhedged position may be a long underlying position or it may be a short underlying position.

Hedgers offset the price risk in the underlying asset by taking an opposite position in the futures market. So, someone who is long the underlying asset will sell the equivalent number of futures contracts to hedge the risk (a short hedge). However, although the cash and futures prices are strongly correlated, there is some flexibility in that relationship. Basis changes will affect the performance of the hedge. This is termed the basis risk of the hedge.

3.1 Cheapest to Deliver (CTD)

Learning Objective

8.4.2 Understand the importance of hedging ratios in cheapest to deliver bonds (CTDs): price factors; highest implied repo rate; number of contracts to hedge an exposure to the CTD bond; duration-based hedge ratios for non-CTD bonds

If the long gilt futures (or most other bond futures) contract is used to hedge a portfolio of underlying gilts, any risk is limited to the basis risk (assuming that the appropriate number of contracts are entered into). Remember that the long gilt futures contract has a basket of deliverable gilts, one of which is cheaper to deliver than the others (the cheapest to deliver or CTD).

The CTD bond is the deliverable gilt with the highest implied repo rate. The futures contract price will be very closely correlated to this CTD bond and the number of contracts used to hedge is calculated on the basis of holding the CTD bonds in the portfolio, not any other bonds.

The implied repo rate is a measure of the funding cost implied in futures prices, which reflects the difference between a bond's cash price and the price of a futures contract.

For many products, the number of contracts needed to hedge is simply a matter of dividing the portfolio size/value by the contract size/value. However, with bonds, the price factor of the CTD bond needs to be taken into account. The formula is:

$$\text{Number of contracts} = \text{price factor} \times \frac{\text{nominal value of CTD portfolio}}{\text{nominal value of the contract}}$$

Example 2

You have a portfolio of CTD bonds with a nominal value of £10,000,000 and a market value of £11,500,000. The price factor is 1.1214645. The contract size of the long gilt future is £100,000, nominal. Number of contracts needed to hedge =

$$1.1214645 \times \frac{£10{,}000{,}000}{£100{,}000}$$

$$= 112.15$$

$$= 112 \text{ approximately.}$$

Note that if you did not have a portfolio of CTD bonds, the above formula would need to be adjusted. Hedging non-CTD bonds is outside the exam syllabus.

Exercise 1

An investor has sold short CTD gilts with a nominal value of £15 million and a market value of £15.4 million. The price factor is 1.12486. She wishes to hedge the position using long gilt futures. How many contracts are required and should the investor buy or sell the long gilt futures contracts?

The answers can be found in the appendix at the end of this chapter.

3.2 Hedge Ratio Calculation

Learning Objective

8.4.3 Understand hedge ratio calculation for other short-term interest rate futures: basis point value; number of contracts to hedge an interest rate exposure

8.4.4 Understand hedge ratio calculation for equity futures: stock and portfolio beta; number of contracts to hedge an equity exposure

When using futures to hedge an equities portfolio, its beta is useful when calculating how many contracts you will need to trade to be fully hedged. A share's beta is the measure of its relative volatility or risk versus the market. Therefore a portfolio's beta is the weighted average of the individual betas of the shares that make up the portfolio.

Example 3

If a portfolio has a beta of 1.1 relative to the S&P 500, it means that if the S&P rises by 10%, that portfolio will rise by 11.0%. In other words it is riskier than the index.

Therefore, if this portfolio has a value of US$8.0 million and the fund manager wants to hedge this portfolio using S&P 500 futures, the portfolio's beta is useful in calculating the number of contracts required to fully hedge this portfolio. At the time the S&P 500 index was trading at 1850. The CME S&P 500 contract's size is US$250 times the index.

Number of contracts = $8.0m/($250 x 1850) = 17.3
17.3 x 1.1 = 19 contracts

In the case of STIR futures, the size/tick value relative to a basis point is the key factor when determining the number of contracts that are required to hedge a specific position.

3.3 Basis, Basis Trading and Basis Risk

Learning Objective

8.4.5 Understand basis, basis trading and basis risk: problems caused by changes in basis; how changes in basis can be used to advantage by an investor

Basis and basis trading were covered in Section 1.6 of Chapter 4. Remember that basis is the difference between the cash and futures prices. Basis risk is the risk that the change in futures prices will be different to changes in the cash price. Basis trading is implementing strategies to profit from anticipated basis changes.

Example 4

A fund manager has a portfolio of top UK equities, currently valued at £15,000,000. He hedges the portfolio by selling 250 FTSE index futures at 6930. The FTSE 100 currently stands at 6985. A day later the FTSE 100 has fallen by 20 index points and the future has fallen by 16 points to 6914. The outcome for the fund manager is as follows:

1. Unhedged equity portfolio value = £15,000,000

Day 1	Day 2
$£15{,}000{,}000 \times \frac{(6985 - 20)}{6985}$ =	£14,957,051

2. Futures profit = 250 x (6930 – 6914) x £10 = £40,000
3. Hedged portfolio value loss = £15,000,000 x (20/6985) = –£42,949

Day 1	Day 2
£15,000,000	£14,991,496

4. Difference = loss due to change in basis = –£2,949

4. Hedging Using Options

Learning Objective

8.5.1 Understand the application and effects of delta hedging and be able to establish an investor's net long/short position

8.7.1 Be able to calculate a derivatives position with an underlying market equivalency, either to establish or to hedge a required exposure: long/short through futures; long/short through single options; long/short through option combinations; long/short through simple OTC derivatives; limits to upside and/or downside exposures

The four basic options positions (long call, short call, long put and short put) can be used as hedging instruments against an underlying position.

Remember that the efficiency of hedging using options is dependent upon the delta of the option's position mirroring the delta of the underlying position, in other words, creating a delta neutral portfolio overall.

Broadly, the deltas are as follows:

Position	Delta
Long underlying	+1
Short underlying	–1
Long future	+1
Short future	–1
Long call (deep ITM)	+1
Long call (ATM)	+0.5
Short call (deep ITM)	–1
Short call (ATM)	–0.5
Long put (deep ITM)	–1
Long put (ATM)	–0.5
Short put (deep ITM)	+1
Short put (ATM)	+0.5

So a long underlying position (delta +1) could be hedged by a short, deep ITM call (delta –1) to create a delta neutral portfolio (overall delta = +1 – 1 = 0). Alternatively, it could be hedged by two short ATM calls (–0.5 x 2 = –1), or a deep ITM long put (–1), or even two ATM long puts (–0.5 x 2 = –1).

4.1 Hedging a Long Underlying Position using Options

Learning Objective

8.3.1 Understand the use of derivatives for speculation and hedging: speculation: long calls, short puts (bullish); speculation: short call, long puts (bearish); hedging: covered calls and protective puts; recognise diagrammatic representation of each strategy; maximum upside and downside for each strategy

This is best illustrated by examples. Also see the notes on **covered calls** in Section 4.3 of this chapter.

4.1.1 Buy a Put Option

Example 5

Investor A owns a portfolio of FTSE shares with a current value of £550,000. The FTSE index stands at 7155. He is exposed to a fall in the value of the shares. To hedge the risk he needs an options position that will make a profit if the index falls – for example, a long put position.

If his worries are borne out and the index falls, the loss on the portfolio will be offset by the profit on the put option. Remember that the premium paid on the put will never be refunded, so the hedge has a cost (unlike a futures hedge).

However, if the index were to rise, the long underlying position can still show an overall profit once the cost of the put premium has been recouped.

How many contracts are needed to hedge?

The contract size of a FTSE option on ICE, London is the index level x £10 per point.

With the put option exercise price at, say, 7100, each contract hedges £71,000 of shares (7100 x £10 per point).

So the number of contracts needed = £550,000 ÷ £71,000 = 8 contracts.

4.1.2 Sell a Call Option

Example 6

An aluminium producer does not have forward sale agreements for all of its production over the next six months. One way to hedge against a possible fall in the cash price would be to sell calls on the LME's primary aluminium futures. The contract size is 25 tonnes. If the amount of the unsold December production is 100 tonnes, the producer can sell four primary aluminium calls with a strike price of $1,900, its budgeted sale price. By selling this covered call, since the producer has the underlying metal, the premium received will partially offset any price fall that might occur. But if the price rises, the producer will only receive $1,900 – the strike price – plus the premium for the option he has sold, if the option expires in-the-money (ITM).

4.2 Hedging a Short Underlying Position Using Options

The following illustrates how a short position might be hedged:

4.2.1 Buy a Call Option

Example 7

Investor B needs to buy 500oz of gold for June; gold is currently trading at $1,205.00 per ounce in the cash market.

The investor is exposed to an increase in gold's price. One way to hedge the risk is to buy a gold futures call option for June, a position that will make a profit if the price of gold rises. To be fully hedged, investor B will have to buy five calls, since each option has a value of 100oz per contract.

If the price of gold rises, the extra cost of buying it in the cash market will be offset by the profits on the call option. But remember that the premium paid to buy the call will not be refunded, therefore this method of hedging has an initial cost (unlike a futures hedge).

But if the price of gold falls, investor B will be able to buy gold at a lower price and reduce their costs, after recouping the premium paid for the call.

4.2.2 Sell a Put Option

See notes on covered short puts in Section 4.3 of this chapter.

It is useful to note the following:

- Unlike a futures hedge, an options hedge will underperform because of the premium paid.
- In contrast to a futures hedge, an options hedge provides flexibility. It allows overall profits to be made if the price of the underlying moves in the investor's favour instead of against him, because the loss on the option is limited to the premium paid.

4.3 Covered Options Positions

Learning Objective

8.3.1 Understand the use of derivatives for speculation and hedging: speculation: long calls, short puts (bullish); speculation: short call, long puts (bearish); hedging: covered calls and protective puts; recognise diagrammatic representation of each strategy; maximum upside and downside for each strategy

8.7.2 Understand the uses and advantages of covered calls and covered puts: motivation for the writer of a covered call; motivation for the buyer of a protective put; risks/maximum losses; use in different market conditions

4.3.1 Covered Short Call

A covered short call is sometimes referred to as a **buy-write** strategy. It is constructed by combining a long underlying position with a short call position.

The following example illustrates the potential outcome of a covered short call strategy.

Example 8

An investor is long 1,000 ABC plc shares. Current share price is 407. He sells an ABC plc 425 call for a premium of 11 (each contract is for 1,000 shares).

Analysis of outcome at expiry

If the share price is unchanged at expiry, the option is abandoned. The investor keeps the premium, thereby creating a positive return on investment.

If the share price drops, the premium helps to cushion the fall. The investor is hedged to the extent of the premium. If the fall is less than the premium, the investor is still better off. If the fall is greater than the premium, the investor loses the excess above the premium.

If the share price rises to 425, the investor will make a profit on the shares and keep the premium (18 on the underlying and 11 on the premium = 29). This is the **point of maximum profit**. The return on investment is 18 (425 – 407); since the premium of 11 that was received for the call reduces the initial investment to 396, that return is (425 – 407)/396 x 100 = 4.55% over the period.

If the price rises above 425, the option will be exercised against the investor. He will deliver the share for 425. He has effectively capped his maximum potential profit at 29 (ignoring dividends paid on the shares).

In summary, the motivation is to enhance returns in a stagnant market and, at the same time, to partly hedge a long underlying position. If the market remains static, an investor will enhance the return on the asset, since he has collected the option's premium and it will expire unexercised. In a falling market, the premium will reduce the loss, but will not provide a true hedge. In a rising market, overall gains will be limited, since the call will be exercised and any further gains above the strike price will not be realised, since the investor no longer owns the asset.

Exercise 2

Mr Z holds 1,000 shares in XYZ, with a current price of 215p. He writes a single call option (on 1,000 shares) with an exercise price of 220p and for a premium of 9p. What is the outcome for Mr Z if the price of XYZ shares at expiry is:

a. 194p
b. 208p
c. 230p

The answers can be found in the appendix at the end of this chapter.

Note that selling call options without owning the asset is known as creating a naked short call position or naked writing. This is more of a speculative position, where the investor may be happy to sell the asset at that price, based on the outlook that its price will fall later. Again, receiving the premium does raise one's break-even level, but this strategy has created an open risk that the asset's price will continue to rise.

4.3.2 Covered Short Put

A covered short put position is constructed by selling a put but, at the same time, holding sufficient funds to buy the asset if necessary or already having a short position, such as being short the futures contract, then writing/selling a put on the futures contract.

Example 9

The ABC plc share price is 407p. An investor leaves the funds (£4,070) on deposit and sells the 400 put for 20p per share.

Analysis of outcome at expiry

If the share price is unchanged at expiry, the option is abandoned by the long put and the investor keeps the premium. This increases the return on his funds by the premium retained.

If the share price rises, although the investor is enhancing the return on his funds by the premium received, he has forgone the opportunity to make a profit on the shares he could have purchased. There is an opportunity cost for the investor.

If the share price falls below 400, the option will be exercised against the investor. He will have to buy the shares at 400p. The investor has effectively reduced the cost price of the shares to 400p, less the amount of the premium. That is 380p (400 – 20).

The point of maximum profit is at 400. The investor will make 20 on the premium, plus the interest on the funds, and be able to buy the shares at 400 rather than 407.

In summary, the motivation is to enhance the return on funds in a stagnant market and to partially hedge a short underlying position. It is also an attractive method of taking profit on a short position. But it does limit gains on that short position, since, once the put is exercised, the investor no longer has a short position in that asset and therefore will no longer profit from further falls in its price.

Exercise 3

Mrs P enters into a covered short put position on the shares in QRS plc. She writes a 700p put option for a premium of 12p at the time QRS plc shares are trading at 718p. What is the outcome for Mrs P if the price of QRS shares at expiry is:

a. 690p
b. 718p
c. 750p

The answers can be found in the appendix at the end of this chapter.

5. Options Spreads

Learning Objective

8.7.1 Be able to calculate a derivatives position with an underlying market equivalency, either to establish or to hedge a required exposure: long/short through futures; long/short through single options; long/short through option combinations; long/short through simple OTC derivatives; limits to upside and/or downside exposures

An options spread involves the simultaneous purchase and sale of options in the same class, ie, calls or puts on the same underlying asset.

There are three different types of options spreads that are constructed as follows:

1. **Vertical spread** – buying and selling calls (or puts) with different strikes, but the same expiry, eg, buy April 200 call and sell April 220 call or buy September 500 put and sell September 550 put.
2. **Horizontal (calendar) spread** – buying and selling options with the same strike, but different expiry months, eg, buy April 200 call and sell May 200 call or sell September 500 put and buy December 500 put.
3. **Diagonal (diagonal calendar) spread** – buying and selling options with different strikes and different expiry months.

5.1 Vertical Spreads

Learning Objective

8.3.3 Understand the characteristics and effects of vertical spreads: bull call and bear call spreads; bull put and bear put spreads; use in differing market conditions; anticipating modest market rises/falls (bull/bear markets); risks

8.3.5 Be able to calculate maximum profits/losses in simple examples of the above strategies

Vertical spreads can be split into two basic types: **bull spreads** and **bear spreads**.

In a bull spread, the investor buys the lower strike and sells the higher strike: for example, buying the 500 call and selling the 600 call (a bull call spread); or, alternatively, buying the 500 put and selling the 600 put (a bull put spread).

The opposite is true for a bear spread, where the investor sells the lower strike and buys the higher strike, for example, selling the 500 call and buying the 600 call (a bear call spread); or, alternatively, using put options by selling the 500 put and buying the 600 put (a bear put spread).

All vertical spreads attempt to profit from a directional movement in the underlying. However, unlike an outright purchase of a call or put, spreads are moderately bullish/bearish strategies.

Example 10

The current price of ABC plc is 550 and the options available with the premium (PM) at a range of exercise prices are as follows:

Call PM	Strike	Put PM
70	500	18
49	525	23
37	550	35
25	575	47
19	600	67

Rationale

Suppose an investor is bullish on ABC shares. He could buy the 550 call and pay a premium of 37. However, he is moderately bullish and does not think the shares will rise beyond 590 by expiry.

So he sells the 600 call at the same time. He receives a premium of 19, which reduces his net outlay to 18. This is known as a bull call spread.

Analysis

If the price remains at 550 or below, both options will expire OTM and be abandoned. The loss will be limited to the net outlay of 18.

If the price rises to between 550 and 600, he will exercise the 550 call and collect the IV (the 600 call will be abandoned). To make a net profit on the trade, the intrinsic value of the 550 call needs to be greater than 18, his initial net outlay. The break-even point is 568.

If the price rises beyond 600, both calls are ITM and will be exercised. In effect, the investor will exercise the 550 call and will be obliged to deliver the ABC shares at 600. The profit will be capped at 32 ((600 – 550) – 18). Looked at another way, once ABC shares are above 600, all the extra profit made from the 550 call is taken away by the short 600 call.

All vertical spreads work in a similar way. A bear spread is essentially the other side of a bull spread.

Exercise 4

Mr Z buys a 500 put in ABC plc shares for 18p and sells a 550 put at 35p. What is the outcome at expiry if the price of ABC plc shares is:

a. 490p
b. 530p
c. 575p

The answers can be found in the appendix at the end of this chapter.

5.1.1 Summary of Vertical Spreads

Bull Call

Motivation	Moderately bullish.
Construction	Buy at lower strike price, sell at higher strike price.
Net premium	Paid out.

Maximum risk	Net premium paid.
Maximum reward	Difference in strike prices less the net premium paid.
Break-even point	Lower strike price + net premium paid.

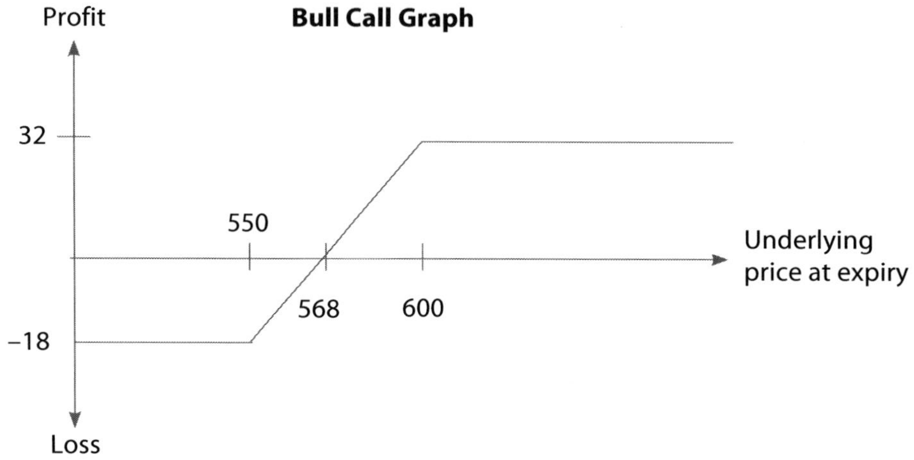

Bear Call

Motivation	Moderately bearish.
Construction	Sell at lower strike price, buy at higher strike price.
Net premium	Received.
Maximum risk	Difference in strike prices less the net premium received.
Maximum reward	Net premium received.
Break-even point	Lower strike price + net premium received.

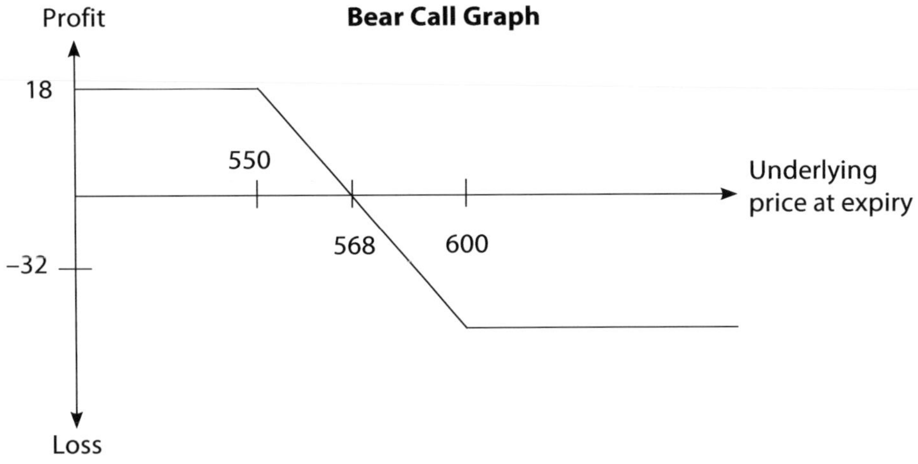

Bull Put

Motivation	Moderately bullish.
Construction	Buy at lower strike price, sell at higher strike price.
Net premium	Received.
Maximum risk	Difference in strike prices less net premium received.
Maximum reward	Net premium received.
Break-even point	Higher strike price less net premium received.

The shape of the bull put graph will be identical to the bull call graph.

Bear Put

Motivation	Moderately bearish.
Construction	Sell at lower strike price, buy at higher strike price.
Net premium	Paid out.
Maximum risk	Net premium paid.
Maximum reward	Difference in strike prices less net premium paid.
Break-even point	Higher strike price less net premium paid.

The shape of a bear put graph will be identical to the bear call graph.

Exercise 5

Mr Z buys a 500 put in ABC plc shares for 18p and sells a 550 put at 35p. What is the break-even point and what is the maximum profit on this trade?

The answers can be found in the appendix at the end of this chapter.

5.2 Horizontal and Diagonal Spreads

Learning Objective

8.3.6 Understand the uses, characteristics and effects of horizontal and diagonal spreads: use in differing market conditions; anticipating modest market rises/falls (bull/bear markets); risks

Horizontal spreads are also known as calendar spreads. They are motivated by expected moves in volatility. There are two basic types of horizontal spreads. The first is based on the view that **volatility will fall**, and involves selling a shorter maturity and buying a longer maturity option on the same asset with the same strike price. This type of spread takes advantage of the fact that short-dated options will lose their time value faster, and therefore react more quickly to a fall in volatility, than the longer-dated option.

Example 11

The GBP/USD spot rate is currently quoted at 1.2500/05; the following options, with ATM strike prices, are currently quoted in the market.

Expiration	Call PM	Strike Price	Put PM
1 month	45	1.2525	50
3 months	130	1.2550	145
6 months	280	1.2550	295
12 months	575	1.2550	585

Rationale

Based on the viewpoint that currency rates will remain steady over the near term and that the slight premiums the sterling short-term puts have will decrease, an investor will sell the one-month 1.2525 put and buy the six-month 1.2550 put, for a net cost of 245. This is known as a horizontal spread.

Analysis

If the spot GBP/USD exchange rate remains fairly steady and looks set to settle into a trading range, the implied volatility combined with the larger time decay will cause the premium on the shorter-term GBP put to fall faster than that of the longer maturity.

After two weeks, when the premiums of these same options have fallen to, say, 20 for the two-week and 275 for the five-and-a-half month GBP put, the investor will receive a net premium of 10, since he is able to unwind the spread and receive a net payment of 255, compared to the initial cost of 245.

The second type of horizontal or calendar spread is based on the view that volatility, particularly short-term volatility, will rise. It involves buying a shorter maturing option and selling a longer maturity option, again on the same underlying asset with the same strike price. This strategy is used most often ahead of key announcements, such as companies' earnings reports or central bank meetings, to take advantage of any dramatic short-term moves that may occur from the news.

Diagonal spreads are directional depending on market view. They will be constructed with call options if the investor's view is bullish or put options if bearish by selling shorter-dated options and buying longer-dated and further OTM options. Diagonals are difficult to compute as, once again, they use differently dated expiries.

Both these strategy types take advantage of the different rates of time decay for options with different expiries. Essentially, the trades are designed to take advantage of changes in volatility.

There will be no calculation questions in the exam on horizontal and diagonal spreads.

6. Options Combinations

Learning Objective

8.3.4 Understand the characteristics and effects of long and short straddles and strangles: use in differing market conditions; anticipating modest market rises/falls (bull/bear markets); risks

8.3.5 Be able to calculate maximum profits/losses in simple examples of the above strategies

8.7.1 Be able to calculate a derivatives position with an underlying market equivalency, either to establish or to hedge a required exposure: long/short through futures; long/short through single options; long/short through option combinations; long/short through simple OTC derivatives; limits to upside and/or downside exposures

A combination strategy involves the simultaneous purchase/sale of calls and puts. (Although synthetic positions also involve the use of calls and puts, they will be treated separately.)

The two major strategies are straddles and strangles. They attempt to profit from a change in the volatility of the underlying asset. Long positions anticipate an increase in volatility and short positions anticipate a decrease. Both strategies will be illustrated using the following example:

Example 12

The current price of DEF shares is 550p and the following options are available:

Call PM	70	49	37	25	19
Strike	500	525	550	575	600
Put PM	18	23	35	47	67

6.1 Long Straddle

Rationale

An investor is unsure about the direction of movement in DEF shares. Perhaps a major announcement is due. Good news will push the share price higher; bad news will push it lower. By buying a 550 call for 37 he will profit if the price rises, and by buying a put for 35 he will profit if the share price falls. By doing both, a long straddle position is created for a net premium outlay of 72 (37 + 35).

Analysis

If the news is good, and the share price rises to, say, 660 by expiry, the investor will exercise the call (110 IV) and abandon the put. He has paid 72 for the strategy, giving a net profit of 38. For the strategy to make a net profit, the price has to rise above 622 (550 + 72).

If the news is bad and the share price falls to 500, the investor will exercise the put (50 IV) and abandon the call. The price move has not been large enough to offset the premium paid. The price will have to fall below 478 (550 – 72) before the strategy shows a net profit.
There is a profit potential on this trade in either direction, as long as the price movement is large enough (high volatility) to overcome the cost of both premiums. The strategy has two break-even points, an upside and a downside break-even.

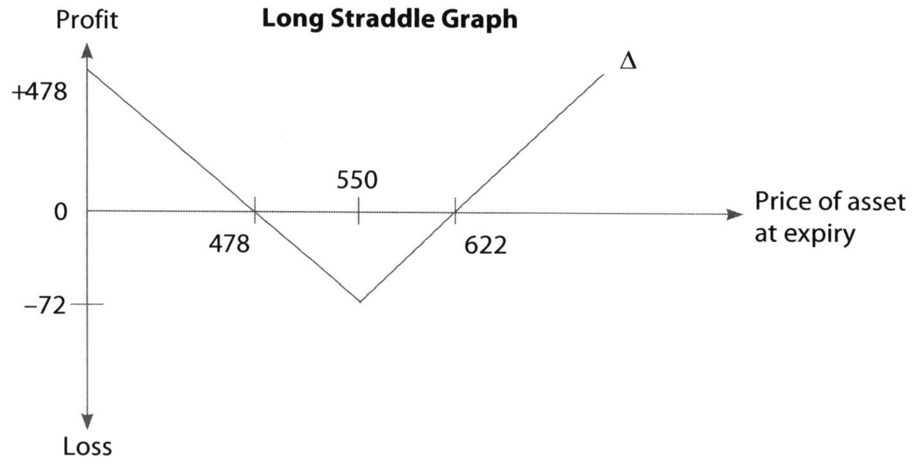

Motivation	Expectation of increase in volatility.
Construction	Buy a call and a put with the same strike and expiry.
Maximum risk	Total sum of premiums paid.
Maximum reward	Unlimited.
Break-even point	Downside: strike price less total premium paid. Upside: strike price plus total premium paid.

Exercise 6

What is the break-even range for the buyer of a put and a call on XYZ plc shares, where the 500p call has been purchased for 18p and the 500p put has been purchased for 7p? See the appendix at the end of this chapter.

6.2 Short Straddle

Rationale

Taking the opposite view, an investor who is unsure as to directional movement, but is convinced that the price will not move too far away from the current price, will be looking to sell both call and put, ie, taking a short straddle position. This is simply the other side of the long straddle, for example, an investor selling a 550 call for 37 and selling a 550 put for 35.

Analysis

The investor will have received a net premium of 72 (call = 37, put = 35).

If the share price rises, the investor will have the call exercised against them and lose the IV. As long as this is less than 72, the investor is still making a net profit. A movement above 622 will produce a net loss.

If the share price falls, the investor will have the put exercised against them and lose the IV. As long as this is less than 72, the investor will still be making a net profit. A movement to below 478 will produce a net loss.

The point of maximum profit will be at 550. Here, both options will be abandoned and the seller of the straddle will keep the total premium. You can see that there is a profit potential on this trade in either direction, as long as the price movement is not large enough (low volatility) to outweigh the net premium received.

Short Straddle Graph

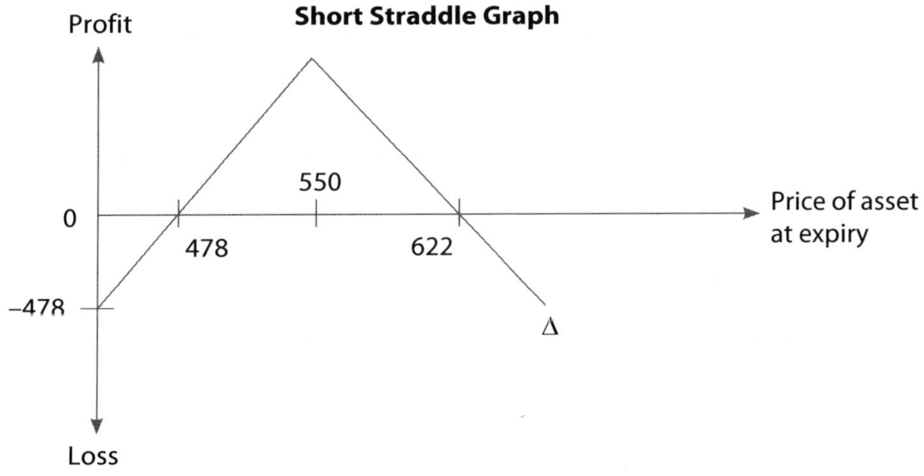

Motivation	Expectation of decrease in volatility.
Construction	Sell a call and a put with the same strike price and expiry.
Maximum risk	Unlimited.
Maximum reward	Limited to the sum of the premiums received.
Break-even point	Downside: exercise price minus premiums. Upside: exercise price plus premiums.

6.3 Long Strangle

A strangle is a variation of a straddle undertaken for the same purposes, ie, expectation of changes in volatility. For example, buying a 500 put for 18 and buying a 600 call for 19.

The differences between a long strangle and a long straddle are as follows:

- A strangle involves the purchase of a call and a put with the same expiry but different strike prices (normally constructed with the put strike lower than the call strike).
- The premium outlay on a strangle will usually be lower than on a straddle.
- The strategy needs more volatility to succeed.
- The maximum loss on a long position will be crystallised over a range (between the two strike prices) where neither option will be worth exercising.

Long Strangle Graph

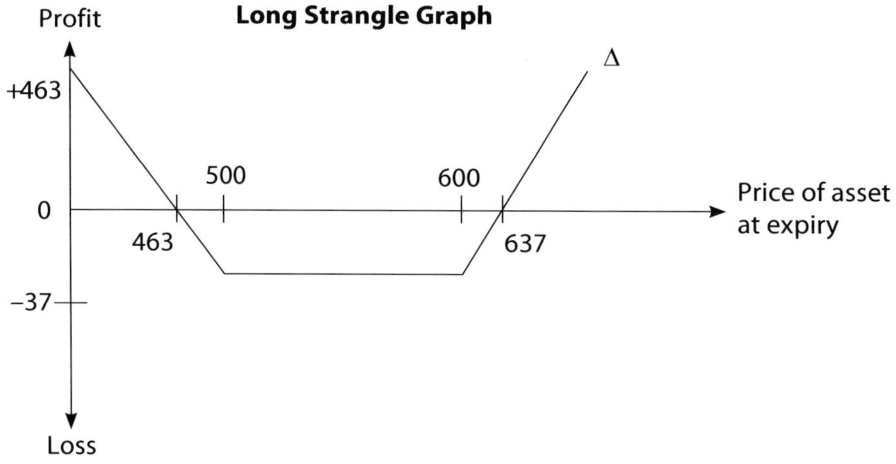

Motivation	Expectation of large increase in volatility.
Construction	Buy a call and a put with the same expiry but with different strikes.
Maximum risk	Total premium paid. (Call strike price higher than the put.) (If constructed with the call strike lower than the put, this will be limited to the premium less the difference between the strike prices.)
Maximum reward	Unlimited.

Break-even point	Downside: lower strike price less total premiums paid. Upside: higher strike price plus total premiums paid. (Call strike price higher than the put.) (If constructed with the call strike lower than the put, these will be reversed.)

Exercise 7

What is the breakeven range for the buyer of both a 400 put at 17p and a 450 call for 8p?

The answer can be found in the appendix at the end of this chapter.

6.4 Short Strangle

A short strangle is the other side of a long strangle strategy. For example, it will be created by selling a 500 put for 18 and selling a 600 call for 19.

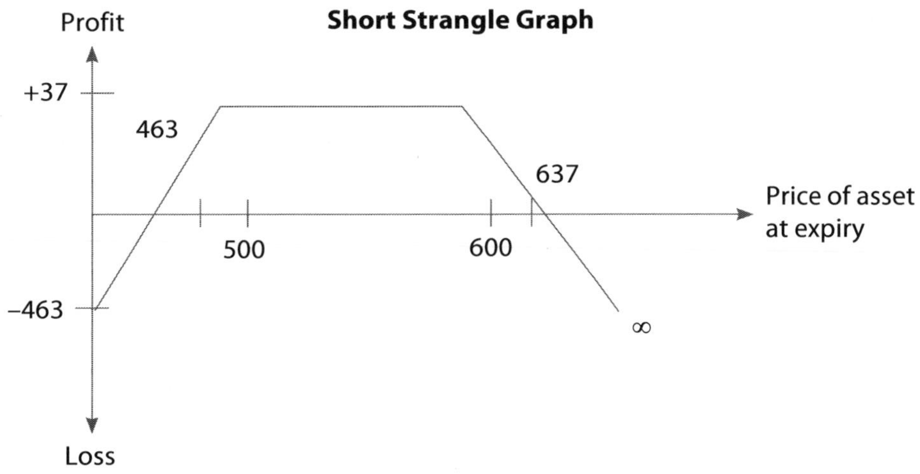

The differences between a short strangle and a short straddle are as follows:

- A short strangle involves the sale of a call and a put with the same expiry but different strikes (normally constructed with the put strike lower than the call strike).
- The total premium received on a strangle will usually be lower than on a straddle.
- The strategy can withstand more volatility before losses are incurred.
- The maximum profit on a short position will be crystallised over a range (between the two strikes) where neither option will be worth exercising against the seller.

Motivation	Expectation of a large decrease in volatility.
Construction	Sell a call and a put with the different strike prices but same expiry.
Maximum risk	Unlimited.
Maximum reward	Total premium received. (Premiums received less difference between the strikes if call strike is lower than the put.)
Break-even point	Downside: lower strike price minus premiums. Upside: higher strike price plus premiums. (Put strike lower than the call.) (If the call strike is lower than the put, these will be reversed.)

7. Synthetics

Learning Objective

8.3.2 Understand and be able to create basic synthetic options and futures: synthetic long; synthetic short; synthetic put; synthetic call

8.3.5 Be able to calculate maximum profits/losses in simple examples of the above strategies

By combining futures and options, it is possible to create positions synthetically. There are six basic synthetics that you should be familiar with:

1. Synthetic long future = buy a call and sell a put with the same strike and expiry.
2. Synthetic short future = sell a call and buy a put with the same strike and expiry.
3. Synthetic long call = buy a future and buy a put. (Note this is the same as having a hedged long position.)
4. Synthetic short call = sell a future and sell a put. (Effectively a short call position.)
5. Synthetic long put = buy a call and sell a future. (Note this is the same as a hedged short position.)
6. Synthetic short put = sell a call and buy a future. (Effectively a short put position.)

The reason for using synthetics might be to create positions that may not be available on the underlying asset. For example, if no futures are available, the investor could create a futures position synthetically, as long as options are available.

However, the main reason for the use of synthetics is arbitrage. The put/call parity formula encountered earlier (Chapter 4, Section 2.2) defined the relationship between call and put premiums and the price of the underlying asset. If call and put premiums are out of line with one another, it is possible to lock in riskless profits. This is illustrated in the following examples, both creating synthetic futures.

Example 13

The long gilt future is currently trading at 114.14. The premium of the 114.00 call is 0.45 and the premium of the 114.00 put is 0.39.

What should you do?

Buy the call and sell the put for a net premium outlay of 0.06. This gives you a long futures position (synthetically) at 114.06.

But the actual future is trading at 114.14, so sell the future to **lock in** the difference of 0.08.

The whole trade is known as a **reversal**.

Example 14

The long gilt future is currently trading at 114.14. The premium of the 114.00 call is 0.51 and the premium of the 114.00 put is 0.31. What should you do?

Sell the call and buy the put for a net premium receipt of 0.20. This gives you a short futures position (synthetically) at 114.20. But the actual future is trading at 114.14, so **buy the future** to **lock in** the difference of 0.06.

The whole trade is known as a **conversion**.

Both OTC and exchange-traded derivatives can be used in the wide range of trading strategies discussed in this chapter. Many include both types as part of the same strategy.

The same factors that an investor or fund manager uses when deciding which type of contract to use in a basic position are also used in these strategies. The most basic is: which type of contract best fits the goal of the strategy? If it is a hedge, does the flexibility of an OTC contract better suit the hedge? Or does the extra liquidity and ease of trading an exchange-based product better suit one's goal?

While they are important, they are just some of the many factors that are used when deciding what type of contract is best.

8. Exchange-Traded Versus Over-the-Counter (OTC) Derivatives Hedges

Learning Objective

8.6.1 Understand the advantages and disadvantages of using exchange-traded versus OTC products in hedge management: exposure flexibility versus contract specification; ease/cost of closing OTC transactions versus exchange-traded positions; margins versus collateral processes; counterparty exposure versus centralised clearing; price transparency; best execution; documentation; settlement mechanism

Exchange-traded (ETD) and OTC derivatives each have their advantages and disadvantages with respect to speculative and hedging strategies.

	Advantages	Disadvantages
Exchange-Traded	More liquidity. Full price transparency. Counterparty credit risk limited to the exchange's clearing house.	Margin payments required. Standardised contracts.
Over-the-Counter	Flexible contracts to fit any exposure. No margin required, collateral depends on counterparty.	Counterparty credit risk. Limited price transparency. Higher transaction costs.

Note that best execution depends more on the client's relationship with their broker. While the increased price transparency associated with ETD contracts does give them a slight advantage, in this aspect it is more of a case-by-case basis.

When comparing an OTC to an exchange-traded derivative, any investor has to weigh up the advantages and disadvantages. One of the key advantages of OTC is the flexibility that this type of contract gives to an investor. An OTC derivative can be negotiated and customised to meet the specific needs of an individual investor, including contract amount, maturity/expiration date and contract price. This flexibility is key to OTC derivatives, but there is a trade-off, since OTC derivatives have several disadvantages compared to exchange-traded derivatives.

OTC contracts tend to have more counterparty risk, and less market transparency – this might result in limited liquidity and higher transaction costs.

Since most exchange-traded contracts have standard specifications, their documentation and trade processing and clearing is also fairly standard. In contrast, while some OTC derivative counterparties can have netting and other agreements that will enable them to reduce the associated trade documentation, the fact that the OTC derivatives are individual means that, for most, the trade documentation process is more involved, usually meaning higher transaction and processing costs.

The same is true for settlement agreements/procedures. The fact that the clearing house is the counterparty to every trade means that there are specific and standard delivery procedures for those exchange-traded derivatives that do go to delivery. This again reduces counterparty risk, as well as delivery costs. Recent regulatory changes have increased the level of standardised or straightforward processing of a wide range of OTC derivatives. Several market-based organisations, such as ISDA have established settlement best practices and procedural guidelines for their members to use to improve the settlement time and risk management of their OTC derivatives exposure.

OTC derivatives' flexibility with regard to contract maturity/expiration also extends to its delivery mechanism. When an OTC derivative is negotiated, either counterparty can include specific delivery arrangements that meet his specific requirements. For example, a buyer of a silver call may have included, as part of the contract agreement, specific details of where the seller will deliver the silver, if the buyer chooses to exercise the call. This flexibility should be priced into the call's premium.

9. Indirect Investment

Most investors are unlikely to become involved directly in the derivatives markets, but there are numerous instruments that they do invest in which indirectly involve the use of futures and options.

There are two main routes for most customers wanting to invest in derivatives, accounts and pooled funds.

1. **Accounts**
   A discretionary account operates where the client entrusts money to a regulated firm, which then undertakes to manage the funds according to the client's objectives, perhaps subject to restrictions on the types of instruments that can be used by the manager. Wealthy individuals normally use such funds. The key advantage of such accounts is that the client benefits from professional management and oversight. The client also benefits from profits, but is equally liable for losses on the portfolio that can be more than the funds invested.
2. **Pooled Funds**
   These are collective investment schemes (CISs) managed by regulated fund management companies on behalf of investors whose money is pooled together and invested. These CISs can include derivatives. An investment pool is specific to the US and relates to small, highly regulated funds. The maximum loss to the investor is restricted to the amount they invest. Their main advantage is that, by pooling the funds, risk is diversified. The number of investors in a pooled fund is usually small, normally 20–30, and management fees are relatively high.

9.1 Investment Style of Derivatives-Based Funds

The investment style/objectives of derivatives-based funds vary, but can be categorised by three main types:

1. **Speculative** – highly geared funds investing in derivatives to produce high returns, at a high risk. Clients cannot lose more than the funds invested.
2. **Guaranteed** – funds that lock in the investor for a minimum period and provide exposure to a market but guarantee that, at worst, the investor will get their money back (or a preset amount, eg, 95%). Typically, most of the funds will be invested in ZCBs, or cash, with the balance being used to buy options, eg, FTSE put options for an index bear fund. These are low-risk because investors'

capital is safe. However, the lock-in periods can be quite long (one to seven years). If after five years an investor only received their money back, the cost is the lost returns they could have received elsewhere, for example bank interest. This is known as opportunity cost.

3. **Synthetics** – funds designed to replicate the performance of an index. They use the techniques described in Section 6 of this chapter to achieve their objectives. Typically, the funds are invested on risk-free deposit and the relevant numbers of futures contracts (representing the value of the funds) are purchased. Note that, even though futures are being used, there is no gearing in these funds.

9.2 Derivatives-Based Funds

CISs are a means of investing money alongside others, benefiting from professional fund management. The prime vehicle is the unit trust, which pools funds placed by investors.

There are two types of unit trusts: authorised and unauthorised. The authorisation comes from the FCA. The significance of authorisation is that it dictates the marketability of the fund to private customers. Authorised unit trusts (AUTs) can be freely advertised and marketed; unauthorised unit trusts cannot.

9.3 Offshore Funds

Investors can invest in CISs established within the UK (onshore funds) or outside the UK (offshore funds). Offshore funds may provide the UK investor with greater choice and may be tax-efficient; however, the regulatory protections may be less substantial and the charges may be higher than in an equivalent UK fund. Most are based in an offshore financial centre, such as Luxembourg, the Cayman Islands or the British Virgin Islands.

10. Application – Different Uses

Learning Objective

8.7.3 Analyse the relative attractiveness of derivative positions or investments to specific client circumstances: private client investment portfolios; individual portfolios; institutional asset managers; corporate treasurers; hedge funds; sovereign wealth funds

Derivatives can be used to reduce risk as a hedge, or increase risk as a way of increasing profit – speculation. We also know derivatives are leveraged, some more than others. The following provides an overview of how different types of clients/investors are most likely to use derivatives.

Private Client Investment/Portfolios

Also widely known as private investors or retail clients, their use of derivatives can range from never and for hedging existing investment positions to moderately speculative depending on their knowledge/understanding of the markets, as well as their arrangements with their bank/broker. The institutions that execute trades for these clients are bound by the FCA, the EU and the US and other regulators to know their customers and not missell or misrepresent the risk associated with any trades, particularly those that involve derivatives (see Chapter 7). In addition, private clients will find that their speculative use of derivatives may be restricted by their banks/brokers, since they must ensure that clients have sufficient assets/credit facilities to meet all of their obligations, which range from margin calls to the liabilities associated with writing a naked option. There are also regulations that restrict private client use of derivatives, particularly when it is related to self-managed individual pension accounts.

Individual Portfolios

This classification of client is defined by a wide range of regulations – FCA, MiFID and SEC guidelines, to name a few (see Chapter 9). The most com mon and widely used definition of an individual, private or retail client or investor is one that is neither a professional nor is considered to be an eligible counterparty. While each of the specific guidelines for each agency differs slightly regarding benchmarks where an individual investor is no longer considered to be a retail investor, this category is provided with the highest level of protection by them and all are considered to be non-professional investors. The main reason for this level of protection is the view that these investors have the lowest risk tolerance and many have a limited understanding of the risks associated with many investments.

Most banks/brokers have their own in-house parameters to classify an individual investor or private client. They usually define an individual as high net worth when they have a minimum amount of assets to invest, such as £10 million or £15 million of assets that the client can deposit with the specific institution. While slightly more relaxed, the know your customer rules still apply since, with these sums, the regulators are concerned about money laundering as well as client protection.

Given their increased assets, this class of client will normally have a wider range of derivative products available for their use. They tend to have a higher risk tolerance, therefore their use of derivatives is more speculative than that of private retail clients. In summary, high net worth clients normally take riskier derivative positions, depending on their wealth; these can sometimes match those of the small hedge funds.

This class of investor will normally be more restricted by the limits placed upon them by their banks/brokers, who must ensure that they have sufficient funds/credits to cover any margin calls or funds to cover the exercise of any naked written option position held by these clients.

Institutional Asset Managers

Collective investment or fund managers use derivatives to both reduce risk (hedge) and increase it (speculate), as a means to increase the return of their fund. Each will have specific guidelines within which they must operate. While UCITS III has allowed OTC funds to increase their use of derivatives, as long as they report and account for such use and manage it within their guidelines, institutional asset managers, for the most part, will be more conservative in their use of derivatives than hedge fund managers.

In summary, while it very much depends on their individual fund's guidelines, most institutional asset managers' use of derivatives will be more speculative than a corporate treasurer's, but less than a hedge fund's.

Corporate Treasurers

Most companies are not in the business of speculating in derivatives as a way of generating profit. Therefore, most corporate treasurers will use derivatives as a hedge in order to reduce risk. Their use of derivatives ranges from buying or selling futures (both financial and commodities) to reduce any price risk associated with their line of business. For example, a mining company might sell copper futures when planning their budget to lock-in the future price they will get for the copper they produce. Corporate treasurers may also buy options, such as FX options, if they are involved in international transactions, in order to reduce any currency risk.

In summary, corporate treasurers are most likely to be among the most conservative users of derivatives.

Hedge Funds

There is a wide range of hedge funds, each with its own goal and risk parameters. Funds' use of derivatives will range from hedging, to reduce risk and lock-in profits, to highly geared speculative positions. Again, their use of derivatives depends on their investment goals and specific guidelines. Recent regulations, such as UCITS III, have made the use of derivatives by OTC funds less restrictive, while also ensuring that these funds report their use properly and remain within their guidelines' limits.

In summary, hedge funds can be found along the full spectrum of derivative use, from hedging to highly geared speculative positions, such as naked options writing.

Sovereign Wealth Funds (SWFs)

These are pools of money derived from a country's reserves, which are set aside for investment purposes that will benefit the country's economy. The funding for a Sovereign Wealth Fund (SWF) comes from central bank reserves that accumulate as a result of budget and trade surpluses.

The types of acceptable investments included in each SWF vary from country to country; they include stocks, bonds, property, precious metals and other financial instruments (which in some cases include derivatives).

Some countries have created SWFs to diversify their revenue streams. For example, the UAE relies on oil exports for its wealth. Therefore, it devotes a portion of its reserves to an SWF that invests in other types of assets that can act as a shield against oil-related risk.

Some SWFs may be held by a central bank, which accumulates the funds in the course of its management of a nation's banking system; this type of fund is usually of major economic and fiscal importance. Other SWFs are simply the state savings schemes that are invested by various entities for an attractive investment return.

The accumulated funds may have their origin in, or may represent, international currency deposits, gold, special drawing rights (SDRs) and International Monetary Fund (IMF) reserve positions held by central banks and monetary authorities, along with other national assets such as pension investments, oil funds, and other industrial and financial holdings. Such investment management entities may be set up as official investment companies, state pension funds, or sovereign oil funds.

The following is a list of the 10 largest SWFs as of March 2017:

Fund's name	Country	Size of fund – USD bn
Government Pensions Fund	Norway	922.1
China Investment Company	China	813.8
Abu Dhabi Investment Authority	Abu Dhabi	792.0
Kuwait Investment Fund	Kuwait	592.0
SAMA Foreign Holdings	Saudi Arabia	514.0
Hong Kong Monetary Authority Investment Portfolio	Hong Kong	456.6
SAFE Investment Company	China	441.0
Government of Singapore Investment Corporation	Singapore	350.0
Qatar Investment Authority	Qatar	335.0
National Social Security Fund	China	295.0

Appendix

Answer to Exercise 1

Number of contracts required =

$$\text{Price factor} \times \frac{\text{Nominal value of CTD portfolio}}{\text{Nominal value of the contract}}$$

Number of contracts needed to hedge =

$$1.12486 \times \frac{£15{,}000{,}000}{£100{,}000}$$

$$= 168.729$$

$$= 169 \text{ contracts approx.}$$

Because the investor has short sold the gilts, she should buy 169 long gilt futures.

Answer to Exercise 2

a. There is a loss on the shares of 21p (215p – 194p); however, the option is not exercised, so Mr Z keeps the premium of 9p, resulting in an overall loss of 21p – 9p = 12p per share.

b. There is a loss on the shares of 7p (215p – 208p); however, the option is not exercised, so Mr Z keeps the premium of 9p, resulting in an overall profit of 9p – 7p = 2p per share.

c. The gain on the shares would have been 15p (230p – 215p), but the option is exercised, so Mr Z needs to deliver his shares at 220p, a gain of only 5p (220p – 215p). However, he also keeps the premium of 9p, resulting in an overall profit of 9p + 5p = 14p per share.

Answer to Exercise 3

a. The option is exercised and Mrs P has to pay 700p under the terms of the option. But since she was short of the shares at 718p, that will give her 18p of profit, which, combined with the premium received from writing the covered put, results in a total profit of 30p.

b. The option is not exercised and Mrs P keeps the 12p premium.

c. While the option is not exercised, Mrs P will realise a loss of 32p (the difference between the share's price of 750p and where she is short, 718p). But that will be reduced by the 12p premium that she received for writing the put, which results in a net loss of 20p.

Answer to Exercise 4

a. The 550 put will be exercised, so Mr Z will buy the ABC shares at 550p each and he will be able to sell them for 500p under the terms of the put option he holds. The loss will be 50p, but Mr Z has received a net premium of 17p (35p – 18p), so in overall terms he has lost 33p (50p – 17p).

b. The 550 put will be exercised, so Mr Z will buy the ABC shares at 550p each and he will be able to sell them for 530p on the market. The loss will be 20p, but Mr Z has received a net premium of 17p (35p – 18p), so in overall terms he has lost 3p (20p – 17p).

c. Neither option will be exercised, so Mr Z will keep the net premium of 17p (35p – 18p).

Answer to Exercise 5

This is a bull put spread.

The break-even will be when the share price reaches 533p. At this price the holder of the 550 put will exercise, so Mr Z will lose 17p (buying shares for 550p that are only worth 533p). However, there is also the net premium receipt of 17p to consider (35p – 18p), so overall Mr Z will break-even.

The maximum profit will occur at 550p or above. At 550p, Mr Z will keep the premium of 35p, having spent a premium of 18p on the bought put with the lower exercise – a net profit of 17p.

Answer to Exercise 6

This is a long straddle, and the break-even range is the strike plus and minus the two premiums, here 7p + 18p = 25p. So, in this instance the shares need to fall below 475p (500p – 25p) or rise to above 525p (500p + 25p) to bring about a profit for the investor.

Answer to Exercise 7

The underlying share has to rise above 450 plus the two premiums or fall below 400 minus the two premiums. So the break-even range is from 375 to 475.

End of Chapter Questions

1. What is a market-linked product?
   Answer reference: Section 1

2. What are intra-market spreads based on?
   Answer reference: Section 2.1

3. When using futures to hedge an equities portfolio, how is its beta useful?
   Answer reference: Section 3.2

4. What is covered short call?
   Answer reference: Section 4.3.1

5. From what do vertical spreads attempt to profit?
   Answer reference: Section 5.1

6. How do straddles and strangles work?
   Answer reference: Section 6

7. What is the main reason for using synthetics?
   Answer reference: Section 7

8. Identify the key advantage of OTC derivatives hedges.
   Answer reference: Section 8

9. What are two main routes for most customers wanting to invest in derivatives?
   Answer reference: Section 9

10. Who are most likely to be among the most conservative users of derivatives?
    Answer reference: Section 10

Chapter Nine

Regulatory Requirements

This syllabus area will provide approximately 7 of the 100 examination questions

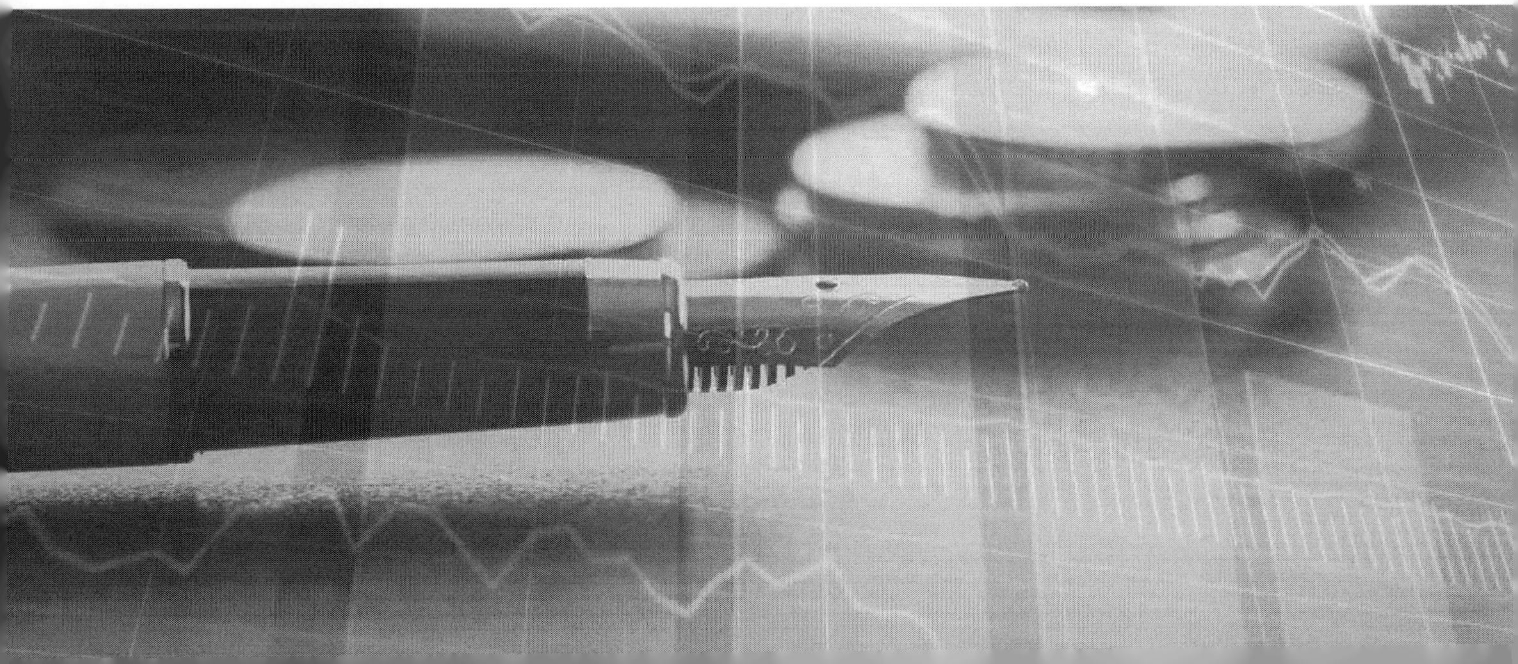

1. The Scope of Regulation

Learning Objective

9.1.1 Understand in general terms the scope and purpose of regulation of derivatives and the main activities of regulators: Europe (MIFID, FCA, other regulators); US (Fed, SEC & CFTC); Far East (Hong Kong, Singapore and Japan); orderly markets; consumer protection; education; combating financial crime; regulation of individuals, companies; supervision; sanction processes; passporting regulated status; classifications/exemption; OSC commitments to regulators for OTC derivatives

9.1.2 Know the primary requirements of a regulated exchange

This chapter covers some of the key aspects and the role of market regulators in relation to derivatives in some of the main markets. It is followed by a review of UK, European Union (EU) and US regulations and a brief review of the international accounting rules that apply to derivatives.

1.1 Main Market Regulators

Europe	European Banking Authority (EBA) European Securities and Markets Authority (ESMA) and the European Insurance and Occupational Pensions Authority (EIOPA) UK – Prudential Regulation Authority (PRA) and Financial Policy Committee (FPC) (part of the Bank of England) and the Financial Conduct Authority (FCA)
Asia	Hong Kong – Securities and Futures Commission India – Securities and Exchange Board of India (SEBI) Singapore – Monetary Authority Japan – Financial Services Authority (FSA) China – China Securities Regulatory Commission (CSRC)
US	Federal Reserve (Fed) Securities and Exchange Commission (SEC) Commodity Futures Trading Commission (CFTC)
Latin America	Argentina – Comisión Nacional de Valores (CNV) Brazil – Comissão de Valores Mobiliários (CVM) Mexico – Secretaría de Hacienda y Crédito Público (SHCP)

The main purpose and aims of regulation, in all markets globally, are to:

- maintain and promote the fairness, efficiency, competitiveness, transparency and orderliness of the securities and futures industry
- promote understanding by the public of the operation and functioning of the securities and futures industry
- provide protection for members of the public investing in or holding financial products
- minimise crime and misconduct in the securities and futures industry
- reduce systemic risks in the securities and futures industry, and
- assist in maintaining the market's financial stability by taking appropriate steps in relation to the securities and futures industry.

All of the above-mentioned are the requirements that all regulated markets must fulfil, in order to receive the approval of their respective national regulator. Without these, any market will not be considered by local and international investors as safe and fair and therefore will eventually disappear.

While they are not recognised as official market regulators, two other organisations play a significant role in the development of financial market regulation.

The International Organization of Securities Commissions (IOSCO) is an association of organisations that regulate the world's securities and futures markets. Its membership is made up of the main securities commissions and/or financial regulators from each country. IOSCO members currently regulate more than 90% of the global securities markets. Its role is to assist its members to promote high standards of regulation and act as a forum for national regulators to cooperate with each other and other international organisations. Its three main goals are to:

- promote high standards of regulation for the sake of orderly and efficient markets,
- share information among exchanges and assist them with technical and operational issues,
- establish standards towards monitoring global investment transactions across borders and markets.

The International Swaps and Derivatives Association (ISDA) is a trade organisation, whose members are the main participants in the global OTC derivatives markets. Some of its main accomplishments are the acceptance and use of a standardised contract (the ISDA Master Agreement) for a wide range of derivatives transactions. ISDA also manages FpML, an XML message standard for the OTC derivatives industry. For more details, see Chapter 5, Section 11.6.

1.2 UK and EU

While each country has its own financial regulator (such as the PRA and FCA in the UK, which sets out the rules for all the UK markets, including the derivatives markets) the EU, through MiFID and EMIR, has introduced more extensive rules and regulations regarding the conduct of business and operational and risk management requirements of firms within the financial industry.

While the results of the June 2016 referendum and the formal start of the Brexit process in March 2017 (that the UK will leave the EU) will change the relationship between the EU regulators and the UK, the fact that London is expected to maintain its position as a key international financial centre, since the continued globalisation of the financial markets continues, will require that the high level of cooperation between EU and UK regulators is expected to remain strong. Therefore, any changes to current and planned future EU-based regulations that apply to the UK will remain as is during the negotiations and will most likely apply after the details of the final Brexit agreement has been settled.

The Investment Services Directive (ISD) was issued in 1993. Broadly, it specified that if a firm had been authorised in one member state to provide investment services, this single authorisation enabled the firm to provide those investment services in other member states without requiring any further authorisation. This principle was, and still is, known as the passport. The state providing authorisation is where the firm originates and is commonly referred to as the home state. States outside the home state where the firm offers investment services are known as host states.

The ISD was repealed and replaced by MiFID. MiFID provisions came into force in the UK on 1 November 2007. One of the key aims of MiFID was to provide investor protection rules across the EEA. Investor protection is ensured, *inter alia*, via the obligation to obtain the best possible result for the client, information disclosure requirements, client-specific rules on suitability and appropriateness and rules on inducements.

MiFID has been designed to support two key policy goals of the EU. These are:

- extending the scope of the passport to include a wider range of services, and
- removing a major hurdle to cross-border business, by way of the application of host state rules to incoming passported firms.

Previously, under the ISD, firms were only able to passport a limited range of investment services into other host states. MiFID widens the range of passportable activities – for example, it now includes:

- investment advice (which under the ISD was only permitted where it was an **ancillary service** to some other core service being provided – for example, dealing in investments)
- some underwriting activities
- operating an MTF
- investment activities relating to commodity derivatives, credit derivatives and CFDs, since MiFID has extended the scope of the passport to cover these instruments for the first time
- investment research, where it is an ancillary service to some other core service.

Not all firms authorised by the Bank of England are directly subject to the requirements of MiFID: whether they are or not will depend on the nature of their activities. Very broadly, all those firms which were subject to the ISD form the core of the MiFID population – but, as we have seen, MiFID broadens the range of activities caught within its scope, so many new firms which were not previously ISD firms became MiFID firms on 1 November 2007.

Broadly, the range of UK firms which are classified as MiFID firms is as follows:

- firms dealing and managing investments
- firms operating an MTF
- venture capital firms that meet certain criteria.

A key feature of MiFID is that it improves the passport of regulated firms by clarifying any differences between the home and host markets' regulations. It also sets out a **Capital Requirements Directive (CRD)**, which sets requirements for the regulatory capital a firm must hold. This is to ensure orderly markets and improve client protection.

1.2.1 MiFID II

In April 2014, the European Parliament voted through MiFID II. Its new measures will be implemented on 3 January 2018. An overview of the main elements of the proposals is set out below:

- The scope of MiFID will be expanded:
  - MiFID will also apply to the advised and non-advised sale of structured deposits by credit institutions.
  - MiFID will apply to all transactions (including spot transactions) in emissions allowances (until now only certain derivative transactions in emissions allowances fell within the scope of MiFID).

    - MiFID II clarifies that the MiFID rules also apply to investment firms and credit institutions selling their own securities at the moment of their issuance when not providing advice.
    - The scope of the existing exceptions for investment firms that deal on their own account will be narrowed. For instance, investment firms that deal on their own account will require a licence if they are a member of a regulated market or an MTF.
    - The scope of the existing exceptions for entities active in commodity derivatives trading will be narrowed.
    - Custody of financial instruments will become an investment service. Currently, this is merely an ancillary activity. This means that entities that provide custody services without providing other MiFID services will require a licence.
- The proposals create a new regime for investment firms based in non-EU/EEA countries. Pursuant to this regime, investment firms based in non-EU/EEA countries will be able to benefit from a European passport. This requires, among other things, the establishment of a branch in the EU/EEA when offering services to non-professional clients.
- Amendment of the rules regarding client classification:
    - The proposals provide that municipalities and other local authorities do not qualify as professional investors.
    - Additional obligations will apply with respect to services offered to eligible counterparties.
- New rules with respect to investor protection:
    - Firms giving investment advice will be required to disclose whether the advice is provided on an independent basis, whether it is based on a broad or on a more restricted analysis of the market, and whether the firm will provide the client with the ongoing assessment of the suitability of the financial instruments recommended. In order to qualify as advice provided on an independent basis, the firm must meet certain requirements.
    - Investment firms providing advice on an independent basis or providing asset management services may not receive fees, commissions or other monetary benefits from a third party in relation to the provision of the service to clients.
    - The exception with respect to the 'know your customer' (KYC) requirement for execution-only business will be narrowed by limiting the categories of financial instruments for which this is permissible.
    - The proposals introduce specific information obligations in respect of bundled products.
    - The proposals contain additional information obligations with respect to order execution policies.
    - The proposals prohibit the conclusion of title transfer financial collateral arrangements with non-professional clients.
- Additional corporate governance requirements will be imposed on investment firms, including requirements with respect to the members of the management board and the supervisory board:
    - The existing requirement to have sufficiently experienced members is expanded: members will be required to commit sufficient time to discharge their duties. The proposals include limits on the number of directorships a person can have at any one time.
    - The proposals require, where appropriate, the establishment of a nomination committee.
    - Investment firms must take into account diversity as one of the criteria for selection of members of the management board and the supervisory board.
- The proposals provide that investment firms must record certain telephone conversations and electronic communications (for instance email).
- The proposals, based on MiFIR (Markets in Financial Investments Regulation) which is set to go live in January 2018, will introduce new rules with respect to the infrastructure of trading venues:
    - A new trading venue is to be provided for the organised trading facility (OTF). This is a trading venue other than a regulated market or MTF, that brings together multiple third party

buying and selling interests (an example of an OTF is a broker crossing system). OTFs require authorisation from the regulator. In addition, OTFs must meet certain ongoing requirements that also apply to regulated markets and MTFs, but will also be subject to certain investor protection rules. OTFs may not execute orders against their own capital.
    - The regime for systematic internalisers will no longer be limited to shares, but will also extend to other financial instruments. In addition, the proposals contain additional rules for systematic internalisers.
    - Additional requirements will apply with respect to regulated markets (MTFs and OTFs), including the requirement to provide annual information on the execution quality, more extensive transparency and reporting obligations and rules with respect to data consolidation.
- The proposals introduce rules with respect to algorithmic trading: investment firms that engage in algorithmic trading must comply with additional requirements.
- Mandatory exchange trading of derivatives: in line with EMIR, MiFID requires that transactions in derivatives that have been identified by ESMA may in principle occur only on a regulated market, MTF, OTF or equivalent third country trading venue.
- The proposals provide for additional powers for the regulators: regulators will have the power to require any person to reduce its derivatives position, or, with respect to commodity derivatives, to limit the ability of any person to enter into a commodity derivative. In addition, regulators will have the power to prohibit or restrict the marketing, distribution or sale of particular financial instruments or a type of activity.
- The proposals introduce new rules with respect to sanctions: there will be minimum requirements that the member states must implement, including the provision that the maximum penalty must be at least 10% of the total annual turnover in the case of a legal entity and €5,000,000 in the case of a natural person or twice the amount of benefit derived from the violation.

1.3 Over-the-Counter (OTC) Derivatives

The Operations Steering Committee (OSC, previously the Operations Management Group or OMG) of ISDA has targets to improve the operational infrastructure and regulation of the OTC derivatives industry. The OSC, whose membership includes OTC broker-dealers, buy-side firms and industry associations such as ISDA, has made a commitment to regulators to increase the number and types of OTC products that will be centrally cleared, such as single-name credit default swaps (CDSs) and overnight index swaps (OISs).

In addition, the OSC has increased its emphasis on collateral management. It has implemented daily reconciliation of all collateralised inter-dealer positions in excess of 500 positions. This should cover 70% of the markets covered.

The group has also set a goal that at least 50% of equity derivatives traded can be matched, processed and cleared electronically. Equity derivatives are the least standardised of all OTC derivatives, making operational standardisation the most difficult.

1.4 European Regulators

1.4.1 The European Banking Authority (EBA)

The European Banking Authority (EBA) is a regulatory agency whose activities include conducting stress tests on EU banks with the goal of increasing transparency within the European financial system, and identifying weaknesses in banks' capital structures. The EBA has the power to overrule any national regulators if they fail to properly regulate their banks, and it can prevent regulatory arbitrage, which should allow banks to compete fairly throughout the EU.

Other tasks set out in the EBA's mandate include investigating alleged incorrect or insufficient application of EU law by national authorities, mediating to resolve disagreements between competent authorities in cross-border situations, and promoting transparency, simplicity and fairness in the market.

1.4.2 The European Securities and Markets Authority (ESMA)

The European Securities and Markets Authority (ESMA) is one of the three European Supervisory Authorities. Its main role is to establish an EU-wide financial markets overseer by first assessing risks to investors, markets and financial stability, and then composing a single rulebook for EU financial markets, promoting supervisory convergence among EU members and directly supervising credit rating agencies and trade repositories. A single rulebook will enhance the EU's single market by creating a level playing field for investors and issuers across the EU.

ESMA is mandated to take an active role in building a common supervisory culture among national competent authorities to promote sound, efficient, and consistent supervision throughout the EU. This is known as supervisory convergence and is the consistent implementation and application of the same rules using similar approaches across EU member states, and implies sharing best practices and realising efficiency gains across the financial industry.

ESMA's position in the European System of Financial Supervision also makes it qualified to conduct peer reviews, set up EU-wide market data reporting requirements, thematic studies and common work programs, draft opinions, guidelines and Q&As.

1.4.3 Member Regulators

Cyprus – Cyprus Securities and Exchange Commission (CySEC)

CySEC is the financial regulatory agency of Cyprus, and was launched in 2001. When Cyprus became an EU member state, in 2004, CySEC became a part of MiFID regulation, which granted firms registered in Cyprus access to all European markets. However, joining the EU and adopting the euro has caused significant changes to Cyprus' financial structure, since it had been considered a tax haven. This, in turn, has caused some major policy changes by CySEC.

France – Autorité des Marchés Financiers (AMF)

The AMF is an independent public body which regulates and monitors the participants and products of France's financial markets, with its main focus on the Paris Bourse and Euronext Paris Matif. It safeguards investments in financial products and maintain orderly financial markets. It also carries out investigations and issues sanctions for any violation of its rules and ensures that investors receive all required information and provides a mediation service to assist them in disputes.

Germany – Federal Financial Supervisory Authority (BaFin)

BaFin is an independent financial regulatory body that supervises all aspects of the German financial system. It supervises around 2,700 banks, 800 financial services institutions and 700 insurance companies, and ensures that their financial condition of solvency and liquidity are met. BaFin ensures that Germany's securities and derivatives markets operate in accordance with the Securities Trading Act, including the prevention of insider trading and other market abuses, such as price and market manipulation. BaFin also has a wide range of enforcement powers.

Netherlands – Netherlands Authority for the Financial Markets (AFM)

The AFM is the financial services regulator for the Netherlands, and its role and the way it operates is comparable to that of the SEC in the US. It is the sole regulator of all Dutch financial markets. It was set up in 2002 by legislation which significantly expanded its responsibilities to cover all financial products, including savings, investments, loans, insurance and accounting.

Spain – Comisión Nacional del Mercado de Valores (CNMV)

The CNMV is the independent agency responsible for the regulation of securities markets in Spain. The reforms that established the CNMV in 1988 defined its powers and responsibilities, and were key to establishment of a regulatory framework that would meet EU standards. The aim of the CNMV is to ensure the stability and transparency of Spain's financial markets, protecting investors and insuring that brokers and intermediaries behave correctly.

1.5 Non-EU Europe Regulators

Switzerland – Swiss Financial Market Supervisory Authority (FINMA)

FINMA is the Swiss financial regulator. It is an independent body with responsibilities including the supervision of Swiss banks, insurance companies, stock exchanges, futures exchanges, securities dealers, and financial intermediaries. FINMA is responsible for combating money laundering and, where necessary, it conducts financial restructuring and bankruptcy proceedings.

2. Different Regulatory Approaches

Learning Objective

9.2.1 Understand in general terms the importance of the principles-based approach to regulation: client classification; treating customers fairly; suitability and appropriateness of the transaction/product; best execution

9.2.2 Understand the differences between rules-based and principles-based regulation

2.1 Principles-Based Regulation

Principles-based regulation means moving away from reliance on detailed, prescriptive rules and relying more on high-level principles to set the standards by which regulated firms must conduct business.

In the UK, the FCA has continued an approach to market regulation that is similar to its predecessor, the FSA. Three key elements in the FCA's current approach are:

- broad-based standards in preference to detailed rules
- outcomes-based regulation
- increasing senior management responsibility.

Many proponents of the principles-based approach feel that it better fits today's changing financial markets, by allowing the flexibility that is required, given the new developments in technology and financial products that are now available.

The key point of results- or outcomes-based regulation is such that its proponents state allows it to be applied to client-based services. They claim that if a firm does not treat customers fairly, or adhere to the best execution rules, or sells products to investors that are not appropriate or suitable, the poor results/performance that these clients will have will result in their using other firms, thereby damaging the firm's reputation and, in the long run, their overall performance.

Rules-based regulation is based on strict, clearly defined but inflexible one size fits all rules that must be followed. In contrast, principles-based regulation allows for flexibility and judgement, as broadly based guidelines/standards are the norm. While many feel that the latter can cause confusion and problems, its proponents claim that it is better suited for today's financial markets.

2.2 FCA Principles for Businesses

The FCA's Conduct of Business Sourcebook (COBS), which replaced the FSA's sourcebook, still includes 11 key Principles for Businesses ('the Principles'), which authorised firms must observe. If a firm breaches any of the Principles that apply to it, it will be liable to disciplinary sanctions.

The 11 Principles for Businesses are:

1. **Integrity** – a firm must conduct its business with integrity.
2. **Skill, care and diligence** – a firm must conduct its business with due skill, care and diligence.

3. **Management and control** – a firm must take reasonable care to organise and control its affairs responsibly and effectively, with adequate risk management systems.
4. **Financial prudence** – a firm must maintain adequate financial resources.
5. **Market conduct** – a firm must observe proper standards of market conduct.
6. **Customers' interests** – a firm must pay due regard to the interests of its customers and treat them fairly.
7. **Communication with clients** – a firm must pay due regard to the information needs of its clients and communicate information to them in a way which is clear, fair and not misleading.
8. **Conflicts of interest** – a firm must manage conflicts of interest fairly, both between itself and its customers, and between customers and other clients.
9. **Customers: relationships of trust** – a firm must take reasonable care to ensure the suitability of its advice and discretionary decisions for any customer who is entitled to rely upon its judgement.
10. **Clients' assets** – a firm must arrange adequate protection for clients' assets when it is responsible for them.
11. **Relations with regulators** – a firm must deal with its regulators in an open and cooperative way and must disclose to the FCA appropriately anything relating to the firm of which the FCA would reasonably expect notice.

2.3 Treating Customers Fairly (TCF)

It should be apparent from a reading of COBS that there is a general theme of overriding fair play. This is coupled with a recognition that there is often an information imbalance between the firm and its customers (since the firm usually has a higher level of expertise in its products and services than its customers). This theme is reinforced through the FCA's Treating Customers Fairly (TCF) initiative. This was originally launched by the FSA in response to some work it undertook in 2000/01, to look at what a fair deal for customers should actually mean. The FCA defines six consumer outcomes to explain to firms what it believes TCF should do for its consumers. These are that:

1. Consumers can be confident that they are dealing with firms where the fair treatment of customers is central to the corporate culture.
2. Products and services marketed and sold in the retail market are designed to meet the needs of identified consumer groups and are targeted accordingly.
3. Consumers are provided with clear information and are kept appropriately informed before, during and after the point of sale.
4. When consumers receive advice, the advice is suitable and takes account of their circumstances.
5. Consumers are provided with products that perform as firms have led them to expect, and the associated service is both of an acceptable standard and as they have been led to expect.
6. Consumers do not face unreasonable post-sale barriers imposed by firms to change product(s), switch provider, submit a claim or make a complaint.

A key part of the FCA's approach is that all advisers adhere to its 'good practice in your behaviour' policy. A key part of this is that all advisers ensure that TCF is a core part of their business by following these practices:

- making sure the fair treatment of customers is a crucial part of your business philosophy
- remembering that TCF is your responsibility and that it cannot be delegated away
- if you use a compliance consultant, ensure their advice is evaluated and applied with your knowledge of your customers and the issues in your business
- ensure your own knowledge, training and competence are up-to-date

- making yourself aware of changes in the market, and
- being conscious of regulatory changes that may affect you or your business.

2.4 Client Categorisation

A firm is required to categorise its clients if it is carrying on designated investment business. MiFID lays down rules as to how client categorisation has to be carried out for MiFID business.

The FCA's COBS define a **client** as someone to whom a firm provides, intends to provide or has provided a service in the course of carrying on a regulated activity; and, in the case of MiFID or equivalent third country business, anything which is an ancillary service.

The term includes potential clients. In addition, in relation to the financial promotions rules, it includes a person to whom a financial promotion is communicated, or is likely to be communicated.

Under COBS, clients may be categorised as:

1. a retail client
2. a professional client, or
3. an eligible counterparty.

The categories are relevant principally in terms of the level of protection afforded them: retail clients receive the highest level of regulatory protection.

New clients must be notified of how the firm has classified them. They must also, before services are provided, advise them of their rights to request recategorisation and of any limits in their protections that arise from this.

1. A retail client is any client who is not a professional client or an eligible counterparty. Note: The term customer means retail clients and professional clients.
2. Professional clients may be either elective professional clients, or per se professional clients. An elective professional client is one who has chosen to be treated as such. Per se professional clients are, generally, those which fall into any of the following categories – unless they are an eligible counterparty, or are categorised differently under other specific provisions.
   The categories are:
   - an entity required to be authorised or regulated to operate in the financial markets.
   - large undertakings – companies whose balance sheet, turnover or own funds meet certain levels.
   - governments, certain public bodies, central banks, international/supranational institutions/ similar organisations, and
   - institutional investors whose main business is investment in financial instruments.
3. Finally, COBS contains a list of the types of clients that can be classified as eligible counterparties (ECPs). Each of the following is an ECP (per se). This includes entities that are not from an EEA state that are equivalent to any of the following (unless and to the extent it is given a different categorisation under COBS 3).
   - a credit institution
   - an investment firm

- another financial institution authorised or regulated under EC legislation or the national law of an EEA state (that includes regulated institutions in the securities, banking and insurance sectors)
- an insurance company
- a collective investment scheme authorised under the UCITS Directive or its management company
- a pension fund or its management company
- a national government or its corresponding office, including a public body that deals with public debt
- a supranational organisation
- a central bank
- an undertaking exempted from the application of MiFID under either Article 2(1)(k) (certain own account dealers in commodities or commodity derivatives) or Article 2(1)(l) (locals).

The list is, to a certain extent, identical to the per se professional client; however, the ECP category is narrower as it does not include large undertakings.

Policies, Procedures and Records

A firm must implement appropriate written internal policies and procedures to categorise its clients. A firm must make a record of the form of each notice provided and each agreement entered into. This record must be made at the time that the standard form is first used and retained for the relevant period after the firm ceases to carry on business with clients who were provided with that form.

Recategorisation of Clients

Many of the COBS rules do not apply when the client is an eligible counterparty; the result of this is that the ECP will not benefit from the protections afforded by these rules. Having said that, the majority of ECPs are large firms who are very familiar with the financial markets, or are themselves large players in the financial markets, and do not need such protections anyway. Some ECPs, however, will have rather more protection by voluntarily asking to opt-down a client category and become elective professional or even retail clients. Firms must allow eligible counterparties to request recategorisation, so as to benefit from the different protections afforded to retail clients or professional clients (as applicable).

Alternatively, a professional client may be treated as an elective ECP if it is a company and it is:

- a per se professional client (other than one which is only a professional client because it is an institutional investor), or
- it asks to be treated as such and is already an elective professional client (but only for the services for which it could be treated as a professional client), and
- it expressly agrees with the firm to be treated as an ECP.

A retail client may be treated as an elective professional client both for MiFID and non-MiFID business only if:

- the firm has assessed his (or its) expertise, experience and knowledge and believes it can make his own investment decisions and understands the risks involved (this is called the qualitative test), and
- any two of the following are true (this is called the quantitative test)
  - the client carried out, on average, ten significantly sized transactions on the relevant market in each of the past four quarters

  - the size of the client's financial portfolio exceeds €500,000 (defined as including cash deposits and financial instruments)
  - the client works or has worked as a professional in the financial services sector for at least a year on a basis which requires knowledge of the transactions envisaged.

For MiFID business, a client may be treated as an elective professional client if it meets both the qualitative test and the quantitative test. If a firm becomes aware that a client no longer fulfils the initial conditions that were made for categorisation as an elective professional client, the firm must take appropriate action. Where the appropriate action involves recategorising the client as a retail client, the firm must notify that client of its new categorisation.

Recategorisation may be carried out for a client on a general basis; or on more specific terms, for example in relation to a single transaction only. A firm can classify a client under a different client classification for different financial instruments in respect of which they may trade/undertake transactions. However, this will mean complex internal arrangements for firms.

2.5 Best Execution

The rules on best execution apply to MiFID and non-MiFID firms and business. The best execution rules under COBS require firms to execute orders on the terms that are most favourable to their client. Specifically, they require that firms take all reasonable steps to obtain, when executing orders, the best possible result for their clients taking into account the execution factors. These factors are price, cost, speed, likelihood of execution and settlement, size, nature or any other consideration relevant to the execution of an order.

Best execution is not merely how to achieve the best price. Any of the other factors mentioned above should be considered and, depending on the criteria or characteristics, may be given precedence.

2.6 Suitability

The COBS rules on the suitability requirements apply when firms:

- make personal recommendations relating to designated investments
- manage investments.

There are specific rules relating to the provision of basic advice (personal recommendations on stakeholder products); firms may, if they choose, apply those rules instead of the more general rules on suitability when advising on stakeholder products. The suitability rules exist to ensure that firms take reasonable steps to ensure that personal recommendations (or decisions to trade) are suitable for their clients' needs.

In order to make a suitability assessment, a firm should establish, and take account of, the client's:

- investment objectives
- knowledge and experience in the investment relevant to the specific type of designated investment or service
- level of investment risk they can bear financially that is consistent with their investment objectives.

In order to do so, a firm should gather enough information from its client to understand the essential facts about them. It must have a reasonable basis to believe that, bearing in mind its nature, the service or transaction:

- meets their investment objectives
- carries a level of investment risk that they can bear financially, and
- carries risks that they have the experience and knowledge to understand.

In terms of assessing the client's knowledge and experience, the firm should gather information on:

- the types of service/transaction/investment with which they are familiar
- the nature, volume, frequency and period of their involvement in such transactions/investments, and
- their level of education, profession or relevant former profession.

Firms are not required to ask clients to provide information or assess appropriateness if:

- the service is execution-only, or for the receipt and transmission of client orders, in relation to particular financial instruments (see below) and at the client's initiative, and
- if the client has been clearly informed that the firm is not required to do so in this particular case, and that they will, therefore, not get the benefit of the protection under the rules on assessing suitability, and
- the firm complies with its obligations regarding conflicts of interest.

The particular financial instruments are:

- shares listed on a regulated market or an equivalent third country market
- money market instruments, bonds or other forms of securitised debt (providing that they do not have embedded derivatives)
- holdings in UCITS funds, and
- other investments meeting a definition of non-complex investments.

A financial instrument is non-complex if:

- it is not a derivative
- there is sufficient liquidity in it
- it does not involve liability for the client that exceeds the cost of acquiring the investment, and
- it is publicly available and comprehensive information is available on it.

In regard to derivatives, therefore, it can be seen that assessment will always be necessary.

3. Principal Differences Between UK, EU and US Regulators

Learning Objective

9.2.2 Understand the differences between rules-based and principles-based regulation

One of the key differences between EU/UK versus US regulations is their different regulatory approach. While EU and UK regulators very much follow outcomes- or principles-based approaches, such as MiFID, their US counterparts follow the rules-based approach.

Rules-based regulation is based on strict, clearly defined but inflexible one size fits all rules that must be followed. In contrast, principles-based regulation allows for flexibility and judgment, as broadly based guidelines/standards are the norm. Principles-based regulation means less reliance on detailed, prescriptive rules, relying more on high-level principles and objectives to set the standards by which regulated firms must conduct business.

A good example of this can be seen from the EU's introduction of MiFID, which allows individual member authorities to opt out of certain aspects of the regulations if they see fit, while the introduction of the Sarbanes-Oxley Act in the US is very much in line with its more rules-based approach. This act sets out strict regulations on how a company manages its derivatives use and exposure as well as reporting it. These regulations are strict requirements for any company that wishes to list its shares on a US exchange. The fallout from this act has seen US exchanges losing listings of international companies to UK and European exchanges, owing to their different regulatory environment.

3.1 UK Regulators

Learning Objective

9.3.1 Know the role of European regulation on EU derivatives markets including the UK: MiFID and the Transparency Directive; clients' money; clients' accounts; margining practices; unregulated markets; access to overseas markets; access to overseas clients

In the UK between 2001 and 2013, the FSA, a quasi-judicial body, was responsible for the regulation of the financial services industry. While its board was appointed by the Treasury, it operated independently of government. It was a limited company and was fully funded by fees charged to the financial services industry.

Due to perceived regulatory failure of the banks during the financial crisis of 2007–08, the UK government decided to restructure financial regulation and abolished the FSA. On 19 December 2012, the Financial Services Act 2012 received royal assent, abolishing the FSA with effect from 1 April 2013. Its responsibilities have been split between two new agencies: the FCA and the PRA (which is part of the Bank of England).

The FCA's main goal is to ensure that there is fair competition among financial firms and that they are all sound. While it reports to Parliament, it, like its predecessor the FSA, is funded by the firms that it regulates. In light of its structure and goals, it is more focused on maintaining a healthy and competitive retail financial industry.

The FCA focuses on:

- **conduct** – for the market to thrive, firms must behave ethically, stick to the rules and meet regulatory standards
- **competition** – it encourages healthy competition between firms to keep the market buoyant and help the economy grow
- **reducing market abuse** – firms need to have procedures to help them identify and stop market abuse practices, such as insider dealing and share price manipulation.

The FCA's responsibility covers all UK financial markets, including the derivatives markets and, therefore, works closely with its EU counterparts and is active in the implementation of MiFID II and all other international regulations.

The PRA, which is part of the Bank of England, is now the UK's prudential regulator for deposit-takers (banks, building societies and credit unions), insurers and designated investment firms. It derives its responsibilities and its powers from the Financial Services and Markets Act 2000 (as amended by the Financial Services Act 2012), and the relevant EU directives for which it is a competent authority.

Its main focus is to ensure that all companies that are part of any aspect of the UK-based financial markets are financially sound. While it is not the PRA's role to ensure that no firms fail, it is its responsibility to ensure that, should this happen, it does so in a way that avoids any major disruption to the supply of critical financial services.

Therefore, both its authority and involvement in the regulation of the derivatives markets is mainly on an indirect basis.

Since the UK has a major international financial market, the FCA works closely with other regulators to improve the market standards. Since the UK is part of the EU, approximately 70% of the FCA's policies are based on EU initiatives, particularly the Financial Services Action Plan.

Two of the key parts of this are MiFID II and the Transparency Directive (TD). MiFID is discussed in Section 1.2 of this chapter.

The TD is designed to enhance transparency on EU capital markets by establishing minimum requirements on periodic financial reporting and on the disclosure of major shareholdings for issuers whose securities are admitted to trading on a regulated market in the EU. The directive also deals with the mechanisms through which this information is to be stored and disseminated.

The TD distinguishes between the concepts of home and host member state regulation, allowing the issuer's home country regulator to impose more stringent disclosure requirements than those set out in the directive, but restricting the host competent authority from doing the same.

The TD establishes disclosure requirements on an ongoing basis about issuers who have securities admitted to trading on a regulated market situated or operated within the EU, for investors who invest in these securities.

There are three broad areas covered under the directive:

1. The minimum content of annual, half-yearly and interim management statements.
2. The notification requirements of both issuers and investors in relation to the acquisition and disposal of the major holdings in companies.
3. The method of disseminating and storing the information covered in 1 and 2 on a pan-European basis.

3.1.1 Clients' Money and Clients' Accounts

FCA rules relating to the custody and safeguarding of client money and client assets are contained in the Client Assets Sourcebook (CASS). They exist to ensure that firms take adequate steps to protect those client assets for which they are responsible. Within CASS, the requirement to segregate client money from a firm's own money is aimed at ensuring that, if the firm fails, that money will not be used to repay its creditors. Usually this is done by ensuring that it is placed promptly in a separately designated client money account with a bank and that the bank treats it as separate from the firm's own.

CASS, in general, applies to every firm, with some specific exemptions (see below). CASS applies directly in respect of activities conducted with or for all categories of client, ie, retail clients, professional clients and eligible counterparties. CASS was substantially updated for the MiFID changes that took effect from 1 November 2007.

CASS 6 contains the custody rules that apply when a firm holds financial instruments of a client in the course of MiFID business and when it is safeguarding and administering investments in the course of non-MiFID business.

CASS 7 (client money and distribution rules) applies to a MiFID investment firm either when:

- it holds client money in the course of its MiFID business or in respect of any investment agreement entered into, or to be entered into, with or for a client, or
- in the course of non-MiFID business, it opts to comply with the MiFID client money rules.

Firms must, when holding safe custody assets belonging to clients, make adequate arrangements so as to safeguard clients' ownership rights. Firms must also introduce adequate organisational arrangements to minimise the risk of loss or diminution of client's safe custody assets. Firms must take the necessary steps to ensure that client money deposited in accordance with the requirement of CASS 7.4.1 (depositing client money) is held in an account or accounts identified separately from any accounts used to hold money belonging to the firm.

There are a number of circumstances when the client money rules will not apply, for example, where money is held in connection with a delivery versus payment (DVP) transaction (unless the DVP does not occur by the close of business on the third business day following the date of payment of a delivery obligation) or where it becomes due and payable to the firm. Bank deposits are also exempted.

Reconciliation of Client Assets

Firms must keep such records and accounts as necessary to enable it at any time and without delay to distinguish safe custody assets held for one client from safe custody assets held for any other client, and from the firm's own assets.

CASS 6.5 sets out the obligations of firms to perform internal and external reconciliations. Broadly, reconciliations should be made as often as necessary to ensure the accuracy of a firm's records and accounts, between its internal accounts and records and those of any third parties by whom those safe custody assets are held. If possible, they should be done by someone who has not been involved in the production or maintenance of the records being reconciled.

If the reconciliation shows a discrepancy, the firm must make good (or provide the equivalent of) any shortfall for which it is responsible. If another person is responsible, the firm should take reasonable steps to resolve the position with that person.

Firms must inform the FCA without delay of any failure to comply with the reconciliation requirements, including reconciliation discrepancies and making good any such differences.

Reconciliation of Client Money

Firms must keep such records and accounts as necessary to enable it at any time and without delay to distinguish client money held for one client from client money held for any other client, and from its own money. **CASS 7.6** sets out the obligations of firms to perform internal and external reconciliations.

- **Internal Reconciliations**

Performing an internal reconciliation means cross-checking the records showing each client's entitlement to client money against the records of client money the firm holds in client bank accounts and client transaction accounts. Firms can choose how often they perform internal reconciliations, subject to the requirement that they do so as often as is necessary – and as soon as reasonably practicable after the date to which the reconciliation relates. A remittance made up of client money and money intended to pay the firm's fees is classified as client money. The FCA has set a method of reconciliation of client money balances called the standard method of client reconciliation.

- **External Reconciliations**

This means cross-checking the internal client money accounts against the records of third parties (eg, banks) with whom client money is held. Firms must perform external reconciliations as often as is necessary and as soon as reasonably practicable after the date to which the reconciliation relates. If there is a discrepancy, the firm must investigate and correct it as soon as possible. If it cannot do so and the firm should be holding a greater amount of client money, it must pay its own money into the client bank account pending resolution of the discrepancy, which it must correct as soon as possible. If a firm has not complied with these requirements, or is for some reason unable to comply in a material aspect with a particular requirement, it must inform the FCA in writing.

The FCA believes that an adequate method of reconciling client money balances with external records is as follows:

- a reconciliation of a client bank account as recorded by the firm with the statement issued by the bank (or other form of confirmation issued by the bank)
- a reconciliation of the balance on each client transaction account as recorded by the firm, with the balance of that account as set out in the statement (or other form of confirmation) issued by the person with whom the account is held.

Exemptions from CASS

CASS does not apply to, *inter alia*:

- Investment companies with variable capital (ICVCs)
- incoming EEA firms other than insurers, for their passported activities
- UCITS qualifying schemes
- a credit institution (eg, a bank) under the Banking Consolidation Directive, in relation to deposits held
- coins held for the value of their metal
- money transferred under title transfer collateral arrangements
- money held in connection with a DVP transaction (unless payment does not occur after three business days)
- money due and payable to the firm
- where a firm carries on business in its name but on behalf of the client when that is required by the very nature of the transaction and the client is in agreement, or
- the custody rules [CASS 6] do not apply if a client transfers full ownership of a safe custody asset to a firm for the purpose of securing or otherwise covering present or future, actual contingent or prospective obligations.

Specific rules within CASS may be disapplied depending on the nature of a firm's activities; the details are set out within the individual rules.

3.1.2 Margin Practices

The initial margin requirement is the amount required to be collateralised in order to open a position. Thereafter, the amount required to be kept in collateral until the position is closed is the maintenance requirement. The maintenance requirement is the minimum amount to be collateralised in order to keep an open position. It is generally lower than the initial requirement. This allows the price to move against the margin without forcing a margin call immediately after the initial transaction.

On instruments determined to be especially risky, however, the regulators, the exchange or the broker may set the maintenance requirement higher than normal or equal to the initial requirement to reduce their exposure to the risk accepted by the trader.

When the margin posted in the margin account is below the minimum margin requirement, the broker or exchange issues a margin call. The investors now either have to increase the margin that they have deposited or close out their position. They can do this by selling the securities, options or futures if they are long and by buying them back if they are short. But if they do none of these, the broker can sell his securities to meet the margin call.

The amount of variation margin is determined by the exchange and the clearing house where exchange-traded contracts are settled – such as LCH.Clearnet in the UK.

3.1.3 Access to International Markets

Investors can undertake derivative contracts on any regulated market, providing that they have suitable arrangements set up with agents in each country (ie, bank, securities account, broker-dealer).

Subject to meeting local regulatory requirements, investors are not prohibited from undertaking derivatives contracts just because they are not domiciled in that country.

3.1.4 Access to International Clients

UK-authorised and -regulated firms are permitted to engage with non-UK clients. However, what is key is where the legal agreement is signed and where the relationship exists. This will determine the extent of the conduct of business requirements of the host state.

There may however still be some local regulatory requirements that exist even though no business services are conducted in the home country, but rather are carried out in the UK. The firm will have to classify the client and also undertake the appropriate 'know your customer' requirements, adhere to the FCA's conduct of business rules on suitability and appropriateness, and also provide the client with relevant information about the firm, its charges and risk warnings.

3.2 EU Regulators

Learning Objective

9.3.1 Know the role of European regulation on EU derivatives markets including the UK: MiFID and the Transparency Directive; clients' money; clients' accounts; margining practices; unregulated markets; access to overseas markets; access to overseas clients

The basic details of EU regulation have been discussed in Sections 1.1 and 1.2 of this chapter.

The EU regulation on the OTC derivatives markets that established central counterparties and trade repositories (TRs) that operates in parallel with individual National Regulatory Authorities (NRAs), is covered by EMIR.

EMIR was introduced to improve the transparency and reduce some of the risk associated with the OTC derivative markets that contributed to the financial crisis of 2007–08. EMIR also establishes common organisational, conduct of business and prudential standards for all central counterparties and other trade repositories.

The EMIR requires all those who enter into any form of derivative contract, including interest rate, FX, equity, credit and commodity derivatives, to:

- report every derivative contract that they enter to a trade repository

- implement new risk management standards, including operational processes and margining, for all bilateral OTC derivatives, ie, trades that are not cleared by a central counterparty, and
- clear, via a central counterparty, those OTC derivatives subject to a mandatory clearing obligation.

EMIR has tightened up various operational areas of OTC derivatives operations, including confirmations, collateral management, portability, reconciliations, dispute resolution and portfolio compression. ISDA terms and protocols continue to operate between transacting counterparties as they have done for over 35 years. ISDA therefore operates in parallel with EMIR.

European Market Infrastructure Regulation (EMIR)

EMIR introduced:

- **Reporting obligation for OTC derivatives** – the aim is to establish greater transparency within the OTC derivatives market, since it requires that all trades are registered with a trade repository (TRs).
- **Central counterparties for all OTC derivative trades** – the aim is greater market safety by reducing both counterparty credit and operational risks.

The scope of EMIR is that it applies to all types of OTC derivatives. It applies both to financial firms who use OTC derivatives and also to non-financial firms that have large positions in OTC derivatives. It also applies to central counterparties and trade repositories.

An important aspect of EMIR is its ongoing focus on reducing the risks associated with OTC derivatives. One aspect of this is its current recommendation that EMSA has proposed the introduction of a one-day margin period of risk for all CCP client accounts, reducing it from two days.

3.3 US Regulators

3.3.1 The Securities and Exchange Commission (SEC)

Learning Objective

9.3.2 Know the role of the Securities and Exchange Commission (SEC) in the regulation of derivatives: what is the SEC; regulated investments; regulated exchanges

Although a major regulator of US securities markets, the SEC has a limited role in the regulation of derivatives markets. The SEC regulates the following:

1. Options on currencies undertaken on exchanges (eg, currency options on PHLX).
2. Options on individual stocks.
3. Options on stock indices.
4. The Chicago Board Options Exchange (CBOE) – a major centre for equity-based options.
5. The International Securities Exchange (ISE) – the world's largest equity options exchange.

Note that the SEC does not regulate any futures products or exchanges.

3.3.2 The Commodity Futures Trading Commission (CFTC) and National Futures Association (NFA)

Learning Objective

9.3.3 Know the role of the Commodity Futures Trading Commission (CFTC) and the National Futures Association (NFA): what is the CFTC; what is the NFA; NFA-delegated functions including screening and registration of all firms and individuals who want to conduct futures-related business with the public; regulated investments; regulation of other entities; dispute resolution

9.3.4 Know the prohibitions of CFTC Part 30 (Foreign Futures and Segregation of Customer Funds)

The Commodity Futures Trading Commission (CFTC) regulates all on-exchange derivatives transactions that are not covered by the SEC. It regulates all futures products and exchanges (including PHLX) and all of the options not covered by the SEC (including currency options on the CME).

It draws its powers from the Commodity Exchange Act and is also responsible for overseeing the National Futures Association (NFA). The NFA is a self-regulatory organisation registered by the CFTC and was formed in 1982.

The CFTC has delegated powers to the NFA to oversee firms operating in the derivatives industry and, as such, is similar to the UK's FCA in this regard.

The NFA provides regulatory programmes that safeguard the integrity of the derivatives markets. It is a not-for-profit organisation, financed exclusively from membership dues and fees and assessments paid by users of the futures markets. Every firm or individual that conducts business with the public on any US futures exchange is required to be registered with the CFTC and be a member of the NFA. The key part of the process is the registration and clearing process that the NFA requires. The NFA has approximately 4,200 members and 50,000 associate members (salespersons employed by NFA member firms).

CFTC Part 30

Within the CFTC rules, CFTC Part 30 specifies that it is illegal to trade with US customers on a US exchange without the relevant authorisation from the NFA, unless the trade is conducted via an NFA firm. Non-US firms are prohibited from dealing with US customers on any non-US exchange, unless they trade via a US-registered firm or have been granted exemption. Firms are prohibited from trading non-US products for US customers, unless the products have been approved by the CFTC.

The above restrictions are designed to give US customers an adequate level of protection.

Part 30 Exemption

Non-US firms can seek exemption from Part 30, but only in respect of derivatives trades on non-US exchanges.

To obtain the exemption, UK firms regulated by the FCA must agree to the following:

- Funds from US clients must be placed into segregated accounts, ie, all clients' funds are subject to the client money rules.
- All US customers must sign two-way risk disclosures.
- To abide by recognised investment exchange (RIE)/designated investment exchange (DIE) rules and FCA conduct of business rules.
- Must provide the FCA with information and access to records that may be required under Part 30. The FCA can then provide these to the CFTC.
- Must consent to join the NFA arbitration scheme.
- Must agree to jurisdiction in the US under the Commodity Exchange Act.

Note that not all US citizens are automatically considered as US customers. While all US citizens living within the US are considered as US customers, those living abroad are not automatically classed as US customers under this rule.

3.3.3 Commodity Futures Modernization Act 2000

Learning Objective

9.3.5 Know of the Commodity Futures Modernization Act 2000 and the principles governing trading of single stock futures in the US: physical delivery or cash settlement; market regulators; restrictions

The Commodity Futures Modernization Act is seen as a major step forward in the creation of a flexible structure for the regulation of futures trading, by formalising an agreement between the CFTC and the SEC to repeal the 18-year-old ban on trading single stock futures, as well as providing legal guidelines for the OTC derivatives markets.

The law, reauthorising the CFTC for five years, also clarifies the Treasury amendment exclusion and specifically grants the CFTC authority over retail foreign exchange trading.

One of the key changes with this law is that it legalised trading in single stock and narrowly defined stock-index futures under the joint jurisdiction of the SEC and CFTC.

A single stock future (SSF) is a futures contract on an individual share. An SSF has a set maturity and amount of shares, and most of those traded in the US on the OneChicago exchange are settled through physical delivery. In addition to those traded in the US, SSFs are also traded in the UK, Spain, India, Singapore and Australia.

3.3.4 Dodd-Frank Act

On 15 July 2010, after a lengthy and sometimes contentious legislative process, the US Senate approved the Dodd-Frank Wall Street Reform and Consumer Protection Act (the act). Title VII of the act sets forth the new legislative framework for derivatives.

The act creates an extensive new regulatory framework for swaps and security-based swaps, capturing substantially all derivatives transactions that previously were exempt from regulation under the Commodity Futures Modernization Act.

The act contemplates mandatory clearing and trading on regulated facilities for many derivatives contracts, with an exception for non-financial end users.

Swap dealers and major swap participants are subject, among other things, to capital and margin requirements, business conduct rules and special duties in their dealings with governmental entities, the Employee Retirement Income Security Act (ERISA) and governmental plans and endowments. While many end users will not be directly regulated, they will often be affected indirectly as their counterparties become subject to new requirements, in particular with respect to margin rules.

Other significant provisions include the swaps pushout rule, collateral segregation and real-time swap transaction reporting requirements, position limits and large trader reporting, and the application of the securities laws to security-based swaps.

Significant uncertainties remain to be clarified in rule making proceedings.

As part of this ongoing process, as of May 2013, the SEC has adopted the following updates under Title VII:

- joint rules with the CFTC regarding the definitions of swap and security-based swap dealers, and major swap and security-based swap participants
- rules relating to mandatory clearing of security-based swaps that establish a process for the clearing agencies to provide the SEC with detailed information covering the security-based swaps that the clearing agencies plan to accept for clearing
- joint rules with the CFTC regarding:
    - the definitions of the terms swap, security-based swap, and security-based swap agreement
    - the regulation of mixed swaps, and
    - security-based swap agreement record-keeping
- rules that establish standards for how clearing agencies should manage their risks and run their operations.

Swaps and Security-Based Swaps

The act aims to sweep the universe of previously unregulated derivatives into the new regulatory framework, and divides this universe into two broad categories:

1. **Swaps** – the term swap is defined broadly and includes options, swaps and other transactions based on rates, commodities, securities, debt instruments, indices, quantitative measures and other financial or economic interests, subject to certain exceptions. Building upon the definition of previously exempt swap agreements under Section 206A of the Gramm-Leach-Bliley Act, the act brings previously unregulated derivatives into the new framework. Swaps are subject to CFTC jurisdiction. Swaps do not include security-based swaps, as discussed below.
2. **Security-based swaps** – security-based swaps are swaps based on individual securities or loans, on narrow-based securities indices, or on events affecting individual issuers of securities or issuers of securities in a narrow-based securities index. Security-based swaps are subject to SEC regulation.

The act seeks to establish parallel rules for swaps and security-based swaps. Mixed swaps, which combine features of swaps and security-based swaps, are to be regulated jointly by the CFTC and SEC. Parties seeking to list or trade novel derivatives products, having both commodities and securities features, may petition the CFTC and SEC for a determination of the product's regulatory status. The CFTC and SEC are required to consult and coordinate with one another (and with the federal banking regulators) in exercising their jurisdiction over swaps, and may challenge each other's actions in court in the event of a dispute.

While the basic approach is comprehensive and quite straightforward, the definitional provisions are complex in detail. Care must be taken in evaluating the status of individual derivatives products. For example, the swap definition excludes certain transactions that are already regulated as securities, including options on securities and FX options traded on registered securities exchanges. Other exclusions remove from the scope of the act commodity and security futures, leverage contracts, and forward transactions for non-financial commodities intended for physical settlement, as well as deposit and savings accounts, certificates of deposit and other identified banking products. Swaps based on government securities (other than municipal securities) are excluded from the security-based swap definition and thus are subject to regulation by the CFTC.

FX swaps and forwards, which were the subject of considerable debate during the legislative process, will be considered swaps. The Treasury Secretary may, however, make a reasoned determination based on specified criteria that such transactions, to the extent they are not cleared or traded through regulated facilities, should be exempt. Even if that determination is made, reporting requirements and certain business conduct standards still apply.

Clearing and Trade Execution

The effort to require central clearing and exchange trading for many derivatives transactions is at the heart of two basic purposes of the act – reducing systemic risk and increasing market transparency. At the same time, the mandatory clearing and exchange trading provisions have been controversial, in particular due to the increased margin requirements (and hence increased costs) associated with central clearing.

The act contemplates that the CFTC and SEC will, on an ongoing basis, review swaps and categories or classes of swaps with a view to determining whether clearing should be mandatory. Factors to be considered include the existence of significant outstanding exposures, trading liquidity and the availability of appropriate operational expertise and resources. Where the CFTC or SEC determine that a particular type of swap should be cleared but no clearing organisation accepts the swap for clearing, the CFTC or SEC are directed to investigate and take appropriate action. Mandatory clearing will not be applied to existing swap positions, so long as the positions are reported to swap data repositories in a timely fashion under rules to be promulgated by the CFTC and SEC.

Clearing organisations will be required to offset swaps with the same terms and conditions on an economically equivalent basis within the clearing organisation, and to provide for non-discriminatory clearing of transactions executed bilaterally or on unaffiliated facilities. In a similar vein, the act calls on the CFTC and SEC to adopt rules, including possible ownership and control limitations, to mitigate conflicts of interest that may arise in relation to ownership of regulated clearing and trading facilities by bank holding companies, certain non-bank financial institutions, swap dealers and major swap participants.

Joint Study

The Act called upon the CFTC and SEC to conduct a joint study of the regulation of swaps and clearing agencies in the US, Asia and Europe and report to Congress. The key recommendations of its 31 January 2012 report, to ensure compliance with the Dodd-Frank Act, were:

- CFTC and SEC staff should continue to monitor developments at national level across jurisdictions and should communicate with fellow regulators involved in efforts to regulate OTC derivatives.
- CFTC and SEC staff should continue to participate in international forums and actively contribute to initiatives that are designed to develop and establish global standards for OTC derivatives regulation.
- CFTC and SEC staff should continue to engage in bilateral dialogues with regulatory staff in the EU, Japan, Hong Kong, Singapore and Canada, and should consider dialogues with additional jurisdictions, as appropriate.

The report goes on to state that regulation of OTC derivatives is still in its beginning stage, and that further co-operation among regulators will ensure a well-functioning market that in turn will ensure global financial stability.

4. Regulators – Other Markets

4.1 Asia

4.1.1 China

The China Securities Regulatory Commission (CSRC) is a ministerial-level public institution that was created by China's first comprehensive securities law, which became effective on 1 July 1999, granted it the 'authority to implement a centralised and unified regulation of the nationwide securities market in order to ensure their lawful operation.' The CSRC oversees China's centralised securities supervisory system, its powers include the regulation and supervision of securities issuers, as well as to investigate, and impose penalties for, 'illegal activities related to securities and futures'. It governs all securities exchanges and futures markets activity within the People's Republic of China and its functions are similar to that of the Securities and Exchange Commission in the United States.

The CSRC's responsibilities include:

- creating and reviewing securities legislation
- regulating the trading, issuing, and settlement of stocks, fixed income securities, and securities funds
- supervising the conduct of shareholders and securities brokers, and
- overseeing the issuance of non-Chinese company listings and offerings (such as H-Shares listed on the Hong Kong Exchange).

4.1.2 Hong Kong

The Securities and Futures Commission (SFC) of Hong Kong is the independent statutory body charged with regulating the securities and futures markets in Hong Kong. The SFC is responsible for ensuring the orderly functioning of Hong Kong's securities and futures markets, to protect investors and to promote

Hong Kong as an international financial centre and a key financial market in China. Even though it is considered to be a branch of the government, it is run independently under the authorisation of the laws relating to securities and futures.

The SFC is one of four regulatory organisations that make up financial regulators in Hong Kong. The others are the Hong Kong Monetary Authority (HKMA), Office of the Commissioner of Insurance (OCI) and the Mandatory Provident Fund Schemes Authority (MPFA). The SFC is responsible for securities and futures markets including the Hong Kong Exchange and Clearing (HKEX).

4.1.3 India

The Securities and Exchange Board of India (SEBI) is the regulator for the stock exchange and all other securities market in India. It was granted its statutory powers on 12 April 1992 through the SEBI Act, 1992. The board plays a key role in maintaining stable and efficient financial and investment domestic markets by creating and enforcing effective regulation in India's financial marketplace. India's SEBI function is similar to that of the US Securities and Exchange Commission.

4.1.4 Philippines

The Securities and Exchange Commission (SEC) is an independent government regulatory agency that is charged with supervision over the corporate sector, capital market participants, the securities and investment instruments market. Created on 26 October 1936 by The Securities Act, the SEC is tasked to regulate the sale and registration of securities, exchanges, brokers, dealers and salesmen. Subsequent laws have been enacted to broaden the commission's mandates and powers and in recent years, to give greater focus on the SEC's role in domestic capital market development, by fostering good governance and enhancing investor protection.

The SEC's main role in the supervision of the securities markets, is to oversee the operations of the Philippine Stock Exchange (PSE) and its members, and ensure their compliance with the provisions of the securities act. It is also involved in the development of a capital markets development plan.

4.1.5 Singapore

The Monetary Authority of Singapore (MAS) is Singapore's central bank as well as its financial regulatory authority. It administers all of the regulations that pertain to money, banking, insurance, securities and the financial sector in general, as well as currency issuance.

4.1.6 Sri Lanka

The Central Bank of Sri Lanka (CBSL) was established in 1950 and is responsible for the conduct of monetary policy in Sri Lanka and also has wide supervisory powers over the banking sector and the domestic financial system. Its main role is regulating the domestic banking system, to ensure that it is stable and a favourable environment for investors and borrowers. As key aspect of its goal of financial system stability is FX rare management as well as working with the other domestic regulators.

The Securities and Exchange Commission (SEC) of Sri Lanka was established in 1987, and has had its role and function further defined by Parliamentary acts in 1991, 2003 and 2009.

4.2 Middle East

4.2.1 United Arab Emirates (UAE) and Dubai

The UAE includes two separately regulated financial centres: the Dubai International Financial Centre (DFSA) and the rest of the UAE. The DFSA is the financial regulatory agency of the special economic zone, the Dubai International Financial Centre (DIFC). The remainder of the UAE has its own independent financial regulatory system. The DFSA provides a regulatory environment of international standards, including its own civil, commercial and criminal laws, and all regulated firms and their employees are subject to strict fraud and money laundering laws. The DFSA regulates the two markets in the DIFC: NASDAQ Dubai and the Dubai Mercantile Exchange (DME). In contrast, the regulatory role within the rest of the UAE is divided among its Central Bank, which manages monetary policy, the monetary system and banking Laws.

4.2.2 Qatar

In December 2012, the Emir and the Qatar Central Bank (QCB) enacted a law that defined more clearly the roles of the QCB, the Qatar Financial Centre (QFC) Regulatory Authority (QFCRA) and the Qatar Financial Markets Authority (QFMA). While all remain independent regulators, the law promotes increased co-operation among the three. The QCB's Financial Stability Committee provides the formal structure for the co-ordination among Qatar's regulatory bodies; it also identifies any risks to the financial sector and makes recommendations on how to manage and avoid such risks. The QFMA is responsible for the regulation and supervision of Qatar's financial markets, while the QFC's main role is to regulate the Qatar Financial Centre.

4.3 Russia

The main role of the Central Bank of the Russian Federation (CRB) is to manage and publish the official exchange rates of other currencies against the ruble. It is an independent entity whose primary responsibility is to protect the ruble's stability in global FX markets. It is the main regulator of the Russian banking industry, responsible for banking licenses, rules of banking operations and accounting standards, serving as a lender of last resort for credit organisations. The structure of regulation of Russia's banking and financial markets was changed significantly in 2013 when the CRB became the country's main financial market regulator. In addition to the CBR's supervision of commercial banks, it also regulates non-bank financial institutions such as insurance companies, asset management companies, investment and pension funds, brokers and exchange intermediaries, as well as microfinance institutions.

4.4 South Africa

The Financial Services Board (FSB) oversees the non-banking financial services industry. It is the government of South Africa's independent financial regulatory agency whose goal is to promote and maintain sound and stable financial investment in the economy. Its mission is to promote the fair treatment of consumers of financial services and products, the financial soundness of financial institutions, the systemic stability of financial services industries, and the integrity of financial markets and institutions. The South African Reserve Bank is responsible for ensuring the financial stability of the local banking system. It relies on market forces to achieve this stability. A third financial regulator is the

National Credit Regulator (NCR) which is responsible for the regulation of the South African domestic credit industry.

5. International Accounting Rules

Learning Objective

9.4.1 Know the requirements under IAS 32 and IFRS 9 such as to disclose derivative positions held and report the fair value: the impact and risk implications that fair value accounting may have on the derivative activities of banks and corporates

9.5.1 Know the need to include derivative positions in calculations affecting merger & acquisition activities

IAS 39 Financial Instruments: Recognition and Measurement became part of the mandatory International Financial Reporting Standards (IFRS) in 2005 and was adopted on a global basis. It requires that an entity must report all financial assets and liabilities on its balance sheet. IAS 32 Financial Instruments: Presentation was established to complement IAS 39. Its objective is to establish principles for presenting/reporting financial instruments as liabilities, equities and for offsetting financial liabilities and assets. The classifications defined by IAS 32 are from the perspective of an issuer.

The International Accounting Standards Board (IASB) published the final version of IFRS 9 in July 2014. The mandatory effective date when IFRS 9 will replace IAS 39 in its entirety is for annual periods beginning on or after 1 January 2018.

The IASB developed IFRS 9 as a replacement for IAS 39. The process of developing IFRS 9 began in 2001 and has been developed based on feedback received by the IASB.

This process was split into five key phases:

- classification and measurement of financial assets
- classification and measurement of financial liabilities
- impairment methodology
- hedge accounting
- asset and liability offsetting.

Key differences between IAS 39 and IFRS 9 approach:

IAS 39 Classification	IFRS 9 Classification
Rule-based	Principle-based
Complex and difficult to apply	Classification based on business model and nature of cash flows
Multiple impairment models	One impairment model

IAS 39 Classification	IFRS 9 Classification
Own credit gains and losses recognised in profit or loss for fair value option (FVO) liabilities	Own credit gains and losses presented in other comprehensive income (ICO) for FVO liabilities
Complicated reclassification rules	Business model-driven reclassification

IAS 32 and 39, along with IFRS 9, define a derivative as a financial instrument:

- whose value changes in response to the change in an underlying asset, such as interest rates, currencies, commodities, individual shares or an index (later amended to include weather- and climate-related factors)
- that requires no initial investment, or one that is smaller than would be required for a cash market contract, which has similar gains/losses to market/price movements – in other words, a geared instrument
- that is settled on a future date.

Both IAS 39 and IFRS 9 include embedded derivatives in this definition and treatment, if they produce a cash flow, that is similar to a stand-alone derivative. Embedded derivatives require the same type of treatment as any other derivative.

The key requirement of IAS 39, as it pertains to derivatives is that it requires that all derivatives held by an institution, except those that are designated as a hedge, must be stated in all accounting statements at their fair value. Fair value is defined as the value for which an asset or contract can be exchanged, or a liability settled, between knowledgeable and willing parties in an arm's length transaction.

In other words, all derivatives must be marked to market and stated at their current market value in all financial reports.

The main exception to IAS 39's fair value derivatives rule, which the EU opted out of, is the requirement of stating those derivatives that are reported as a hedge on financial statements at their fair value. Therefore, any derivative that is stated to be a hedge does not have to be shown at its fair value, since they are expected to be held until maturity or the early settlement of the related transaction.

In contrast, IFRS 9 uses a single approach to determine whether a derivative contract is measured at its amortised cost or fair value, replacing the many different rules in IAS 39. The approach in IFRS 9 is based on how an entity manages its financial instruments (its business model) and the contractual cash flow of its financial assets. Gains and losses on those financial assets classified as measured at fair value are recognised in profit or loss except where an entity has elected to recognise these gains and losses on an equity investment in other comprehensive income.

IFRS 9 does not change the basic accounting model for financial liabilities that exists under IAS 39 – the two measurement categories continue to exist: fair value through profit or loss and amortised cost.

But IFRS 9 does require any gains and losses on financial liabilities designated as fair value through profit or loss to be split into: the amount of change in the fair value that is attributable to changes in the credit risk of the liability, and the remaining amount of change in the fair value of the liability, which is presented in profit or loss.

All derivatives are measured at fair value, unless the hedging provisions of IAS 39 are applied. Embedded derivatives are only separated from the host contract where that contract is not an asset within the scope of IFRS 9. Otherwise the entire hybrid contract is accounted for as one instrument.

The additions that were put in place in November 2013 set out a new model for hedge accounting that closely aligns the relevant accounting treatment with risk management activities.

This new model:

- replaces the IAS 39 hedge effectiveness test with an objectives-based test that focuses on the economic relationship between the hedged item and hedging instrument
- allows that a risk component is designated as the hedged item for non-financial items as well as financial items
- allows the designation of more groups of items as the hedged item
- allows items such as the time value of an option to be accounted for as a cost of hedging
- introduces more extensive and meaningful disclosure requirements.

End of Chapter Questions

1. Who manages FpML?
   Answer reference: Section 1.1

2. What is FINMA responsible for?
   Answer reference: Section 1.5

3. List the three key elements in the FCA's current approach.
   Answer reference: Section 2.1

4. Name the 11 Principles for Business.
   Answer reference: Section 2.2

5. Under COBS, what are the three categories of client?
   Answer reference: Section 2.4

6. When considering best execution, what factors must be taken into account?
   Answer reference: Section 2.5

7. Where are the FCA rules relating to the custody and safeguarding of client money and client assets contained?
   Answer reference: Section 3.1.1

8. In the USA, what does the SEC regulate?
   Answer reference: Section 3.3.1

9. In the Republic of the Philippines, what is the role of Bangko Sentral ng Pilipinas?
   Answer reference: Section 4.1.4

10. In 2013 who became Russia's main financial market regulator?
    Answer reference: Section 4.3

Glossary and Abbreviations

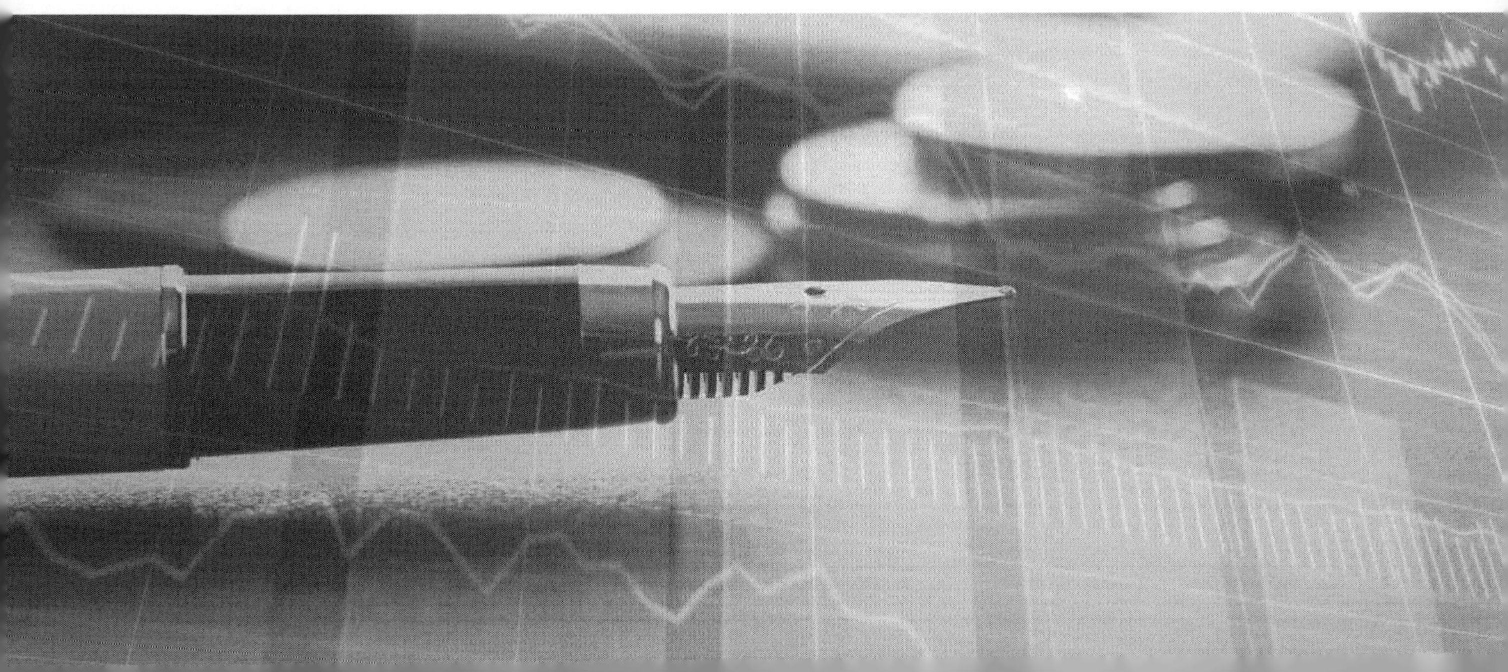

Abandon

The decision of the holder of an option not to exercise his rights, due to the fact that the option is either OTM or the transaction costs are greater than its IV.

Accrued Interest

The calculation of entitlement to interest on a bond, usually done on a daily basis. This needs to be reflected in the invoice amount in a bond future.

Allocation

Assigning a completed derivatives trade to its originator, including registration into the correct account.

Alternative Delivery Procedure (ADP)

The agreement that allows the buyer and seller in a futures contract to change the delivery procedure from the exchange's standardised procedure.

American Depositary Receipt (ADR)

Represents ownership in the shares of a non-US company trading on US financial markets. ADRs are priced in US dollars, they pay dividends in US dollars and they can be traded like the shares of US-based companies. Their price is close to the price of the international share in its home market, adjusted for the ratio of ADRs to international company shares.

American-Style

An exercise style of an option. An option that can be exercised on any business day up to expiry on the last trading day.

Arbitrage

Trading simultaneously in one asset in two different markets to profit from short-term price differentials.

Asian Option

An option whose strike price is set at its expiration date. Its strike price is based on the average price of the underlying asset. The calculation is based on a pre-agreed fixing over the period.

Assign

Refers to options – following exercise by the option holder, the exercise is matched with a short position. Assignment is initiated when the exchange clearing house notifies the writer by an assignment notice.

At-the-Money (ATM)

An option with an exercise price that is the same as, or very near to, the current underlying asset price.

Backwardation

When cash prices are higher than futures prices. Unusual for equity futures because of positive cost of carry. Normal for bond futures because bond yields are normally higher than money market yields (there is a negative cost of carry). Opposite of **Contango**.

Barrier Option

An option that is activated or deactivated once the underlying asset's price reaches a set level. There are two main types, knock-in and knock-out barrier style options.

Basis

The difference between the present cash price and the nearby futures price of an asset. Calculation is cash minus futures. Basis will be negative in a **contango** market, and positive in a **backwardation** market.

Bear

An investor who believes the market in general, or a particular investment, will fall.

Bear Spread

A moderately bearish strategy. Uses call or put options for the same month but at different strikes (ie, vertical spreads), eg, buy 350 June calls, sell 300 June calls.

Bermudan Option

An exercise style of an option, which lies between a European and American, in that it can be exercised on any various specified dates between the purchase date and the option's expiry.

Bond

A security issued by an organisation such as a government or corporation. Bonds pay regular interest and repay their principal or face value at maturity. One of the most common underlying assets for derivative contracts.

Bull

An investor who believes the market in general, or a particular investment, will rise.

Bull Spread

An options trade for the moderately bullish investor. Uses call or put options for the same month but at different strikes (ie, vertical spreads), eg, buy a 300 June call, sell a 350 June call. Can also be done with put options.

Buy-Write

An investment strategy involving buying a security and, simultaneously, selling calls against it.

Call

A type of option that gives the buyer the right, but not the obligation, to buy the underlying asset at an agreed price within a specific time for a set premium. Call sellers may be obliged to sell a specific asset at the set price if the call's holder chooses to exercise.

Cap

An option, which puts a ceiling to the interest rate at which a client borrows. A common term is quarterly over three years. If the reference rate (eg, LIBOR) is above the cap, the writer pays compensation. Allows the borrower to manage interest rate risk. Also used in FX.

Cash Settlement

Method of settlement where the underlying asset is not exchanged, just the cash difference between the contracted price and the official settlement price. Often known as a contract for difference. STIRs and equity index futures are settled by cash payment rather than physical delivery.

Central Counterparty

An entity that sits between the buyer and seller and acts as a guarantor of contracts, reducing counterparty risk. Until recently, they were only involved in exchange-traded transactions, but new regulation (EMIR) means that they may also be used to clear some OTC derivative trades, if these trades are eligible.

Collar

The purchase of a cap, financed by the sale of a floor.

Combination

Strategy involving a variety of individual positions, such as puts and calls (eg, straddle, strangle).

Contango

A market where futures prices are higher than the cash price because of a positive cost of carry. Opposite of **Backwardation**.

Contingent Liability

A potential liability for loss, over and above the amount invested, the amount of which cannot be established at the outset of a derivatives contract. For example, the seller of a future does not know how high the price may move against him – he is in a contingent liability situation.

Contract for Difference (CFD)

A contract involving the exchange of difference between the pre-agreed price and the closing price of the underlying instrument (such as an index or a share price). A contract involving cash settlement.

Convertible Bond

A bond that is convertible into another instrument, sometimes another type of bond, but more commonly into a company's shares at the set price which usually is above the current share price at the time of its issue.

Cost of Carry

The cost of holding an asset over time. Comprises borrowing costs and, for physical commodities, storage/insurance costs. For equities, cost of carry will be reduced by dividends earned from the shares.

Covered Call

A short call option position that is covered because the writer also owns the underlying asset.

Credit Risk

The exposure to loss associated with the payment default or failure on a payment due from a transaction/trade by a counterparty. It is also known as counterparty risk.

Delivery

The settlement of a contract (such as a future) by delivery of the asset by the seller to the exchange clearing house. The long position holder takes delivery from the clearing house against payment.

Delta (Δ)

The measure of change in an option's premium or futures price given a change in the underlying asset. In options, delta can be thought of as the probability that the option will be ITM at expiry. The delta of futures will generally be about 1 or 100%. A £3 change in the cash price should cause the future to move by about £3 (3/3 = 1).

Derivative

Instruments whose price is derived from another asset. Examples include futures, options, FX forwards and swaps.

Electronic Communication Networks (ECNs)

Term used in financial circles for a type of computer system that facilitates trading of financial products on OTC markets. The main products that are traded on ECNs are equities and FX.

Equity Indices

Indices of blue-chip (ie, large) companies in various national or regional markets. Examples include S&P 500, FTSE 100, Euro Stoxx. Major indices are used as the basis for derivatives contracts.

Euronext

A European stock exchange based in Amsterdam, Brussels, London, Lisbon and Paris.

European-Style

An exercise style of an option. An option, which can only be exercised by the holder at expiry.

Exchange Delivery Settlement Price (EDSP)

The price at which maturing futures are settled (an ICE and Euronext term).

Exchange for Physical (EFP)

The exchange of a future's position for a physical position. Also known as **Against Actual**.

Exercise

The decision by a holder of an option to take up their rights. In a call option, exercise involves buying the asset; in a put option, exercise involves selling the asset.

Exercise (or Strike) Price

Refers to options – the price at which assets can be bought (call) or sold (put). In exchange-traded options, the exchange determines the intervals between strike prices.

Fair Value

The theoretical price of a future, ie, cash price plus cost of carry.

Financial Conduct Authority (FCA)

The new UK financial regulator that has assumed most of the authority of the FSA.

Flex Option

Exchange-traded options, where the investor can specify within certain limits, the terms of the options, such as exercise price, expiration date, exercise type, and settlement calculation.

Floor

An OTC option which guarantees a minimum return. If the reference rate (eg, LIBOR) falls below the floor level, the buyer of the floor receives compensation. See also **Cap** and **Collar**.

Foreign Exchange (FX)

The name given to the general aspects of currency trading.

Forward

An OTC derivative on, for example, FX. Forward prices are based on the spot price and the interest rate differential of the two currencies, in the same way as exchange-traded FX futures.

Forward Rate Agreement (FRA)

An agreement where the client can fix the rate of interest that will be applied to a notional loan or deposit, drawn or placed for an agreed period in the future. Traded OTC.

FTSE 100

The London Stock Exchange's main share index of 100 largest listed companies.

Future

An exchange-traded contract that is a firm agreement to make/take delivery of a standard quantity of a specified asset on a fixed future date at a price agreed today.

Gamma

Measures the speed of change of delta on a derivative for a given change in the price of the underlying asset. Gamma is at its maximum for ATM options.

Gearing

An important feature of derivatives. Because only a small percentage of an asset's value is required when a contract is entered into (initial margin or premium), a small change in the underlying asset's value can lead to large percentage gains or losses relative to the initial investment. Also known as leverage.

Global Depositary Receipt (GDR)

The non-US version of **ADRs** that are traded on non-US exchanges such as the London Stock Exchange.

Hedge

A strategy to protect or minimise a potential loss to an existing position or known commitment resulting from adverse price movements. For example, those owning assets can hedge by buying put options, protecting against a fall in value of that asset.

InfolectTM

The LSE's market data service, which provides information ranging from real-time data on individual share price movements to company announcements.

Initial Margin

A good faith deposit (in the form of collateral or cash) lodged with the broker or clearing house against potential liabilities on an open position. It is returned when the position is closed out.

In-the-Money (ITM)

An option with **IV**, eg, a call whose strike is below the underlying asset price.

Intrinsic Value (IV)

Indicates how much an option is ITM. One of the two components that make up an option's value.

The IV represents the absolute minimum premium for an option. For example, a £1 call option will be worth at least 25p if the underlying asset's price is £1.25. Options which are ITM have IV. Intrinsically, a £2 put will be worth at least 50p if the underlying asset is trading at £1.50.

Invoice Amount

The amount a futures buyer pays to the exchange clearing house at delivery, for the underlying physical asset.

Last Notice Day

The last day for issuing of notices of intent to deliver against a futures contract.

Last Trading Day

The last day for trading futures within the current delivery month. All contracts outstanding/open at the end of the last trading day must be settled by delivery or by cash settlement.

LMEsword

A secure electronic transfer system for LME warrants.

LMEX

A cash-settled index-based futures contract that is based on the weighted average of the price of the LME's six primary metals.

London Inter-Bank Offered Rate (LIBOR)

The average rate at which banks will lend sterling, dollars, euros, yen and other currencies to each other for periods of, eg, one month, three months. Established by a daily survey by ICE, who also ask for bid rates enabling LIBID (London Inter-Bank bid rate) to be calculated, which is how much banks will pay to borrow funds.

Long

The buyer of an asset is long the asset. Futures buyers are long the futures. Options buyers or holders are long the options.

Margin

Collateral paid to the clearing house by the counterparties to a derivatives transaction to guarantee their positions against loss. Initial margin is a security deposit that must be handed to the exchange clearing house by a broker (and to the broker by their client) for futures or short options. See also **Variation Margin**.

Mark to Market

The process of adjusting the value of investments to reflect their current market price. See also **Variation Margin**.

Marketing of Financial Instruments Directive (MiFID II)

The European Union legislation requiring firms to maintain and operate effective organisation and administrative arrangements to take all reasonable steps designed to prevent conflicts of interest from adversely affecting the interests of its clients. (Replaces the original MiFID).

Netting

A system or agreement whereby all outstanding contracts of the same specification maturing, on the same date, between two counterparties can be settled on a net basis. This is an efficient way of reducing both settlement and counterparty risks.

Novation

The legal process whereby the exchange's clearing house becomes the counterparty to both the buyer and seller of futures contracts, substituting the original contract.

Omgeo OASYS, formerly OASYS

A US financial markets trade allocation and acceptance service that communicates trade and allocation details between investment managers and broker-dealers.

Open Interest

The number of contracts that have not been closed out by being offset.

Open Outcry

Trading system where participants meet face-to-face and cry out their prices and sizes to the others on the floor. Used in many US exchanges.

Option

A contract that gives the buyer the right, but not the obligation, to sell or buy a particular asset at a particular price, on or before a specified date. Options are set at an agreed price (exercise or strike price) and the exercise style will normally be American-style or European-style. The class of option either gives holders the right to buy (call) or the right to sell (put).

Out-of-the-Money (OTM)

A term used to describe an option whose strike price is less advantageous/profitable than the asset's current market price. For example a £1 call if the asset is trading at 85p. An OTM option has no IV – a premium may well be payable, but it will comprise only time value.

Over-the-Counter (OTC)

Transactions between banks and their counterparties not on a recognised exchange.

Par Value

The face value of a bond.

Pip

A pip is the smallest change that a given exchange rate can make.

Physical Delivery

Where the settlement of a futures contract is by delivery of the physical underlying asset. Certain futures (eg, gilt futures, copper) will run through to physical delivery for final settlement. Other futures (eg, stock index futures and short-term interest rates) are cash-settled.

Premium

The money paid by option buyers to option sellers. The price paid for the option.

Prudential Regulation Authority (PRA)

The part of the UK financial regulator that is now part of the Bank of England.

Put

A type of option that gives its buyer the right, but not the obligation, to sell the underlying asset at an agreed price within a specific time for a set premium. Put sellers may be obliged to buy the specified asset at the strike price if the put's holder chooses to exercise.

Put/Call Parity

The theoretical relationship between put premiums and call premiums for the same strike and expiry. The relationship (for European options) is:

Call premium – put premium =
underlying asset's price – strike price
(discounted to the present value)

Series

Options of the same class (ie, calls or puts) with the same strike, date and underlying (eg, calls – 950, June, HSBC).

Settlement Risk

The risk that an expected payment of an asset/security or cash will not be made on time or at all. This type of risk can be significantly reduced by establishing a netting system.

Short

1. To need an asset.
2. Another term for selling futures or selling/writing puts.
3. To hold a net sold position.

Short-Term Interest Rate (STIR) Derivatives

Common contracts for difference derivative contracts, based on the interest on a notional sum of money for three months. For example, Euronext Liffe's June short sterling contracts are based on the interest on a notional cash deposit of £500,000 for the three months from June (ie, July, August and September). Priced as 100 minus the predicted rate, thereby replicating the inverse pricing behaviour of bonds and bond futures.

Single Stock Futures (SSFs)

Futures contracts whose underlying assets are individual stocks/shares. Traded on several exchanges, such as OneChicago, where the contract size is 100 shares in an individual company.

Softs

Soft commodities are goods that are grown.

Sovereign Wealth Fund

A state-owned and state-funded investment company that invests in a wide variety of domestic and international assets.

Spot

A term used to describe the current price of an asset. Also known as underlying or cash. Also used in FX where spot rates are the exchange rates for deals which settle right away.

Spread

1. In futures – buying and selling different months of the same asset (intramarket spread) with a view about changes in basis.
2. In futures – buying and selling futures in different assets (intermarket spread). For example, a fund manager could increase his effective weighting of US stocks by buying S&P 500 futures and simultaneously selling FTSE 100 futures.
3. In options – see **Vertical Spreads**.
4. The difference between the bid and offer price.

Standard Portfolio Analysis of Risk (SPAN)

SPAN is a scenario-based risk programme, designed by the CME, used for calculating daily initial margins across a portfolio. Essentially, it looks at the impact on a position if the price and volatility of the underlying change by set amounts.

Stop Loss

An order placed by an investor to buy or sell a security when it reaches a certain price. A stop loss order is designed to limit an investor's loss on an existing position.

Straddle

A combination of a put and a call option at the same strike. Buyers profit from volatility in the underlying asset.

Strangle

A combination of a put and a call option at different strikes. Buyers profit from **Volatility** in the underlying asset.

Strike

See **Exercise**.

Swap

A contract to exchange a series of payments with a counterparty, eg, fixed for floating interest rates, currency A for currency B, income from asset C for income from asset D.

Swaption

An option to enter into a swap.

Synthetic

Manufactured position, eg, a synthetic future can be created by buying a call and selling a put option on the future.

Theoretical Intermarket Margining System (TIMS)

TIMS is a method used by the OCC and other clearing houses to determine the margin requirements for mixed portfolios of derivatives, particularly options.

Theta

The measure of the decline in an option's value compared with the continuous decrease in time to expiry.

Tick

The smallest permitted variation between prices quoted to buy and sell on derivatives exchanges. For example, the tick for gold is 10 cents so prices of $390.00, $390.10, $390.20 can be quoted, but not $390.13. **Tick value** is the profit or loss that arises when prices move by one tick.

Time Value

An option's value that represents its time to expiry and the **Volatility** of the underlying asset's cash price. It is the option's premium, less any IV. Time value will be higher the longer the option has to maturity. Sometimes known as extrinsic value.

Treasury Inflation Protected Securities (TIPS)

A treasury security that is indexed to inflation in order to protect investors from the negative effects of inflation. TIPS are considered an extremely low-risk investment since they are backed by the US government and their par value rises with inflation, as measured by the consumer price index, while their interest rate remains fixed. The coupon on TIPS is paid semi-annually.

Variation Margin

Margin is transferred from the account of the loser to the winner as prices move on a daily basis and positions are marked to market. The total accumulated variation margin equates to the profit or loss when a position is closed out.

Vega

The measure of how a 1% change in **Volatility** affects an option's price/value.

Vertical Spreads

Calls (or puts) for the same month but at different strikes. For example, buy a 300 June call, sell a 350 June call. See also **Bull Spread** and **Bear Spread**.

Volatility

The measure of the probability of an asset's price moving. Usually calculated as annualised standard deviation. Volatility has an important impact on the pricing of options.

Warrant

1. A securitised **Option**. An example is a security, which can be converted into shares in a company.
2. A document of title to goods; for example, warrants are used to satisfy the physical delivery of metals on the LME.

Yield Spread

Yield (or credit) spread is the difference between the quoted rates of return on two different bonds, which have the same or very similar maturities. It reflects the market's view and is based on the market's/investor's perception of the different credit quality between the two borrowers.

Δ
Delta

ABS
Asset-Backed Security

ADP
Alternative Delivery Procedure

ADR
American Depositary Receipt

ADSM
Abu Dhabi Securities Market

AFM
Authority for the Financial Markets (Netherlands)

AMF
Autorité des Marchés Financiers

API
Application Programming Interface

APS
Assured Payments Service

ATM
At-the-money

AUT
Authorised Unit Trust

BaFin
Bundeszentrale für Finanzdienstleistungsaufsicht (Bundesbank and German Financial Supervisory Authority)

BBA
British Bankers' Association

BM&F
Brazilian Mercantile & Futures Exchange

Bps
Basis Points

BTPs
Buoni del Tesoro Poliennali

CAC 40
French stock market index

CASS
Client Assets Sourcebook

CBO
Collateralised Bond Obligation

CBOE
Chicago Board Options Exchange

CBOT
Chicago Board of Trade (now part of the CME Group)

CBRC
China Banking Regulatory Commission

CBSL
Central Bank of Sri Lanka

CCP
Central Counterparty

CD
Certificate of Deposit

CDD
Cooling degree days

CDOs
Collateralised debt obligations

CDO
Credit Default Option

CDS
Credit Default Swap

CESR
Committee of European Securities Regulators

CFD
Contract for Difference

CFFEX
China Financial Futures Exchange

CFTC
Commodity Futures Trading Commission (US derivatives regulator)

CHF
Swiss Franc

CIRC
China Insurance Regulatory Commission

CIS
Collective Investment Scheme

CLN
Credit Linked Note

CME
Chicago Mercantile Exchange (now part of the CME Group)

CMO
Collateralised Mortgage Obligation

CMS
Constant Maturity Swap

CNMV
Comisión Nacional del Mercado de Valores

CNY
Chinese Yuan

COB
Conduct of Business

COMEX
A division of the New York Mercantile Exchange

CP
Commercial Paper

CP
Committed Principal

CPI
Consumer Prices Index

CRB
Central Bank of the Russian Federation

CRD
Capital Requirements Directive

CSA
Credit Support Annex

CSRC
China Securities Regulatory Commission

CTD
Cheapest to Deliver

CySEC
Cyprus Securities and Exchange Commission

DCO
Designated Clearing Organisation (US)

DFM
Dubai Financial Market

DGCE
Dubai Gold and Commodities Exchange

DIE
Designated Investment Exchange

DME
Dubai Mercantile Exchange

DMO
Debt Management Office (UK)

DTCC
Depository Trust & Clearing Corporation

DTC
Depository Trust Company

DTSS
Derivatives Trading and Settlement System

DVP
Delivery Versus Payment

EBA
European Banking Authority

ECB
European Central Bank

ECN
Electronic Communications Network

ECP
Eligible Counterparty

ECS
Extensible Clearing System

ECX
European Climate Exchange

EDSP
Exchange Delivery Settlement Price (ICE and Euronext)

EFP
Exchange for Physical

EFS
Exchange for Swap

EMIR
European Market Infrastructure Regulation

EONIA
Euro OverNight Index Average

ERISA
Employee Retirement Income Security Act

ESMA
European Securities and Markets Authority

ETD
Exchange-Traded Derivative

EU
European Union

EUR
Euro

FCA
Financial Conduct Authority

FCM
Futures Commission Merchant

FDIC
Federal Deposit Insurance Corporation

FEC
Front End Clearing

Fed
Federal Reserve Bank

FFA
Forward Freight Agreement

FFABA
Forward Freight Agreement Brokers' Association

FFMS
Federal Financial Markets Service (Russia)

FIFO
First-In, First-Out

FINMA
Swiss Financial Market Supervisory Authority

FLEX

FLexible EXchange

FOK

Fill or Kill

FPC

Financial Policy Committee

FpML

Financial products Markup Language

FRA

Forward Rate Agreement

FRN

Floating Rate Note

FSA

Financial Services Authority (former UK regulator)

FX

Foreign Exchange

GBP

Pound Sterling

GCM

General Clearing Member

GDP

Gross Domestic Product

GDR

Global Depositary Receipt

GFD

Good for the Day

GIS

Good in Session

GRY

Gross Redemption Yield

GTC

Good 'til Cancelled

GUI

Graphical User Interface

HDD

Heating Degree Days

HKEx

Hong Kong Exchanges and Clearing

IASB

International Accounting Standards Board

IBA

ICE Benchmark Administration

ICE

Intercontinental Exchange

ICE EURIBOR

Euro Interbank Offered Rate

ICE LIBID

London Inter Bank Bid Rate

ICE LIBOR

London Inter Bank Offered Rate

ICM

Individual Clearing Member

ICVC

Investment Company with Variable Capital

IDB

Inter-Dealer Broker

IFRS

International Financial Reporting Standards

IOSCO

International Organization of Securities Commissions

IPE
International Petroleum Exchange of London (now renamed ICE Futures Europe)

IPO
Initial Public Offering

IRP
Interest Rate Parity

IRS
Interest Rate Swap

ISD
Investment Services Directive

ISDA
International Swaps and Derivatives Association

ISE
International Securities Exchange

ITM
In-the-money

ITP
ICE Trading Platform

IV
Intrinsic Value

JADE
Joint Asian Derivatives Exchange

JGB
Japanese Government Bond

JPY
Japanese Yen

JSE
Johannesburg Stock Exchange

KRX
Korea Exchange

KYC
Know Your Customer

LIBID
London Interbank Bid Rate

LIBOR
London Interbank Offered Rate

LIFO
Last-In, First-Out

LME
London Metal Exchange

LSE
London Stock Exchange

MAS
Monetary Authority of Singapore

MBS
Mortgage-Backed Security

MCX
Multi Commodity Exchange of India (Mumbai)

MDS
Market Data System

MEFF
Spanish Exchange for Financial Futures and Options

MiFID
Markets in Financial Instruments Directive

MIT
Market if Touched

MOC
Market on Close

MOO
Market on Open

MTF
Multilateral Trading Facility

MTM
Mark to Market

NASDAQ
National Association of Securities Dealers Automated Quotations

NCDEX
National Commodity & Derivative Exchange (India)

NCR
National Credit Regulator (South Africa)

NDF
Non-Deliverable Forward

NFA
National Futures Association (US)

NLV
Net Liquidation Value

NOM
NASDAQ Options Market

NRA
National Regulatory Authority

NSCC
National Securities Clearing Corporation

NYBOT
New York Board of Trade

NYMEX
New York Mercantile Exchange

NYSE
New York Stock Exchange

OAS
Option-Adjusted Spreads

OATs
Obligations Assimilables du Trésor

OATS
Order Audit Trail System

OCC
Office of the Comptroller of the Currency

OCC
Options Clearing Corporation

OI
Overnight Index

OIS
Overnight Index Swap

OPEC
Organisation of the Petroleum Exporting Countries

OPL
Open Position Limit

OSC
Operations Steering Committee

OSE
Osaka Securities Exchange

OTC
Over-the-Counter

OTF
Organised Trading Facility

OTM
Out-of-the-money

PHLX
Philadelphia Stock Exchange

PM
Premium

POM
Public Order Member

PPP
Purchasing Power Parity

PPS
Protected Payments System

PRA
Prudential Regulation Authority (part of the Bank of England)

PTM
Panel on Takeovers and Mergers

PSBR
Public Sector Borrowing Requirement (UK)

PSNCR
Public Sector Net Cash Requirement (UK)

QCB
Qatar Central Bank

RBI
Reserve Bank of India

RNS
Regulatory News Service

RCH
Recognised Clearing House (UK)

RIE
Recognised Investment Exchange (UK)

RPI
Retail Prices Index

SABR
Stochastic Alpha, Beta, Rho pricing model

Safex
South African Futures Exchange

S&P
Standard & Poor's

SCM
SwapClear Clearing Member

SDRs
Special Drawing Rights

SDRT
Stamp Duty Reserve Tax (UK)

SEAQ
Stock Exchange Automated Quotation System (UK)

SEBI
Securities and Exchange Board of India

SEC
Securities and Exchange Commission (US securities regulator)

SESC
Securities and Exchange Surveillance Commission

SETS
Stock Exchange Electronic Trading Service

SFC
Securities and Futures Commission (Hong Kong)

SGX
Singapore Exchange

SHFE
Shanghai Futures Exchange

SONIA
Sterling OverNight Index Average

SPAN

Standard Portfolio ANalysis of Risk

SPE

Special Purpose Entity

SPV

Special Purpose Vehicle

SSA

Sovereign, supranational and agency counterparties

SSF

Single Stock Future

STANS

System for Theoretical Analysis and Numerical Simulations

STIR

Short-Term Interest Rate

STP

Straight-Through Processing

STRIP

Separate Trading of Registered Interest and Principal

SWF

Sovereign Wealth Fund

SWIFT

Society for Worldwide Interbank Financial Telecommunication

SwML

Sign-writing Markup Language

TAPO

Traded Average Price Option (LME)

TCF

Treating Customers Fairly

TD

Transparency Directive

TIMS

Theoretical Intermarket Margining System

TIPS

Treasury Inflation Protected Securities

TIW

Trade Information Warehouse

TOIS

Tom/Next Indexed Swap

TR

Trade Reporting

TR

Trade Repository

TRS

Trade Registration System

TRS

Total Return Swap

TSE

Tokyo Stock Exchange

TSX

Toronto Stock Exchange

TV

Time Value

UAE

United Arab Emirates

UCITS

Undertakings for Collective Investment in Transferable Securities

UCP

Universal Clearing Platform

USD

United States Dollar

USF

Universal Stock Futures

UTP

Universal Trading Platform

WMBA

Wholesale Markets Brokers' Association

XML

Extensible Markup Language

ZCB

Zero Coupon Bond

Multiple Choice Questions

The following questions have been compiled to reflect as closely as possible the standard that you will experience in your examination. Please note, however, they are not actual exam questions.

1. One of the differences between a contract for difference and a spread bet is that a:
   A. spread bet does not have a specific maturity
   B. contract for difference has a single price differential, while a spread bet has at least four
   C. contract for difference is legally defined as gambling
   D. contract for difference does not have a specific maturity

2. A speculator is anticipating an increase in lead prices and purchases 30 contracts for delivery in three months' time at $3,500 per tonne. The contract size is 25 tonnes. At expiry the position is closed out when the price has risen to $3,525 per tonne. What is the profit?
   A. $6,250
   B. $7,500
   C. $12,500
   D. $18,750

3. How are members' contributions to the member default fund determined?
   A. According to the volume of clearing activity
   B. As an annual flat fee
   C. As a percentage of the firm's fees
   D. According to the status of the firm

4. A shipping company is concerned that rising fuel prices will push up its costs and reduce profits. What should the company consider doing?
   A. Sell an oil futures call
   B. Sell oil futures
   C. Go long oil futures
   D. Buy an oil futures put

5. The automatic exercise by ICE Clear Europe of ICE Futures options is prevented by filing:
   A. an assignment notice
   B. a give-up notice
   C. a registration notice
   D. a suppression notice

6. Under the FCA's Conduct of Business rules, a firm's customers are defined as those clients:
   A. that are considered to be retail clients only
   B. that are considered to have a limited understanding of the markets
   C. that are considered to be retail and professional clients, but not eligible counterparties
   D. with assets of less than £1 million, no matter what their understanding of the market

7. Which of the following best describes the contract size for a futures contract?
   A. A variable quantity of the underlying negotiated with the futures exchange
   B. A standardised quantity of the underlying set by the futures exchange
   C. A standardised quantity of the underlying set by the buyer
   D. The price of an agreed quantity of the underlying set as standard by the futures exchange

8. A call option has a strike price of £4. If the share is currently trading at £3.85, what is the intrinsic value of this option today?
   A. −15p
   B. Nil
   C. 5p
   D. 20p

9. Which of the following is a distinctive feature of cumulative preference shares?
   A. Dividends are paid before other preference shares
   B. Unpaid dividends from previous years must be paid before any dividends on ordinary shares
   C. Dividends are accumulated and paid once every two years
   D. Dividends received are equal to the cumulative dividends paid on other types of preference shares

10. The type of swap that allows an investor to exchange the returns on an equity-based investment for the return on another equity-based investment is known as?
   A. a mark to market swap
   B. an equity swaption
   C. a commodity/equity swap
   D. a volatility swap

11. An investor has purchased a cocoa futures option on ICE that can be exercised at any time. What kind of option does he have?
   A. American
   B. Asian
   C. European
   D. Exotic

12. If you sell a straddle, what are you seeking to profit from?
   A. Time value
   B. Decreasing volatility
   C. Increasing volatility
   D. A rise in the price of the underlying

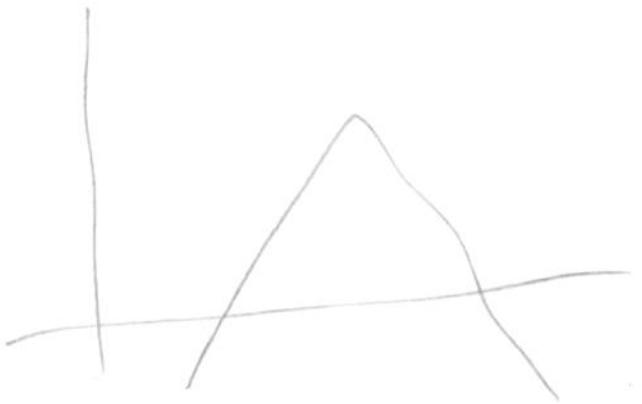

13. One of the reasons why a bank might apply a haircut to the collateral that a client has deposited with them is:

    A. regulatory requirements that apply to certain types of derivative contracts
    B. exchange-based regulations that apply to all clearing members
    C. protection from movements in the market
    D. provision for the client to exercise any options

14. If a futures contract is trading significantly below its fair value, what strategy will an arbitrageur use?

    A. Spread
    B. Cash and carry arbitrage
    C. Reverse cash and carry arbitrage
    D. Reversal

15. A member default fund is funded by:

    A. bank guarantees
    B. cash contributions
    C. margin deposits
    D. collateral deposits

16. Which of these options will best hedge a short underlying position?

    A. A short future
    B. A long, deep-in-the-money put
    C. Two long at-the-money puts
    D. Two long at-the-money calls

17. Which of the following BEST describes how IAS 39 requires that all derivatives held by firms be reported?

    A. All derivatives contracts must be stated showing their fair value
    B. All derivatives contracts, except those designated to be held to maturity, must be stated at their fair value
    C. All derivatives contracts, except those that are embedded in other contracts, must be stated at their fair value
    D. All derivatives contracts, except those that are designated as a hedge, must be stated at their fair value

18. An investor is long a coffee future at £17 a tonne and ideally wants to make a profit of at least £10 and limit any loss to £7. What instructions should be given to the dealer?

    A. Sell at limit £27, buy at £10 stop
    B. Sell at limit £10, sell at £7 stop
    C. Sell at limit £10, buy at £7 stop
    D. Sell at limit £27, sell at £10 stop

19. When do UK Treasury bills typically mature?
    A. 15 days
    B. 31 days
    C. 91 days
    D. 121 days

20. Who has the choice of where to deliver soft commodity products?
    A. The buyer
    B. The clearing house
    C. The exchange
    D. The seller

21. What type of option gives the holder the right to sell?
    A. Put option
    B. Call option
    C. Long option
    D. Short option

22. Which of the following is the option premium?
    A. Strike price minus time value
    B. Intrinsic value plus strike price
    C. Time value plus strike price
    D. Intrinsic value plus time value

23. Which of the following would be accepted as collateral by a broker to take against a written GlaxoSmithKline put option?
    A. GlaxoSmithKline shares
    B. Undated bonds
    C. Certificate of deposit
    D. Swiss bonds

24. What action will an investor take if he expects volatility to rise?
    A. Sell a call and buy a call on the same underlying
    B. Sell a put and buy a put on the same underlying
    C. Sell a call and sell a put on the same underlying
    D. Buy a call and buy a put on the same underlying

25. Which of the following option positions is MOST likely to be exercised before its expiry date?

A. Long-dated, deep-in-the-money, European-style

B. Long-dated, out-of-the-money, American-style

C. Short-dated, deep-in-the-money, American-style

D. Short-dated, out-of-the-money European-style

26. What function does a pit observer have in relation to cross trades in an open outcry market?

A. To allocate the position to the relevant account

B. To confirm time of execution

C. To input trades into the trade reporting system

D. To verify and sign off trades

27. What sum should a client's portfolio exceed before they can be treated as an elective professional client?

A. €250,000

B. €200,000

C. €400,000

D. €500,000

28. If the price of a future rises out of the arbitrage channel, what will arbitrageurs do?

A. Sell the underlying and buy the future

B. Sell the future and buy the underlying

C. Buy the underlying and sell it at a profit

D. Buy the underlying and buy the future

29. What are TIMS and SPAN used to calculate?

A. Daily settlement prices

B. Initial margins

C. Maintenance margin

D. Value of collateral

30. Who pays the premium on an option?

A. The holder of a put

B. The writer of a put

C. The writer of a call

D. The seller of a put

31. Which of the following government bonds has an annual coupon?
    A. BTP - Italy
    B. JGB
    C. OAT - France
    D. Treasury bond

32. Which of the following is an example of backwardation?
    A. Futures price at fair value, slightly higher than the cash value of the underlying
    B. Futures price below fair value, but above cash value
    C. Futures price below cash value
    D. Futures price has risen out of the arbitrage channel

Future > FV = contango
FV = cash + cost of carry
+ C

33. Which of the following statements most accurately defines the arbitrage channel?
    A. The range of prices within which transaction costs outweigh any potential arbitrage profits
    B. The range of prices within which arbitrage can be carried out profitably
    C. The range of prices within which the derivative is trading at less than its fair value
    D. The range of prices within which the derivative is trading at more than its fair value

34. How many bond futures must be traded to hedge an anticipated holding of €50 million nominal of the cheapest to deliver (CTD) bond assuming the contract size is €250,000, the price factor of the CTD is 1.112233 and the notional coupon is 6%?
    A. 180
    B. 200
    C. 222
    D. 247

35. Which organisation regulates options on stock indices in the US?
    A. Chicago Board Options Exchange
    B. Commodity Futures Trading Commission
    C. National Futures Association
    D. Securities and Exchange Commission

36. What is a key element of principles-based regulation?
    A. Well-defined rules that all regulated firms can easily apply
    B. Well-defined rules that all firms can tailor according to the scope of their business
    C. Broad-based guidelines that are applied by each regulated firm according to the scope and nature of their business
    D. Broad-based guidelines that each EU member state translates into its own well-defined rules

37. What is the rate quoted for accepting deposits in the interbank market?
    A. LIBID
    B. LIBOR
    C. LIMEAN
    D. LISTIR

38. If you sell a 240 put option for 17, what is your maximum profit?
    A. 17
    B. 233
    C. 240
    D. Unlimited

39. What is a European-style option?
    A. An option traded only in the European markets
    B. An option which can be executed at any time
    C. An option which can only be exercised at expiry
    D. An option on a European share

40. To liquidate a long position when the price falls below the prevailing market price requires which of the following orders?
    A. Sell stop
    B. Buy stop
    C. Sell limit
    D. Buy limit

41. A member firm executes, confirms and matches a trade, which it pre-registers to allocate the trade to another member firm. What is the term for this action?
    A. Assign to
    B. Call-up
    C. Give-in
    D. Give-up

42. Which of the following is TRUE about EFP trades?
    A. Counterparty credit risk increases when an EFP replaces an existing OTC trade
    B. EFP transactions can be negotiated and registered on a round-the-clock basis
    C. OTC and futures positions can be swapped even if they differ substantially in value
    D. Margin and credit limits can be reduced by netting OTC and futures positions

43. By which method does a clearing house become the counterparty to every trade?
    - A. Assignment
    - B. Novation
    - C. Offsetting
    - D. Registration

44. Which of the following is typically the most conservative users of derivative products?
    - A. Hedge funds
    - B. Pension funds
    - C. Corporate treasurers
    - D. High net worth individuals

45. Which of the following types of margin covers the risk of default during the delivery process?
    - A. Intra-day margin
    - B. Maintenance margin
    - C. Spot month margin
    - D. Variation margin

46. The benefit of a mark to market swap is:
    - A. its regular payments reduce any market risk from the underlying asset
    - B. after each settlement date, any credit risk that has built up is removed
    - C. it allows the value of the underlying principal to fluctuate after every settlement date
    - D. the regular principal repayments fit its use as a hedge for bonds

47. Which category of member is restricted to trading only for third parties?
    - A. Brokers
    - B. Broker-dealers
    - C. Dealers
    - D. General clearing member

48. Which is TRUE of price-takers?
    - A. They are buyers of financial securities only
    - B. Always have to pay away the market spread
    - C. Price-takers determine and deal on their own price
    - D. Always get to deal on their own price

49. How is a yield curve described when short-term rates are the same as long-term rates?
    - A. Concave
    - B. Flat
    - C. Inverted
    - D. Normal

50. If volatility rises, what will this do to options prices?
    A. Call and put premiums will rise
    B. Call and put premiums will fall
    C. Call premiums will rise, put premiums will fall
    D. Call premiums will fall, put premiums will rise

51. An option that can be exercised by its holder at any time to up its expiration date is known as:
    A. American
    B. Asian
    C. Bermudan
    D. European

52. If an investor buys a call with a higher strike and a put with a lower strike on an oil future, what is this strategy called?
    A. Short straddle
    B. Long strangle
    C. Bear spread
    D. Bull spread

X B

53. Which of the following is involved in a long hedge?
    A. A stop order
    B. Selling short
    C. Buying futures
    D. An intra-market spread

54. Which of the following is the main regulator of futures exchanges in the US?
    A. Commodity Futures Trading Commission
    B. National Futures Association
    C. Securities and Exchange Commission
    D. Treasury and Exchange Department

55. A CBO is considered investment grade and a portfolio of junk bonds is not because the CBO:
    A. offers an extremely attractive yield
    B. has a Moody's rating of BBB or higher
    C. includes a pool of several types of credit-quality bonds
    D. includes a pool of bonds with different maturities

X C

56. A Japanese investor expects to receive USD income from his portfolio of US government bond investments in three months' time. How might he hedge currency risk relating to this income?
    - A. Buy yen spot value
    - B. Sell a yen call/USD put option with a three-month expiration
    - C. Buy yen versus the USD forward, with a three-month maturity
    - D. Sell the US Treasury bonds

57. If you buy an option, what is the effect, if any, of gearing for a given price change in the underlying asset?
    - A. A similar proportionate change in the option value
    - B. A greater proportionate change in the option value
    - C. A smaller proportionate change in the option value
    - D. None

58. Which order type on ICE Futures Europe is to be executed at the best price available?
    - A. Basis order
    - B. Market on open order
    - C. Market order
    - D. Normal limit order

59. An investor is short a future and buys a put. To achieve delta neutrality, what should the investor do?
    - A. Buy calls
    - B. Sell calls
    - C. Buy puts
    - D. Sell futures

60. According to the two most widely used option pricing models, an option's value will fall when the underlying asset's:
    - A. volatility rises faster than market volatility
    - B. price moves below the call's strike price
    - C. price moves below the put's strike price
    - D. price moves above the call's strike price

61. What price is used to mark to market all positions?
    - A. Opening traded price
    - B. Daily settlement price
    - C. Mid-market traded price
    - D. Weighted average traded price

62. Which of the following applies to broker margins?
    A. They can be greater than those of the corresponding clearing house
    B. They are 15% of the underlying contract value
    C. They are based on SPAN
    D. They must be equal to the margin determined by the clearing house

63. What is the main purpose of the Capital Requirements Directive introduced as part of MiFID?
    A. To ensure orderly markets and improve client protection
    B. To make it easier for firms wishing to take advantage of passporting opportunities
    C. To implement tougher sanctions against firms
    D. To improve trading liquidity across the EU

64. What is a gilt strip?
    A. The tax element of a coupon payment
    B. The separation of the interest payments and the principal amount
    C. The best bid-offer spread shown on a gilt dealing screen
    D. A tap issue of gilts by the Debt Management Office

65. Which of these describes a situation in which the futures price is lower than the cash price of the underlying?
    A. Positive basis
    B. Carrying
    C. Negative basis
    D. In contango

66. An investor buys a January £5 call option at 25p. At the expiry, the stock is at £4.75. How much will the investor lose per share?
    A. 25p
    B. 50p
    C. £4.75
    D. £5.00

67. If an investor goes long a call on three S&P 500 index futures where the premium is $1,500, what additional margin needs to be paid (if any)?
    A. $1,500
    B. $3,500
    C. $4,500
    D. Nothing

68. FLEX options are hybrid products in what way?

    A. OTC-traded, but with standardised contract specifications

    B. Exchange-traded, but with choice of two exercise styles

    C. Exchange-traded, but with freely negotiable terms

    D. Options that can freely trade either on- or off-exchange

69. Where permitted, what does a credit line cover?

    A. Margin requirements of members' clients

    B. Tax liabilities when in default

    C. Purchase of the underlying asset on exercise

    D. Settlement payments of members

70. A dealer buys £10 million nominal of gilts, and sells gilt futures to the same value. What type of trade has he just executed?

    A. A FLEX trade

    B. A basis trade

    C. An exchange for physical

    D. A block trade

71. Certificates of deposit are issued:

    A. at deep discount to their face value

    B. with maturities typically between six and 12 months

    C. at a slightly lower rate of interest compared with Treasury Bills

    D. with the possibility of withdrawal prior to maturity, but usually at a cost

72. Which ONE of the following government bonds is settled on a T+1 basis?

    A. BTP

    B. Bund

    C. OAT

    D. Treasury bonds

73. A sugar refiner bought 15 white sugar futures contracts on ICE Futures Europe at $275 per tonne. The contract size was 50 tonnes. The position was later closed out when the price was $270 per tonne. What was the loss?

    A. $750

    B. $1,875

    C. $3,750

    D. $4,125

74. Which of the following is accepted by ICE Clear Europe as collateral?

A. Australian dollars in cash

B. Equities that are traded on AIM

C. Japanese bonds

D. US dollar certificates of deposit

75. ICE Clear Europe calculates the amount of initial margin required to cover all contracts for each member by using the:

A. difference between the settlement price and variation margin

B. gross value of all positions

C. marked to market value of net positions

D. net liquidation values

76. MarkitWire is an:

A. industry-backed straight-through processing system for OTC derivatives

B. exchange-based derivatives clearing and margin system

C. industry-backed straight-through netting and payments system for OTC derivatives

D. exchange-based derivative netting and payments system

77. What use, if any, will arbitrageurs make of a future when it is in the arbitrage channel?

A. Sell it to capitalise on its low value in relation to the underlying

B. Buy it to capitalise on its low value in relation to the underlying

C. Buy it to capitalise on its high value in relation to the underlying

D. None

78. What is the term used when a trader closes out a position for a nominal amount to crystallise a loss?

A. Abandonment

B. Assignment

C. Cabinet trade

D. Basis trade

79. When is a change in basis profitable for the short hedger (short the future, long the underlying)?

A. Cash prices go down while futures remain steady

B. Cash prices move from a premium over to a discount under futures

C. Futures and cash move in unison

D. Future prices go down while cash prices remain unchanged

80. Under which of the following circumstances will the FCA or an exchange set a maintenance margin higher than a position's initial margin?
   A. When the broker is dealing with an offshore client, to ensure that they have sufficient funds to meet any margin calls
   B. When the contract is considered to have a higher than normal risk or is very volatile
   C. If the broker is actively managing the client's portfolio and therefore does not maintain a separate client account
   D. When the client plans to hold the position to or close to its maturity, to avoid any additional margin calls

81. The current exchange rate is \$1.65 = £1 and the interest rates in the US and UK for the next year are 3% and 4% respectively. What is the one-year forward rate of exchange using interest rate parity?
   A. \$1.6341 = £1
   B. \$1.6540 = £1
   C. \$1.6995 = £1
   D. \$1.7165 = £1

82. A call option has a strike price of £3. If the share is currently trading at £3.30, what is the intrinsic value of this option today?
   A. 10p
   B. 25p
   C. 30p
   D. 35p

83. If a borrower wants to hedge the risk that the floating rate on their loan will rise above a certain level, they will buy a:
   A. floor
   B. collar
   C. swaption
   D. cap

84. Which of these statements is most accurate in relation to trading in options?
   A. The buyer buys the underlying from the seller of the option
   B. The seller sells the buyer the right to buy the underlying
   C. The buyer buys the right either to buy or sell the underlying
   D. The buyer buys the right to either buy or sell a single option

85. Which of the following describes the activity of an arbitrageur?
   A. Using the cash market to reduce gearing
   B. Using derivatives to minimise risk on a position
   C. Seeking to profit from mispricings between markets
   D. Mainly trading contracts on the same underlying but different maturities

86. How does ICE Clear Europe collect margin due on positions from members?

A. By assigning collateral lodged by members

B. By payments through a Bank of England account

C. By requesting cash or collateral for each transaction

D. By debiting members' accounts via the Protected Payments System

87. Which of the following is normally used to settle a contract for difference?

A. Exchange of documents

B. Exchange of financial futures

C. Exchange of the underlying

D. Cash

88. What action will an investor take if he is anticipating a change in the difference between a futures price and the cash price of its underlying asset?

A. Naked purchase

B. Basis trade

C. Intermarket spread

D. Naked sale

89. What did the Commodity Futures Modernization Act 2000 permit?

A. FLEX options

B. Single stock futures

C. Swap futures

D. Synthetic futures

90. What is a block trade?

A. A large transaction between an exchange member and a wholesale client, negotiated away from the central order book and reported after completion

B. A large transaction between an exchange member and a wholesale client, according to the terms of the central order book and reported after completion

C. An off-market transaction that involves the swapping of an OTC position with a futures position

D. An off-market transaction that involves the swapping of an OTC position with a series of futures contracts

91. If you buy a 100 put for a premium of 13, what will your maximum potential profit be?

A. 13

B. 87

C. 100

D. Unlimited

92. An increase in which of the following factors will cause all option premiums to increase?

    A. Time to maturity

    B. Risk-free interest rate

    C. Lower strike price

    D. Price of the underlying

93. Which of the following applies to segregated accounts?

    A. The customer has the same protection as non-segregated customers

    B. The transaction ends up in a house account, separate from all other customers

    C. Assets are protected in the event of a default by the firm

    D. Assets are held in a single portfolio

94. What is the purpose of marking to market?

    A. To calculate the value of collateral

    B. To calculate any variation margin due

    C. To establish the daily settlement price

    D. To establish the spread margin requirement

95. Which of the following is TRUE when comparing the price of an ETD with an OTC derivative?

    A. The OTC price will always have a tighter bid/offer spread

    B. Both are usually the same, since both are reported to the market

    C. The ETD price spread is wider, since it includes the initial margin

    D. The ETD price is more transparent, since it is quoted via the market

96. A covered call is closest to which of these?

    A. Synthetic short put position

    B. Synthetic short call position

    C. Synthetic long call position

    D. Synthetic long put position

covered call : $-P = -C + S$ sell future

97. An investor bought 1 June 100 call for 22 and sold 1 June 120 call for 6. What market expectation did he have?

    A. Neutral

    B. Volatile

    C. Moderately bullish

    D. Bearish

Long call 100 22
Short call 120 6
Bull call

98. Assume that S&P 500 index futures are currently priced at $1,600 and the contract size is $250. How many index futures contracts will be required to hedge a $15 million portfolio of US equities that has a beta of 1.12?

A. 15

B. 19

C. 38

D. 42

99. If tick size is half a point for a future on the FTSE 100 index and is valued at £5, what is the profit for an investor who goes long with the index at 4260 and then settles at expiry with the index at 4300?

A. £20

B. £200

C. £400

D. £4,260

Buy 42600
sell 43000

100. Which of the following services does SWIFTNet FpML provide?

A. A payments netting system across a range of OTC contracts

B. A real-time matching system for a range of OTC confirmations

C. A straight-through payment system for FX and swap transactions

D. A real-time position and credit limit monitoring system

101. Within what time period following verbal agreement must a block trade be reported on ICE Futures Europe?

A. 3 minutes

B. 5 minutes

C. 10 minutes

D. 30 minutes

102. If a UK exporter wants to hedge the risk associated with the euro-denominated receipts for its products, which of the following will provide an effective hedge?

A. EUR FRA

B. GBP swaption

C. EUR/GBP forward contract

D. EUR/GBP swap

UK
Receive euro
X C

103. If you buy a 100 call for a premium of 13, what is your maximum potential profit?

A. 13

B. 87

C. 100

D. Unlimited

104. A speculator can avoid taking delivery of an underlying asset in their long futures position by:
   - A. selling an option on the underlying
   - B. extending the terms of the future
   - C. selling an equivalent future
   - D. renegotiating the contract

105. Which formula is generally used to calculate the invoice amount on a physically delivered contract?
   - A. EDSP x scale factor x number of contracts
   - B. (EDSP/scale factor) x number of contracts
   - C. (Settlement price/scale factor) x number of contracts
   - D. Traded price x scale factor x number of contracts

106. The most effective way to change the interest rate and/or the currency exposure of a specific investment, is to enter into:
   - A. an asset swap
   - B. a currency swaption
   - C. a collar
   - D. an interest rate swap

107. What is the purpose of variation margining?
   - A. To settle profits or losses over a period
   - B. To remunerate traders
   - C. To act as a one-off initial deposit
   - D. To take account of changing interest rates

108. A UK, FCA-authorised firm is approached by a US resident. Which of the following is the firm allowed or required to do?
   - A. Trade all contracts whether UK or US
   - B. Trade UK contracts if the firm does not have CFTC Part 30 exemption
   - C. Provide a segregated account
   - D. Trade US contracts if the firm has CFTC Part 30 exemption

109. How is a bear spread constructed?
   - A. Selling a put and buying a call with a higher strike price
   - B. Buying a call and selling a call with a higher strike price
   - C. Selling a put and buying a put with a higher strike price
   - D. Buying a put and selling a put with a higher strike price

110. Which of the following might be a likely scenario for a futures hedge?

A. An investor notices that grain futures can be purchased more cheaply in London than in Chicago

B. A company dealing in a commodity wishes to capitalise on the rising price of that commodity

C. A company requiring a commodity wishes to protect itself against possible price rises

D. An investor anticipates a rise in bond yields following an interest rate change

111. Which of the following is a type of calendar spread?

A. Vertical spread

B. Temporal option

C. Directional spread

D. Horizontal spread

112. If a dealer wants to open a position by buying at the best available price, once a limit has been reached, what kind of order should be given?

A. Limit stop order

B. Limit order

C. Market if touched order

D. Spread order

113. What is the value of a 760 index put when the value at expiry of the underlying index is 772?

A. –12

B. 0

C. 12

D. 760

114. When might the price of emissions contracts be expected to rise?

A. When heavy polluters buy more contracts in order to hedge their exposure to pollutants

B. If emissions in a specific pollutant increase

C. As regulation tightens and pollution targets are reduced

D. As pollution targets are reached

115. An investor has bought 25 Brent Crude Oil futures contracts on ICE Futures at $63.25 per barrel and later closes out when the price is $64.30 per barrel. The contract size is 1,000 barrels. What is the profit?

A. $6,250

B. $10,050

C. $16,075

D. $26,250

116. A long put option is normally considered to have the potential for:
   A. unlimited profit and unlimited loss
   B. limited profit and limited loss
   C. unlimited profit and limited loss
   D. limited profit and unlimited loss

117. Which of the following types of margin is exclusively paid by a client to the member?
   A. Intra-day margin
   B. Maintenance margin
   C. Spread margin
   D. Variation margin

118. An investor sells a July 100 call and buys a July 90 call on the same underlying. What strategy is this?
   A. Vertical spread
   B. Horizontal spread
   C. Diagonal spread
   D. Simple spread

119. Which of the following is the usual procedure when a futures contract is being physically delivered?
   A. The buyer nominates the time and place of delivery
   B. The clearing house gives instructions on delivery
   C. The exchange stipulates the delivery time
   D. The seller gives notice of intention to deliver

120. Which of the following distinguishes ICE Clear Europe as operating a mutual guarantee system?
   A. A collective default fund
   B. Financial Services Compensation Scheme eligibility
   C. Insurance cover
   D. Balance sheet reserves

121. A basis trade is agreed on ICE Futures Europe at 11.00am. By what time must the trade have been reported?
   A. 11.03am
   B. 11.05am
   C. 11.15am
   D. 11.30am

122. A European put option has a strike price of 350p and the current price of the underlying instrument is 275p and the premium 65p. What is the best course of action for an investor?

A. Buy the option and sell the underlying

B. Sell the option and buy the underlying

C. Buy the option and buy the underlying

D. Sell the option and sell the underlying

123. Which of these statements is TRUE in relation to intrinsic value and for time value?

A. Time value is based on the length of an option's risk period

B. Time is value measured by gamma

C. Intrinsic value is negative for puts and positive for calls

D. Time value can fall to zero as expirations get closer

124. What classification is given to a UK government bond that an investor has held from issue five years ago and which is due to be redeemed in six years' time?

A. Short-dated

B. Medium-dated

C. Long-dated

D. Dual-dated

125. Which of the following is an example of an intramarket spread?

A. Buying 250 June calls, selling 250 September calls

B. Selling 200 June puts, selling 220 September calls

C. Buying 240 June calls, buying 260 September calls

D. Buying September futures, buying November futures

126. An advantage of exchange price feeds is to:

A. allocate limit orders

B. display clearing information

C. match trading parties

D. provide real-time prices

127. What are the key advantages of a FLEX facility?

A. Standardised terms with customised settlement, between wholesale counterparties

B. Standardised terms with OTC delivery, between retail and wholesale counterparties

C. Customised terms with standard exchange settlement, between wholesale counterparties

D. Customised terms with standard exchange settlement, between retail or wholesale counterparties

128. What method is used by London SPAN to assess volatility in options positions?

A. Basis

B. Deltas

C. Gammas

D. Net liquidation values

129. What measurement of an option is also known as the hedge ratio?

A. Beta

B. Delta

C. Gamma

D. Vega

130. What type of margin represents daily movements on open positions in derivatives?

A. Variation

B. Realised

C. Initial

D. Spread

131. How do you create a synthetic long future?

A. Buy a call and buy a put

B. Buy a call and sell a put

C. Sell a call and sell a put

D. Sell a call and buy a call

132. The only credit risk associated with OTC options trading exists for a:

A. bank that has sold an in-the-money put to a client

B. customer who has sold an at-the-money call to its broker

C. bank that has sold an in-the-money call to another bank

D. broker who has bought an out-of-the-money call from a client

133. An important feature of a master agreement is that it:

A. enables banks to swap offsetting contracts to reduce their total exposure

B. allows the netting of all amounts due between two parties upon early termination of contracts covered by the agreement to one single payment

C. allows two parties to share information and net any outstanding contracts with a common third party

D. provides a set and accepted framework that allows several parties to measure their risk to a specific type of contract

134. What type of option gives the holder the right to buy?

A. Put option

B. Call option

C. Long option

D. Short option

135. Which of the following is a type of wholesale trade recognised by ICE Trading Platform?

A. Basis trade

B. Stop trade

C. Cross trade

D. Limit trade

136. The interest rate parity theorem states that:

A. in FX forward rates, the higher interest rate currency commands a premium in the FX forward market

B. in FX swaptions, the lower interest rate currency commands a lower premium payment

C. in FX forward rates, the lower interest rate currency commands a premium in the FX forward market

D. FRA rates are determined by the relative swap rates of the two currencies involved in an FX FRA

137. An option's vega is useful in that it is a measure of:

A. the relationship between an option's time decay and market sentiment

B. an option's sensitivity to both market sentiment and current market conditions

C. an option's hedge ratio and how it changes relative to price movements

D. an option's sensitivity to market interest rates

138. Which of the following best describes when a put option is out-of-the-money?

A. When the strike price plus the premium is greater than the current market price

B. When the strike price plus the premium is less than the current market price

C. When the strike price minus the premium is less than the current market price

D. When the strike price is less than the current market price

139. What is the approximate delta of a deep in-the-money short call position?

A. –0.5

B. +0.5

C. –1.0

D. +1.0

140. The type of option that combines the benefits of customisation of an OTC product with the advantages of being listed on an exchange is known as:

A. an average rate option

B. a Bermudan option

C. a FLEX option

D. a lookback option

141. The writer of an option who agrees to buy the underlying at a given date and price is described as having done what?

A. Gone short a call option

B. Gone long a call option

C. Gone long a put option

D. Gone short a put option

142. The strike price of a put option is £2.00 and the current price is £2.20. The premium when this option was purchased was 15p and it is now 12p. What is the time value of this option today?

A. 3p

B. 12p

C. 20p

D. 32p

Answers to Multiple Choice Questions

1. D Chapter 5, Section 2.2

Contracts for difference do not have a fixed maturity.

2. D Chapter 3, Section 4

The speculator has made a profit of $25 per tonne after buying at $3,500 and selling at $3,525. The total profit = $25 x 25 tonnes x 30 contracts = $18,750.

3. A Chapter 6, Section 1.3

Every clearing member contributes in cash to the member default fund according to the volume of its clearing activities.

4. C Chapter 2, Section 6.3

This is a hedge: rising oil prices mean rising fuel prices. The company should therefore go long oil futures, locking into the cheaper oil price.

5. D Chapter 7, Section 2.5

If an ICE Futures option is not to be automatically exercised by ICE Clear Europe, a suppression notice must be filed.

6. C Chapter 9, Section 2.4

The FCA's Conduct of Business rules (COBS) define a client as someone to whom a firm provides, intends to provide, or has provided a service in the course of carrying on a regulated activity; and, in the case of MiFID or equivalent third country business, anything which is an ancillary service. For COBS this does not include eligible counterparties, although for CASS it means all clients.

7. B Chapter 1, Section 2.1

The futures exchange sets contract terms at specific quantities of the underlying, so investors can buy multiples of that amount but not fractions – investors cannot buy part of a contract.

8. B Chapter 4, Section 2.1.1

The intrinsic value is the difference between the current share price and the strike price, but only if that is a positive figure. The intrinsic value is zero.

9. B Chapter 2, Section 5.2.1

A cumulative preference shareholder will not only be paid this year's dividend before any ordinary shareholders' dividends, but also any unpaid dividends from previous years.

10. D Chapter 5, Section 6.10

Volatility or equity swaps are the most popular method of switching the returns on equity or equity index-based investments.

11. A Chapter 1 Section 3.2

An American option may be exercised at any time. Cocoa futures options on ICE are American-style.

12. B Chapter 8, Section 6.2

Straddles are volatility trades, and an investor selling a straddle will profit if the underlying price is stable.

13. C Chapter 5, Section 10.1.1

A haircut is applied to any type of collateral, to ensure that the broker/bank is fully covered as the value of the collateral changes. Therefore the more volatile the collateral, the larger the haircut.

14. C Chapter 4, Section 1.7.2

He will buy the future as it is relatively cheap and sell the cash asset – a reverse cash and carry arbitrage.

15. B Chapter 6, Section 1.3

Every clearing member contributes in cash to the member default fund according to the volume of their clearing activities.

16. D Chapter 8, Section 4

A short underlying position has a delta of –1, so can be hedged by two long ATM calls (+0.5 x 2 = +1).

17. D Chapter 9, Section 4

The key requirement of IAS 39, as it pertains to derivatives, is that all derivatives held by an institution, except those that are designated as a hedge, must be stated in all accounting statements at their fair value. Fair value is defined as the value for which an asset or contract can be exchanged, or a liability settled, between knowledgeable and willing parties in an arm's length transaction. In other words, all derivatives must be marked to market and stated at their current market value in all financial reports.

18. D Chapter 4, Section 3.2

'Sell at £27 limit' is an instruction to sell at no less than that figure, and 'sell at £10 stop' indicates that the investor wants to sell as soon as the price goes to or drops below £10.

19. C Chapter 2, Section 4.2

UK Treasury bills are issued by the DMO and have a maturity of 91 days.

20. D Chapter 2, Section 6.1

For soft commodity products, the sellers choose where to deliver based on the exchange's specified delivery points.

21. A Chapter 1, Section 3.2

A put option is an option to sell an asset for a specified price at a specified date or range of dates.

22. D Chapter 4, Section 2.1

The price paid for an option is made up of two parts, how much in-the-money the option is (intrinsic value) and expectation that it will move more into-the-money before expiry (time value).

23. C Chapter 6, Section 4

The writer of a GlaxoSmithKline (GSK) put option has an obligation to take delivery of the shares and therefore needs cash to pay for those shares. If the put is exercised, it will be because the value of GSK shares is falling. Neither undated bonds nor Swiss bonds are acceptable.

24. D Chapter 8, Section 6.1

Calls and puts are bought in combination if volatility is expected to rise, creating a long straddle or long strangle.

25. C Chapter 7, Section 2.6

American-style options can be exercised before their expiry date. It is feasible to exercise early when the following three criteria are met: i) American-style; ii) deep-in-the-money – having intrinsic value; and iii) close to expiry or short-dated, with very little time value left.

26. D Chapter 4, Section 3.1.6

Cross trades in an open outcry market must be verified and signed off by pit observers when the order is executed.

27. D Chapter 9, Section 2.4

A retail client may only be treated as an elective professional client if the size of their portfolio exceeds €500,000.

28. B Chapter 4, Section 1.7.3

Arbitrage works by buying whichever thing is cheaper and selling the other to generate a risk-free profit.

29. B Chapter 6, Section 3.2.1

They are both scenario-based risk programs used for calculating initial margins.

30. A Chapter 1, Section 3.2

The buyer (holder) of any kind of option must pay the premium to the writer (seller) of the option.

31. C Chapter 2, Section 2.1

OATs and Bunds have annual coupons whereas BTPs, JGBs and T-bonds have semi-annual coupons.

32. C Chapter 4, Section 1.4

The market is said to be in backwardation when the futures prices are lower than the cash prices. If futures prices are higher than cash prices the market is said to be in contango.

33. A Chapter 4, Section 1.7.3

The futures price can move away from its fair value without there being any arbitrage activity, as long as the movement is less than the trading costs that will be incurred. This creates an arbitrage channel – a range of prices within which there will be no possibility for arbitrage owing to transaction costs outweighing any potential benefits.

34. C Chapter 8, Section 3.1

To calculate the number of contracts needed the price factor is multiplied by the nominal value of the CTD portfolio divided by the nominal value of the contract. Therefore, in this case, 1.112233 x (€50m / €250,000) = 222.

35. D Chapter 9, Section 3.3.2

The SEC regulates most US option products and option exchanges but does not regulate futures products or exchanges. The CFTC regulates options not covered by the SEC.

36. C Chapter 9, Section 2.1

While each member state is permitted to implement MiFID according to parameters that are agreed between the EU and each home state, the approach of having broad-based guidelines must be preserved.

37. A Chapter 2, Section 4

The rate at which banks will accept deposits (bid) is LIBID whereas LIBOR is the rate at which they will make funds available (offer).

38. A Chapter 1, Section 3.4

The maximum profit for the writer of a put option is the premium.

39. C Chapter 1, Section 3.2

European-style options are traded all over the world and may only be exercised at expiry, in contrast to American-style options which may be exercised at any time.

40. A Chapter 4, Section 3.2

The stop will not necessarily be executed at the stop level – it will become a market order when the price falls to the stop level. A sell limit order could sit on the order book and remain unsatisfied.

41. D Chapter 4, Section 4.2

Give-ups are the sending of a trade to another member of the exchange. The member to whom the trade is given-up is said to be performing a 'give-in'.

42. **D** **Chapter 3, Section 2**

Margin and credit limits can be reduced by netting out OTC and futures positions; similarly, counterparty credit risk decreases as a result of an EFP trade. They can be negotiated on a 24-hour basis but must be registered during explicit times set down by the exchange. OTC and futures positions can be swapped only if they are substantially similar in value and/or quantity.

43. **B** **Chapter 6, Section 1.1**

Novation is the legal process whereby the clearing house becomes the counterparty to all trades.

44. **C** **Chapter 8, Section 10**

Hedge funds and high net worth individuals tend to have a greater appetite for risk than pension funds, which may also be constrained in their investment activities either through legislation or the client mandate. Corporate treasurers are the most risk-averse and will typically use derivatives to hedge price or currency risk associated with normal business activities.

45. **C** **Chapter 6, Section 3.2.1**

A clearing house will try to minimise the speculative and delivery pressures by increasing the initial margin for those contracts where final settlement is by physical delivery. This is known as a spot month margin. This ensures that those position-holders contemplating taking the contract to delivery have either the underlying asset to deliver or have allocated sufficient funds to effect settlement.

46. **B** **Chapter 5, Section 6.8**

The payment of any changes in market value removes any credit risk between the two swap counterparties on a regular basis.

47. **A** **Chapter 3, Section 1.2**

Brokers may only trade for third parties. Dealers may trade for their own account and trade for other members. Broker-dealers are entitled to trade for both third parties and their own account. General clearing members are able to clear for their own principal trades, on behalf of their clients and on behalf of other non-clearing members.

48. **B** **Chapter 1, Section 7**

A price-taker is a market participant who either requests the price, or deals through an intermediary on another participant's price. Thus, they do not set the price themselves. Many market participants including market makers may find themselves as price-takers in some circumstances, and price-makers or price-givers in others.

49. **B** **Chapter 2, Section 2.1.4**

If short-term interest rates are the same as long-term rates, the yield curve is said to be flat.

50. **A** **Chapter 4, Section 2.1.3**

The more volatile the price of an asset, the greater the uncertainty so the higher the time value and hence the premium. Premiums rise to compensate the writer for this additional risk.

51. A Chapter 5, Section 8.1

There are three popular exercise styles for options. The American-style allows its owner to exercise it at any time, up to its expiration date.

52. B Chapter 8, Section 6.3

Strangles are constructed using calls and puts with different exercise prices. Here, the options are bought, so it is a long strangle.

53. C Chapter 8, Section 3

'Long' means 'buy' in derivatives jargon. Hedgers will offset risk by taking an opposite position in the futures market.

54. A Chapter 9, Section 3.3.2

Although a major regulator of US securities markets, the SEC has a limited role in the regulation of derivatives markets. The CFTC regulates all on-exchange derivatives transactions that are not covered by the SEC. It regulates all futures products and exchanges (including PHLX) and all of the options not covered by the SEC (including currency options on the CME).

55. C Chapter 5, Section 7.4

A CBO is a derivative security that creates an investment-grade bond from a pool of junk bonds (high risk). These junk bonds are typically not investment grade, but, because a CBO includes a pool of several types of credit quality bonds together, they offer enough diversification to be considered investment grade.

56. C Chapter 2, Section 3

If USD were to weaken against JPY over the three months, the amount of yen that the investor would receive would fall. Therefore, it would make sense to fix the exchange rate as soon as possible, to hedge any exchange rate risk. This is best done using a three-month forward contract.

57. B Chapter 1, Section 4

The option value, or premium, is much smaller than the price of the underlying so a change in the value of the underlying will tend to produce a much greater proportionate change in the value of the option.

58. C Chapter 3, Section 2

Market orders are to be executed at the best price available. Normal limit orders are to be executed at the stated price or better.

59. A Chapter 4, Section 2.3

Short future and buy put are negative delta positions. Therefore a positive delta trade is required, so buy calls is the right choice.

60. **B** **Chapter 5, Section 8.1**

According to any option pricing model, a call's price will fall as the price of its underlying asset falls below its strike price, thus making it further out-of-the-money.

61. **B** **Chapter 6, Section 3.2.2**

At the close of each trading day, all positions are marked to market based on the daily settlement price. The daily settlement price can be referred to as the closing price as it is established at the end of the trading day. Other markets have different methods for calculating the daily settlement price.

62. **A** **Chapter 6, Section 3.2.1**

Broker margin must be at least equal to the margin required by the clearing house. As long as they meet this requirement, all other aspects are determined by the broker.

63. **A** **Chapter 9, Section 1.2**

The main purpose of the Capital Requirements Directive is to set out regulatory requirements for capital that a firm must hold. This ensures orderly markets and improves client protection.

64. **B** **Chapter 2, Section 2.1.2**

Stripping a gilt involves trading the interest (each individual coupon) and the principal (the nominal value) separately.

65. **A** **Chapter 4, Section 1.6**

Positive basis describes a situation in which the futures price is in backwardation, ie, below the cash price. Basis is calculated by subtracting the futures price from the cash price, resulting in a negative basis if the market is carrying/in contango.

66. **A** **Chapter 1, Section 3.3.1**

Rather than exercise the option, the investor abandons it and loses his premium: 25p.

67. **D** **Chapter 4, Section 2.5**

There is no initial margin payment on the purchase of an option because the counterparty's risk is covered by the premium.

68. **C** **Chapter 1, Section 3.6**

FLEX options are exchange-traded, but the key parameters such as exercise price, expiry date and exercise style are customised. Compared with OTC options, they have lower credit risk due to the exchange's use of a central clearing house.

69. **A** **Chapter 6, Section 4.2**

Some exchanges allow their members to extend credit to their clients to cover margin requirements. These credit lines are subject to regulatory rules.

70. **B** **Chapter 3, Section 2**

A basis trade is the simultaneous exchange of a financial asset or instrument (eg, a government bond or a basket of shares), together with an appropriate offsetting number of futures contracts, in a privately negotiated transaction between two parties. Similarly to block trades, the exchange allows the futures part of the basis trade to be executed outside the central order book.

71. **D** **Chapter 2, Section 4.3**

CDs are issued at face value at maturities usually between three and six months, and they pay a slightly higher rate of interest over government-issued T-bills to compensate for the additional risk. Because CDs are a form of time deposit, withdrawals are subject to a penalty.

72. **D** **Chapter 2, Section 2.1**

US T-bonds are settled on a T+1 basis. OATs, Bunds, JGBs and BTPs are settled on a T+2 or T+3 basis.

73. **C** **Chapter 2, Section 6.1**

There is a loss of $5 per tonne after buying at $275 and selling at $270. Each contract represents 50 tonnes. Therefore $5 x 50 tonnes x 15 contracts = $3,750.

74. **D** **Chapter 6, Section 4.1**

Certificates of deposit denominated in sterling or US dollars are acceptable. Cash must be in one of eight approved currencies.

75. **D** **Chapter 6, Section 3.3.3**

Because initial margin requirements are based on the net positions held by the member firm and there may be a variety of positions held, the calculation of the amount due is based on the NLVs of the constituent parts of the portfolio.

76. **A** **Chapter 5, Section 11.1**

MarkitWire is an industry-backed STP system for OTC derivatives, which enables the affirmation of direct transactions and brokered deals between counterparties.

77. **D** **Chapter 4, Section 1.7.3**

When a future is in the arbitrage channel it is either at its fair value, or transaction costs cancel out any gains that can be made from engaging in arbitrage.

78. **C** **Chapter 7, Section 2.4**

A trader may need to crystallise a loss for tax or accounting purposes and instead of abandoning the option will close out the position for a nominal amount. This is known as a cabinet trade.

79. D Chapter 8, Section 3.3

Basis is the difference between the cash and futures prices. The short hedger has sold the future and holds the physical asset. Therefore he will benefit if he can close out his position by buying back the future at a lower price while still getting the same cash price for the underlying physical asset.

80. B Chapter 9, Section 3.1.2

The maintenance requirement is the minimum amount to be collateralised in order to keep an open position. It is generally lower than the initial requirement. This allows the price to move against the margin without forcing a margin call immediately after the initial transaction. On instruments determined to be especially risky, however, the regulators, the exchange or the broker may set the maintenance requirement higher than normal or equal to the initial requirement to reduce their exposure to the risk accepted by the trader.

81. A Chapter 2, Section 3.1

The forward rate in one year's time will be based on the spot rate adjusted by the relative interest rates. So US$1.65 x 1.03 will be equivalent to £1 x 1.04. The one-year forward rate will be based on US$1.6995 = £1.04. Dividing both sides by 1.04 = US$1.6995/1.04 = £1.04/1.04. The one-year forward rate = US$1.6341 = £1.

82. C Chapter 4, Section 2.1.1

The intrinsic value is the difference between the current share price and the strike price. Therefore the intrinsic value is 330p – 300p = 30p.

83. D Chapter 5, Section 5

Caps are a type of option that allow the buyer to set a maximum rate on an underlying borrowing/loan.

84. C Chapter 1, Section 3.2

An option buyer buys either an option to buy (call) or an option to sell (put) the underlying from or to the seller (or writer) for a premium.

85. C Chapter 4, Section 1.7

Arbitrage involves spotting mispricings between any two markets, including derivative markets, and profiting from the price differential.

86. D Chapter 6, 3.1

ICE Clear Europe calls on members for margin payments as necessary and these are paid through the Protected Payments System, an automatic debit from members' bank accounts.

87. D Chapter 7, Section 1.4.2

A contract for difference can only be settled in cash.

88. B Chapter 8, Section 3.3

Basis traders profit from the fluctuating difference between a futures price and the cash price of its underlying asset – that is, the basis. They take the form of intramarket, not intermarket, spreads.

89. B Chapter 9, Section 3.3.3

In the US, single stock futures were permitted under the Commodity Futures Modernization Act 2000.

90. A Chapter 3, Section 2

Block trades offer the opportunity to negotiate terms privately, providing that the order is reported into the exchange once completed. C and D relate to EFP and EFS transactions.

91. B Chapter 1, Section 3.4

The maximum gain on a long put = strike price – premium (100 – 13 = 87).

92. A Chapter 4, Section 2.1.4

An increase in interest rates and the price of the underlying will cause call premiums to rise, and put premiums to fall. For all options, an increase in the time to maturity means that the option has a longer life and therefore will increase its value/premium.

93. C Chapter 4, Section 4.1

Customers whose accounts are segregated are protected from having to meet a defaulting firm's liability. All of the customers' accounts that are not segregated are treated as if they are the firm's house positions. As a result, they will not be protected in the event of default by the firm.

94. B Chapter 6, Section 3.2.2

At the close of each trading day all positions are marked to market based on the daily settlement price. The profit/loss on the day is measured and must be paid/received from the clearing house as variation margin.

95. D Chapter 1, Section 6

The prices of all exchange-traded contracts are highly transparent, since they are listed by the exchange and have full public dissemination. All exchange members have access to all prices quotes at any given time.

96. A Chapter 8, Section 4.3.1

A long underlying and a short call together create the profit and loss profile of a short put. A synthetic short put is where an investor sells a call and buys a future – effectively a covered short call position.

97. C Chapter 8, Section 5.1

The investor has bought the call with the lower strike price, and sold the call with the higher strike price, creating a bull spread.

98. D Chapter 8, Section 3

The correct formula is (portfolio value / (futures price x contract size)) x portfolio beta. Therefore, the correct answer is ($15m / (1600 x $250)) x 1.12 = 42 contracts.

99. C Chapter 3, Section 4

The profit is the tick value (£5) times the number of ticks moved. Because the tick size is half a point, the number of ticks moved is twice the number of points moved (40). So the equation is £5 x 40 x 2 = £400.

100. D Chapter 5, Section 11.4

SWIFTNet FpML is a real-time confirmation and exception monitoring system for FX, money market and OTC derivative confirmations, whose main goal is to increase the efficiency of users' straight-through processing of OTC derivative confirmations.

101. B Chapter 5, Section 9.1

On NYSE Liffe, block trades must be reported to the exchange within five minutes of verbal agreement being reached. Basis trades are to be reported within 15 minutes of the time the trade was organised.

102. C Chapter 5, Section 3

Forward FX contracts are a good means of hedging currency risk.

103. D Chapter 1, Sections 3.3.1

Loss is limited to the premium paid, but for the buyer of a call, profit is potentially unlimited.

104. C Chapter 1, Section 2.1

A trader can remove any delivery obligations by taking an equal and opposite position before the expiry. This will crystallise any gains or losses.

105. A Chapter 7, Section 1.4.1

For physically delivered contracts, the futures buyers will receive an invoice for the asset and have to pay the amount stated in the invoice. This is calculated using the formula EDSP x scale factor x number of contracts. For bond futures, the calculation differs to include the price factor and accrued interest.

106. A Chapter 5, Section 6.1

An asset swap is the most effective way to change the total exposure of an asset.

107. A Chapter 6, Section 3.2.2

Variation margining helps protect against default by settling the profit or loss on a position daily.

108. C Chapter 9, Section 3.3.2

The UK firm is only allowed to deal in UK contracts with CFTC Part 30 Exemption. The US resident must always be provided with a segregated account.

109. C Chapter 8, Section 5.1

For a bear spread you buy the high strike and sell the low strike.

110. C Chapter 8, Section 3

This is the typical reason for a hedge. If the company goes long a future in the commodity it wishes to purchase, then even if the price goes up, the value of the future will go up too, offsetting the extra expenditure the company will have to make on the commodity in the spot market. This is a long hedge.

111. D Chapter 8, Section 5.2

A horizontal spread is one type of calendar spread, involving buying and selling the same option across different expiry months.

112. C Chapter 4, Section 3.2

An MIT order is an order to open a position that becomes a market order once the limit has been reached.

113. B Chapter 3, Section 4

At expiry, the put has no value, as the strike price is below the underlying price.

114. C Chapter 2, Section 6.4

Emissions contracts are initially bought by companies in order to offset levels of emissions that exceed set targets such as those established in the Kyoto Accord. The contracts will become more valuable when these pollution targets are reduced.

115. D Chapter 3, Section 4

The investor has made a profit of $1.05 per barrel after buying at $63.25 and selling at $64.30 and each contract represents 1,000 barrels. $1.05 x 1,000 barrels x 25 contracts = $26,250.

116. B Chapter 1, Sections 3.3.3

Loss is limited to the premium paid. Profit is limited to the exercise price, less the premium (as the underlying price cannot fall below zero).

117. B Chapter 6, Section 3.2.3

Maintenance margin is an arrangement between the member firm and its client. A firm will usually require a client to deposit more than the initial margin and allows for the payment of some variation margin to avoid referring back to the client every day. Once the credit breaches a preset limit, the member will issue a margin call expecting the client to replenish the account.

118. A Chapter 8, Section 5.1

Vertical spreads, or price spreads, take place when an investor buys and sells options that have varying strike prices, but have the same expiry date. This investor has created a vertical, bull spread.

119. D Chapter 7, Section 1.4

Futures sellers give notice declaring their intention to deliver the asset to the clearing house. The clearing house assigns the assets to the futures buyers and, if there is any flexibility in the contract, the seller can nominate what, where and when to deliver.

120. A Chapter 6, Section 1.3

All members of ICE Clear Europe contribute to a member default fund, which is available to cover the liabilities of a defaulting member. This system is known as a mutual guarantee system.

121. C Chapter 5, Section 9.1

On NYSE Liffe, basis trades are to be reported within 15 minutes of the time the trade was organised.

122. C Chapter 4, Section 2

Exercise price (350p) – underlying price (275p) = intrinsic value (75p). The premium is 10p under its intrinsic value. The investor takes advantage of the low premium to buy both the option and the underlying so as to be able to deliver the underlying for a risk-free profit of 10p.

123. A Chapter 4, Section 2.1.1

The intrinsic value is the difference between the strike value and the market price. Since the buyer is not obliged to exercise, the intrinsic value cannot be negative. Time value increases in proportion to the length of time the writer is at risk from the buyer exercising.

124. A Chapter 2, Section 2.1

A UK gilt with less than seven years to redemption is classified as short-dated.

125. A Chapter 8, Section 2.1

Spreads require buy and sell transactions on the same underlying asset. Intramarket spreads are trades based on the simultaneous buying and selling of futures with different expiry dates on the same underlying asset.

126. D Chapter 5, Section 9.2.1

Exchanges disseminate the trade reporting information through a price feed. Real-time prices and trade information are included in the feed that is available to exchange members through quote vendors.

127. C Chapter 3, Section 2

The FLEX facility combines the flexibility of the OTC market in customising a transaction, with the clearing and other advantages of exchange trading. This reduces some of the risks normally associated with OTC trading. Typically this facility is only open to exchange members, ie, for wholesale business.

128. B Chapter 6, Section 3.3.1

Options positions will be affected by volatility, and London SPAN uses deltas to calculate the equivalent number of futures to quantify any potential offset.

129. B Chapter 5, Section 8.1

Delta is the Greek measure or ratio that measures how the change in the underlying asset's value changes the option's value. It has a range of zero to one, positive or negative.

130. A Chapter 6, Section 3.2.2

Initial margin is the amount paid by both parties at the outset of a contract to the clearing house. Variation margin is the amount calculated against daily price movements and paid by whomever the price is moving against.

131. B Chapter 8, Section 7

A synthetic long future results where matching short put and long call options positions are taken on a future. An investor will buy a call and sell a put with the same strike price and expiry.

132. D Chapter 5, Section 8.1

Since an option buyer usually buys the premium upfront, the only credit risk lies with any option buyer, no matter what type of option has been purchased.

133. B Chapter 5, Section 10.1

One of the main advantages of a master agreement is the fact that is has two netting features, which helps to reduce credit risk.

134. B Chapter 1, Section 3.2

A call option is an option to buy an asset for a specified price at a specified date or range of dates.

135. A Chapter 3, Section 2

A basis trade is one of two types of wholesale trade recognised by NYSE Liffe's UTP. It is the simultaneous exchange of a financial asset or instrument together with an appropriate offsetting number of futures contacts in a privately negotiated transaction between two parties.

136. C Chapter 5, Section 3.1

The interest rate parity theorem is the basis for the FX forward market, to ensure that arbitrage opportunities do not exist.

137. B Chapter 4, Section 2.4.2

Vega is the measure of how a 1% change in volatility affects an option's value relative to changes in both expected or implied volatility and current market conditions.

138. D Chapter 4, Section 2.1.1

An out-of-the-money option is where there is no intrinsic value. The intrinsic value is the difference between the strike price and the underlying asset price. If the strike price is less than the current market price, a put option is out-of-the-money.

139. C Chapter 4, Section 2.3

Delta equals the change in option premium divided by the change in price of the underlying. Therefore, delta = –1 x 1 = –1.0.

140. C Chapter 5, Section 8.1.1

FLEX options are exchange-traded options that allow buyers to customise key contract terms.

141. D Chapter 1, Section 3.2

The writer sells (goes short) the option for the buyer to sell him the underlying at a fixed price in the future, hoping the price will rise and the buyer will abandon the option, leaving the writer with the premium.

142. B Chapter 4, Section 2.1.2

The premium is calculated as intrinsic value plus the time value. Because the premium is 12p and the intrinsic value is nothing (because the option is out-of-the-money) the time value must be 12p.

Syllabus Learning Map

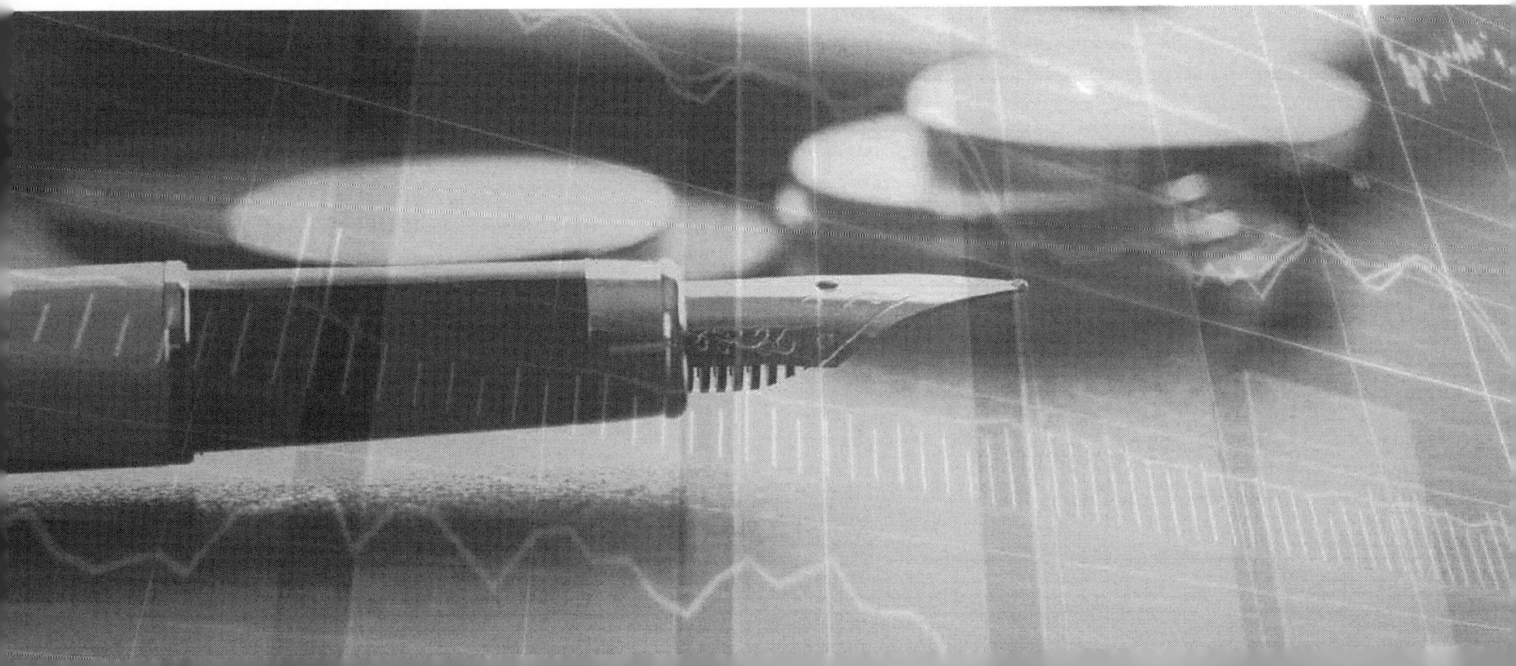

Syllabus Unit/ Element		Chapter/ Section
Element 1	**Introduction to Derivatives**	**Chapter 1**
1.1	**General** On completion, the candidate should:	
1.1.1	understand the basic concepts and fundamental characteristics of: • forward and futures contracts • contracts for differences	2
1.1.2	understand the basic concepts and fundamental characteristics of options contracts, including: • basic puts and calls • options on cash equities and forwards • American, European, Asian, Bermudan • common path-dependent and average pricing options	3
1.1.3	understand the risks and rewards associated with derivatives: • counterparty risk • market risk • liquidity risk • risks to the buyer of options • risks to the writer of options • operational risk	2.6 2.7 3.4
1.1.4	understand the significance of gearing to exchange-traded derivatives: • how margin facilitates gearing • effect on derivative positions • reward versus outlay • reward versus risk	4
1.1.5	understand the principles and differences between the two major measures of exchange-traded liquidity (open interest and volume)	5
1.1.6	understand the main features and differences of over-the-counter (OTC) traded products in contrast to exchange-traded products: • how an OTC-traded product is traded • standard versus bespoke OTC contracts • set maturity or expiry dates versus bespoke OTC contracts • margin requirements versus collateral • central clearing versus counterparty risk • liquidity from standard versus bespoke OTC contracts • risk profile of actively managed exchange-traded versus OTC hedging • market transparency versus confidential transactions	6

Syllabus Unit/ Element		Chapter/ Section
1.1.7	understand the trading mechanisms by which OTC and exchange-traded markets meet: • block trades • EFPs/EFSs • flex products	3.6
1.1.8	understand how to interpret basic options diagrams (long call, long put, short call, short put)	3.3
1.1.9	understand the main markets and stakeholders: • FX, money markets, equity, fixed income, commodity • regulators in major markets • quote driven versus order driven • floor versus voice versus electronic • buy-side • sell-side • price givers – central banks, banks, major market corporates • price takers – central banks, banks, corporates, asset managers, insurance companies, private clients	7
1.1.10	understand the role of liquidity providers: • intermediaries – IDBs • prime brokers • FCMs • executing brokers • clearing brokers	7.1

Element 2	Underlying Markets	Chapter 2
2.1	**Government Debt/Corporate Debt** On completion, the candidate should:	
2.1.1	understand the reasons for the government issuing bonds • public sector finance requirements • financing long-term debt • the role of national debt in government finances	2.1
2.1.2	understand the different categories of gilts and their special features (short, medium and long dated / undated / index linked / coupons and strippable)	2.1
2.1.3	know the main overseas government bonds and their main features (T bonds/JGBs/Bunds/OATs): • settlement • coupon • maturities • countries • spreads between different government bonds	2.1

Syllabus Unit/ Element		Chapter/ Section
2.1.4	understand the relationship between return and maturity shown by yield curves: • normal yield curves • inverted yield curves • flat yield curves	2.1.4
2.1.5	know the main features of the corporate bond market	2.2
2.1.6	understand the relationship between government and corporate bonds: • yield spread over government bonds • high grade and high yield bonds • bond ratings, transition and default	2.2
2.2	**Foreign Exchange Contracts** On completion, the candidate should:	
2.2.1	understand the nature of the spot market and the trading and settlement of spot transactions: • purpose of the market • what is the spot market • contract value dates • settlement periods and timescales	3
2.2.2	understand the nature, characteristics, markets and uses of currency forward contracts: • what is a currency forward contract including non-deliverable forwards • commercial and speculative uses • hedging uses in portfolio management • effect of time on open positions	3, 3.2
2.2.3	understand the factors that determine forward rates and how forward rates are quoted (in terms of premiums and discounts): • what are premiums and discounts • what are forward points • how prices are quoted (may be tested by the use of simple calculations) • effect of interest rate differentials • the relationship between the spot market and the forward market	3
2.2.4	be able to calculate forward foreign exchange rates using interest rate differentials	3, 3.1

Syllabus Unit/ Element		Chapter/ Section
2.3	**Money Market Contracts** On completion, the candidate should:	
2.3.1	know the basic characteristics of treasury bills: • term • how and when issued • issued at a discount • promissory note • redeemed at par	4.2
2.3.2	know the uses and requirements of inter-bank deposits: • what are inter-bank deposits • why do they exist • determination of inter-bank offer rates • LIBOR, LIBID, EURIBOR, EONIA, SONIA	4
2.3.3	know the basic characteristics of certificates of deposit: • term • how and when issued • issued at a discount/par • redeemed at par/premium	4.3
2.3.4	understand the risk implications of trading in the money market contracts: • as a depositor • as a source of funding	4.1
2.4	**Equity Markets** On completion, the candidate should:	
2.4.1	know the principal features and characteristics of ordinary shares and non-voting shares: • ranking in a liquidation, for dividends • voting rights • partly paid shares and calls	5.1
2.4.2	understand the differences and principal characteristics of the following classes of preference shares: cumulative, participating, redeemable, convertible: • valuation techniques given (eg, Gordon's Growth Model)	5.2

Syllabus Unit/ Element		Chapter/ Section
2.4.3	understand equity warrants and equity options and know their differences: • what is an equity warrant • what is an equity option • benefits to an investor or speculator • time to expiry • reasons to issue • who issues them • where traded • strike prices • effect of exercise • settlement • gearing against the underlying	5.3
2.4.4	understand the effect of corporate actions on equity warrants: • rights issues • bonus issues • stock splits • mergers and acquisitions	5.3
2.5	**Softs and Agriculturals** On completion, the candidate should:	
2.5.1	know the main softs and agriculturals and the influences on supply: • coffee, cocoa, white sugar, soya bean, wheat, rape seed oil, grains, livestock • change in demand • change in production, weather • holding cost	6.1
2.6	**Base and Precious Metals** On completion, the candidate should:	
2.6.1	know the main base and precious metals and the influences on supply: • copper, nickel, aluminium, zinc, tin, lead, gold and silver • change in demand • change in production • marginal costs of mining • changes in industry • political or strategic • holding cost	6.2

Syllabus Unit/ Element		Chapter/ Section
2.7	**Energy** On completion, the candidate should:	
2.7.1	know the main energy products and the influences on price (crude oil and natural gas): • change in demand • change in production • marginal costs of production • delivery costs • political or strategic • OPEC	6.3
2.8	**Exotics** On completion, the candidate should:	
2.8.1	know the main products and the influences on price: • freight • emissions • weather • hybrids	6.4

Element 3	**Exchange-Traded Futures and Options**	**Chapter 3**
3.1	**Exchanges** On completion, the candidate should:	
3.1.1	know the structures, physical and electronic trading processes, clearing mechanisms and main products of the following exchanges: • LME, ICE Futures Europe, LSE, Eurex, MEFF, B-ClearPHLX, CBOE, OneChicago, NYBOT (ICE), CME Group • SGX, Osaka, TSE, KOFEX • BSE, NSE, MCX	1.1
3.1.2	know the membership structures (brokers, dealers and broker/ dealers, general clearing, individual clearing and non-clearing) and their principal rights: • executing trades for third parties • executing trades for their own account • executing trades for other members • capacity as broker • capacity as dealer • capacities of clearing members	1.2

Syllabus Unit/ Element		Chapter/ Section
3.2	**Trading Platforms** On completion, the candidate should:	
3.2.1	know the essential details of the trading mechanisms: • open outcry, telephone and electronic platforms • whether quote or order driven • how the trading host matches orders • the order types accepted by the markets • the trading strategies that are recognised • record-keeping	2
3.2.2	know the essential details of wholesale trading facilities: • block trades and basis trades • exchange for physical, exchange for swaps • flex facilities	2
3.2.3	understand the significance, implications and uses of wholesale trading facilities	2
3.3	**Clearing Mechanisms** On completion, the candidate should:	
3.3.1	understand the matching and clearing arrangements: • trade capture processes/order matching processes • how contracts are delivered and settled • physical or cash • establishment of settlement price • options into futures • sellers initiate delivery	3
3.3.2	understand how the physical delivery methods for commodities operate and where they differ from other derivatives: • warehouses, warrants and good delivery • large position reporting • price discovery – official and closing prices	3
3.3.3	know the main exchanges and contracts that have common settlement prices and links and the extent to which these allow investors to transfer open positions from one exchange to another: • CME Group and its global partners • SGX	3
3.3.4	be able to calculate the profit/loss on delivery/expiry of futures and options	4

Syllabus Unit/ Element		Chapter/ Section
Element 4	**Principles of Exchange-Traded Futures and Options**	**Chapter 4**
4.1	**Futures Pricing** On completion, the candidate should:	
4.1.1	understand the mechanisms for futures pricing and the relationship with the underlying cash prices together with the significance of contributing factors: • contango and backwardation • price convergence at maturity • the concept of fair value according to IAS	1
4.1.2	understand the implications of the cost of carry and what may be included in these: • what is cost of carry • interest rates and asset yields • storage costs, insurance and interest costs	1.2
4.1.3	be able to calculate the fair value of a future from relevant cash market prices, yields and interest rates	1.3.1
4.1.4	understand the importance of basis: • behaviour at expiry • significance of changes • basis risk	1.6
4.1.5	understand the principles of cash/futures arbitrage: • what should be included in arbitrage calculations • cash and carry arbitrage • when arbitrage opportunities exist • arbitrage possibilities • arbitrage risk	1.7
4.2	**Options Pricing** On completion, the candidate should:	
4.2.1	understand the factors of options pricing: • option premium • time value • intrinsic value • what affects time and intrinsic values • in-the-money, out-of-the-money and at-the-money	2
4.2.2	understand the factors determining option premiums: • volatility • interest rates • strike or exercise price • time to expiry • the underlying asset price • dividends/coupons	2.1.3

Syllabus Unit/ Element		Chapter/ Section
4.2.3	be able to calculate the put/call parity theorem: • what is the put/call parity theorem • identifying arbitrage opportunities • risk-free interest rate	2.2
4.2.4	understand the qualitative characteristics of the following Greeks and their uses: • delta • gamma • theta • vega • rho	2.4
4.2.5	be able to calculate the sensitivity of the option premium to changes in price by applying delta values to cumulative positions: • what is delta • uses of delta	2.3
4.2.6	know the requirements of, and process for, premium payment: • when paid, immediately or marking to market • the roles of the clearing house and broker • what the seller receives	2.5
4.3	**Order/Instruction Flow and Order Type** On completion, the candidate should:	
4.3.1	know the principles of order flow: • how clients, brokers and exchange members are linked • electronic and open outcry markets • audit trail	3.1
4.3.2	know the definition, significance and differences between principal and agency orders (ie, of dual capacity versus agency orders): • dealing as a principal • cross trading • advantages to the client	3.1
4.3.3	understand the range of types of orders, their uses and effects: • market order • limit order • market if touched order • opening and closing orders • good 'til cancelled • immediate or cancel/fill or kill order • stop order • stop limit order • day order	3.2

Syllabus Unit/ Element		Chapter/ Section
4.4	**Trade Registration** On completion, the candidate should:	
4.4.1	know the processes involved in trade registration, trade input and trade matching and differing requirements of electronic and open outcry markets	4
4.5.2	understand the purpose and importance of give-ups/allocations: • reasons to allocate a trade to an account • use of give-up agreements • risk implications	4.2
4.5.3	understand the use of different types of accounts: • use of house accounts • customer accounts – segregated and non-segregated	4.1

Element 5	Principles of OTC Derivatives	Chapter 5
5.1	**Concepts and Characteristics** On completion, the candidate should:	
5.1.1	understand the basic concepts and fundamental characteristics of: • forwards • caps • floors • collars • swaps	 2 2 5 5 4
5.1.2	understand the basic concepts and fundamental characteristics of interest rate swaps and swaptions: • underlying (fixed/fixed, fixed/floating, floating/floating) • interest calculation (compared to bond markets)	4
5.1.3	understand the basic concepts and fundamental characteristics of foreign exchange and currency forwards, swaps and swaptions: • FX forward (outrights quotes v pips) • Currency swap/swaption	3
5.1.4	understand the basic concepts and fundamental characteristics of equity forwards, swaps and swaptions: • equity baskets/index • equity forwards • equity swaps/swaptions	6.1.0
5.1.5	understand the basic concepts and fundamental characteristics of commodity forwards, swaps:	6.9
5.1.6	understand the basic concepts of total return and asset swaps	6
5.1.7	understand the basic concepts and fundamental characteristics of zero coupon inflation products	6.12

Syllabus Unit/ Element		Chapter/ Section
5.1.8	understand the basic concepts and fundamental characteristics of credit derivatives and the main credit events: • default events • ratings transitions	7
5.1.9	understand how spread betting differs from other contracts for differences	2.2
5.1.10	understand the basic concepts and fundamental characteristics of flex options: • how they differ from standard exchange-traded options • how they differ from OTC options	8.1.1
5.1.11	understand the basic concepts and fundamental characteristics of CFDs	2.2
5.2	**ISDA Documentation** On completion, the candidate should:	
5.2.1	know the main ISDA documents supporting OTC derivative activities: • master agreements • credit support annex documentation • confirmations • ISDA protocols	10
5.3	**Forwards and Swaps** On completion, the candidate should:	
5.3.1	understand the mechanisms for OTC derivative pricing and the relationship with the underlying cash prices together with the significance of contributing factors: • forward and forward/forward rates • cash flow analysis and the zero curve • the role of interest rates and yields • other factors affecting pricing	2
5.4	**Credit Default Swaps** On completion, the candidate should:	
5.4.1	know the common credit derivative instruments and their relationships to other markets and products: • credit default swaps • credit-linked notes • collateralised debt obligations/collateralised bond obligations • synthetic CDOs • option adjusted spreads	7.1 7.1 7.4 7.4 7.3

Syllabus Unit/ Element		Chapter/ Section
5.4.2	understand the mechanisms for pricing credit derivatives and the relationships with asset swap prices	7.1
5.5	**Other Swap types** On completion, the candidate should:	
5.5.1	know the common equity swap instruments and their relationship to other markets and products: • total return • volatility • variance • dividend swaps	6.10
5.5.2	know the common interest rate swap features and their relationships to other markets: • amortising • accreting • rollercoaster • forward start	4, 6
5.6	**Inflation Swaps and Structured Products** On completion, the candidate should:	
5.6.1	understand how structured products utilise embedded derivatives to achieve a risk/return profile: • convertible bonds • index linked notes • capital protected products • callable/puttable bonds	8.2
5.6.2	know the basic purpose of the following • commodity swaps • property swaps • environmental swaps	6.9 6.11 6.11
5.7	**Options** On completion, the candidate should:	
5.7.1	know the common OTC option products: • European, American, Bermudan, Asian • lookbacks and variants • ratchets/cliquets	8.1

Syllabus Unit/ Element		Chapter/ Section
5.7.2	understand the mechanisms for option pricing and the relationship with the underlying cash prices together with the significance of contributing factors: • structure • arbitrage restrictions • valuation inputs • SABR model • Black Scholes model • binomial model	8.1
5.7.3	know the requirements of, and process for, premium payment: • when paid • credit exposure • the collateral process	8.1
5.8	**Market Transparency, Trade Reporting and Monitoring** On completion, the candidate should:	
5.8.1	know the purpose and requirements of trade reporting in markets: • information to be reported • process for reporting • responsibility for reporting	9.1
5.8.2	know the advantages and main sources for exchange price feeds: • price transparency • current bids and offers • trade prices • high/low prices • last night closing price • traded volume	9.2
5.8.3	understand the importance of monitoring volume and open interest information and settlement: • purpose of monitoring open interest • breach of credit limit • guarantee in the event of settlement failure • effect of client's failure to monitor open interest	9.3
5.9	**Market Platforms and Trade Processing** On completion, the candidate should:	
5.9.1	know the trading mechanisms and platforms for common OTC derivatives along with processing requirements and platforms: • Markit Wire/Markit SERV • DTCC Deriv/SERV and TIW • SwiftNet FpML • TriOptima • ICE LINK • DTCC AffirmXpress	11

Syllabus Unit/ Element		Chapter/ Section
5.10	**Settlement and Processing of OTC Contracts** On completion, the candidate should:	
5.10.1	know the importance of accurate and timely settlement processes for OTC products: • deal tickets and term sheets • trade confirmations • reconciliation processes (internal and external) • cashflow/asset movement instructions and control processes • close out or maturity instructions	10.2 12 12 12 12
5.10.2	understand the main control process: • front to back office reconciliation • trade validation • profit and loss reporting	12
5.11	**OTC Collateral Processes** On completion, the candidate should:	
5.11.1	understand the potential impact of credit exposures on OTC positions: • nature of OTC contracts • mark to market and potential exposures • term of OTC derivatives • acceptable forms of collateral (certainty and currency of asset) • the collateral process (mark to market, hurdle, minimum cash flow, parties involved)	10.2

Element 6	**Principles of Clearing**	**Chapter 6**
6.1	**Definition and Purpose of Clearing** On completion, the candidate should:	
6.1.1	understand the purpose of clearing and the function of novation: • mutual offset system • principal to principal • broker's position	1.1
6.1.2	understand the risks usually associated with the clearing process and the implications of default: • settlement risk • counterparty risk • currency risk	1.1
6.1.3	understand the role played by the clearing house in the clearing process: • clearing house relationship with members in settlement • transfer of payments	1.2

Syllabus Unit/ Element		Chapter/ Section
6.1.4	understand the backing arrangements in place in the event of a member default: • novation • guarantee of performance of the contract • default fund • members' contributions • principal to buyer and seller • control of funds to clearing members' accounts • requirement for members to use an approved bank	1.3
6.1.5	understand the relationship between clearing members and non-clearing members: • clearing versus non-clearing member • use of general clearing members to clear trades	1.2
6.1.6	understand the principles of mutual and independent guarantees: • mutual guarantees versus independent guarantees • purpose of the guarantees • funding of the default fund at the clearing house	1.3
6.1.7	understand the services offered by prime brokers as they relate to derivatives: • borrowing and lending securities • financing positions • providing custody and safekeeping of assets • clearing and settling trades • administering onshore and offshore funds • corporate actions • capital introductions • risk management • regulation of prime brokers	1.4
6.1.8	know which exchanges/clearing houses offer OTC clearing arrangements and for which major products	1.5
6.1.9	understand how OTC products can be centrally cleared: • eligibility and credit standing of counterparts • constraints placed upon contract terms • the margin processes • advantages and uses of centralised clearing of OTC products • setup of the clearing fund	1.5
6.1.10	understand how centrally cleared products are executed	1.5

Syllabus Unit/ Element		Chapter/ Section
6.2	**Position and Price Limits** On completion, the candidate should:	
6.2.1	understand price limits and position limits and the effects of their application: • price limits • what are position limits • who imposes limits • purpose of price and position limits • action in the event of breach	2
6.3	**The Principles of Margin** On completion, the candidate should:	
6.3.1	understand the differences between initial and variation margin and the significance of marking to market and withdrawal of variation margin profits: • marking to market • trigger levels • offsetting long and short positions • when paid	3.2
6.3.2	know the means by which exchanges establish settlement prices: • what are settlement prices • closing ranges/prices	3.2.2
6.3.3	understand the nature and use of offsets for spread/spot month margining: • purpose of offsets • what is spot month margin • purpose of spot month margins • purpose of spread margins	3.2.1
6.3.4	understand why the clearing house might call intra-day margin: • purpose of intra-day margin • when is intra-day margin paid	3.2.1
6.3.5	know methods of margining involving delta and SPAN and their implications: • use of delta • use of SPAN • effect of price change in the underlying • use of net liquidation value	3.3
6.3.6	know methods of margining for centrally cleared OTC products and their implications: • how exposure is calculated • what margins are applied • how and when margin payments are made	3.2

Syllabus Unit/ Element		Chapter/ Section
6.3.7	understand how a firm deals with margin payments for its own positions and for its clients' positions through its books: • use of house accounts • use of client segregated accounts • use of client non-segregated/pooled accounts	3.1
6.3.8	understand the difference between the clearing house's margin and that of the broker and the collection/payment process: • amounts paid by clearing member and its clients • flow of margin	3.1
6.4	**Collateral/Credit** On completion, the candidate should:	
6.4.1	know the definition, purpose and uses of collateral and the major types of acceptable collateral (cash versus non-cash)	4.1
6.4.2	understand the significance of credit lines: • purpose of credit lines • what credit lines cover • deals in excess of a credit line • significance of collateral	4.2
6.4.3	understand the mechanisms of collateral management • valuation and pricing • credit support annex (CSA) • One-way CSAs • thresholds • haircuts • minimum transfer amount	Chapter 6, 4.3 and Chapter 5, 10.1

Element 7	Delivery and Settlement	Chapter 7
7.1	**Aspects of Delivery** On completion, the candidate should:	
7.1.1	understand the purpose of the exchange delivery settlement price (EDSP) and the factors affecting it: • purpose of EDSP • auction process • factors included in calculating the EDSP value • reasons for the exchange to set the EDSP • no EDSP on the last notice day	1.5

Syllabus Unit/ Element		Chapter/ Section
7.1.2	understand the differences between cash settlement and physically delivered contracts and the final payment process: • what is cash settlement • what is physical delivery • factors used in ascertaining the invoice amount • who calculates the invoice amount • differences between financial and commodity products	1.3
7.1.3	Know the role of alternative delivery procedures (ADPs) in physical delivery	1.3
7.1.4	understand the importance and implications of the delivery of open contracts at expiry and the significance of the short position: • purpose of open contracts • physical versus cash delivery • financials versus commodities • avoidance of delivery – reasons and methods • advantages and disadvantages of cash delivery • asset delivery to the clearing house • seller's choice of delivery time and method • relevance of first notice day, last notice day and delivery day or period	1.3
7.1.5	know the role of the clearing house as counterparty in delivery: • when the clearing house becomes the counterparty • role of the clearing house as counterparty • role of the clearing house as guarantor • counterparty risk • assignment • use of warrants in delivery	1.1
7.1.6	understand the purpose and uses of LME closing contracts	1.2

Syllabus Unit/ Element		Chapter/ Section
7.2	**Exercising Options** On completion, the candidate should:	
7.2.1	understand the significance and implications of the exercise of options, the assignment of obligations, abandonment and expiry: • purpose of assignment of obligations • instigating an assignment notice • receiving an assignment notice • abandonment • which options are most likely to be exercised before expiry • exercise at expiry • European, American and Asian options • action upon exercise • reasons for assignments • effect of assignment • advantages to the investor • probability of assignment	2
7.2.2	understand the significance of automatic exercise: • purpose of automatic exercise • options that may be subject to automatic exercise • reasons for clearing houses to adopt automatic exercise • benefits to members and holders of long positions • prevention of automatic exercise	2.5
Element 8	**Trading, Hedging and Investment Strategies**	**Chapter 8**
8.1	**Derivative Users** On completion, the candidate should:	
8.1.1	understand the categories of users of derivatives and structured products and their respective use of derivative products: • hedger • speculator • arbitrageur	1
8.2	**Futures Spread Trading** On completion, the candidate should:	
8.2.1	know the distinctions between intramarket spreads and intermarket spreads and the scenarios in which they may be appropriate: • use in differing market conditions • situations resulting in profitability/loss	2
8.3	**Options Strategies** On completion, the candidate should:	

CISI
CHARTERED INSTITUTE FOR SECURITIES & INVESTMENT

Syllabus Unit/ Element		Chapter/ Section
8.3.1	understand the use of derivatives for speculation and hedging: • speculation: long calls, short puts (bullish) • speculation: short call, long puts (bearish) • hedging: covered calls and protective puts • recognise diagrammatic representation of each strategy • maximise upside and downside for each strategy	4.1, 4.3
8.3.2	understand and be able to create basic synthetic options and futures: • synthetic long • synthetic short • synthetic put • synthetic call	7
8.3.3	understand the characteristics and effects of vertical spreads: • bull call and bear call spreads • bull put and bear put spreads • use in differing market conditions • anticipating modest market rises/falls (bull/bear markets) • risks	5.1
8.3.4	understand the characteristics and effects of long and short straddles and strangles: • use in differing market conditions • anticipating modest market rises/falls (bull/bear markets) • risks	6
8.3.5	be able to calculate maximum profits/losses in simple examples of the above strategies	5.1, 6, 7
8.3.6	understand the uses, characteristics and effects of horizontal and diagonal spreads: • use in differing market conditions • anticipating modest market rises/falls (bull/bear markets) • risks	5.2
8.4	**Basics of Hedging (Futures)** On completion, the candidate should:	
8.4.1	know the characteristics and implications of long and short positions	3
8.4.2	understand the importance of hedging ratios in cheapest to deliver bonds (CTDs): • price factors • highest implied repo rate • number of contracts to hedge an exposure to the CTD bond • duration-based hedge ratios for non-CTD bonds	3.1

Syllabus Unit/ Element		Chapter/ Section
8.4.3	understand hedge ratio calculation for other short-term interest rate futures: • basis point value • number of contracts to hedge an interest rate exposure	3.2
8.4.4	understand hedge ratio calculation for equity futures: • stock and portfolio beta • number of contracts to hedge an equity exposure	3.2
8.4.5	understand basis, basis trading and basis risk: • problems caused by changes in basis • how changes in basis can be used to advantage by an investor	3.3
8.5	**Basics of Hedging (Options)** On completion, the candidate should:	
8.5.1	understand the application and effects of delta hedging and be able to establish an investor's net long/short position	4
8.6	**Comparison of Exchange-Traded and OTC Hedges** On completion, the candidate should:	
8.6.1	understand the advantages and disadvantages of using exchange-traded versus OTC products in hedge management: • exposure flexibility versus contract specification • ease/cost of closing OTC transactions versus exchange-traded positions • margins versus collateral processes • counterparty exposure versus centralised clearing • price transparency • best execution • documentation • settlement mechanism	8
8.7	**Applications of Derivative Strategies** On completion, the candidate should:	
8.7.1	be able to calculate (through the knowledge gained above), a derivatives position with an underlying market equivalency, either to establish or to hedge a required exposure. • long/short through futures • long/short through single options • long/short through option combinations • long/short through simple OTC derivatives • limits to upside and/or downside exposures (Sufficient contract/product information will be provided to candidates in the exam to enable the required calculations)	4, 5, 6

Syllabus Unit/ Element		Chapter/ Section
8.7.2	understand the uses and advantages of covered calls and covered puts: • motivation for the writer of a covered call • motivation for the buyer of a protective put • risks/maximum losses • use in different market conditions	4.3
8.7.3	analyse the relative attractiveness of derivative positions or investments to specific client circumstances: • private client investment portfolios • individual/portfolios • institutional asset managers • corporate treasurers • hedge funds • sovereign wealth funds	10

Element 9	**Regulatory Requirements**	**Chapter 9**
9.1	**Scope of Regulation** On completion, the candidate should:	
9.1.1	understand in general terms the scope and purposes of regulation of derivatives and the main activities of regulators: • Europe (MiFID II, FCA, ESMA, EMIR, other regulators) • US (Fed, SEC and CFTC) • Far East (Hong Kong, Singapore and Japan) • orderly markets • consumer protection • education • combating financial crime • regulation of individuals, companies • supervision • sanction processes • passporting regulated status • classifications/exemption • OSC commitments to regulators for OTC Derivatives	1
9.1.2	know the primary requirements of a regulated exchange	1
9.2	**Rules Based versus Principles Based Regulation** On completion, the candidate should:	
9.2.1	understand in general terms the importance of the principles-based approach to regulation: • client classification • treating customers fairly • suitability and appropriateness of the transaction/product • best execution	2

Syllabus Unit/ Element		Chapter/ Section
9.2.2	understand the differences between rules-based and principles-based regulation	2, 3
9.3	**US – Principal Differences Between EU and US Regulations** On completion, the candidate should:	
9.3.1	know the role of European regulation on EU derivative markets including the UK: • MiFID and the Transparency Directive • clients' money • clients' accounts • margining practices • unregulated markets • access to overseas markets • access to overseas clients	3.1, 3.2
9.3.2	know the role of the Securities and Exchange Commission (SEC) in the regulation of derivatives: • what is the SEC • regulated investments • regulated exchanges	3.3.1
9.3.3	know the role of the Commodity Futures Trading Commission (CFTC) and the National Futures Association (NFA): • what is the CFTC • what is the NFA • NFA delegated functions including "screening and registration of all firms and individuals who want to conduct futures-related business with the public." • regulated investments • regulation of other entities • dispute resolution	3.3.2
9.3.4	know the prohibitions of CFTC Part 30 (Foreign Futures and Segregation of Customer Funds)	3.3.2
9.3.5	know of the Commodity Futures Modernization Act 2000 and the principles governing trading of single stock futures in the US: • physical delivery or cash settlement • market regulators • restrictions	3.3.3
9.4	**International Accounting Standards** On completion, the candidate should:	
9.4.1	know the requirements under IAS 32 and IFRS 9 such as to disclose derivative positions held and report the 'fair value': • the impact and risk implications that fair value accounting may have on the derivative activities of banks and corporates	5

Syllabus Unit/ Element		Chapter/ Section
9.5	**Merger and Acquisition Activities** On completion, the candidate should:	
9.5.1	know the need to include derivative positions in calculations affecting merger and acquisition activities	5

Examination Specification

Each examination paper is constructed from a specification that determines the weightings that will be given to each unit. The specification is given below.

It is important to note that the numbers quoted may vary slightly from examination to examination as there is some flexibility to ensure that each examination has a consistent level of difficulty. However, the number of questions tested in each unit should not change by more than two.

Element number	Element	Questions
1	Introduction to Derivatives	7
2	Underlying Markets	12
3	Exchange-Traded Futures and Options	9
4	Principles of Exchange-Traded Futures and Options	16
5	Principles of OTC Derivatives	16
6	Principles of Clearing	10
7	Delivery and Settlement	7
8	Trading, Hedging and Investment Strategies	16
9	Special Regulatory Requirements	7
Total		100

Assessment Structure

A two-hour examination of 100 multiple choice questions.

Candidates sitting the exam by computer based testing will have, in addition, up to 10% additional questions as trial questions that will not be separately identified and do not contribute to the result. Candidates will be given proportionately more time to complete the test.

CISI Associate (ACSI) Membership can work for you...

Studying for a CISI qualification is hard work and we're sure you're putting in plenty of hours, but don't lose sight of your goal!

This is just the first step in your career; there is much more to achieve!

The securities and investments sector attracts ambitious and driven individuals. You're probably one yourself and that's great, but on the other hand you're almost certainly surrounded by lots of other people with similar ambitions.

So how can you stay one step ahead during these uncertain times?

Entry Criteria:
Pass in either:

- Investment Operations Certificate (IOC), IFQ, ICWIM, Capital Markets in, eg, Securities, Derivatives, Advanced Certificates; or
- one CISI Diploma/Masters in Wealth Management paper

Joining Fee: £25 or free if applying via prefilled application form **Annual Subscription (pro rata):** £125

Using your new CISI qualification* to become an Associate (ACSI) member of the Chartered Institute for Securities & Investment could well be the next important career move you make this year, and help you maintain your competence.

Join our global network of over 40,000 financial services professionals and start enjoying both the professional and personal benefits that CISI membership offers. Once you become a member you can use the prestigious ACSI designation after your name and even work towards becoming personally chartered.

* ie, Investment Operations Certificate (IOC), IFQ, ICWIM, Capital Markets

Benefits in Summary...

- Use of the CISI CPD Scheme
- Unlimited free CPD seminars, webcasts, podcasts and online training tools
- Highly recognised designatory letters
- Unlimited free attendance at CISI Professional Forums
- CISI publications including *The Review* and *Change – The Regulatory Update*
- 20% discount on all CISI conferences and training courses
- Invitation to the CISI Annual Lecture
- Select benefits – our exclusive personal benefits portfolio

The ACSI designation will provide you with access to a range of member benefits, including Professional Refresher where there are currently over 100 modules available on subjects including Anti-Money Laundering, Information Security & Data Protection, Integrity & Ethics, and the UK Bribery Act. CISI TV is also available to members, allowing you to catch up on the latest CISI events, whilst earning valuable CPD.

Plus many other networking opportunities which could be invaluable for your career.

Professional Refresher

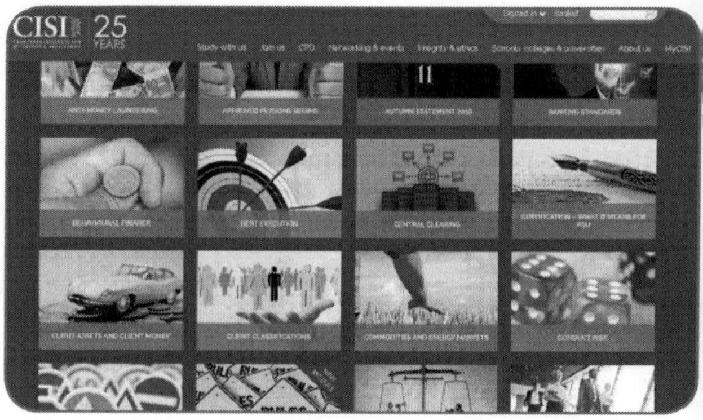

Self-testing elearning modules to refresh your knowledge, meet regulatory and firm requirements, and earn CPD.

Professional Refresher is a training solution to help you remain up-to-date with industry developments, maintain regulatory compliance and demonstrate continuing learning.

This popular online learning tool allows self-administered refresher testing on a variety of topics, including the latest regulatory changes.

There are currently over 100 modules available which address UK and international issues. Modules are reviewed by practitioners frequently and new topics are added to the suite on a regular basis.

Benefits to firms:

- Learning and testing can form part of business T&C programme
- Learning and testing kept up-to-date and accurate by the CISI
- Relevant and useful – devised by industry practitioners
- Access to individual results available as part of management overview facility, 'Super User'
- Records of staff training can be produced for internal use and external audits
- Cost-effective – no additional charge for CISI members
- Available to non-members

Benefits to individuals:

- Comprehensive selection of topics across sectors
- Modules are regularly reviewed and updated by industry experts
- New topics added regularly
- Free for members
- Successfully passed modules are recorded in your CPD log as active learning
- Counts as structured learning for RDR purposes
- On completion of a module, a certificate can be printed out for your own records

The full suite of Professional Refresher modules is free to CISI members, or £250 for non-members. Modules are also available individually. To view a full list of Professional Refresher modules visit:

cisi.org/refresher

If you or your firm would like to find out more, contact our Client Relationship Management team:

+ 44 20 7645 0670
crm@cisi.org

For more information on our elearning products, contact our Customer Support Centre on +44 20 7645 0777, or visit our website at cisi.org/refresher

Feedback to the CISI

Have you found this workbook to be a valuable aid to your studies? We would like your views, so please email us at learningresources@cisi.org with any thoughts, ideas or comments.

Accredited Training Partners

Support for exam students studying for the Chartered Institute for Securities & Investment (CISI) qualifications is provided by several Accredited Training Partners (ATPs), including Fitch Learning and BPP. The CISI's ATPs offer a range of face-to-face training courses, distance learning programmes, their own learning resources and study packs which have been accredited by the CISI. The CISI works in close collaboration with its ATPs to ensure they are kept informed of changes to CISI exams so they can build them into their own courses and study packs.

CISI Workbook Specialists Wanted

Workbook Authors

Experienced freelance authors with finance experience, and who have published work in their area of specialism, are sought. Responsibilities include:

- Updating workbooks in line with new syllabuses and any industry developments
- Ensuring that the syllabus is fully covered

Workbook Reviewers

Individuals with a high-level knowledge of the subject area are sought. Responsibilities include:

- Highlighting any inconsistencies against the syllabus
- Assessing the author's interpretation of the workbook

Workbook Technical Reviewers

Technical reviewers to provide a detailed review of the workbook and bring the review comments to the panel. Responsibilities include:

- Cross-checking the workbook against the syllabus
- Ensuring sufficient coverage of each learning objective

Workbook Proofreaders

Proofreaders are needed to proof workbooks both grammatically and also in terms of the format and layout. Responsibilities include:

- Checking for spelling and grammar mistakes
- Checking for formatting inconsistencies

If you are interested in becoming a CISI external specialist call:

+44 20 7645 0609

or email:

externalspecialists@cisi.org

For bookings, orders, membership and general enquiries please contact our Customer Support Centre on +44 20 7645 0777, or visit our website at cisi.org

17.95 - ON

SERVICING THE HONDA

CIVIC

MOTOR CAR

1974 Edition

Published by

TRACTOR & MECHANICAL PUBLICATIONS

405 Pitt Street Sydney. N.S.W. Phone 212.4486
P.O. Box 311, North Sydney. N.S.W. 2060 Australia